CALCULATED RISK
THE SUPERSONIC
LIFE AND TIMES OF GUS GRISSOM

CALCULATED RISK
THE SUPERSONIC
LIFE AND TIMES OF GUS GRISSOM

BY GEORGE LEOPOLD

PURDUE UNIVERSITY PRESS / WEST LAFAYETTE, INDIANA

Cataloging-in-Publication Data available at the Library of Congress.

Hardback ISBN: 978-1-55753-745-4
ePub ISBN: 978-1-61249-459-3
ePDF ISBN: 978-1-61249-458-6

Cover credit: Ralph Morse/The LIFE Picture Collection/Getty Images

For my father, who taught me to look up.

Robert George Leopold
Sergeant
301st Bombardment Group
Fifth Bombardment Wing
15th Air Force
US Army Air Corps

CONTENTS

PREFACE

By the end of the 1960s, twelve human beings had traveled to the moon; four had walked on its barren, untouched surface. Eight more American astronauts would reach the lunar highlands in the early 1970s. The American people and NASA had accomplished what they said they would do: land men on the moon by the end of the decade and bring them back. And it was done in front of the entire world. When asked what it all meant a few weeks after his return from the moon in July 1969, *Apollo 11* command module pilot Michael Collins put this singular human achievement into perspective: "I think it [was] a technical triumph for this country to have said what it was going to do a number of years ago, and then by golly do it just like we said we were going to do."[1]

In the decades since the final US moon landing, most of America's early astronauts recorded their stories for posterity. In one form or another, these early space pioneers published their memoirs, mostly with the help of professional writers or aerospace journalists who covered their exploits. (Notable exceptions include Collins, undoubtedly the finest writer ever sent into space, and Walter Cunningham, who chronicled the early years of NASA along with his own career as an Apollo astronaut.)

From Shepard to Glenn, Armstrong to Cernan, these men were able to shape the public's perception of these early astronauts' lives and careers. While Virgil Ivan "Gus" Grissom managed to coauthor one book about his role in the Gemini program before his death (completing a draft manuscript weeks before the *Apollo 1* fire on January 27, 1967), most of what we know or think about the third human being to fly in space, if we think of him at all, was shaped by press accounts, documentary snippets, and a few interviews given by the press-shy Grissom to trusted newspaper and television reporters. In the early days of the Space Race, inhabited as it was with ultra-competitive men with enormous egos, Gus Grissom was often a footnote.

Aside from a 1968 self-published tribute by the Grissom family's pastor and a 2004 biography that focuses heavily on Grissom's Indiana years, no comprehensive survey exists of this simultaneously simple and complex man, his supersonic life, and his tragic and unnecessary death. This volume is intended to fill that gap in the historical record, to examine the life and career of Gus Grissom, to reconsider his place in the annals of space exploration as well as in the history of the Cold War struggle between the United States and the Soviet Union.

Grissom was a Cold Warrior in the truest sense. No geopolitical rivalry better defines this period of human history than the competition between the United States and the Soviet Union for supremacy in space exploration. The first waypoint was a manned lunar landing. Soviet Premier Nikita Khrushchev and President John F. Kennedy understood this instinctively. America, Kennedy concluded early in his administration, could not survive if the Soviet Union controlled outer space.

By hanging their hides out on the line, Grissom and his fellow Mercury astronauts became the instruments, the business end, of US Cold War strategy. Grissom was an eager, willing participant, agonizing over every Soviet space spectacular, and then redoubling his own efforts to keep pace and eventually pass the Soviets in a race to the moon.

By the mid-1960s, with planning for lunar missions well under way and technological development moving at a breakneck pace, Grissom had emerged from the pack as the odds-on favorite to be the first human being to walk on the moon. He would focus all of his energies on that goal. He and his family would pay the ultimate price for his unswerving dedication.

The reticent test pilot and astronaut from downstate Indiana was more than willing to do the tedious testing and other unglamorous engineering work required to reach the moon by the end of the 1960s. He was utterly uninterested in tickertape parades and White House ceremonies, unimpressed, as fellow astronaut Wally Schirra later observed, with personal prestige. Gus Grissom did not care. He just wanted to fly. And the best place to go was 238,000 miles from Earth.

ACKNOWLEDGMENTS

Charles Watkinson, former director of Purdue University Press, launched this project. Charles took a chance on a first-time author, ably pointing me in the right direction until his departure to greener pastures (the University of Michigan Press) in 2014. Charles embodies the "gentleman and scholar" ideal.

Charles's successor, Peter Froehlich, has been equally encouraging since taking the reins at Purdue University Press in 2015. Peter and his able staff saw this project through to completion. Special thanks go to editor Katherine Purple, who repeatedly saved me from myself. Editors do the unglamorous work of untangling prose and helping authors tell their stories in ways that are accessible to a broad audience. Beloved American classics such as *To Kill a Mockingbird*, we have recently discovered, would have been far less appreciated without the steady hand of a wise book editor.

As this project took shape, I was struck by a deep and abiding affection for Gus Grissom. He connected on a visceral level with average Americans in a way the other astronauts, placed as they were on pedestals, could not. Gus was the everyman. Americans rooted for him. Among the reasons were his humble beginnings along with his determination and willingness to size up situations and take risks. Gus's youngest brother, Lowell, gives greater meaning to the phrase "brotherly love." Lowell has kept the memory of his big brother alive through the decades. He was gracious with his time and straightforward in discussing the meaning of his brother's life and deeds. Gus would be proud of his kid brother.

Few researchers know more about the career of Virgil Grissom than Rick Boos. As a student in the 1960s, Rick corresponded with the astronaut in the heyday of American spaceflight. Those letters from Grissom had a profound effect on Rick, who made it his life's work to document the astronaut's contributions and correct the misconceptions about his career. Rick willingly shared his years of research, particularly the controversial ending of Grissom's Mercury spaceflight and profound tragedy that killed the crew of *Apollo 1*. Rick and I talked for hours; I have done my level best to accurately convey the results of his extensive research. I am in Rick's debt.

To the present day, we continue to ponder the watershed events of the 1960s, especially the remarkable early days of human spaceflight. The families of the men who challenged the vacuum of space also were key actors in mankind's greatest adventure. Kris Stoever, the erudite daughter of Malcolm Scott Carpenter and coauthor of her father's memoir, *For Spacious Skies*, was a treasure trove of institutional memory about the American space program and its toll on the astronauts' families. While many of us watched it unfold on television, Kris was on the other side of the camera, caught in the unsparing glare of astronaut celebrity. She saw and recorded it all, passing along my queries to her ailing mother, Rene Price Carpenter. Kris's guidance was indispensable.

Those who crossed paths with Gus Grissom at Purdue, the Air Force, and NASA, folks with a sense of history and Gus's place in it, graciously provided reminisces, anecdotes, and photos tucked away in dusty albums. I thank them all.

The human beings who journeyed to another world and walked on the moon are like no other creatures on Earth. These men possess an utterly unique perspective on our place in the universe. Several helped with this project, honoring the memory of their fallen comrade Gus Grissom. Thanks especially to Alan Bean, who gave up precious time at the easel painting his memories of walking on the lunar surface to talk about Grissom. Thanks also to Walt Cunningham, Tom Stafford, and Al Worden. John Young's 2012 memoir was indispensable in my research.

The staff of the NASA History Office in Washington, DC, also provided yeoman service. John Norberg supplied invaluable guidance and helped me avoid gimbal lock. The documentary filmmaker David Sington provided inspiration.

Ellen Seefelt, my wife and companion of thirty-five years, has endured the writer's life since we decamped from the Midwest a week after our honeymoon to New York City. There, she supported me while I studied journalism. Over the intervening years, Ellen prodded me to come up with a book idea that would synthesize a lifelong interest in space exploration. It turned out to be the life of Gus Grissom. As we walked the dog each day, she listened to my latest travails and was unfailing in her encouragement. Without her love, support, and understanding, this project would never have left the ground.

INTRODUCTION: PURE OXYGEN

Men have become the tools of their tools.
—Henry David Thoreau

The crew cabin of the new American moon ship, the Apollo command module, was already getting "fat" in 1962. That meant engineers at Apollo prime contractor North American Aviation and their NASA managers in Langley, Virginia, were under growing pressure to "keep the spacecraft on a diet," as spacecraft designer Caldwell Johnson indelicately put it.[1] Despite the fact that the five-engine first stage of the Saturn V moon rocket would generate an astounding 7.5 million pounds of thrust, every engineer working on every component of the booster was looking for some way to shed weight. The moon rocket would eventually weigh in at about 6 million pounds, enough mass to pulverize the special gravel roadbed designed to transport the vehicle to Pad 39 at Cape Canaveral.[2] It was an enormous undertaking. Hence, the mantra for NASA and its contractors was simple: "Weight is everything."

All that machinery would be stacked on a thirty-six-story-high, three-stage rocket generating the equivalent of a small nuclear explosion. In the early days of Apollo, the machine was getting heavier by the day. (It eventually fell to North American Aviation engineers in California designing the booster's second stage to develop a weight-saving common bulkhead between two huge propellant tanks that finally allowed the mighty rocket to "make weight" and get off the ground.[3])

To shave a few more pounds from the command module, NASA managers decided during the critical summer of 1962—months after John Glenn's historic orbital flight—to use a simpler, lighter, single-gas atmosphere inside the Apollo cabin rather than a complex oxygen-nitrogen design. That fateful decision, based largely on the success of a handful of

American manned flights that all used a pure oxygen atmosphere in the spacecraft, would reduce the weight of the Apollo environmental control system by eliminating the need for a tangle of complex plumbing, including regulators and a sensor needed to maintain a proper mix of oxygen and nitrogen. A pure oxygen atmosphere had been used on the Mercury program, which was now sending astronauts into orbit without incident. It would again be used in the upcoming Gemini program.

It turned out that NASA and its Apollo contractors were literally playing with fire.

The designers of the conical-shaped Apollo ship believed they understood the inherent danger of a cabin fire when using a high-pressure oxygen atmosphere. Besides weight, there were plenty of sound engineering reasons for using pure oxygen. There were also plenty of risky trade-offs. It was generally understood that reducing the amount of flammable material in the cabin was essential. More importantly, NASA engineers, struggling to find a way to reach the moon by the end of the decade, concluded that using a pure oxygen environment could save about thirty precious pounds, not to mention reduce the complexity of arguably the most complicated flying machine ever built.

Pure oxygen had never been used in a ship as large as the three-man cabin of the Apollo spaceship, a volume measuring about 210 cubic feet. Aware of the extreme fire hazard, British scientists advising the space agency recommended that NASA install nitrogen containers in the cockpit that could be released in the event of an oxygen-fed fire to help extinguish the flames.[4]

NASA managers ignored these and other warnings about the dangers of pure oxygen under pressure.

With that decision, one of countless engineering trade-offs made by NASA designers in the frantic early days of the Apollo program, CM-012, the *Apollo 1* spacecraft commanded by US Air Force Colonel Virgil I. "Gus" Grissom more than four years later, would use a pure oxygen cabin atmosphere at a pressure of 16.7 pounds per square inch. The overpressure would equalize the cabin with normal outside pressure (14.7 psi) while allowing for inevitable leakage. It would also ensure that a cork-like inner hatch would remain sealed on the voyage to the moon.

Gus Grissom endorsed the design. A tight seal on the hatch was one fewer thing to worry about as the astronauts and engineers struggled to build and test a machine that could send men to the moon and get them back alive. It was a calculated risk Grissom was willing to take. Then, it was on to the next, and the one after that. This was the reality of early space exploration.

Not everyone agreed with NASA's decree to use pure oxygen, even when the spacecraft was still on the launchpad. "It's the wrong thing to do," insisted North American Aviation's Charles Feltz. Feltz was the legendary chief designer of the spectacularly successful X-15 rocket plane. His opinion carried much weight. The record-breaking performance of the X-15 had played a major role in NASA's political decision to hand the huge Apollo contract to North American Aviation. Despite his peerless reputation as a designer of rocket planes, Feltz was overruled by NASA officials and ordered to install a pure oxygen system.[5]

Others familiar with the arcane world of hyperbaric environments wondered later why NASA would risk using a pure oxygen cabin atmosphere that brings with it well-understood fire hazards. Curt Newport, the underwater salvage expert who retrieved Gus Grissom's *Liberty Bell 7* spacecraft from the Atlantic Ocean in 1999, was unequivocal in stating that pure oxygen would "never" be used in deep underwater vessels that closely simulate a spaceship.

The difference, of course, was that the early version of the Apollo command module, known as a Block I, was crammed full with miles of electrical wiring and other electronic gear. Making matters worse, Grissom and his crew had been allowed to attach flammable material, like Velcro, throughout the cabin.[6] Each crew customized their ship, and Velcro was the preferred method of keeping everything in the cabin from floating around. Weightlessness was exhilarating, but it also had its practical drawbacks.

John Young, the only astronaut to fly in space with Grissom aboard *Gemini 3* in March 1965, was at the time of the *Apollo 1* fire also helping to get the troubled Block I version of the spacecraft off the ground. Young noted that the first-generation Apollo command module contained no fewer than 640 switches, circuit breakers, event indicators, and computers.[7]

Young had learned plenty about aircraft wiring during his days as a test pilot at Patuxent River Naval Air Station. What he saw in the Block I command module shocked him. Wire bundles as big as a man's arm bending around corners where they would surely fray. "I knew [bad wiring] when I saw it, and I saw it in spades in the Block I command module," Young recalled. "Big wire bundles lay against the aluminum stringers with no support," he added. "We saw many instances of wiring where insulation was already frayed. In pure oxygen this was not good."[8]

Young has asserted in the decades since the *Apollo 1* fire that he asked Grissom why the commander, a meticulous test pilot and engineer who fully understood the risks inherent in spaceflight, said nothing to his NASA bosses about the bad wiring in his ship. "If I say anything about it," Young claims Grissom replied, "they'll fire me."[9] Whether this meant Grissom believed he would be relieved of his command, and with it his chance to perhaps be the first man on the moon, or that he would be dismissed from the American space program altogether has never been fully explained.

Grissom, however, *did* complain to anyone who would listen about other obvious shortcomings of his ship. He also complained bitterly about the Apollo simulator used for crew training. Personnel in charge of the simulator simply could not keep up with the never-ending modifications and engineering changes being made to the first manned Apollo spacecraft.

Astronaut Michael Collins, who at the time of the *Apollo 1* fire was nursing along another of the early command modules, accurately referred to the mess that was the Block I spacecraft as "one big potential short circuit."[10] That meant there were countless potential ignition sources in a pure oxygen atmosphere.

Never one to pull his punches during his long career as an astronaut and NASA administrator, Young has been even more outspoken about the fatal decision to use pure oxygen in the Block I spacecraft, especially during full dress rehearsals on the launchpad. "Today it's hard to comprehend how ignorant some of our early spacecraft management teams actually were" about pure oxygen. "Even if the bad wiring and the danger of testing in 100 percent pure oxygen had been laid out in front of them as plain as day, NASA might not have changed course, short of a catastrophe."[11]

Unfortunately, Young was correct: it took a catastrophe to fix the fatal design flaws and shoddy program management that produced the death trap that was the first Apollo spacecraft.

Referring to the use of pure oxygen under pressure at sea level, salvage expert Newport wrote in his 2002 account of the successful *Liberty Bell 7* salvage: "Even before the mid-1960s, no competent diving company would have ever dreamed of filling a deck decompression chamber up with 100 percent oxygen and putting three men inside. Yet, our premier scientific agency in the United States misjudged a technical issue known to any qualified diving supervisor."[12]

Along with designer Feltz of North American Aviation, others working for the Apollo prime contractor were equally wary of pure oxygen. Maxime Faget, the brilliant mechanical engineer and NASA's chief spacecraft designer, dismissed their concerns. Faget, along with Caldwell Johnson and other Apollo designers, remained fixated on reducing the weight of the Apollo spacecraft.

Weight, the gravitational force to be overcome by a powerful rocket, would outweigh all other technical considerations in the early 1960s. Apollo was a "crash program" with the sole purpose of beating the Soviets to the moon. This Cold War imperative trumped nearly every engineering decision in the early days of the race to the moon.

Part of the obsession with weight stemmed from an unassailable fact of the Space Race: the Soviets possessed rockets that could hurl more mass into space. The Vostok spacecraft that carried Major Yuri Gagarin into Earth orbit on April 12, 1961, was believed to be three times heavier than the American Mercury capsule. Gagarin's ship was equipped with a two-gas system that supplied the cosmonaut with a mixture of oxygen and nitrogen similar to the air we breathe at sea level. The Soviet system was heavier but safer. This was a luxury the Americans believed they could not afford.[13]

The design of the early Mercury spacecraft was therefore limited by the marginal thrust generated by the American Redstone and Atlas rockets. Concerns about the American shortfall in rocket thrust went all the way to the top: presidential candidate Senator John F. Kennedy insisted in the earliest days of the Space Race that he would gladly trade color television for bigger rockets. "I will take my television black and white. I want to be ahead of [the Russians] in rocket thrust."[14]

Despite the fact that former Nazi rocket engineer Wernher von Braun was in the process of building multistage Saturn rockets larger than anything the Soviets had yet tested, Apollo engineers remained fixated on reducing weight. This failure of imagination would unnecessarily put future Apollo crews at risk.

These trade-offs were made despite ample evidence from the biomedical and aerospace communities that pure oxygen could be deadly. Most of this research, including at least one oxygen atmosphere study,[15] was readily available to NASA managers. Still, Apollo engineers bent on beating the Russians pressed on with the single-gas system. Such design changes would hold up the program, they argued. Unbeknownst to the Americans, the Soviets had already lost one cosmonaut in a training accident involving pure oxygen. Fires linked to pure oxygen under pressure also occurred during US military tests. None of this mattered; NASA was in a hurry, trying to keep its lunar-landing program on schedule.

Hence, the space agency proceeded in January 1967 with a launchpad test in which the *Apollo 1* spacecraft commanded by Grissom would be switched to internal power at the end of a simulated countdown. It was called a "plugs-out" test. This meant Grissom's crew would be throwing electrical switches in a pure oxygen environment with the hatches sealed. NASA managers, lulled into complacency about the use of pure oxygen, classified the fatal launchpad test as "routine."

Today, some of Grissom's Apollo colleagues insist he should have known better. Ultimately, Grissom's impeccable credentials as an aeronautical engineer, test pilot, and veteran of two space flights were insufficient to counteract the shortcuts employed to beat the Soviets to the moon. Grissom understood by 1966 he had a flawed spacecraft on his hands. He calculated the risks and concluded that somehow the problems could be fixed before launch. By virtue of being the first to command the flight of a new machine, Grissom would retain his coveted position at the top of the exclusive astronaut pecking order.

The hard-charging, no-nonsense engineer and test pilot had made a conscious decision to play the hand he was dealt in the hope that he could nurse his deeply flawed spacecraft into orbit on its maiden flight. Half joking, he remarked in the weeks before his scheduled Apollo launch that his crew would be relieved to simply survive. Then, if a series of Apollo shakedown flights succeeded, Grissom might be in line to command the first attempt to land and walk on the moon.

Nearly a decade of unrelenting testing, factory tours, insufferable press interviews, and separation from his wife and two sons could perhaps culminate in man's greatest adventure. Grissom was all in.

At the monthly Apollo spacecraft design review meeting in July 1962, NASA officials formerly directed the spacecraft contractor to install a pure oxygen atmospheric system. The fire hazard was acknowledged but rationalized: "The answer to this problem appeared to be one of diligent effort on the part of spacecraft designers to be aware of the fire hazard and to exercise strict control of potential ignition sources and material selection."[16]

NASA's directive to use a single-gas system in the Apollo crew cabin was officially transmitted to North American Aviation[17] in August 1962, about a year after Grissom's first spaceflight. The Apollo prime contractor was ordered to drop its proposal for a two-gas system and change the Apollo cabin atmosphere to "pure oxygen and [delete] nitrogen system provisions." NASA's mandate to use pressurized pure oxygen in the sealed Apollo spacecraft on the launchpad was officially transmitted to the command module prime contractor on August 28, 1962.[18]

From that day forward, until the terrible winter evening in early 1967, the fate of Virgil "Gus" Grissom, father of two young boys, one of the original Mercury Seven astronauts, the very embodiment of "The Right Stuff," as well as the fates of two crewmates aboard the *Apollo 1* spacecraft, were sealed.

They were doomed.

1

1926

First, inevitably, the idea, the fantasy, the fairy tale. Then, scientific calculation.
—*Konstantin Tsiolkovsky*

The year of Virgil Ivan Grissom's birth would be a watershed in the history of rocketry. The future astronaut was born on April 3, 1926. Eighteen days earlier, some eight hundred miles to the northeast at Auburn, Massachusetts, the original American rocket scientist, Robert Hutchings Goddard, had successfully launched the world's first liquid-fueled rocket. The brief flight was eventually considered "as significant to history as that of the Wright Brothers at Kitty Hawk" twenty-three years earlier.[1] Grissom's birth and Goddard's rocket illustrated how the arc of technological progress had coincided perfectly with the arrival of a generation of men who would become humankind's first space travelers.

Indeed, the year of one's birth seems to have played a critical role in determining the pecking order that emerged some thirty years later among the future American astronauts. Birth dates and fate would determine who played what role in the coming Cold War drama that was the race to the moon.

Michael Collins, a member of the first lunar landing crew, noted that he and crewmates Neil Armstrong and Buzz Aldrin were all born in 1930. "How lucky can you get?" Collins remarked. "We just happened to come along at the right time."[2]

Four years earlier, Goddard pierced the sky with his primitive rocket. The 11.3-foot-tall collection of steel tubes and propellant weighed just over ten pounds. It rose that momentous day 41 feet above his aunt's farm, covering a horizontal distance of about 184 feet before landing in his Aunt Effie's cabbage patch. The flight lasted 2.5 seconds. Maximum velocity was sixty miles per hour.[3]

Anticipating the names bestowed on later rockets, Goddard called his prototype "Nell."[4]

Less than a month later, the first son of Dennis David Grissom, a signalman for the Baltimore & Ohio Railroad, and Cecile King Grissom entered the world on the evening of April 3. The boy was born at about 8 p.m. in the Grissom's Sixth Street home in the southern Indiana town of Mitchell.

The Grissom's first child, a daughter named Lena, was either stillborn (according to an early chronicler of the family's history) or died shortly after her premature birth in March 1925. Hence, the expecting mother was "excessively anxious" about her second pregnancy.[5] Virgil Ivan was small but arrived healthy. A daughter and two more sons would follow over the next seven years, quickly filling up the modest, white wood-frame house the Grissoms moved into a year after Virgil's birth.

Lowell Grissom, the youngest of Virgil's three siblings, has no idea why Dennis and Cecile picked such an unusual name for their first son. (Lowell believes he was named for Lowell Thomas, the popular American newsman, commentator, and adventurer from neighboring Ohio.) The choice of "Ivan" as a middle name was even more curious and would prove particularly vexing for Virgil in the chilliest days of the Cold War when he would emerge on the world stage as a key protagonist.

What mattered more than the boy's name, of course, was the time and place of his birth. Never was this fact more relevant than the coming age of aviation and space exploration.

That same year, 1926, toiling in isolation a world away, the legendary rocket theorist Konstantin Eduardovich Tsiolkovsky was completing his treatise, *Plan of Space Exploration*. Tsiolkovsky, Goddard, and the Austro-Hungarian-born German physicist Hermann Oberth would emerge as three of the greatest rocketeers of the age, fleshing out the theoretical underpinnings of spaceflight.

Goddard too continued to work mostly in isolation. Beyond some financial backing from the Smithsonian Institution, the work of the mythic Clark University physicist who earned 214 patents went largely unnoticed in the United States. Goddard later managed to attract the attention of Charles Lindbergh, who helped arrange the financial support of millionaire financier Harvey Guggenheim. That backing allowed Goddard to move to the wide-open spaces of New Mexico to continue his research in secrecy. His work would eventually be put to use during World War II by German rocketeers led by a team that included the young Wernher von Braun. They would build the Nazi's *V-2* rocket used against civilians in England and continental Europe.

Near Roswell, New Mexico, Goddard's path crossed with a local lad who walked along a white gravel road past the rocket scientist's encampment each day on his way to school. "Though I have no recollections of rockets flaring into the night skies or the ignition of exotic new fuels, there were stories that circulated among the natives of Roswell—stories of fire and brimstone igniting the heavens, strange machinery, and a quiet, reclusive mind assembling it all," the schoolboy later recalled. "This was a man who would loom large in my imagination, a man of the proportions of my grandfather. He was mythic, and I now see how his life ran so counter to the setting he must have found himself in. Here was a man of science, a man from that ungodly world beyond the perimeter of Roswell. By any standard, Robert Goddard was part of the scientific lore of the times."[6]

That New Mexico schoolboy was Edgar Dean Mitchell, who, like Virgil Grissom, would grow up to become a top military test pilot. Mitchell would go on to earn a PhD in aeronautics and astronautics from the Massachusetts Institute of Technology. With impeccable credentials, he was eventually selected as an astronaut, becoming the sixth human to walk on the moon.[7]

The US Army's Redstone booster, a modified version of the *V-2* rocket von Braun and his men built for Hitler and based on Goddard's work, would eventually launch two American astronauts into space. One was Virgil Grissom.

The eldest Grissom son arrived at the dawn of the Rocket Age. Just as significant, Virgil's birthplace teemed with machinery, manufacturing, and tinkering. Mitchell was a rural town seemingly situated in the middle of nowhere. There was no significant river or body of water nearby. But it was a railroad junction, a fact that in the early twentieth century often determined whether a small American town survived and thrived or died on the vine. The Baltimore & Ohio Railroad, Dennis Grissom's employer for forty-seven years, ran East-West through Mitchell. The Chicago, Indianapolis, and Louisville Railroad, affectionately known in the Hoosier State as the "Monon," ran North-South.

The freight trains that passed one block from the Grissom's first home on Sixth Street were a constant part of the town's background noise, along with the cicadas of the steaming summer months. The train whistles were among the first mechanical sounds young Virgil Grissom heard. "Watch out for the trains, [and] don't play on the tracks!" Cecile warned her son when he was old enough to explore the neighborhood.[8]

The family had moved to a larger house on Baker Street when Virgil was a year old and Cecile was pregnant with her second child. As his family grew, filling the small wood-framed house, Dennis Grissom somehow managed to hang on to his twenty-four dollar a week job with the B&O as the Great Depression deepened. By today's standards, the Grissom home would have seemed cramped. During the Depression, it was cozy.

Virgil would grow up among machines and men who fixed them when they broke down. Even today, the neighborhoods of Mitchell are dotted with makeshift repair shops. The boy quickly learned that he would first have to earn the money for a bicycle, and then would have to make his own repairs.[9] Like several of his future astronaut colleagues, Virgil also would eventually earn the money required to take his first airplane ride.

But first he had to be raised and educated while finding his place as the eldest son of a growing family in a small, isolated but relatively prosperous town that was equal parts midwestern and southern. The citizens of Mitchell were described by a local historian as "not overly ambitious, but they do show vitality."[10] From an early age, it was clear Virgil was different: he exhibited both ambition *and* vitality. He would not be content with a quiet, safe, nine-to-five existence. There was too much to accomplish. The train whistles reminded him there was a larger world beyond State Route 37, the main road through town, one that a boy born in the middle of a vast continent would one day view from the high ground of space.

A description of the first human in space also could have been applied to Virgil Grissom. "Was he special?" remembered Yuri Gagarin's foreman at the Lyubertsy Steel Plant in Moscow, the future cosmonaut's first apprenticeship. "No, but he was hard-working."[11]

Mitchell, seventy or so miles west and north of the mighty Ohio River, also was nothing special. But its citizens were mostly industrious, thrifty, self-reliant, and insular.[12] Mitchell also was nearly flat—a "rolling plateau," an ancient seabed. Hence, it was a perfect location for a railroad junction. The town was laid out in 1853 and surveyed by Ormsby McKnight Mitchel, a West Point graduate, University of Cincinnati professor, and Union Army major general. The town of Mitchell (the second "L" was added later) was incorporated in 1864.

Dennis David Grissom was born in Martin County, just southwest of Mitchell, on October 14, 1903, the son of John Wesley and Melissa Stroud Grissom. The Grissom men were all of Hoosier stock. John Wesley was born in Martin in 1877. Virgil's great-grandfather, Thomas Elsworth Grissom, whose last name may have been changed from "Grisham," according to some genealogical records, was born in Orange around 1853. The Grissom family name may also have been derived from "Gresham," a surname associated with Virgil's great-great grandfather, John, a North Carolinian born in 1824. John eventually made his way over the Appalachians, across the Ohio River, and married Ruth Hopper of Orange in 1845.

Indeed, many of the first settlers of the southern part of the Indiana Territory arrived around 1815 from North Carolina and Virginia. Others, like the Lincolns of Rockingham County, Virginia, chose to settle first in Kentucky. There, the future sixteenth president of the United States was born in a log cabin at Sinking Springs Farm, near the present-day Hodgenville, on February 12, 1809. Title disputes and, legend has it, abhorrence of slavery prompted Thomas Lincoln to move his family in 1816 to the wilderness of Spencer County, Indiana. It was at Pigeon Creek Farm that Abe Lincoln learned to wield an ax and split rails.

By the time of the western migration, the legendary Shawnee leader Tecumseh and his failed tribal confederacy had been subdued after opposing the United States during the War of 1812. The territory appropriately christened "Indiana" in 1800 was also home to the Chippewa, Delaware,

Erie, Huron, Iroquois, Kickapoo, Mahican, Miami, Mohegan, Nanticoke, and Potawatomie tribes. Indiana, or "land of Indians," entered the union on December 11, 1816, as the nineteenth state in the Union.[13]

Cecile King was nearly two years older than her husband, who had moved to Mitchell in 1924. Dennis and Cecile were married there in March of that year. Cecile's parents, Charles Asbury "Charlie" King and Sarah Alice "Sally" Beavers were still alive when the Grissom children were born; Sally died in 1932 at the age of fifty-four.

Like the Grissoms, the King family's roots were in North Carolina: Cecile's great-grandfather William A. "Billy" King, born in 1824, apparently moved his family west and died in Lawrence County, Indiana, in 1873. His son, John Wesley King, married Margaret Elizabeth "Betty" Terrell in Mitchell in 1867. Their son, "Charlie" King, Cecile's father, was born in November 1871.[14]

After moving to Mitchell, Virgil's father went to work as a signalman for the B&O Railroad, eventually providing his new wife with a modest but comfortable single-story home within easy walking distance of the town's schools. Virgil's sister Wilma was born in 1927, followed by Norman in 1930 and Lowell, the youngest, in 1934.

In the forty years, nine months, and twenty-four days of Virgil Grissom's life, he was to play a central role in some of the greatest technological advances in human history. All this seemed improbable when the oldest son of a railroad signalman was born in an obscure southern Indiana town a few years before the Great Depression.

The future Gus Grissom would later describe his hometown as "small and unhurried."[15] It remains so today. Growing up in Mitchell, he also recalled, one was likely to encounter characters like Penrod Schofield and Sam Williams, the rascals immortalized in the Indiana author Booth Tarkington's 1916 bestseller, *Penrod and Sam*. Virgil undoubtedly read Tarkington's popular children's book and saw in himself the mischievous, restless Penrod. Grissom and his future high school friend Bill Head, paired together in school by the sheer coincidence of alphabetical order, would become Mitchell's version of Penrod and Sam. Virgil represented the former, viewing school as "merely a state of confinement" and, upon seeing his first brass band, "anxious to Make a Noise in the World."[16]

Mitchell was a town of tinkerers. If you needed a mechanical part, you made it yourself. If farm machinery broke down, you fixed it yourself. If you yearned for the fastest hot rod, you tore down the engine and put it back together. If there were parts left over, you did it again.

Mitchell, Bedford, and the university town of Bloomington up the road on Route 37 were situated over one of the richest deposits of limestone bedrock on the planet. By the early 1900s, thousands of big-city workers— Italians, Germans, and Scandinavians—flocked to the region to labor in the limestone quarries. Two-thirds of the nation's building limestone came from Lawrence and Monroe counties. The choicest sections were shipped east to decorate the facades of skyscrapers and government buildings. The inferior grades were used for cement or crushed into gravel.

The Lehigh Portland Cement Company opened a plant in Mitchell in 1902, initially covering the town in a cloud of dust.[17] Automation after World War II eliminated much of the dust but also trimmed the payroll. When flying jet fighters out of Dayton, Ohio, as an Air Force test pilot, the future Gus Grissom would scan the Indiana skies for the cement plant's dust cloud before buzzing his hometown.[18]

Shortly before Virgil's birth, another manufacturer arrived in Mitchell— the Carpenter Body Works. Its founder, Ralph Carpenter, had operated a blacksmith shop on the same street Virgil was born. In 1922, he opened a factory to build buses for the local school district. Bare chassis were delivered to the factory where workers installed yellow school bus bodies.

After his discharge from the Army Air Corps in 1945, Grissom would spend several months installing doors on busses while contemplating his future.

The self-reliant men and boys of Mitchell had grease under their fingernails and calluses on their hands. When their noses weren't under the hood or repairing farm equipment, a few were in the air gazing at the occasional flying machines seen in those parts in the early 1930s. The Grissom family radio and the *Indianapolis Star* brought news of great aviation exploits, most notably Charles Lindbergh's transatlantic flight a year after Virgil was born.

The eldest Grissom son arrived in an America mad for aviators and their flying exploits. Airplanes had become a way to break the bonds of Earth and see the world from an entirely new perspective. Then there were the Buck Rogers comic strips, launched in 1929, and, debuting in 1932, the radio show. Cartoonist Dick Calkins fired the imagination of a generation of American boys with lines like this from the Buck Rogers strips: "That cosmo-magnetic hurricane hurled us down the curvature of space—into a different universe!"[19]

Like other boys his age, Virgil was fascinated with the tools of war: airplanes, guns, tanks. Later, Grissom the astronaut would profess indifference toward futuristic space fantasies. "I had never been much of a science-fiction or Buck Rogers fan. I was more interested in what was going on right now than in the centuries to come."[20]

A contemporary of Grissom growing up in rural Virginia, the future newspaper columnist and wit Russell Baker, summed up the fantasies of many of America's boys in the early days of aviation: "I had been in love with the romance of flying since first hearing as a small boy about Charles A. Lindbergh, the Lone Eagle, Lucky Lindy, who'd flown all the way to France by the seat of his pants. The pinups over my bed had been Captain Eddie Rickenbacker, Wrong-Way Corrigan, Roscoe Turner, Wiley Post, and Amelia Earhart."

After much struggle, Baker would eventually become a Navy flyer. Like Virgil Grissom, he would be too late to get into World War II. "In my fantasies I flew over the trenches on the dawn patrol, white scarf streaming behind me in the wind as I adjusted my goggles and maneuvered the Fokker of Baron [Manfred] von Richthofen [the German World War I ace, also known as the "Red Baron"] into my gun sights," recalled Baker.[21]

Nearly all the future astronauts built model airplanes or pinned pictures of Rickenbacker, Post, and Earhart on their bedroom walls. Virgil too built balsa wood models and suspended them to the ceiling in one of the rooms he shared with his siblings. There was a need to give form and substance to dreams of flight, to be going somewhere, anywhere.

U pon entering the boyhood home of Virgil Grissom at 715 West Grissom Avenue, one immediately understands that the future astronaut had no problem with cramped spaces. The modest, one-story house included five rooms, a covered front porch, a small back entrance, an attic, and little else. The house was situated on a deep lot, allowing for a family garden the Grissom children tended. Cecile canned the produce for use during the winter. At one time, six Grissoms lived in these five rooms: a parlor/living room, a decent-size kitchen, and three adjacent bedrooms. With each new child, Virgil moved to another bed, eventually sleeping on the living room couch.

By Depression standards, however, the home was comfortable and close to everything in Mitchell, a primarily Protestant town of about three thousand souls roughly midway between Indianapolis and Louisville, Kentucky. Up Route 37 about thirty miles, past the limestone quarries of Bedford, is the college town of Bloomington. (Native son and Indiana University law school graduate Hoagy Carmichael, having quickly tired of the law, was writing the music for *Stardust*, one of the great popular tunes of the twentieth century, at the Book Nook on South Indiana Avenue in Bloomington the year after Virgil was born.)

In his spare time, Dennis worked on home improvements, upgrading Cecile's kitchen with cupboards he built himself. His eldest son certainly observed this early example of sweat equity and may have pitched in himself to help with the project.

Virgil entered Riley School in 1933, at that time Mitchell's main elementary school, just a block or so from the Grissom homestead. The school was presumably named for the Hoosier poet James Whitcomb Riley, the "Children's Poet" famous for appealing to young readers. Whether Virgil gave much thought to Riley's sentimental poems is unknown. He was, it turned out, an unremarkable student with an aptitude for numbers. Mrs. Myrtle McKeever, Virgil's first grade teacher, thought him conscientious, as was expected by his parents. He was neat, his ears were clean, and by all appearances he was an earnest lad.[22] Virgil read books but remained more interested in numbers, popular science, and machines than in English grammar or rustic poetry.

After Virgil's death, the local librarian remembered that the boy was his father's son in appearance and demeanor. "They were both alike," Mrs. Fiscus, the Mitchell librarian, said of Dennis and his eldest son. "They both had a sparkle about their personalities."[23]

Grissom was intelligent; his IQ was said to have been 145. But IQ was only one measure of intelligence. Virgil also possessed a native intelligence that was focused primarily on problem solving and to a lesser extent on abstractions. His elementary school report cards and grades in high school and college reflected the way his brain was wired. He was more interested in acquiring practical knowledge than boosting his grade point average. He took what he needed and discarded the rest. What no metric could quantify was his restless energy and determination to succeed at something. The question was, What?

Grissom's early interest in flight showed that he could focus intensely on something he was passionate about, and then channel his energies and intelligence to achieve the goal of becoming a flyer. It was in instances like this that the reserved boy who was small for his age would emerge from his shell and display a measure of self-assurance and confidence. For example, the conventional wisdom holds that the pugnacious Grissom harbored a sense of inferiority about his small stature—five feet, seven inches when fully grown. He would nevertheless turn his compact body into an asset when he became a pilot and astronaut. Indeed, his size would aid him as a flyer and eventually help save his life at the end of his first space flight. Similarly, the British test pilot Eric Brown, who also stood five-foot-seven, claimed he would have lost his legs on at least three occasions had he not been able to curl them beneath his seat.[24]

While Virgil was described by his earliest biographer as a "mild introvert"[25]—Lowell Grissom considered his older brother a "mild extrovert"[26]—Virgil also was a "joiner" in every sense of the word: he made things, carefully assembling the pieces of a model airplane. He also joined organizations, beginning with the Riley Elementary Safety Patrol and Boy Scout Troop 46, where he reached the level of "star scout" and leader of the troop's Honor Guard.

A 1938 photo of the Riley School Safety Patrol shows an earnest group of crossing guards in spotless white rain gear under the customary guard's sash and belt. Standing at attention in the center of the front row is a stern-looking twelve-year-old boy holding the flag used to signal oncoming traffic or pedestrians to halt. Virgil and his classmates took their duties seriously.

Later, the tendency toward fellowship expressed itself by enlisting in the Army Air Corps, joining the Hi-Twelve, a student branch of the Masons, reenlisting in the US Air Force, and eventually joining Masonic Lodge No. 228 in Mitchell. There, he rose to the rank of Master Mason. According to the frequently inscrutable code of Free Masonry, the Master Mason "has symbolically, if not actually, balanced his inner natures and has shaped them into the proper relationship with the higher, more spiritual parts of himself. His physical nature has been purified and developed to a high degree. He has developed stability and a sure footing. His mental faculties have sharpened and his horizons have been expanded."[27]

Whether the Master Mason Grissom actually believed these words is unknown. But his actions from an early age tended to support the view that he would attempt to live his life in accordance with the ideals expressed by the Masons. His faculties were indeed "sharpened" far beyond what any of his teachers expected and his horizons surely would be "expanded" far beyond Mitchell, Indiana.

A central reason was flight. As daring aviators followed Lindbergh's lead in the 1930s, breaking one distance record after another, the serious business of model-airplane building began in earnest across the country. Virgil was an avid and meticulous model builder, suspending the balsa woods airplanes from ceilings. It was the making that interested him, at least initially, not the starry-eyed dream of flight.

But model airplanes and the supplies needed to make them did not grow on trees. Nor did the schoolbooks that Virgil was expected to help pay for. When old enough, the eldest son rose at 4 a.m. to deliver the morning newspaper, the big-city *Indianapolis Star.* There were the usual hardships of slogging through high drifts in winter along with the mundane tasks associated with the paper route. Among them was knocking on doors on Saturdays collecting subscription fees from annoyed customers who were more often than not falling behind on their payments. Virgil was on the hook for all those newspapers—the Sunday edition cost twice as much—until he could persuade his customers to pay up. Then there were the dogs that snarled at mailmen, paperboys, and traveling salesman. Virgil maintained his bicycle himself so he could speed up deliveries and outrace the howling neighborhood hounds.

Two determined brothers from Dayton, Ohio, invented the world's first powered flying machine.[28] One of the coincidences in the early days of the American space program was the fact that many of the astronauts either grew up in the Midwest or attended an engineering school in the Big Ten conference. Indeed, the state of Indiana alone has so far produced about a dozen astronauts.

Raised in rural Michigan, the childhood of another astronaut was likely similar to Grissom's. "As a little kid, I had a lot of freedom," recalled Al Worden, who circled the moon on *Apollo 15*, becoming the first human to climb out of a spacecraft and float in cislunar space—the void between the earth and the moon. Born in 1932 in Jackson, Michigan, Worden remembered wandering along the railroad tracks to watch the steam engines go by. "I did my own thing, followed my own interests, and didn't rely on others," Worden wrote of his idyllic youth. "From an early age, I could take care of myself, and I knew it."[29]

In those Depression Era days, country boys and those who lived in small towns like Mitchell wandered the fields and woods alone, making up their own games and adventures. They were accustomed to, even welcomed, being on their own. They were free, and the life of the mind was unleashed. The result for boys like Al Worden and Virgil Grissom was self-reliance.

2

WORK

I'd been biding my time, waiting in numb hope for some unknown,
defining reality finally to pop up that would clarify the course I
should follow. . . . We had not thought it would be a war.
—Joseph Heller[1]

Young Virgil Grissom did not have the same wide-eyed love affair with flying associated with many of the early astronauts. There were no World War I–era barnstormers flying through Mitchell needing to be refueled, offering boys their first plane ride. Indeed, airplane sightings around the railroad junction of Mitchell were rare in his youth. Grissom made his share of model airplanes but did not spend his boyhood with his nose in the air dreaming of the wild blue yonder. There was no time. He was too busy for idle thoughts, and his nose instead remained always to the grindstone.

Classmate Jenny Leonard, a dignified, unassuming woman no town can do without, knew Virgil well enough that he signed her high school yearbook. Precisely summing up Grissom's early life, she remembered: "He just worked."

An early biography noted that Virgil's parents had developed in all the Grissom children a "balance of discipline and pleasure." Dennis and Cecile had stressed the "harm of excesses and the value of thrift." Most important, they "exemplified the *importance of work*."[2]

Growing up during the Depression, the Grissom children learned early if they wanted something, they had to earn it. Virgil did eventually scrape together the fifty cents, or perhaps it was a dollar, his brother Lowell recalled, for his first plane ride with money earned delivering the *Indianapolis Star* in the morning and the evening *Bedford Times*. Another classmate and lifelong friend Bill Head remembered that his friend had swapped something to get an early plane ride at the small airport in nearby Bedford. Years later, it would be renamed Virgil I. Grissom Municipal Airport.

Virgil "must have been twelve or fourteen, somewhere in there," when he took his first airplane ride, according to Lowell. His reactions to this experience are unknown, but they certainly gave the now wide-eyed Indiana lad a completely new perspective on the world beyond Lawrence County. Up amidst the cold, dry air, he gazed down on the farmland of southern Indiana and likely considered what lay beyond the horizon. Leaving the ground in the 1930s to see what relatively few had seen would change the boy who was becoming a man. Flying above the earth would ignite a spark in Virgil, something that would smolder until it caught fire, eventually changing the course of his terrestrial life. He would fly again, someday.

Back on the ground, he continued building model airplanes, becoming angry one day when his younger brother Norman sat on one. It was unusual for the easy-going eldest brother to show anger. Norman and Lowell looked up to Virgil, but they never found a reason to fear him. The model was promptly repaired, hinting at his growing passion for airplanes and flight. A handmade version of an early American fighter jet, the sleek F-86 Sabre, the plane Virgil would fly with distinction in Korea, still hangs from the ceiling of his boyhood home.

"I suppose I built my share of model airplanes, but I can't remember that I was a flying fanatic,"[3] Virgil recalled years later. Still, the Mitchell of Grissom's youth echoed with the sound of train whistles, metal benders, lathes, and a collection of neighborhood do-it-yourselfers making with their own hands parts they couldn't afford to buy.

In the days before American manufacturing was largely shipped overseas, fellows like Grissom were getting their hands dirty repairing bicycles and equipment, or even fashioning spare parts. Not for nothing was the mechanically inclined Virgil originally tagged with the nickname "Greasy."

Mitchell developed its own version of the Yankee workshop based on midwestern notions of self-reliance. If a part broke, you fixed it yourself. This ethic was engrained in Virgil as a schoolboy. He would later take it with him when he ventured off to college to study mechanical engineering.

It turned out that flying was a natural extension of Virgil's interest in machines and what made them tick. It was the same for other star-crossed boys across America who would one day become "astronauts," a term not yet invented, or space travelers. As long as he could remember, the future astronaut Michael Collins said, he too was intrigued with "mechanical objects in the sky."[4] Eventually, small engines were mounted on the balsa wood contraptions. "Some of them actually flew," Collins recalled.

As his interest in aviation grew, Grissom spent more time hanging around the Bedford airport, just up State Road 37 from Mitchell. (An apocryphal story has it that a local attorney who owned a small plane taught Grissom the basics of flying at a dollar a lesson. Brother Norman doubts this is true. More likely it was a family trip to Vincennes, just over sixty miles to the west, during which Virgil took his first ride in an airplane.[5]) Later, he reportedly traded an air rifle for another ride at the Bedford airport.[6]

During the prewar summers of the late 1930s, amid the profound economic depression that gripped the nation and much of the world, Virgil doubled his workload picking cherries and peaches in orchards outside Mitchell. Idleness was never an option, and, like Tarkington's *Penrod and Sam*, boredom was to be avoided at all costs. Therefore, he also put in time at the local grocery and dry goods stores, worked occasionally at a gas station, and even tried his hand at the fading art of blacksmithing. Like many of his generation, Dennis and Cecile's oldest son was a striver who realized early on that he had to earn the money for extravagances like movie tickets or flying lessons. Fun-loving as well as self-reliant, he also preferred to have some spending money in his pocket for Cokes at the Cargas Candy Kitchen on Main Street.[7]

W hen not laboring or spending, Virgil took a passing interest in his studies. He was a high school sophomore on December 7, 1941. The Japanese attack on Pearl Harbor forced American teenage boys to grow up quickly. Of far greater importance now was completing a year of pre-cadet training for the US Army Air Corps. Grissom listed mathematics and machine shop as his high school "majors" on one of a series of job applications. Mostly, he coasted through high school. Either he had little use for other classes or there simply were not enough hours in the day for further study. Either way, he was, by his own admission, "drifting and not knowing what [he] wanted to make of [him]self."[8]

He eventually concluded that making something of himself required a mate. In the months before Pearl Harbor, Grissom made the acquaintance of a freshman named Betty Lavonne Moore, a drummer in the Mitchell High School band. She had noticed him in the hallway between classes and recognized Virgil as the member of the Boy Scout Honor Guard presenting the colors along with the school band at basketball games. Virgil eventually got around to introducing himself to Betty during halftime in the fall of 1941.

"I was told he said, 'That's who I'm going to marry,'" Betty recalled fifty years after her husband's first space flight. "I don't know whether he really said it or not, but I heard that. It seemed like we just kept staying on together; he was mostly at my house. If he wasn't at my house he was working or in school. It always seemed like he had a job."[9]

Virgil's work ethic impressed Betty as much as hers would make an impression on him when she labored at a shirt factory after high school and, later, as a switchboard operator in West Lafayette while Virgil attended Purdue University. Betty's suitor spent most of his earnings taking her to movies in Mitchell, usually the late show. The newsreels provided updates on the war, including the air combat over Europe and the Pacific. What little free time they had was usually spent at the Moore's home outside Mitchell. Betty's parents were suspicious of boys from town; Virgil had to pass muster before being accepted by the Moores. (Claude Moore, Betty's father, would eventually treat Virgil as if he were his own and was shattered when his son-in-law was killed.) Dinner at the Moore's helped fill out his thin frame, and Virgil was known to leave his bike behind as an excuse to return the next day.

The couple eventually became inseparable, and Virgil soon concluded that, as far as girls were concerned, meeting Betty "was it, period, exclamation point!"[10]

By the time he enrolled at Purdue, Virgil claimed to weigh 140 pounds, standing five feet seven inches. During high school, he and diminutive high school classmate Bill Head were joined at the hip as the shortest, skinniest students in mandatory physical education courses. "When we started in high school in '40, we were the two smallest guys in our class, and you had to take one year of phys ed, so they paired [us] up together. I think he weighed 99 and I weighed 98 pounds," Head recollected. "When we were sophomores, [President Franklin Roosevelt] declared that all males would take [a] physical fitness program in high school, so there we were for three more years. So, we were always buddied together 'cause we's the two smallest guys," Head recalled on a torrid July day outside the Masonic Temple in Mitchell.

Undeterred, Head and Grissom (who stood only five feet, four inches when he entered high school) both tried out for the varsity basketball team. Even a seat on the bench was frequently a ticket to social mobility in high school, especially in the basketball-crazy Hoosier State. After a week of practice, Head recalled, "the coach decided it was time to 'cull.' There was another Grissom in our class, so when [the coach] read off the names, he said, 'Head, Grissom, and Grissom!' That's the three that got cut. That was the end of our athletic" careers.

Not quite. Virgil, it turned out, was better suited to other athletic pursuits, like boxing. (After becoming an astronaut, he was considered an ace handball player, fished near Cape Canaveral whenever he could find the time, and was a competent water and snow skier.) Mitchell High School offered intramural boxing during the lunch period. The buddies signed up, recalled Head, who would eventually become the Lawrence County, Indiana, agriculture agent. They were among four "flea weights." Both won their first-round matches. "That made me and [Virgil] for the final championship of the flea weights. Well, I'd boxed him a little in phys ed so I knew to stay away from him, but I made one mistake. I got through the first round all right, and the second one just started, and I made a mistake in not running backwards and he hit me, floored me, and when I looked up all I saw was black spots." Virgil was tough as nails—and extremely competitive. Head had discovered this fact the hard way.

An early biographer, Carl Chappell, had a unique perspective as a neighbor of the Grissoms and pastor of the First Baptist Church of Mitchell. His theory was that the oldest Grissom son "sensed his inferior size," compensated for it, and "learned to excel in ways that did not demand height and weight."[11] Virgil's stature did him no harm when he set his sights on becoming a pilot and an astronaut. Years later, he would be the fastest in and out of the cramped cabin of his Mercury spacecraft in a life-or-death situation.

Grissom literally did not stand out in a crowd, and his schoolmates remembered a somewhat reserved but approachable young man. Classmate Jenny Leonard first met Virgil in sixth grade. "He was always just friendly. He wasn't too much with the girls" in high school. "Of course he had Betty from the time he was a sophomore [so] he couldn't mess around girls very much. But if you asked him something, he'd be glad to talk to you; he was very friendly, very quiet and"—her cadence slowing—"a . . . *lot* . . . more . . . mischievous I have found out than I ever thought he was."[12]

The mischief during high school mostly involved "cutting up" in class with Head and, undoubtedly, Friday night hijinks like tipping over outhouses. More than anything, the classroom antics reflected boredom, uninspiring teachers, and restless energy.

Earlier, as a member of Robert Pingrie's Boy Scout Troup 46, Virgil was said to be practicing the fine art of knot tying when his scoutmates decided to rig a hangman's noose. They slipped it over Virgil's head, tossed the other end over a rafter, and pulled it to see if the knot would hold. The victim's face was turning blue when he was finally cut down.[13]

Like much of the country, Mitchell during World War II experienced firsthand the deprivations of a world ablaze. There was no question during the war years that every citizen of Mitchell would willingly sacrifice to aid the war effort. Bill Head remembered: "God, everything was rationed, you know, [even] turning the street lights out at night." The war rationing, the newsreels—the need to do something concrete to help the war effort fueled Virgil's now-burning desire to join the military after graduation. He must also have understood that the tide of war in Europe had turned after the decisive Allied invasion of Western Europe on June 6, 1944. About to graduate from high school, he undoubtedly sensed that the Allies had gained control of the skies over most of Europe. Perhaps, he may have thought, there was still a chance to fly in the Pacific, where the titanic struggle with Japan seemed as if it could go on indefinitely. Or so it seemed.

What no one save a few top American officials along with a team of physicists knew was that a secret weapon was being readied in New Mexico, a weapon so fearsome that it could end the war with Japan in a single flash brighter than the sun.

Having studied just enough to earn his diploma, Grissom graduated from Mitchell High School in May 1944. A month earlier, he had turned eighteen, and he was now eligible to enlist. At this turning point in his life, however, classmates like Jenny Leonard and Bill Head agreed later that Grissom was generally considered among the least likely among them to do great things. Still, they admired his work ethic, his devotion to Betty, his genial, if reserved, nature. What they could not see was the fire in his gut that now yearned to break way.

From May until August of 1944, the graduate toiled as a helper in the signal department of the B&O Railroad in Mitchell, undoubtedly using his father's connections. The position quickly proved unsatisfactory. For a young man with brains and ambition, signing up for the US Army Air Corps now seemed the best way for a high school graduate to get into the fight. It was also the quickest way out of a small Indiana town that offered little beyond menial labor and long hours working either for the B&O or installing bus doors at the Carpenter Body Works.

Grissom's outlook was similar to another Air Corps enlistee, Joseph Heller of Coney Island, Brooklyn, who was delivering telegrams in New York City and working other odd jobs when World War II broke out. The future bomber pilot initially believed the war was the greatest thing that had ever happened to him. "We had nothing better to do," the future novelist recalled. Knowing that nineteen-year-olds could soon be drafted into military service, Heller and his friends were "further motivated by the opportunity to choose the branch [they] preferred."

Heller's dreary life in New York would soon be replaced with glory and flight pay if he could earn his wings. He had enough on the ball to become a pilot, but his view of the air war over Europe changed drastically, of course, once his B-25 *Mitchell* bomber started taking antiaircraft fire over Italy.[14] The absurdities of aerial combat nevertheless helped the future novelist place his finger precisely on the horns of the great dilemma of the war-ravaged twentieth century in his existential masterpiece, *Catch-22*.

Unlike Heller and future astronauts Alan Shepard and John Glenn, Grissom's brief stint in the service during World War II would be far less eventful. Shepard served with distinction in the Pacific on a Navy destroyer; Glenn was a fighter pilot with the marines. Born too late to get into the fight, Grissom languished behind a desk but would at least earn the right to attend college under the G.I. Bill of Rights. It seemed insignificant at the time, but Grissom became one of countless World War II veterans who grabbed the opportunity for a college education and made the most of it.

That summer after graduation, Grissom had arranged his priorities: flying, Betty, and escaping Mitchell. In August, he enlisted in the US Army Air Corps (three years later, it would become a separate service branch, the US Air Force). "Flying sounded a lot more exciting than walking," he decided.[15]

Virgil along with two Mitchell buddies, Harrison Conley and Bill Harrison, were inducted into the US military on August 8 at Fort Benjamin Harrison near Indianapolis. After basic training at Sheppard Field in Wichita Falls, Texas, the recruit and his hopes of flying crash-landed behind a desk as a clerk at Brooks Field in San Antonio. There, he rode out the remainder of the wars in Europe and the Pacific.

Near the end of World War II, Bill Head remembered the War Department declaring a series of "draft holidays" as the recruits backed up in barracks waiting to begin basic training. The air war was indeed winding down, and Virgil, the eager enlistee in the Air Corps' Aviation Cadet Program, would not earn his wings.

Private Grissom returned home on leave for the first time during the Christmas holiday of 1944. The visit was uneventful, and Virgil was likely one of several stateside servicemen who had been granted leave from their typewriters. It's likely that Virgil and Betty discussed marriage during the holidays and may have even decided on the date.

Upon his return to Brooks Field, Virgil's disappointment and the drudgery of pencil-pushing would soon be offset by the singular fact that he was now eligible for one of the great American social experiments of the twentieth century, the G.I. Bill of Rights. A typical scenario was described by war veteran and future NASA engineer George Page, who oversaw early spacecraft testing. After the war, "they opened up the G.I. Bill of Rights, [without which] I never would have gone to college because we weren't in the financial situation where we could save money for that kind of stuff." Page eventually graduated with a degree in aeronautical engineering from Penn State and went on to a long career at NASA and the aerospace industry. Page would work closely with astronaut Gus Grissom, overseeing a key spacecraft test on the night of the *Apollo 1* fire.[16]

Officially known as the Servicemen's Readjustment Act of 1944, the G.I. Bill nearly stalled in Congress. Some lawmakers balked at a provision that would give unemployed veterans $20 a week. This "handout" would diminish a veteran's incentive to work, huffed the critics. Others thought college was reserved for the privileged, not battle-hardened veterans.

The veterans of World War II were on the verge of defeating fascism. They weren't looking for a handout. They wanted a job! The desire of a majority of lawmakers to avoid the injustices endured by World War I veterans, who received little more than a sixty-dollar allowance and a train ticket home, finally helped push the G.I. Bill through to passage.[17]

Five and a half million veterans benefited from the G.I. Bill in the decade after World War II. Precisely how many of the 400,000 engineers and technicians who worked on the American space program in the 1960s directly benefited from the landmark legislation is unclear. Without question, the G.I. Bill educated the cadre of engineers who laid the groundwork for the United States to become a postwar superpower.

Seldom had so many fulfilled the responsibilities that entitled them to the right to a college education. Virgil's future as well as the future of countless World War II veterans—indeed, even the course of an emerging global superpower itself—would be transformed by the opportunity to earn a college degree. The G.I. Bill was a form of social mobility and a source of economic prosperity like no other in the middle of the twentieth century. It proved to be one of the best investments America has ever made. Grissom possessed the good sense and the ambition to see that the G.I. Bill was his ticket to a better life for himself and his fiancée.

Anxious now to be discharged from the service, Virgil wrangled enough leave to return home again in time to secure a marriage license on July 3 and marry Betty Moore on a Friday afternoon, July 6, 1945. The ceremony took place in the parsonage of the First Baptist Church of Mitchell, Reverend A. G. Sinclair officiating.[18]

The groom was nineteen, the bride eighteen. Betty's sister Mary Lou was maid of honor. Norman Grissom served as best man. Along with the couple's parents, only a few close friends attended the ceremony. The honeymoon was brief: a quick trip in the Grissom family car to Indianapolis, a night or two at the Washington Hotel, and a day at the amusement park riding the roller coaster and bumper cars, "laughing all the way."[19] The newlyweds had hoped for Niagara Falls, but the expense and wartime gas rationing ruled that out until their first wedding anniversary.

Returning to Mitchell, Virgil caught a train back to his base in Texas. Mrs. Virgil Grissom remained at her parents' home outside Mitchell for the remainder of the war, hanging on to her job at the Reliance Shirt Factory. Virgil waited until November 3 to be honorably discharged from the Army Air Corps. The desire to fly was as strong as ever, but reality had set in: the war was over, and the wings of Franklin Roosevelt's Arsenal of Democracy would soon be scrapped. There had been too many air cadets in the pipeline when Virgil enlisted; they surely would not be needed now. Plans for a flying career were set aside, and he packed his gear and returned home.

The veteran began planning his next move while working in the electrical department at the Carpenter Body Works. The newlyweds had recently moved into a modest upstairs apartment on Main Street. Virgil returned home from work one day in August 1946 and told his wife he had made up his mind: he would enroll as an engineering major at Purdue University in the fall. The decision came as little surprise to Betty, who could already see that a college education was their best option. She was simply waiting for her frustrated husband to come around to the same conclusion.[20]

At a crossroads in their lives together, Virgil and Betty might have played it safe, starting a family in Mitchell and setting down deeper roots. He held a steady job in his hometown, something few veterans could claim. She could remain close to home and family while starting her own. But together they decided to take a risk by moving to the college town of West Lafayette. Perhaps it was not a huge risk in the scheme of things, but for a young married couple striking out on their own it represented a life-altering decision. In so doing, they gained.

Responding to a question in a later job application when asked his reason for leaving his job installing doors on busses, Virgil replied: "To Enter Purdue."

3

PURDUE

I needed more technical training if I was going to get ahead.
So I took time out to go to Purdue University.
—Virgil Grissom

irgil Grissom, a World War II veteran with no combat experience and little to show for his service beyond an honorable discharge from the US Army Air Corps, was nevertheless admitted to Purdue University by virtue of the fact that he had worn the uniform. His acceptance into Purdue's engineering school had little to do with the fact that he was an industrious young man who had finally figured out what to do with his life.

Purdue was an opportunity, and Grissom seized it.

Just the same, it seemed unlikely in the autumn of 1946 that a twenty-year-old veteran with a new wife from a small Indiana town would make much of a mark at Purdue, then among the many American college campuses swarming with war veterans. An opportunity to "get ahead" had presented itself, and Virgil and Betty were ready when it appeared.

Describing his background in a 1962 book promoted as written by "The Astronauts Themselves," Grissom said he realized soon after his discharge from the military with the rank of corporal "that [he] needed more technical training if [he] was going to get ahead." Quickly finding the manual labor in his hometown unfulfilling, the veteran decided to exercise his G.I. Bill of Rights by enrolling at Purdue to study engineering.[1]

By September 1946, American universities were attracting ex-G.I.s in droves. The competition was intense for admission to top engineering schools, meaning a letter of recommendation from a high school principal was an absolute necessity. Grissom and Bill Head, the two cut-ups from Mitchell High School, had a difficult time obtaining the required credentials to gain acceptance to Purdue, the school both had decided to attend. The dubious high school principal George Bishop vividly remembered the buddies were "troublemakers" but nevertheless supplied tepid recommendations that constituted less-than-favorable endorsements of their college prospects.

A Purdue admission official quickly figured out that the "two boys sat too close together" in class, meaning that their average high school grades would normally disqualify them from admission to a top engineering school. Reluctantly, the counselor relented. "Since you are G.I.s, we can't turn you down." Grissom was in—barely. Head would follow a few years later. Neither would waste the opportunity.

Given this less-than-auspicious introduction to higher education, it seemed improbable in September 1946 that a campus engineering building would one day bear Virgil Grissom's name. It would not be the first time he was underestimated. The freshman would now "set aside childish things" and begin working in earnest to build a better life for himself and his family. He would commit himself to the study of a branch of science and technology concerned with designing, building, and using engines, machines, and structures for the progress of mankind. For its part, the university was essentially placing a bet on an unknown quantity: among thousands of new freshman overrunning the Purdue campus, veterans who had grown up quickly, enlisted in the military, some had married and most had mapped out a plan to better themselves.

Grissom's education represented the very essence of the American system of higher education: if you could get in, you would get out of it precisely what you put into it.

Discharged from the service in November 1945 and biding his time at Carpenter Body Works, the restless veteran's thoughts soon turned to college, an engineering degree, and the dream of becoming a test pilot. He quickly understood the opportunity presented by the G.I. Bill. Virgil had encouraged Bill Head to enlist before the war ended, and then immediately applied to Purdue University after he was discharged.

"You'd better go back with me and get your papers in to go to Purdue," Grissom told his friend after Head had completed an eighteen-month hitch as an Army medic.[2] Two years ahead of his friend, Grissom understood it would be difficult for Head to gain admission with the university already bursting at the seams.

When he enrolled at Purdue in the fall of 1946, Grissom was a face in a crowd that totaled 11,462 students—49 percent greater than the previous academic year. Enrollment peaked at 14,674 in 1948. (The previous maximum enrollment at Purdue had been 6,966 students.[3]) These numbers were typical for most US universities by the late 1940s.

The land grant university founded in 1869 and named for its chief benefactor, the successful merchant and philanthropist John Purdue, was packed to the rafters when Grissom enrolled. A residency requirement meant the newlyweds had to scramble to find someplace—anyplace—to live. During his first semester in the fall of 1946, Grissom had to share a room and a double bed with a male roommate while Betty moved back in with her parents. She moved to West Lafayette for the spring semester, and the couple ended up in a basement apartment at 205 Sylvia Street a few blocks north of the Purdue engineering building.[4]

After the relative inactivity of military life as the war wound down, Purdue would now demand even more effort and sacrifice than Virgil and Betty had previously endured. To make ends meet, Virgil flipped burgers for thirty hours a week while taking a full load of undergraduate courses. "I used to carry an engineering textbook along to my job as a hamburger cook," he recalled with a measure of pride.[5]

The G.I. Bill provided a monthly allowance of $65 plus $500 for tuition, books, and fees.[6] Grissom's goal was to earn an engineering degree in less than four years (his short military stint meant the G.I. Bill would only cover part of a college education). Betty was soon holding down the fort working as a telephone operator for the Indiana Bell Telephone Company. Between work and classes, they hardly saw each other.

Grissom could not have picked a more demanding field of study. Today, the attrition rate for undergraduate engineering students is high. Introductory courses are demanding and often seem far removed from the actual engineering profession. "Grissom, like many other postwar veterans flocking to the nation's colleges and universities, was quite different from the ordinary college freshman," a Purdue engineering professor recalled. "He knew exactly what he was going to school for and would let nothing get in his way. He hit the books instead of horsing around."[7]

From 1941 to 1959, Purdue's mechanical engineering program was lorded over by Harry L. Solberg, whose father was credited with constructing the first wind tunnel used by a US engineering school. Solberg helped shepherd the more than 2,200 mechanical engineering students who came through Purdue during the postwar years. "Harry was a crotchety old rooster who talked no nonsense," remembered William Fontaine, who went on to become director of the university's Herrick Laboratories. Solberg turned out to be just what a determined engineering student required, especially one trying to earn his degree in fewer than four years. With the engineering school going "full steam" after the war, Purdue awarded more than seven hundred bachelor's degrees in mechanical engineering during Grissom's years there. Sparse with his praise, Solberg nevertheless proclaimed, "They were the finest group of students we ever had."[8]

As with high school, Virgil's college grades were unspectacular, only slightly above average. This was understandable given the fact that by his senior year at Purdue, he was working long hours at the campus burger joint (after his veterans' benefits ran out). His grades also reflected an intense interest in what practical applications he could derive from his studies. The letter grade was of little consequence.

Slowly, the engineering student was formulating a strategy for what he expected to derive from a college education. A decade later, while overseeing development of a spaceship, Grissom would apply the engineering principles he absorbed at Purdue to develop his own theory of how to get things done. As he watched the engineers fiddling with his spacecraft, he adhered to a plan that had its origins in his practical engineering education.

"It was my theory all along," he observed a decade after graduating from Purdue, "that we ought to have everything working perfectly that could possibly affect our safety or the efficiency of the capsule. But I was convinced that if we waited for all the peripheral equipment to work perfectly, too, we would never get off the ground."[9] In other words, "Perfect is the enemy of the good."

Grissom's engineering professors remembered an "exceptionally determined student" who missed only two classes during his eight semesters at Purdue. He also found time to join several professional and service organizations on campus in hopes of burnishing his academic record. Besides the High Twelve,[10] a kind of fraternity and luncheon club for young Masons, Grissom was a student member of the American Association of Mechanical Engineers and the American Society of Heating and Ventilating Engineers. He also joined the Purdue Independent Association, a service organization and alternative to the campus Greek organizations. The splinter group flourished on the Purdue campus until the mid-1950s, attracting blue-collar veterans who had little use for fraternities.

While hustling to earn a mechanical engineering degree, the earth-bound student never abandoned his goal of flying, perhaps flight-testing fighter jets that would soon enter military service. Out in the high California desert, the Air Force was then evaluating rocket planes. A test pilot named Chuck Yeager had broken the sound barrier in one of them, the Bell X-1, on October, 14, 1947. When word of Captain Yeager's historic accomplishment finally leaked out, Grissom took note. A new word had entered the vocabulary of flying: "supersonic."

As it turned out, the steady presence of the Air Force Reserve Officer Training Corps on the Purdue campus would prove to be Grissom's ticket to flight training. In the meantime, Virgil studied while Betty worked, scrimped, and saved to pay tuition and rent on the basement apartment.[11] Virgil took no summer breaks, pressing on with his engineering studies. He also knew there would be additional work during the summer months that could supplement their meager incomes. While taking more courses, he spent one summer detasseling corn, a character builder if there ever was one. The tedious labor involved walking down long rows of corn and yanking the tassels off ears meant to produce hybrid seeds. The mind-numbing task performed alone amid the cornfields of Indiana afforded the engineering student some time to think about flying. That and the welcome thought of a paycheck at the end of another long week to cover rent, groceries, and textbooks.

In July of 1947, Virgil applied for yet another temporary job as a laborer in the Lafayette roundhouse of the Chicago, Indianapolis, and Louisville Railroad Company—the same "Monon" that ran through Mitchell. He started on the night shift on July 8 at a rate of 82 cents an hour. Virgil was suited to the work, and by the end of the summer he had moved up to lofty positions of pipefitter and machinist's helper.

Working odd summer shifts, Virgil and Betty saw even less of each other, and there was little time for domestic life. In the midst of all this frenetic activity, however, the couple somehow found time to produce a son: Allan Scott Grissom was born on May 16, 1950, three months after his father graduated from Purdue. The boy would be called "Scotty."

Despite the Grissom family's growing independence, not all their ties with Mitchell were cut. For example, the time-honored college tradition of hauling home one's laundry was well under way by the time Grissom reached Purdue. On an accelerated schedule at a crowded campus that meant classes ran through Saturday mornings, Virgil would leave Betty at her switchboard and take off for home on Saturday afternoons. He and Bill Head would carry their laundry in one hand, the thumb of the other extended along the side of the road. It was the heyday of hitchhiking in rural America, and it was relatively easy to get a ride to and from Purdue if one knew the ropes.

Grissom and Head had a sure-fire method of convincing drivers to pick them up. They would strike out to the south on the state highways in the days before the Interstate Highway System carrying a sort of suitcase specifically designed to haul laundry. A "Purdue University" sticker was affixed to the hamper. The hitchhikers displayed it prominently to passing cars and trucks. "Every once in a while, we had [a driver] who didn't like [Indiana University] like we didn't, so we got a ride," Head recalled with a laugh.[12]

It was not exactly the hitchhiking scene from the Clark Gable–Claudette Colbert film of 1934, *It Happened One Night*, but Grissom and Head generally managed to hitch a ride back and forth the one hundred and forty miles between West Lafayette and Mitchell, returning to school in time for classes on Monday morning.

It was indeed a different time in America, a decade when a driver gave not a second thought to picking up a couple of college guys on a pleasant autumn afternoon along a country highway in the middle of Indiana. The war was fading from memory. Things were looking up. The impoverished college students could look forward to a home-cooked meal and, when they returned, a sack of clean clothes.

The dizzying pace of school and work made those college days race by. The hitchhikers' pastoral adventures along the country roads of Indiana helped slow things a bit, allowed the friends to talk about their problems and reflect. "On the road," a phrase that would come to define for some the postwar generation, meant that the college buddies Grissom and Head were temporarily carefree. Someone would eventually stop and ask where they were headed, and home they would go. Making the round trip in a little over a day, the Purdue classmates "spent a lot of time together," a wistful Bill Head remembered sixty years later. "We had a lot of good experiences hitchhiking together."[13]

Grissom's three-and-a-half years at Purdue University transformed him both personally and professionally. Among the transformations wrought by life on campus was an incident that would literally change the engineering student's identity, his view of himself, and the way others—even his own wife—saw him.

What's in a name? Not much. But nicknames, like stage names, can remake, for example, a Marion Robert Morrison into a heroic "John Wayne." They were the same person, but one persona is perceived quite differently from the other. And so it was for Virgil I. Grissom.

There are several differing accounts of how Virgil came to be known as "Gus" Grissom. The conventional version has it that he acquired the sobriquet during a campus card game when the scorekeeper wrote down "Gris" and someone read the notation upside down as "Gus." The nickname stuck, or so the story goes.

Betty Grissom subscribes to this version of the metamorphosis of her husband from Virgil Ivan to "Gus." When asked decades later how she addressed her husband at home, Betty responded, "Probably 'Hey you!'" Joking aside, she added, "At the beginning, 'Gus' was hard for me because he didn't have [a nickname] when we first met."[14] Indeed, most everyone in Mitchell would continue calling her husband "Virgil."

Whether the card game story is apocryphal cannot be proven, but Bill Head has his own version of how his friend and classmate became "Gus." Standing in the shade of a big oak tree near the Virgil I. Grissom Memorial in Mitchell one July morning, Head was deep into his reminiscences about his buddy when he made a point of recounting what he claims is the real story.

"Let me tell you something," he volunteered, anxious to share the tale. "Have you ever known how he got the name Gus?" The version involving "Gris" and the card game was repeated, and the dismissive Head warmed to the subject.

"I'll tell you what he told me: There were two guys in his class [at Purdue]. . . . They were in the same [engineering major] as he was. And there was another kid, I'll say, that for some reason thought Virgil's name was," drawing out the name on the first mention, "Guh-us."

"So he started calling him 'Gus' and following him around when they [would] go to class. And the other two guys that was in his class, they picked it up, they started calling him 'Gus,' then Betty started calling him 'Gus.'"

Head arrived at Purdue in the fall of 1948, moving into another rented basement room about a block and half from the Grissoms. He visited one day, but Virgil was not home. According to Head, Betty confided: "I want to tell you, they call him Gus. No Virgil, it's nothing but Gus." "Well," Head recalled, chuckling at the memory, "he wasn't real sure about this boy that called him 'Gus' that followed him around, so I didn't pursue the issue."[15]

The male engineering student's identity and motive are irrelevant. What mattered was the apparent object of his affection had completed the slow but steady transformation from Virgil Ivan into Gus Grissom. Virgil was the restless boy from Mitchell whose parents had bestowed on him an unusual name for reasons known only to them. ("He wasn't proud of 'Ivan,'" according to Head. "He never put that forward—it was always 'Virgil I.'") Henceforth, he would be known to all and to history as Gus Grissom.

Grissom's engineering education predated the rise of aeronautics and the newfangled science known as astronautics. His undergraduate courses certainly touched on critical aspects of airplane design, but it wasn't until the watershed International Geophysical Year of 1957 and the earth-shaking launch of *Sputnik* in October of the same year that aeronautical engineering really "took off" at American engineering schools.

"The curriculum studied by Mr. Grissom leading to his B.S. in [mechanical engineering] in 1950 was probably not influenced by this new educational interest," a department professor recalled.[16] Only about two doctorates in "space research" were being awarded annually at Purdue in the early 1950s. Fifteen years later, at the height of the Space Race, that total would jump to about a dozen PhDs a year, transforming Purdue into a hotbed of aeronautical engineering. Grissom would be the first in a long line of Purdue graduates to qualify as astronauts, a list that included the first and last men to walk on the moon.[17]

Returning to Purdue, Astronaut Grissom was amazed by what he observed. "When I was studying at Purdue, we learned our thermodynamics from an antique steam engine. When I went back in 1964, I found the laboratories packed with the most modern equipment for the study of thermodynamics, some of which had been built by the students themselves."[18]

Grissom may have been slightly ahead of his time when it came to aeronautics, but he nevertheless gained a solid grounding in the fundamentals of engineering. Moreover, he was by now determined to translate the concepts he had mastered into practicable skills. For him, little that was absorbed was theoretical; he would find a way to apply his knowledge.

On a fateful morning in the fall of 1949, as they made their way to class, Grissom and Head were climbing the steps on the east side of the Purdue Memorial Union when an Air Force recruiter stepped forward and offered each a recruiting pamphlet. "Do you want to be a pilot?" the recruiter inquired.

Grissom, the fourth-year mechanical engineering student, grabbed the pamphlet out of the recruiter's hand, considered his options, and immediately realized this was his ticket. He probably would have gotten around to checking in with an Air Force recruiter when he could find a free moment, but instead, the US Air Force found Gus Grissom.

His brothers recalled later that Gus had reminded them to be ready when an opportunity came along. The elder Grissom leaped at the chance to fly, and, for better or worse, Betty would take the leap with him.

"We were going from his house to the morning class, and we walked up a block across the street and went into the east end of the union building," Head remembered as if it was yesterday. "As we started up the steps, there was an Air Force [officer] and he was handing out some literature, so we took it. And it was saying: 'Would you like to be a pilot?'"[19]

The recruiter asked Grissom and Head what each was studying and when they expected to graduate. When Grissom replied that he was a senior engineering student, the recruiter indicated that he would have little trouble passing the entrance exam. He wasn't as sure about Head.

Each decided to take the Air Force aviation cadet entrance exam that same day. Sure enough, Grissom easily passed the test. Head also received a passing grade, to his surprise. The next step was deciding when to report. The senior expected to graduate three months early, so he picked a date shortly after earning his diploma in February 1950. Head reckoned it was best to get his degree before doing anything as rash as enlisting in pilot training. "That's how it all came about; that's how Gus became a pilot," Head recalled.

From the moment the two students encountered the Air Force recruiter, the course of Gus and Betty's life was set: it would revolve around flying, Air Force bases, the Korean war, and, one day in 1959, a telegram to report for a classified briefing at the Pentagon in Washington, DC, to hear about a plan to send humans into space aboard rockets.

The Air Force would serve as the stepping-stone for Grissom to pursue his dream of flying. He would quickly fall in love with flight. For the new Air Force wife Betty, it meant long separations, constant relocations, and sweating out a combat tour in Korea alone with an infant son followed by a brief period of relatively normal family life while her husband pushed the flight envelope as a test pilot. The Air Force also would serve as another form of social mobility for the Grissoms, one that other future astronauts did not require. Some, like Gus's future Air Force test pilot buddy Leroy Gordon Cooper, were born into military families and had been flying airplanes before they could ride a bike. For Grissom, the Air Force offered a flying career at a time when competition for civilian engineering jobs was intense.

On that autumn morning, on the steps of the Purdue Union, Gus Grissom at last took a moment to look up from the work that had so thoroughly dominated his life. Without consulting the main breadwinner in the family, his wife, Gus determined that he was going to be a flyer. It was the easiest decision of his life.

Nearing graduation, a complication arose. While awaiting word from the Air Force on the date to report for his physical, Grissom made a half-hearted attempt at finding employment in his chosen field. The postwar job market was tight, and new engineering graduates were flooding the nation's labor pool. All Grissom could come up with was an offer as a mechanical engineer at a brewery. After meeting with the Air Force recruiter and quickly passing the test for aviation cadet training, Grissom asked to take his physical in the fall of 1949. There would then be enough time to join the cadet class of February 1950, immediately after graduation. But there was a hitch: Grissom was informed by the captain in charge of cadet "procurement" that he would not be able to take his air force physical before February 1950. Grissom was in a bind because he had a job offer, one more than many engineering graduates, but he was now determined to join the Air Force—this time as a pilot, not a nontypist clerk.

The news that his physical would be delayed was "very disheartening," he wrote to the head of the aviation cadet examining board on July 1, 1949. In pleading his case, Grissom informed the board that he had a very good reason for requesting an early physical: "In so much as jobs are getting hard to obtain I would like to know whether I am going to be accepted for flight training or whether I should accept a job that may be offered to me. The University will not permit me to accept a job on condition, or accept a job [offer] and then refuse to take it. In the latter case the University would discredit me."[20]

Grissom again requested a physical in September 1949 so he could enter the early 1950 aviation cadet class. If not accepted, he offered to travel an hour down the road by car—perhaps even hitchhiking—to Indianapolis to meet with the board president to work something out. Either way, the brewery job was unappealing. He was now determined one way or another to attend aviation cadet school and earn his wings.

The matter may have been settled when Cecile Grissom got wind of the job offer. While her son insisted he would not have to drink the stuff, his teetotaler mother "threw a fit" and shot down the offer.[21]

As it turned out, the timing was critical, and Gus barely made it into flight school: his was the last post–World War II class of cadets to accept married men. A month's delay and he might have remained in Indiana for the rest of his life.

Eighteen years after Grissom left Purdue with his wife to join the Air Force, Gus and Betty's friends, and Gus's colleagues and college classmates returned to West Lafayette in the spring of 1968 to honor Gus and his fallen comrade Roger Chaffee, Purdue class of 1957. The shocking deaths of Grissom, Chaffee, and their *Apollo 1* crewmate Edward Higgins White II just over a year earlier were still fresh in everyone's memory as the families gathered on May 2, 1968, to remember the three astronauts who had died in a launchpad fire on January 27, 1967.

After six years of American space successes, the *Apollo 1* tragedy underscored the substantial risks taken by all the astronauts and cosmonauts. Space was hard, spaceflight could be deadly, and the dangers could not always be engineered out of complex machines.

Purdue and its urbane president Frederick Lawson Hovde, the former Rhodes Scholar and chemical engineer, pulled out all the stops to ensure that its two astronaut alumni would receive the recognition they deserved from their alma mater. The ceremonies and the dedication of an engineering building just north of the Purdue Memorial Union as Grissom Hall and another campus building for Chaffee were fitting tributes to fallen astronauts. Purdue also provided the education for the Grissom sons. "Scott and [younger brother Mark, born in December 1953], are really thrilled that they will be able to attend their father's school," Betty wrote in a thank-you letter to Hovde two months after the fire.

"Mark, the youngest, is practicing his saxophone daily in hopes that he can make the band," added Betty, herself one of the first high school female drummers in the state of Indiana.[22]

Still in mourning, Betty was just then beginning to reflect on her husband's career and what life without him would be like. "Gus served his country most of his life and died in its defense," she replied to Hovde in a handwritten letter. "His life of accomplishment really started at Purdue."[23]

Unlike subsequent memorials for Grissom and his crew, Betty deeply appreciated the honors bestowed on her husband by the university. They included both the christening of Grissom Hall as the home of the School of Aeronautics and Astronautics and scholarships established in the alumni astronauts' names.

Betty confided to Hovde: "Your high esteem for Gus has been more comfort to us than anything else since our great loss."[24] She would eventually find the posthumous medals and other NASA awards to be empty gestures. In thanking Hovde, she was sincere. The university had extended every courtesy to Betty and her sons before, during, and after her visit. These gestures were comforting, and Hovde was especially gracious in offering condolences to Dennis and Cecile Grissom. Still, nothing could alter the fact that the son, the husband, the father was gone.

Accompanying Betty to Purdue for the dedication ceremonies was her friend and neighbor in the Houston suburb of Timber Cove,[25] Adelin Hammack. Adelin was the wife of Mercury project manager Jerome "Jerry" Hammack. Betty and Adelin shared a room that weekend at Purdue's Union Club Hotel, and she helped Betty get through the public ceremonies.

The backdrop for the dedication ceremony included growing student unrest over the war in Vietnam and the military draft. Hovde opened the ceremony dedicating Grissom Hall by noting the *Apollo 1* astronauts' "competence and courage," adding that "they were willing to discipline themselves to meet the challenge of their professional tasks, duties and responsibilities." With rights come responsibilities, the Purdue president emphasized, detouring into a sermon critical of rebellious college students. "The young people are demonstrating for their rights, but I see no one demonstrating for the responsibilities," Hovde declared. "If they continue to ask for their rights but ignore their responsibilities, the very end they seek will elude them."[26]

Among the "ends" Hovde did not mention were cessation of the disastrous war in Vietnam and greater freedom of expression. The nation was in the midst of political turmoil, doubting itself after the deaths of three astronauts. The space program was widely seen as one of a few reasons Americans retained to hold their heads up. A dedication ceremony seemed an inappropriate time to raise a contentious political issue. To Hovde, the astronauts and the protesters represented opposing ideals in a country that would soon be torn apart by war, racial discord, and accompanying inner-city riots and political assassinations. The irony of course was that Gus Grissom had fought in Korea to defend the very rights the students were exercising.

As it turned out, the astronaut scholarship funds established in the names of Grissom and Chaffee would serve as a form of absolution for those who felt responsible for the astronauts' deaths. University records reveal that the largest contributors to the Virgil I. Grissom and Roger B. Chaffee scholarship funds were the very NASA contractors who built the Apollo spacecraft in which they and White were killed.

Donations to the astronaut scholarship funds began pouring into Purdue a month after the *Apollo 1* fire. The list of contributors reflected the affection the nation felt for Grissom and his crew. "T. Chuderski" of Trenton, New Jersey, sent one dollar in cash to each fund. Cub Scout Pack 44 of West Hartford, Connecticut, sent thirteen dollars; another Cub Scout Pack in Maryland sent two dollars. The bridge club that included Blanche Chaffee, Roger's mother, contributed ten dollars. The citizens of Mitchell, Indiana, sent $399.50.

The list of donations to the scholarship funds went on for pages, each carefully recorded by a university clerk. By January 1968, Purdue had received 370 gifts from individuals, groups, and companies totaling $19,000.

Among the NASA contributors were the Astronaut Office and individual space agency employees such as astronaut Harrison Schmitt, spacecraft designer Maxime Faget, and Joe Shea, the NASA engineer responsible for development of the Apollo spacecraft. The astronauts' deaths haunted Shea for the rest of his life.

The largest contributions to the astronaut scholarship funds came from the prime Apollo contractors. The size of their donations to the scholarship funds honoring the dead astronauts reflected the intense guilt company executives felt after the *Apollo 1* fire. John Atwood, president of

Apollo contractor North American Aviation, contributed $500 each to the Grissom and Chaffee scholarship funds. Contractor Martin Marietta sent checks in the same amount. But the biggest contributor by far was Harrison A. Storms, president of North American Aviation's Space and Information Systems unit in Downey, California, the designer and builder of the Apollo spacecraft. As if to ease his suffering over the deaths of the astronauts, Storms sent Purdue a check for the scholarship fund in the amount of $2,000.

Grissom completed his engineering degree in February 1950. Having gained the "technical training" he deemed necessary to advance in his chosen profession, the pace of Gus Grissom's short life would gradually accelerate. Like aviation, his life would soon "go" supersonic. An unexpected encounter with an Air Force recruiter on the steps of the student union put Grissom on a path to earning his wings at last. Scarcely a year after obtaining his engineering degree, the newly minted Air Force pilot would find himself flying a fighter jet in combat over Korea. That test would open the door for the combat veteran with one hundred missions under his belt to begin pursuing his ultimate goal of becoming a military test pilot.

Flying would apply all that Grissom had absorbed in his three-and-a-half grueling years at Purdue. Gus, the striver, Betty, the breadwinner, and their new son were now poised to "get ahead."

4

WINGMAN

Suddenly the [MiG] leader began a sharp turn into us and the hair prickled a little on the back of my neck. One of us wasn't going home.
—*Retired Air Force Major General Frederick C. Blesse, Korean War fighter ace*

Gus Grissom's Air Force career began much like his college education had: he almost didn't make it.

If Grissom had waited another month to join a later class of cadets, he would have failed to gain entrance to flight school. Had he not later insisted on one more training flight with a senior instructor, he would have washed out as a pilot. There would have been no pilot wings, only regrets. After years of toil and sacrifice, Grissom and his wife now had their sights set on his goal. They would not relent until it was achieved.

His pilot wings earned, Lieutenant Virgil Grissom and his family soon embarked on a nomadic life over the following decade that would take them to a succession of Air Force bases and other duty stations. He would soon be tested in combat.

The pace of life had picked up immediately after graduation from Purdue in February 1950. Betty was pregnant for the first time. Before he knew it, Gus was shipped off to Texas for basic training. Less than a year later, the husband and new father would find himself on the other side of the world fighting in the Korean War.

When Air Force fighter pilot and future novelist James Salter arrived in Korea in early 1952 to duel the swept-wing Russian MiG-15s, he sensed immediately the hierarchy of the squadron. "Whatever we were," Salter recalled in his 1997 memoir, "we felt inauthentic. You were not anything unless you had fought." Of those who had flown in combat, Salter wrote: "Their stories were listened to more attentively."[1]

Salter's unit in Korea, among the most distinguished of the war, also included Gus Grissom. Grissom's introduction to the Korean War was similar to Salter's: he arrived in an utterly foreign land in the dead of winter, kept his mouth shut, and paid attention to the veterans, the pilots who had been shot at. Like Salter, Grissom was frequently a wingman. Together, the leader and his wingman were an *element*, the basic combat formation. The wingman's sole job was to stay with the mission leader and cover his rear end—from where the danger usually came. The leader and his wingman were inseparable.

Indeed, the wingman's "duties were nothing less than sacred: to serve as a lookout, especially when the leader was engaged with the enemy, and if needed, to support him with fire. Wingmen who had lost their leaders and vice versa were immediately withdrawn from the combat area," Salter wrote in the introduction to his first novel set in the skies over Korea.[2]

Salter's protagonist in *The Hunters* described a wingman this way: he "was reliable. That was the quality for a wingman."[3]

Years later at a dinner party, a woman challenged the now respected but underappreciated American novelist who died in the summer of 2015 about the virtues of a military life. "I couldn't answer her, of course," Salter remembered. "I couldn't describe . . . what it was like waiting to take off on missions in Korea, armed, nervous, singing songs to yourself, or the electric jolt that went through you when the MiGs came up."[4]

The origins of the Korean War remain controversial.[5] It broke out in June 1950, four months after Grissom graduated from Purdue University. It ended in July 1953 after an estimated five million combatants and civilians were killed. The Korean peninsula remains heavily armed and divided to the present.

The air war over Korea marked the first time jet fighters were operational in war. The clashes pitted Russian pilots flying large numbers of well-armed MiG-15s out of airfields in China against lesser numbers of

American F-86s. What the F-86 Sabre lacked in firepower it made up for with maneuverability and, based on the number of MiGs shot down, better pilots.

The pilots who flew the F-86, built by North American Aviation, loved the plane: "It was the Cadillac of fighters in its day," declared Lieutenant General Charles "Chick" Cleveland, a Korean war jet ace:[6] "I felt very much at home and comfortable and in command in the cockpit."[7]

Grissom and Salter were both assigned to the 334th Fighter Interceptor Squadron based at Kimpo Air Base near Seoul. The pilots preferred the shorthand designation for the place, K-14. Their first commanding officer was among the leading American fighter aces of the Korean War, Major George A. Davis Jr. Salter recalled that on the gloomy, freezing day he arrived at K-14, February 10, 1952, Davis and his wingman had taken on between twelve and fifteen MiG-15s approaching US bombers. The wingman, Lieutenant William "Skosh" Littlefield, remembered thinking he had never seen so many MiGs in his life.[8]

Davis downed his thirteenth and fourteenth MiGs during the engagement but was shot down while going after a third. Littlefield stayed with his leader all the way to the "deck" but survived. Davis was awarded the Medal of Honor for his exploits in Korea and the Pacific during World War II.

Salter and a buddy arrived just in time to hear the bad news. "With the terrible mark of newness on us, we stood in the officers' club and listened to what was and was not fact. We were too fresh to make distinctions."[9] Decades later, Salter told an interviewer: "You want to be like the others, you want to be as good as the others. Or to put it in more classical terms, you want to be highly regarded by the man and admired by the women."[10]

Another second lieutenant in the 334th, twenty-four-year-old William Brown Jr. (eventually, Lieutenant General Brown), was also assigned as a wingman. Brown quickly figured out what the Korean air war was all about: "A group of young people trying to kill another group of young people."[11]

"We flew in flights of four aircraft, in 'fingertip' formation, in two elements of two aircraft," recalled Brown. "The two fellows on the outside are the wingmen. The guy sticking out, whose head is up—who takes responsibility, blame, and credit for everything the flight does—is the leader."

The job of the leader and the wingman was "to find the enemy, seek them out, engage them, maneuver, and kill them. The wingman's job is to help the leader find them, because usually there's an age difference. Some of our leaders were old guys in their thirties, and I was a young twenty-four-year-old. So the difference in eyesight was significant."

Brown continued: "Your job, essentially, was never to lose the leader. You always stayed slightly to the rear and on one side or the other, and as long as the leader was maneuvering, you kept the rear clear. You would call him and tell him, 'you're clear, you're clear,' or, if someone entered that bubble and posed a threat, you would advise him of that. This meant your head was always on a swivel."[12] According to another account, a new wingman informed the lead pilot that the MiGs were indeed "shooting at [them]." "That's OK," the veteran responded. "They're allowed to do that."[13]

The American air force flying F-86 Sabres, one of the first operational US jet fighters with its distinctive swept-back wings, would eventually shoot down 792 MiGs during the Korean War. Only 78 F-86s were lost.

In his diary, Salter also recorded the events leading to the death of the American ace George Davis above the Yalu River, which separates what is now North Korea from China: Davis was "leading the B Flight. Colonel Preston, the group [commanding officer], was leading the squadron. Near the Yalu, Davis dove on fifteen MIGs that were in a climb, got the leader and swung out to try to get another. He did, but was hit with a 37mm [cannon fire] just behind the canopy before [Littlefield] could call a break. He went down in a slow turn, hit and burned."

The flags at the US air base were at half-mast when the squadron returned. Salter's buddy, another pilot named Woody, remarked on the way back to their quarters in the rain: "I'm not going to like it here."[14]

Into this crucible entered Air Force Second Lieutenant Virgil Grissom, who had earned his pilot wings and a commission in March 1951. The passage from a quiet college town to the front lines in far-off Korea produced a steady air force officer and hard-nosed airman who quickly found himself in dogfights with Russian pilots in a deadly game of kill or be killed. Grissom seemingly had little trouble adapting to the situation or his Spartan surroundings and quickly earned a reputation as a proficient pilot and reliable wingman.

A month after graduating from Purdue in February 1950, Grissom rejoined the military as an air cadet. With Betty expecting their first child, the twenty-four-year-old cadet shipped out to basic flight training at Randolph Air Force Base, Texas. He was assigned to the 3510th Basic Pilot Training Wing at the base in San Antonio. Betty moved in with her sister, Mary Lou, in Seymour, Indiana.

Randolph Field was situated not far from the huge White Sands Missile Range outside Las Cruces, New Mexico. There, on February 24, 1949, the early US rocketeers had pulled off what came to be known as the first "space shot." With the help of captured German rocketeers stashed away in the high desert, the Americans had successfully launched a modified V-2 missile fitted with a small WAC-Corporal rocket. The combined vehicle carried a payload of scientific instruments to an altitude of 244 miles.[15]

Arriving at Randolph for six months of basic training, Grissom's experience was likely similar to another air cadet who vividly described the upperclassmen who immediately began hounding the green recruits. A large military truck with a canvas top and benches in the back met Grissom and his fellow cadets at the San Antonio train station. Suitcases were tossed into the back, and the cadets climbed aboard. The truck pulled up in front of Randolph's cadet administrative building. Large numbers of upperclassmen pounced on the new arrivals.

"Form ranks, straighten the line, chin in, suck in that gut, hands along the seam of your trousers!"[16] In other words, "Welcome to the US Air Force, mister."

The constant harassment was of course meant to teach self-control under pressure. It was also an opportunity to dish out some of the abuse the upperclassmen had endured when they arrived six months earlier.

After a trip to the supply building, the new cadets were marched to the barracks and assigned rooms. In between basic flight instruction, the harassment continued, followed inevitably by demerits for minor infractions of air force discipline.

Demerits had to be walked off during what little spare time the cadets had. One new cadet recalled using the exquisite monotony to prepare sarcastic replies to obnoxious upperclassmen. When asked, "What time is it, mister?" the zombie cadet considered this reply: "Sir, I am deeply embarrassed and humiliated that due to unforeseen circumstances over which I have no control, the inner workings and hidden mechanism of my chronometer are in such in-accord with the great sidereal movement by which time is commonly reckoned that I cannot with any degree of accuracy state the correct time, Sir. But without fear of being very far off, I will state, that it is so many minutes, so many seconds, and so many ticks after the 'x' hour."[17]

Grissom too chafed at the peacetime air force discipline and the constant harassment of the senior cadets. Soon the demerits began to pile up for minor spit-and-polish infractions. He spent a fair amount of time at Randolph "walking off a series of demerits," according to Betty.[18]

Offenders marched back and forth on a concrete ramp, a large baking expanse in front of the barracks. A "delinquency report" for being last in formation, for example, would mean an hour walking off the demerit. The new cadets figured they could walk off about six hours' worth of punishments on a weekend while otherwise restricted to base during their first month of training and abuse.

At Randolph, Grissom trained on the T-6 Texan, a single-engine aircraft built by North American Aviation (the same company that would later build the Apollo spacecraft). The T-6, reasonably maneuverable in the hands of an experienced pilot, was deemed even by World War II veterans to be "huge" for a beginner. It had previously served as an advanced trainer.[19] The future Air Force colonel Robert Rogers of Lowell, Massachusetts, reckoned the washout rate during his six-month primary flying program at about 50 percent. Rogers was at Randolph about a year ahead of Grissom. Twenty-nine cadets in Rogers's class were shipped to Williams Field in Arizona for advanced flight training. Nine washed out there.[20]

Soon, Cadet Grissom had bigger problems than demerits: it appeared that he wasn't much of a flyer. During early training, he continually had problems trimming the T-6 prior to landing, a maneuver designed to maintain a certain attitude and air speed, thereby reducing the effort needed to fly the plane. When aircraft elevators are trimmed, a qualified pilot can theoretically fly with a light touch and feel how the aircraft is behaving.

The trimming problem persisted. His instructor advised Grissom it was looking increasingly likely that he would wash out as a pilot and suggested he might want to consider becoming a navigator. The air cadet, his sights set on earning his wings, had not spent the last four years busting his chops at Purdue to become a navigator. He stubbornly dismissed the instructor's suggestion.

Push had come to shove: Grissom sought and gained one last chance with a senior flight instructor to prove his mettle. The trimming problem soon reappeared. The instructor reminded Grissom of two wheels at his knees used to trim the T-6 for landing. This was news to the cadet.

Earlier instructors had apparently neglected to adequately explain the purpose of the trim wheels. "I had no idea what they were for," Grissom admitted. Mystery solved, the student performed enough perfect landings to solo.[21]

At long last, the cadet had mastered the light touch needed to fly an airplane, to become one with the machine. Finally, Grissom had achieved the goal he had pursued since high school. He was a pilot. He would soon fly in combat.

The rising cadet was also about to become a father, albeit an absentee one. There was no money to return home to help Betty through what turned out to be a difficult birth. The couple reasoned that the extra leave would delay his graduation from flight school. Betty was resigned to the fact that they needed to save money for the new baby. She would endure a long and painful delivery on her own. Gus would not see his first son for six months. It would not be the first time his career took precedence over family responsibilities.

In early June, Betty left two-week-old Scotty with new grandmother Cecile and traveled alone by train to San Antonio to see her husband. She visited for ten days, staying in quarters near the base, meeting Gus at the cadet club to spend a few precious hours together. The lonely, "somewhat frightening" return trip to Indiana was miserable.[22]

he future wingman had at last earned his wings. Air Force Second
Lieutenant Grissom then transferred with his cadet class to Williams
Air Force Base in Chandler, Arizona, in September 1950, just seven
months after graduating from Purdue. The fighting in Korea was intensi-
fying. Replacement pilots were needed. Betty and Scott finally caught up
with Gus in Arizona, this time taking their first airplane ride. "So this is
Scotty," Gus chirped as he greeted his wife and son at the Phoenix airport
terminal. "Well, I'll be damned!"[23]

Somehow they survived on his $105 monthly salary. But Grissom's
Air Force pay, like his flying prospects, soared to $400 a month when
he received his commission. "We were practically millionaires!" the
new officer remembered.[24]

Williams Field, outside Phoenix, was another in a series of old World
War II bases the Grissom family would pass through on Gus's way to Korea.
It consisted mostly of wooden buildings and hangars. The main gate greeted
visitors with a sign with a jet fighter and the words: "The United States
Fighter School Welcomes You." Another sign read: "Thru these gates pass
the world's best pilots and airmen. Maintaining this standard is up to you."

Despite the austere surroundings, the renovated barracks at Williams
Field were an improvement over Randolph. An open bay had been converted into small rooms with two beds per room. It was four cadets per
room at Randolph. Robert Rogers, a cadet months ahead of Grissom at both
Randolph and Williams, found the new accommodations "plain but roomy."[25]

It was at Williams, Betty would write years later, that Gus "met the
true love of his life," a jet fighter that could "thrust you up the sky so fast
you could outrun your own sound."[26] Grissom's small frame fit like a glove
in the fighter cockpit. He would spend the next six months in advanced
pilot training, honing his skills to a sharp edge whenever he got the chance
in an F-80 jet trainer. Betty would remember the beautiful Arizona spring
day in 1951 when her husband received his Air Force commission. All the
hard work was beginning to pay off.

The outbreak of the Korean War had caught the Air Force flat-footed,
and its Air Training Command was hustling to fill the needs of a new
ninety-five-wing force, with about seventy-two aircraft per wing. Grissom
had little trouble gaining a combat assignment in Korea.

Following graduation from pilot school in March 1951, Grissom stopped in Indiana and drove with Betty and Scott in a used Buick to an air force base at Presque Isle, Maine. There, he was assigned to the 75th Fighter Interceptor Squadron. Temporary duty at other bases kept the young air force family moving up and down the East Coast. A thirty-day leave in Indiana was a blur. He then returned to Arizona for gunnery training.

Weary of following her husband up and down the East Coast on temporary duty, Betty and a friend decided to pack up the Buick and return to Presque Isle. Her husband was able to fly in occasionally. The Grissoms eventually moved to the top of the base apartment list. Betty wasted little time in ordering furniture.

No sooner had it arrived than they would be again separated: Gus's hard-won piloting skills would be tested in the dangerous skies over the Yalu River, "the line between two worlds,"[27] separating Korea from China.

A few days after the Grissoms moved into their apartment in December 1951, the 75th was ordered to Korea. Gus flew to the West Coast and boarded a transport that would carry the squadron and their planes across the Pacific. Betty packed up again. She and Scott moved back to Indiana to sweat out Gus's one hundred combat missions.

W hat little many of us think we know about the Korean War comes largely from what happened well behind the lines, the war portrayed in the film and television versions of *M*A*S*H*. The air war over Korea in which Grissom and other future astronauts fought was at the front end, the tip of the spear.

Grissom and James Salter were members of the 4th Fighter Interceptor Wing from February to September 1952 but served in different squadrons.[28] Salter had previously served with Grissom in the 75th at Presque Isle. Their wing commander in Korea was Colonel Harrison R. Thyng, himself a fighter ace with five "kills" to his credit. For anyone joining this outfit, the expectations were high. All were expected to be aggressive when the Russian MiGs rose up to meet them over the Yalu River. The 4th wing flew F-86s, then the front-line US fighter.

Salter, a West Point graduate and air force captain when he arrived in Korea, vaguely remembered Grissom during their brief time together in Maine and seemed to have had a clearer recollection of Betty Grissom. "Whatever contact we had other than official was nothing more than at beer calls, softball games," Salter said.[29] Their paths would cross again at Kimpo Air Base, but the tight-knit squadrons had little time to socialize.

Salter, who also flew with other future astronauts, was in a position to observe firsthand the training of American fighter pilots who would a decade later form the cadre of the American Astronaut Corps. One of them, Buzz Aldrin, would walk on the moon. Edward White, who Salter later flew with in Europe as an operations officer, would become America's first spacewalker and eventually perish along with Grissom in the 1967 *Apollo 1* fire.

When Grissom arrived in Korea in the winter of 1952, the 334th Fighter Interceptor Squadron included some of the most distinguished flyers of the war, men like Frederick "Boots" Blesse, a fighter ace who helped reorganize Grissom's squadron. The 334th would eventually be credited with shooting down 142 MiGs. Six pilots from the 334th achieved "ace" status.[30]

Korea also was Grissom's first exposure to outsized personalities and hotshot fighter pilots who weighed the risks of what they were being asked to undertake and took charge. Grissom caught some flak for naming his aircraft "Scotty," after his new son. Others chose what they considered more appropriate monikers, like the names of wives, girlfriends, or Hollywood actresses.

A first lieutenant named Charles "Chick" Cleveland (later Lieutenant General Cleveland) arrived at Kimpo Air Base about the same time as Grissom. Cleveland described the hard-charging Major Blesse this way: "He was there with a purpose, to accomplish something, to contribute and excel. And he did all of the above."[31]

To young pilots like Grissom, men like Blesse "served as [role models] for personal excellence and strong leadership."[32] Along with surviving the war, the new pilots learned how to gauge risk and shoot down MiGs. After all, that's why they were there.

By the time Grissom arrived, the timid pilots had been weeded out of the wing and replaced by aggressive veterans like Blesse, who would retire from the air force as a major general. An oft-repeated story of Grissom's tour of duty described how pilots who had not taken fire in combat remained standing on the bus to the flight line. After his second mission, flying with hard-charging pilots like Blesse, Davis, and Salter, Grissom took a seat on the bus.

Among the veterans, it was important for a new wingman to see action early in his tour. Those who went up to the muddy Yalu River and back—about two hundred miles from Kimpo, twenty minutes or so by air—without seeing the enemy tended to lack the aggressiveness flight leaders desired.[33] The veterans called these missions "sightseeing tours." For Grissom, this was never an issue.

Before a big fight to the north, Colonel Thyng would exhort his fighter pilots to be aggressive against what were expected to be swarms of MiGs but cautioned, "Don't waste your time on long shots." After issuing instructions to the flight and element leaders, Thyng addressed the wingman: "You've got the toughest job of all. Keep your eyes open. Keep your leader cleared. The air is going to be loaded with ships today, so don't be calling a break for some goddamned speck five miles behind you. Make sure that they're MiGs!"

Thyng, who according to Salter looked like a "fading jockey,"[34] then demanded "nothing but kills." He ended with the following: "You can take a look around you right now, because there'll probably be some empty seats here tomorrow. Just make sure it isn't you."[35]

Grissom was not a fighter ace, and he recorded no "kills" during his one hundred missions. Wingmen seldom scored kills. "I never seemed to be in the right place at the right time," he told Betty.[36] The "right place," he understood, was on the leader's wing. That was where Grissom stayed throughout his tour in Korea. Indeed, what mattered most was that Grissom never lost a flight leader in Korea. "We chased the MiGs around, and the MiGs chased us around, and I usually got shot at more than I got to shoot at them," Grissom recalled a decade later. "I never did get hit and neither did any of the leaders that I flew wing for."[37]

Much like his future career as an astronaut, Grissom was workman-like and did not call attention to himself or his flying. He was precisely what a wingman should be: reliable. He would eventually be awarded the Air Medal and the Distinguished Flying Cross for his actions on March 23, 1952, while flying cover during a photoreconnaissance mission.[38] According to the citation, he spotted MiG-15s diving to attack a largely defenseless American reconnaissance plane, peeled off, and helped drive the attackers away. More important than medals, Grissom was promoted to the rank of first lieutenant and cited for his "superlative airmanship."

Occasionally, the harrowing details of the dogfights over Korea seeped into letters to Betty: "I was flying along up there and it was kind of strange. For a moment I couldn't figure out what those little red things were going by. Then I realized I was being shot at," he wrote home early in his tour.[39]

MiG-15s carried two 23-millimeter guns and one 37-millimeter cannon intended primarily to destroy US bombers. The MiG cannon could fire up to 450 1.7-pound rounds a minute. The cannon shells were about the size of a drinking glass.[40] American fighter pilots in Korea reported that they could actually see lethal cannon rounds coming at them "like a Roman candle."[41] By contrast, American F-86s carried only 50-caliber machine guns.

It was the sledgehammer versus the hose, Salter observed.[42]

The MiG-15 could fly higher than the F-86, 50,000 feet compared to 42,000 feet. This provided the Soviet pilots a distinct advantage when engaging the Americans. The MiG also climbed better. Both aircraft were capable of speeds up to 660 miles per hour; however, the F-86 was more maneuverable and could out-dive the MiG-15. Speed, the American pilots understood, was everything.

That capability often prompted American pilots with a MiG on their tail to head for the "deck," skimming the ground in an evasive maneuver that might allow them to regain the advantage in a dogfight.

The 4th Fighter Wing was badly outnumbered in the first year of the air war, with some estimates running as few as forty-four F-86s against more than five hundred MiG-15s. Thyng complained to the Pentagon, resulting in the 51st Fighter Interceptor Wing reinforcing the 4th in December 1951.

Among the pilots in the 51st was Gus Grissom's backup pilot for his first space flight a decade later, Marine Corp Major John Herschel Glenn Jr.[43]

The 4th Fighter Wing was also reinforced with upgraded "E" and "F" versions of the F-86 about the time Gus Grissom arrived at Kimpo. The "F" version, with its "hard wing," added speed and better control at cruising altitude, further improving the odds against the more numerous MiGs.[44] But the F-86 was said to be a "headache" to maintain, meaning a large fraction of the American air strength was "in the shop" at any point during the war. Along with the names painted on the aircraft fuselages, veteran pilots had derisive nicknames for troublesome planes, monikers like "No Go" and "Guzzler."[45]

No two aircraft were the same, Salter claimed, possessing temperaments and traits, "not wholly inanimate."[46]

The missions quickly piled up, and Grissom completed his tour in about six months. During some patrols, Gus wrote Betty, "We'd listen to the Reds over the radio. They'd tell us they were coming over to the field [at Kimpo] to hang us from the barrack rafters." This was no longer flight training, Betty realized. It was kill or be killed.[47]

As the air war heated up, pilots in the 334th often encountered so many Russian fighters coming down from the north that they called them "MiG trains."[48] Once in range, the American pilots would "drop tanks," the F-86's external fuel tanks that inhibited maneuvering and turned into the MiG flights. As they approached, the silver enemy planes were as "silent as a shark."[49] And they were just as deadly.

Between missions, the existence of the American pilots at Kimpo was "a sort of crude colonial life," Salter recalled. Common showers and a latrine were shared all the way up the chain to the wing commander.[50] Still, these Spartan conditions were far better than those endured by the freezing American infantryman at the front, chipping foxholes out of the frozen mud with their spades. "The service is not an intellectual occupation. It's the life of. . . . It's the life of action, of course—action and boredom," he added.[51]

The fighter ace "Boots" Blesse said "Korea made you feel lousy: tired of the huts, roaches, uncomfortable bunks, poor food, and no women. But it was the only place you could get this kind of experience."[52]

It's likely that Lieutenant Grissom reached the same conclusion at the end of his one-hundred-mission tour. He immediately attempted to sign up for twenty-five more. "If you are a shoe salesman," he supposedly said at the time, "you'd want to be where you could sell shoes."[53]

In telling his story as a newly minted astronaut, Grissom summed up his wartime experience in Korea in exactly two paragraphs. "Sometimes a bogey would sneak in and start firing at you before you could spot him," he wrote a decade later. "There was not time in a spot like that to *get* scared. You had just enough time to call your flight leader on the radio—right now—and tell him, in a calm voice that wouldn't rattle him, that it was time to break away fast and get out of there. You also had to remember to tell him which way to break. And you had to make sure to use the correct call sign so you wouldn't get all of the other planes in the flight breaking away at the same time and ruin the mission. This was a lot to do in a split second, and it was good experience." After surviving one hundred missions, Grissom "decided space flight could not be more dangerous than that."[54]

Despite the hardships and the terror of air warfare, Grissom seemed to take it all in stride. After all, he had signed up to fly in combat. His request to re-up for twenty-five more missions was denied; experienced pilots were needed back home to train the next batch of replacement pilots.

During those six months on the front lines of the air war over Korea, the young lieutenant also soaked up the jet fighter ethos. He would eventually display the qualities that less than a decade later would make him a famous astronaut: diligence, hard work, courage, perseverance, and a commanding presence that would make others think twice about challenging him on a technical point.

Grissom likely played as hard as he fought. R&R—rest and recreation—for the American airman fighting in Korea meant a couple days in conquered Japan. The hops over the Sea of Japan were usually miserable, freezing flights in air force transports equipped with nothing more than canvas seats. But Tokyo was full of exotic attractions that usually went well beyond drinking and carousing. Lieutenant Grissom, now in his mid-twenties and on his first tour of Asia, undoubtedly absorbed other ingredients of the fighter jock fraternity in the bars and backstreet hotels of Tokyo. His excursions were unquestionably similar to those recounted later by Salter: during one romp at a favorite spot the pilots called "Miyoshi's," Salter recalled "a girl as smooth as a pear."[55] The bill for the night was 5,000 yen each.[56]

There was time, usually on the last day of leave, for an occasional shopping excursion. A set of dishes and two Japanese robes were shipped home.[57] Then, the long journey back to Korea, perhaps flying a mission the same day they returned.

The routine back at Kimpo seldom changed. The pilots were concerned with "who was scheduled, what was the weather, what had the earlier missions seen?" Salter remembered.[58]

The air war over Korea produced tales of epic battles in the sky, the first involving jet-powered aircraft. It also produced at least one great American writer—Salter—and several American astronauts.[59] Beyond that, little else was accomplished. The stalemate on the Korean peninsula continues to this day.

Returning from Korea in the fall of 1952, the wingman and war veteran would quickly transition to the role of flight instructor. First, Grissom decompressed a bit at the pilot instructor school at Craig Air Force Base in Selma, Alabama. He then moved on to Bryan Air Force Base in Texas. It turned out that teaching cadets was almost as dangerous as aerial combat.

As the need for replacement pilots soared, the air force dropped its requirement for two years of college to qualify for aviation cadet training. By the time Grissom arrived at Bryan at the height of the Korean War, the service was graduating an astounding 7,200 pilots a year. Air force recruiters were enlisting practically every warm body that walked through the office door.[60]

"Some of these kids were pretty green," flight instructor Grissom discovered the hard way. One nearly killed him.[61] Grissom's survival skills rescued him and a young cadet who was practicing a maneuver in which he was instructed to join up on another pilot's wing. The "crazy cadet" came in with too much speed. Grissom was unaware the cadet's identification bracelet had caught in the handle used to control the training aircraft's flaps.[62]

As they zoomed in, one of the flaps snapped off and the aircraft began to roll. Still unaware of what was causing the roll, Grissom, in the backseat, grabbed the controls. "I knew from experience that only one or two things could be causing this to happen." He reached for the flap handle, managed to get one halfway down, regained control of the aircraft, and got the cadet, the aircraft, and his own hide back safely. "It was the kind of situation in which you don't have time to get scared until you're back on the ground," Grissom wrote later. "All you can do is have a beer and think it over."

In two short years, the student had become the teacher. To the cadets, the flight instructor was "God," Grissom said—or, in James Salter's formulation, "gods of tin." "One word from you and they're eliminated." He washed out only one cadet, who later admitted that Grissom had done him a favor.[63]

The incident also illustrated how the combat veteran had developed the instincts to calmly figure out a problem, pull back from the brink, and return his machine "in one piece." The cumulative effect of having served as an air force flight instructor, along with the many hours of flight time logged after returning from Korea, was another incremental step in Gus Grissom's ascent to the top of the pilots' pyramid, joining the brotherhood of those who could handle just about anything thrown at them.

As another test pilot and future astronaut, Edgar Mitchell, noted, bringing back your machine was "a fundamental task."[64] It was among the skills required of a test pilot. Grissom would hone those flying skills after the war as the jets he was piloting went faster and higher. He would take advantage of his rank and situation—the apex of flight testing—to broaden his engineering education to include aeronautics. By the middle of the 1950s, Grissom's thoughts now turned to another school, "the fastest school in the world," in the starkly beautiful Mojave Desert: the US Air Force Test Pilot School.

5

TEST PILOT

You are flying somebody's theory.
—Gus Grissom

With the signing of the truce at Panmunjom ending the Korean War on the morning of July 27, 1953, the United States and the Soviet Union settled in for a "long twilight struggle,"[1] otherwise known as the Cold War. The clash pitted two opposing ideologies, one that the war hero and new US president Dwight David Eisenhower immediately sought to portray as "freedom . . . against slavery, lightness against the dark."[2]

The battle-hardened Eisenhower moved swiftly to extricate war-weary America from the Korean morass. In his first inaugural address, the thirty-fourth president acknowledged the desperate fighting "through the cold mountains of Korea" and posed fundamental questions: "How far have we come in man's long pilgrimage from darkness toward the light? Are we nearing the light, a day of freedom and of peace for all mankind? Or are the shadows of another night closing in upon us?"[3]

For Ike, one of the first steps in inching back toward the light was ending the Korean War on the best possible terms. Six months after his swearing in, the war ended in an uneasy truce.[4]

Far down the chain of command, flight instructor and US Air Force lieutenant Gus Grissom remained stationed at Bryan Air Force Base in Texas when the truce was signed. He would have preferred to stay in Korea to fly another twenty-five combat missions, but the air force was shipping combat veterans to flight instructor schools and stateside air bases to train the next batch of fighter pilots. Grissom left Korea for flight instructor school in June 1952. For a brief time, the Grissom family would be together in Texas. Betty Grissom was pregnant with their second son, Gary Mark, who was born there on December 30, 1953.

As the Korean War ended, Gus Grissom proceeded to pile up as many flying hours as he could get piloting jets cross-country on weekends. The Grissoms somehow found the money to buy a four-seat Stinson Voyager, a single-engine prop plane. Baby Mark sat in the back with Betty while Gus let Scotty take the controls.[5] The family flew the plane north to visit relatives back in Indiana, probably landing at the airport in Bedford, just north of Mitchell, that would one day be named for Virgil I. Grissom.

In November 1953, according to his military personnel records, Grissom received a "top secret" security clearance. Presumably this was required as sensitive and therefore classified technologies were being incorporated into the air force fleet. By August 1954, Grissom had logged more than two thousand hours of flying time in jets, and he now was qualified to fly the top-of-the-line F-100 fighter.[6]

It also appears that Lieutenant Grissom had settled into his air force career after six months of intense aerial combat, acclimating himself to his new surroundings and the harsh Texas climate. His face was more rounded, his slender frame was filling out, and his complexion was listed in his personnel records as "ruddy." The combat veteran returning from the Korean War looked by the end of 1954 to be a self-assured fighter pilot and father who had pretty much figured out where he was headed.

As he accumulated more flying time in advanced fighter jets, Grissom's reputation as a crackerjack flyer grew. The goal since Purdue was to become a test pilot. Grissom applied and was accepted in August 1955 into the Institute for Technology at Wright-Patterson Air Force Base near Dayton, Ohio. A few months later, in November, the veteran, who had survived combat and several close calls as a flight instructor, was promoted to the rank of captain. Things were looking up. Gus, Betty, and the boys would be returning to the Midwest after five years of nonstop moves from Arizona to Maine.

Founded in 1919, the Air Force Institute of Technology was the first step toward earning test pilot credentials. The curriculum was the equivalent of a Bachelor of Science degree in either aeronautics or electrical engineering, which the now-accredited institute began awarding in 1956. Again, Grissom's timing was nearly perfect. Always in a hurry, his plan was to finish the program in one year.

At "Wright-Pat," Grissom met a slow-talking, cocksure pilot from Oklahoma named Leroy Gordon Cooper. Cooper had been flying since he was five and made his first solo flight at sixteen. He later turned down a football scholarship to Oklahoma A&M University to enlist as a rifleman in the US Marine Corps during World War II. Switching to the newly formed US Air Force, Cooper flew fighter jets in Germany while the wingman Grissom was being shot at over Korea.[7]

For the next decade, the fates and military careers of Gus and "Gordo" would be intertwined. One would reach the pinnacle of his profession with little recognition; the other would be hailed as a hero, address Congress, and make the acquaintance of a president but ultimately fall short of his goal. After studying aeronautical engineering all week, the pair would spend most weekends flying. Betty soon grew tired of hearing Cooper's voice on the other end of the phone line inquiring if her husband wanted to fly that weekend. It seemed Gordo always managed to find the time to reserve a plane.[8]

Cooper had developed, almost nurtured, a reputation as a hot dog pilot.[9] On June 23, 1956, at Lowry Field in Denver, he narrowly avoided killing himself and copilot Gus Grissom. The pair flew a two-seat T-33 jet trainer with Cooper at the controls. The thin Denver air at more than five thousand feet above sea level required a long runway and full power to get off the ground. Halfway down the runway on their takeoff roll, according to Betty Grissom, Gus yelled, "Hey Gordo, you're not going to make it!"[10]

Barely off the ground, the T-33 lost power, settled back onto the runway, and the landing gear collapsed. Cooper and Grissom skidded about two thousand feet off the end of the runway where the aircraft crashed and burned. The aspiring test pilots both walked away without a scratch. It was the only flying accident of Grissom's air force career. From then on, regardless of whom he was flying with, Grissom inspected every plane before he flew in it.[11]

If nothing else, the accident forced the careless Cooper to respect his buddy's meticulous approach to flying. Grissom was "a country boy at heart," Cooper wrote years later, "but when it came to flying he was steady and no-nonsense. Of all the astronauts, Gus would have been my choice to fly my wing."[12]

Cooper, the son of an air force officer, entered the US Air Force Institute of Technology a year before Grissom. Gus was again on a fast track to complete his studies. Unlike Cooper, nothing was handed to Grissom. He had to earn it. Press releases issued by the institute today mention its most distinguished graduates, including General Jimmy Doolittle and General Bernard Schriever, architect of the air force ballistic missile and military space programs. Gus Grissom is also mentioned along with Buzz Aldrin. Cooper is not.

Grissom's military records reveal that the institute's assistant director gave the aeromechanical engineering student and aspiring test pilot a glowing recommendation: "Captain Grissom is a bright, alert individual with a pleasing personality. He has an exceptional ability to quickly grasp the essentials of a subject. He displayed originality and initiative in his work. He could always be counted on to complete a task quickly and with consistently excellent results. His cheerful, cooperative manner and active participation made him a valuable team worker. His judgment is considered excellent."[13] It is possible the assessment represented air force boilerplate language, a favorable review added to the personnel file of a deserving and hardworking pilot and engineering student. It also indicated that Grissom, at the age of thirty, was a promising young officer and pilot with a bright future. Either way, the recommendation along with his now-exceptional grades helped open the door to the next critical step in Grissom's career. He and Cooper graduated together from the air force institute in mid-1956 and were both assigned to air force test pilot school. This was the equivalent of a minor league baseball player being called up to the big leagues. In ballplayer parlance, test pilot school was "the show."

The ranks of the US Air Force Test Pilot School in the 1950s and early 1960s were filled with future astronauts and astronaut candidates. The school, tucked away at the sprawling Edwards Air Force Base in California's Mojave Desert, was the place to be for a flyer during the Cold War. The windy high desert thundered with the sonic booms of new generations of jet fighters and experimental rocket planes that were taking "mach buster" test pilots far beyond the speed of sound and to the edge of space. The desert air was dry, the wind was unrelenting, and the pilots' thirst after a long day of flying was nearly unquenchable. The Edwards ethic was to fly all day and carouse most of the night.

It was here, on October 14, 1947, that test pilot Chuck Yeager broke the sound barrier aboard a Bell X-1 rocket plane. Hearing a sonic boom for the first time, some ground observers thought Yeager's ship had exploded.

Class 56D, which entered the school in September 1956, included four air force captains who would become finalists for the future Project Mercury space program. Three were students together at the Air Force Institute of Technology. Two would become astronauts—Captains Leroy Gordon Cooper and Virgil Ivan Grissom.

Just as Grissom and Cooper arrived at the test pilot school, on September 7, 1956, the Korean War ace and test pilot Iven "Kinch" Kincheloe flew the X-2 experimental jet plane to a world record altitude of 126,200 feet. The American press hailed Kincheloe as a "spaceman." Flight test historian Richard Hallion concluded that Kincheloe, "for all practical purposes, [had flown] in space" and was able to observe the curvature of the earth.[14]

Grissom and Cooper had arrived at a time and place where men and machines were routinely traveling more than twice the speed of sound—to the very edge of the earth's atmosphere. Graduation from test pilot school would admit the two pilots to a fraternity of flyers who risked their necks on nearly every test flight.

The test pilot's curriculum consisted of three months of what was called "performance" flying, followed by three more months learning "stability and control" techniques. "You really felt like a select group because the staff treated you that way," wrote Richard Corbett, a member of one of the 1958 classes. "Many of us had only flown F-86Ds [the plane Grissom flew in Korea], but instead of an extensive briefing and ground school you just filled out a simple questionnaire about the aircraft systems and went out and flew it."[15]

The conventional wisdom had it that the key to being a successful test pilot was achieving the mythical "Right Stuff," or what astronaut and moon walker Harrison Schmitt called "an unshakable faith in your own infallibility."[16] This was nonsense, Corbett argued. What was really required was the "right touch," the indefinable melding of man and machine. Corbett, who would rise to the rank of air force colonel, observed: "Most flight test requires precise and smooth stick movement. On the other hand acrobatic flying . . . requires more yank and bank on the part of the wingman."

When the student aviators departed the flight line at Edwards for the day, they could usually be found drinking beer and talking shop at Juanita's Bar and Grill, about twenty miles from the base. Juanita's served as a poor man's version of the legendary test pilot hangout, Pancho's Fly Inn, later the Happy Bottom Riding Club, operated by the foul-mouthed and irrepressible Florence "Pancho" Barnes. Pancho's bar, dance hall, motel, and airstrip just seven miles southwest of Edwards mysteriously burned down in 1953. The year before Grissom and Cooper arrived at the test pilot school, the Society of Experimental Test Pilots was formed at Juanita's.[17]

The fifteen-member Class 56D graduated from the US Air Force Test Pilot School on Grissom's thirty-first birthday, April 3, 1957. Grissom and Cooper stood in the front row of the class graduation picture along with Captain James Wood and Captain Jack Mayo, Wood to Cooper's right, Mayo to Grissom's left. Both would later become astronaut candidates, but neither made the final cut. Wood went on to a highly successful air force career, becoming chief pilot for the service's winged space plane program called Dyna-Soar. Mayo was killed a few months before Grissom's first space flight during a weapons test aboard an F-105D fighter jet over the Gulf of Mexico. His body and the wreckage of his plane were never recovered.[18]

Mayo was among the many test pilots Grissom would come to know who were killed flying high-performance aircraft. Sudden death was now part of the game, and everyone on the flight line, especially the wives, knew it.

With test pilot credentials in hand in the spring of 1957, Grissom and Cooper awaited their next assignments. A world away, Soviet rocket engineers, led by the shadowy and daring chief designer Sergei Pavlovich Korolev, a survivor of Stalin's gulags, were preparing to test the R-7 intercontinental ballistic missile. The first test occurred at the future Baikonur Cosmodrome on the steppes of Soviet Kazakhstan on May 15, 1957. It was a failure, as were the next four test flights.

Finally, on August 21, 1957, the R-7, powered by four clusters of twenty thrust chambers providing more than five hundred metric tons of thrust, flew a ballistic trajectory to the Kamchatka Peninsula in the Russian Far East, about six thousand kilometers, before disintegrating at an altitude of ten kilometers.[19] The rocket carried a dummy hydrogen bomb warhead. Korolev had worked his rocket scientists night and day, and they finally had succeeded in launching the world's most powerful rocket. While the Kremlin leadership viewed the accomplishment in military terms, Korolev had something more audacious in mind: using the R-7 to launch the world's first man-made satellite.

The Soviet scientists working on satellite designs delayed, played for time, to improve reliability. To get around the cautious scientists and, more importantly, beat the Americans into space, the engineers of the Korolev design bureau quickly produced the simplest of satellites. It was called *Prostreishiy Sputnik*, or "PS." "We made it in one month, with only one reason, to be first in space," said Gyorgi Grechko, one of Korolev's top engineers.[20]

The polished 184-pound sphere about the size of a basketball contained four radio antennas and carried only batteries, a radio transmitter, and temperature-measuring instruments. The design was simple but effective.[21] Understanding the significance of what was being attempted, Korolev kept his "PS" on a pedestal draped with velvet during development. "This ball will be exhibited in museums!" he reminded his workers.

Sputnik was mated to the powerful R-7 booster and launched into orbit on October 4, 1957. The world would never be the same. American tracking stations picked up the "beep-beep" transmissions from the world's first man-made satellite, which was surprisingly easy to see from the ground. The Americans had been upstaged, and the Cold War took a dramatic turn.

It is impossible to overstate *Sputnik*'s impact on the world. The Soviet's astounding achievement shocked the West to its core and heightened political tensions while sharpening the military rivalry between the United States and the Soviet Union. In the halls of government, especially the Pentagon, technocrats were scratching their heads and asking each other, "How could this have happened?" The domestic consensus that portrayed the United States as the most technologically advanced people on Earth had been shattered.

Scrambling to respond, President Eisenhower immediately tried to downplay the Russian achievement. The president argued that the small metal sphere orbiting Earth affected US national security not one iota. "Actually, he was probably very worried" since "a rocket that had the power and the accuracy to orbit a satellite [also] had the power and accuracy to send a nuclear warhead across the ocean to a specific target," Neil Armstrong would note decades later.[22]

Sputnik was followed a month later by another audacious space spectacular, *Sputnik 2*, designed primarily to celebrate the fortieth anniversary of the Russian revolution. Its heavier payload included the first living being to be hurled into space, Laika, or "barker," the three-year-old stray dog from the streets of Moscow. *Explorer-I*, the tepid American response, was launched on January 31, 1958.

The sudden thrust into space was a not-entirely-unexpected consequence of a global research effort running from mid-1957 to the end of 1958 called the International Geophysical Year (IGY). At the outset of IGY, the Soviet Union and the United States both announced plans to develop an artificial satellite to be used for scientific observations. Both sides realized that ballistic missiles could be used to boost a satellite into orbit to provide an entirely new perspective on the planet. Such an effort would become the cornerstone of IGY, which was intended to study the geophysics of the oceans, meteorology, the upper atmosphere, cosmic rays, Earth's magnetic field, meteors, and more.

The Russians also realized that being the first nation to orbit a man-made object would confer incalculable scientific prestige, which was fast becoming a new ideological weapon in the Cold War.[23] Neither Cold War rival "would recognize it at the time, but they had started a new competition which eventually became known as the 'Space Race,'" test pilot and astronaut Armstrong noted forty years after walking on the moon.[24]

Even before *Sputnik*, each side had been contemplating the idea of manned space flight. An American aerospace designer named Maxime A. Faget developed the basic blunt-end design for a American manned spacecraft to be called *Mercury* the same year that *Sputnik* was launched. Faget worked for a small but strategic research agency based in Langley, Virginia, called the National Advisory Committee on Aeronautics (NACA). Thanks to the "crisis of confidence"[25] brought about by *Sputnik* and other Soviet space firsts, Congress and the executive branch moved swiftly—at supersonic speed by today's standards—to consolidate NACA and other efforts to explore and *exploit* space under a single civilian agency. Ten days after *Sputnik*, on October 14, Eisenhower received a detailed briefing from the American Rocket Society on the future of space exploration, including manned spaceflight. The society recommended the creation of a civilian research agency similar to NACA but independent of the military.[26]

In April 1958, Eisenhower proposed legislation incorporating the Society's recommendation. Congress, led by Senate Majority Leader Lyndon Johnson of Texas, wasted little time in passing the National Aeronautics and Space Act of 1958 at the end of July. Eisenhower signed the legislation into law on July 29, 1958.

The National Aeronautics and Space Administration (NASA) came into existence with the dawn of the new fiscal year on October 1, 1958.[27] NASA's charter was nothing less than launching humans into space and doing it before the Soviets. In less than a year, the "Space Race" had advanced from a slogan to a Cold War reality. As one chronicler of the competition, space historian Andrew Chaikan, observed, "It was about our own sense of security."[28]

At NASA's core was a brain trust drawn mainly from NACA that came to be called the Space Task Group. Led by Robert Rowe Gilruth, an unassuming but brilliant aerospace scientist and engineer from Duluth, Minnesota, the Space Task Group, headquartered at Langley Air Force Base in Virginia, would lay the groundwork for more than a decade of space firsts that would culminate with twenty-four Americans journeying to the moon and twelve walking on its surface. Korolev, the Russian rocket genius, had met his match. Gilruth had joined NACA in 1937 and by the late 1950s was known to harbor a "scientific obsession with speed."[29] As the Space Race heated up, Gilruth would have far greater economic and political resources at his disposal than Korolev.

Gilruth also was sufficiently astute to appreciate that the test pilots who were selected to fly his space ships, who would risk everything, should be intimately involved in their design.

Bureaucratic dithering followed in the wake of NASA's creation. Agency brass and Eisenhower's advisors could not agree on the necessary physical, psychological, and educational qualifications to fly in space (the term *astronaut*, or "star voyager," had not yet been adopted by the Space Task Group). Among the "intellectual exercises" was an attempt to come up with a hypothetical "superman for space flight."[30] Early in the discussions, stunt men, circus performers, and even racecar drivers were considered as potential candidates.

President Eisenhower settled the matter by ordering that candidates for the new Project Mercury be drawn from a pool of the nation's military test pilots. After all, they were already government employees able to obtain security clearances, available on short notice, and their records were readily available.[31]

At the dawn of the Space Age, Captain Gus Grissom found himself back at Wright-Patterson in May 1957, happily working as an experimental flight test officer assigned to the air force's Fighter Operations Branch. His job was to wring out new jet aircraft. In the two years Grissom spent at Wright Air Development Center, he would rise to become director of flight and all-weather testing, effectively making him one of the air force's top test pilots. While there, he flew most of the future front-line fighter jets in the air force's Cold War arsenal, including updated versions of the F-86 he had flown in Korea along with the F-94. Then came the "Century Series" of supersonic fighters, the F-100 through F-106. Each flew higher and faster than the aircraft it replaced. Mastering each moved Grissom higher up the test pilot pecking order.

Being an "all-weather" test pilot meant flying advanced aircraft in every kind of weather, including "flying blind" using instruments in bad weather and at night. "There wasn't a happier pilot in the air force,"[32] Grissom recalled. His family was in the midst of the most stable, contented time of their lives. Gus and Betty bought a home in the Dayton suburb of Enon. He occasionally made it home in time for dinner.

As the Russians tested their rockets and readied the world's first satellite, Grissom figured he had "one of the best jobs in the air force and . . . was working with fine people." Stationed at the flight test center at Wright-Patterson, "[he] was flying a wide variety of airplanes and giving them a lot of different tests. It was a job [he] thoroughly enjoyed."[33]

The test pilot was now spending a good deal of his waking hours in a cockpit. During his all-weather test pilot days flying out of Patterson Field, Grissom was well on his way to accumulating more than 3,400 hours of flying time, including over 2,500 hours in jets. The "little bear of a man,"[34] as Gordon Cooper described him, seemingly possessed a cast-iron backside.

Later, however, Grissom acknowledged that the glory days of flight testing—Chuck Yeager breaking the sound barrier and dueling with rival test pilot Scott Crossfield to reach the next Mach number milestone— may have passed him by. After being selected as an astronaut, Grissom offered a different assessment on his previous career as an air force test pilot. "By the time I got into test work, it was dying out," Grissom told *Life* magazine staff writer Loudon Wainwright in a March 1961 cover story about "the Astronaut First Team."[35] "It wasn't really flight test at all; it was mostly testing new gadgets," he said. This sudden change in attitude about flight test is difficult to square with the previous decade of intense effort solely directed toward the ultimate goal of becoming a test pilot. This was especially true since Grissom said his initial impression was that Project Mercury, the US effort to put a man in space, "sounded a little too much like a stunt instead of a serious research program."[36]

Still, there was danger even when "testing new gadgets." Grissom mentioned to Wainwright one flight test "just before I got into this thing" and "a lot of people thought the mission was downright suicidal. I wondered the night before the flight if I'd be scared when I got out on the end of the runway, ready for takeoff. As it turned out, I was too busy doing my job to be scared. The best guess I could get was that the plane would fly, and it did." Neither Grissom nor Wainwright elaborated on what happened, but the mission described likely involved a flight test aboard an F-105 fighter.

During his time at Wright-Patterson, Grissom met a recent aeronautical engineering graduate named Samuel T. Beddingfield. The amiable fellow had arrived at the flight test center via the air force ROTC program at North Carolina State University. The two engineers started working closely together, and Beddingfield would remain at Grissom's side until the end.

Beddingfield's father was a druggist in North Carolina. His mother was a nurse. One of his brothers was a doctor. Young Sam said he saw few opportunities for himself in the medical profession. "The only option for me was being an undertaker," he joked.[37]

Working in flight test, Beddingfield spent a good deal of time with Grissom, both on the ground and in the air. "Wright-Pat had one of the better officers' clubs," Beddingfield recalled in a 2010 interview, two years before his death.[38] Grissom usually could be found there at the end of the day, "and he liked his beer."

Of all the test flights they flew together, the last was the most memorable. Taking off in a two-seat F-100F fighter, Grissom and Beddingfield were assigned to escort a B-47, observing the jet-powered bomber while performing tests. Mechanical problems kept the bomber on the ground. Since they were already airborne, Grissom decided to let his copilot check out the fighter jet. "I took over the controls, lit the afterburner, and tried out a few routine maneuvers," Beddingfield recalled. They flew the plane for almost an hour. Grissom was characteristically quiet up front, making only an occasional comment.

The copilot's attention eventually shifted to the fuel gauge, and he attempted to get Grissom's attention. "Hey man, we're down to seven hundred pounds of fuel!" No response from the front seat. Beddingfield then moved the plane's control stick violently to rock the plane side to side. "Where are we?" Grissom finally asked. He had fallen asleep in the front seat of a supersonic fighter cruising at 35,000 feet! "I think we're headed back to base but I can't tell," the nervous copilot replied. Finally awake, Grissom calmly replied, "I've got it." "Patt[erson] Tower, this is Drumhead 5," the pilot radioed, using a call sign that was likely a reference to his flattop haircut. "We're ready to land." Controllers replied that they did not see the aircraft. Still at 35,000 feet, the pilot replied, "You will soon." Grissom put the fighter in a steep bank, entered the flight pattern, landed without incident, and had just enough fuel to taxi back to the ramp. Just another day on the job, Beddingfield figured.

"Looking back," he remarked, "I realize the danger we were in, but at the time I had no concerns. I had total confidence in Gus's abilities—he inspired that kind of confidence. His timing as a pilot was very precise, he knew exactly what he had to do in any circumstance, and knew how to execute the maneuver."[39]

The test pilot had come a long way from the days of uncertainty in basic training and the accompanying fear of washing out when he could not trim his aircraft for level flight. Flying a supersonic fighter jet had by now become second nature. It quickly became obvious to Beddingfield and all who knew him that Grissom had been born to fly.

Despite his future misgivings about the value of flight testing in the late 1950s, Grissom had developed a comprehensive approach for determining why flying machines behaved as they did. In the last year of his life, having flown twice in space and preparing for his next trip, Grissom took a longer view of the value of test pilots. "They don't hand out PhDs in test piloting," he wrote after his *Gemini 3* mission in March 1965, adding, "but you pick up a tremendous amount of scientific and engineering knowledge along the way. After all, when you take up a brand new plane and put it through its paces to see if it will hang together, *you are really flying somebody's theory.* You have to understand that theory pretty well to check it out fully. Every new plane, every test flight, is a brand new challenge. I suspect this is why most of us [astronauts] became test pilots in the first place."[40]

It was. Neil Armstrong, working as a test pilot in the early 1960s piloting the X-15 rocket plane at Edwards Air Force Base, described his job this way: "The test pilot is solving problems. He's looking for inadequacies, or shortcomings, or barriers to substantial safety at increasing performance in flight. And his job is to identify those problems and assist in finding a solution. So it's a problem-solving job, and you're always working with the unknowns. I found that a fascinating part of my career path."[41]

Immersed in the testing of jets and gadgets at Wright Air Development Center, Grissom was summoned one day in early 1959 by an assistant to the base commander. He recalled, "Things were going fine, I figured, until the afternoon I wandered into the squadron operations office and the adjutant asked me, 'Gus, what kind of hell have you been raising lately?'" "None that I know of," the busy test pilot replied, trying to remember if he had failed to salute some general. The desk jockey then asked whom Grissom knew in the nation's capital because he had just been summoned via a top-secret teletype message to report in civilian clothing to an address in Washington, DC.

What Grissom did not know was that the barely six-month-old American space agency, NASA, had come calling. It was scouting for test pilots with at least 1,500 hours of flying time in jets and a university degree in engineering or the physical sciences, and who were under the age of forty and shorter than five feet, eleven inches.

NASA also was scouring the nation's military bases for candidates who possessed a certain intangible quality, men who would be willing to risk their military careers and submit to what turned out to be humiliating biomedical and psychological testing, some of it bordering on torture.

"There is the aggressive response to stress, as we find in the tiger, and the docile response, as exhibited by the rabbit," US Air Force Brigadier General Donald D. Flickinger, a flight surgeon and member of NASA's search committee, told a reporter in 1958. "We're looking for tigers."[42]

The lofting of a silver sphere into space that emitted an ominous *beep-beep* had signaled the dawn of man's exploration of his solar system. The launch of *Sputnik* fourteen months earlier coincided with the rise of a cadre of American test pilots all looking for a way to go faster and higher. It seemed unlikely that a quietly competent air force pilot from a small Indiana town was among them. Then again, it also was a time when a motivated, problem-solving flyer like Gus Grissom could make a name for himself and compete on even terms with the best pilots in the world. Besides, Grissom was curious to find out the reasons behind all the bureaucratic cloak and dagger. "What really intrigued me was the order that I should wear civilian clothing," he remembered, along with explicit instructions to discuss the orders with no one.[43]

Grissom showed up on the appointed day, at the appointed hour, in his civvies. A government functionary ushered him into a room full of equally confused, curious test pilots. "By now I was convinced that somehow I had wandered right into the middle of a James Bond novel," the unsuspecting astronaut candidate wrote in the mid-1960s.[44]

After being led into a separate room and fielding "all sorts of odd-ball questions," Grissom was informed that he was being invited to join Project Mercury. There was no pressure, NASA officials stressed. Astronaut candidates were free to resume their test pilot careers with no repercussions. Several did. There was no need to decide on the spot, he was informed. "Talk it over with your wife and get back to us."[45]

Grissom returned to Enon and laid it all out for Betty. "As I had instinctively known, Betty agreed" that he should volunteer to be catapulted into space atop a ballistic missile. In fact, Betty harbored misgivings but masked them behind the rhetorical question, "What are they going to do? Shoot you up in the nose cone of an Atlas," the air force's most powerful rocket?[46]

Grissom was one of one hundred and ten candidate test pilots summoned undercover to Washington to be briefed about the American effort to put a human in space. Among other things, the invitation validated the fact that Grissom was now among the best test pilots in the world. The years of effort had paid off. Now the question became: Should he risk his air force career for a chance to ride on top of rockets that were blowing up with alarming frequency at Cape Canaveral? The whole scheme seemed, as fellow test pilot and navy aviator Captain Jim Lovell observed, "like a quick way to have a short career."[47]

NASA's invitation was another fork in the road, perhaps *the* turning point in Grissom's test pilot career. He and the other candidates would have to decide whether to delay and possibly jeopardize promising careers as military test pilots to participate in a national effort that in 1958 was little more than a set of drawings on paper. The risk had nothing to do with missiles blowing up. It was all about jeopardizing a hard-won reputation as an elite fighter pilot for what at first blush appeared to be a stunt.

Sensing that the heyday of the air force test pilot was coming to an end, Grissom again stuck his neck out and volunteered for an ill-defined adventure called Project Mercury. He and his young family were in for the ride of their lives.

6

MERCURY SEVEN

We bonded so closely, we were like brothers. Still are.
But sibling rivalry is also part of brotherhood. We had a lot of that.
—Mercury astronaut Walter M. Schirra Jr.

The American response to *Sputnik*, Project Mercury, was officially launched in November 1958, eight weeks after NASA was formed. At year's end, President Eisenhower settled a debate about qualifications, deciding that the first American astronauts would be drawn from the ranks of the nation's military test pilots. Given the strict requirement for at least 1,500 hours of flying time in high-performance aircraft, civilian pilots were effectively ruled out—as were women.[1] Among the other requirements was a bachelor's degree in the sciences, preferably engineering.

For Eisenhower, weary of American rockets blowing up on live television or satellites tumbling out of orbit, secrecy was the highest priority. Most test pilots already held security clearances. Gus Grissom obtained a top-secret security clearance in November 1953. He and the other test pilot candidates also could be counted on to keep their mouths shut and to follow orders. Most important, NASA was in a hurry. (Prior to Project Mercury, the air force had been promoting a scheme called Man In Space Soonest, or MISS. The acronym alone may have doomed the effort.)

With Eisenhower's edict to select only test pilots, NASA quickly formed an eight-man astronaut selection committee headed by Charles J. Donlan, associate director of the new Space Task Group and a twenty-year veteran of NASA's predecessor, NACA. The committee consisted of engineers, flight surgeons, psychiatrists, and psychologists. The panel screened the records of no less than 508 candidates. Of these, 110 test pilots (fifty-eight from the air force, forty-seven from the navy, and five marines) were invited to attend an initial briefing at the Pentagon to hear more about Project Mercury. Only two groups totaling sixty-nine candidates were actually summoned to Washington by mid-February 1959 (Grissom was a member of the second group), and it soon became clear to the selection committee that the nation had plenty of qualified and willing astronaut candidates to choose from within the ranks of its working test pilots. The considerable sums expended over the last decade to train these test pilots would soon bear fruit. The committee's daunting task would be winnowing the list of candidates to a dozen or so—the best of the best, or what General Donald Flickinger, the air force surgeon, referred to as the "premium man."

The winnowing began immediately. Six candidates exceeded the height limit of five feet, eleven inches; fifteen were eliminated during an initial battery of tests along with psychiatric interviews and medical history reviews; and sixteen candidates declined for a variety of reasons, including the expectation that they would soon be receiving command promotions. By early February 1959, the number of candidates had been reduced to thirty-two men who were invited to undergo what NASA later acknowledged as "extraordinary physical examinations" at the Lovelace Clinic in New Mexico. The candidates also were apprised of the fact that they were signing up for "extreme mental and physical environment tests" at Grissom's current base, the Wright Air Development Center in Ohio— that is, the mental and physical probing of the aerospace doctors at the Lovelace Clinic. It would be a kind of athletic competition, a marathon, with a "distinct psychological component," future Mercury astronaut Scott Carpenter concluded.[2] Captain Virgil I. Grissom and the other thirty-one finalists would be competing in what amounted to the final laps of the astronaut selection process.

Some candidates summoned to Washington to hear NASA's pitch came away thinking Project Mercury would amount to little more than what pioneering test pilots like Chuck Yeager derisively called "spam in a can."[3] Air Force captain Thomas Sumner later told space historian Colin Burgess that he too was immediately turned off by the fact that the Mercury "capsule" would have no windows and the astronaut would have virtually no control over the spaceship.

"I thought the whole thing was really ridiculous." In hindsight, he realized that declining NASA's invitation was "maybe one of [his] worst decisions." Sumner had crossed paths with fellow air force captains Gordon Cooper and Donald "Deke" Slayton, and "especially Gus Grissom from Wright Patterson, and [he] often wondered how it might have ended up if [he]'d said 'yes' that day."[4]

Those who did say "yes" began reporting in groups of six (the final group totaled two) to Lovelace Clinic on February 7, 1959. The candidates would now become test subjects. Dr. W. Randolph "Randy" Lovelace II founded the civilian clinic, nestled among a jumble of buildings on what was then the outskirts of Albuquerque. Lovelace was himself a pilot and had previously conducted space medicine testing on American U-2 spy plane pilots.

Physical and radiological examinations and laboratory tests began immediately on arrival. For seven and a half days, the candidates endured the probing of every body cavity, electric jolts to muscles to test reflexes, and had cold water forced into their ears. Blood was repeatedly drawn; urine and stool samples were collected daily. The physiological testing at Lovelace would give new meaning to the phrase "survival of the fittest."

In what was to prove one of the understatements of the Space Age, air force cardiologist Lawrence Lamb acknowledged, "The candidates to become Mercury astronauts were not too happy with the nature of the examinations at the Lovelace Clinic." Lamb, who later assisted NASA with Mercury astronaut selection and eventually became President Lyndon B. Johnson's personal cardiologist, would soon play a central role in the drama surrounding the grounding of astronaut Deke Slayton, Gus Grissom's next-door neighbor when they moved to Virginia to join NASA.[5]

While not playing a direct role in selecting the Mercury astronauts, Lamb and the new breed of "space surgeons" understandably were concerned about the effects of weightlessness on the future space travelers. But even Lamb acknowledged it was difficult to justify some of the more humiliating biomedical tests at Lovelace, including sperm counts. "The purpose of the selection process was to identify the best men available for the [US] man-in-space program, not to do ongoing research with methods that were of unproved validity," Lamb wrote in his 2006 memoir.[6] The results of the thorough biomedical testing were summarized and forwarded to the Aerospace Medical Laboratory at Wright-Patterson Air Force Base, where the next round of stress and psychological tests were conducted.

Grissom's group at Lovelace in early March 1959 included Carpenter, Glenn, and Slayton. Upon arrival at the Albuquerque airport, each was instructed to ask for "Tux" Turner, an air force colonel who directed traffic and delivered the candidates into the gloved hands of the space surgeons at Lovelace.[7] The indignities that followed would prove to be a test of wills among an extremely competitive group of candidates, all determined to show they could handle anything the Lovelace doctors could dish out. The US Navy psychologist Lieutenant Robert B. Voas considered the ordeal to be a "mild test of stress tolerance and motivation."[8]

Voas, a member of the astronaut selection committee and an industrial psychologist, explained: "While the purpose of the medical examinations at Lovelace Clinic had been to determine the general health status of the candidates, the purpose of the testing program at Wright Field was to determine the physical and psychological capability of the individual to respond effectively and appropriately to the various types of stresses associated with space missions."[9]

Voas also was the first NASA official to understand that an extraordinary pilot who managed to survive a trip into space would have much to deal with when he returned. Communication skills would be added to the evaluation list.[10] Others concluded that the process used to select astronauts ultimately came down to whether candidates would make "good heroes." Besides being medically fit and highly motivated, Lamb concluded, "all the astronauts had the ability to present themselves well—when the occasion demanded it, and if they wanted to."[11]

NASA's metrics for selecting astronauts would eventually become a subject of intense scrutiny as it became clear that either the United States or the Soviet Union would one day reach the moon. Walter Cunningham, a member of the third class of astronauts, offered this take on how the process actually worked: "We were slowly waking up to the fact that politics and favoritism were very important," Cunningham recalled. "It wasn't that much different from any other job where personalities play a big part, where it helps to be in the right place at the right time, and where certain factors—service relationships, first impressions, and pressure from friends (pro and con)—created fair-haired boys."[12]

This was less the case in selecting the Mercury astronauts, and Charles Donlan later denied that considerations like the right proportion of air force, navy, and marine flyers played a role in selecting the first group. Neither did it hurt. "In the course of two hours, [we] came up with about a dozen [names] and called in [Space Task Group head Robert] Gilruth; and we just decided on seven, and then the next half hour I had contacted them by phone." Explaining the thinking behind the selections, Donlan added: "If you look at the first seven, you'll find that they all had a little different discipline to contribute. And that was part of the reason they were selected." Donlan also stressed that such swift decision-making would today be impossible.[13]

The astronaut candidates' ordeal at the hands of NASA doctors, what Wally Schirra later described as "a degrading experience" overseen by "sick doctors working on well patients," would not be widely appreciated until the publication of Tom Wolfe's 1979 book, *The Right Stuff*.[14] Other parts of Wolfe's book turned out to be less than accurate.

Unlike the outspoken Schirra, Grissom refrained from bellyaching about his treatment at the hands of the doctors and "headshrinkers." Instead, he went to Lovelace determined to give it the "old school try and take some of NASA's tests." Ever stoic, Grissom's main concern was competing with what he realized were the best of the military test pilots. The opportunity far outweighed the discomfort, and the point was not to be intimidated and to give it his best shot.[15]

The formidable competition included Glenn, whom Grissom may have crossed paths with in Korea when the marine flyer served as an air force exchange pilot. As part of a program called "Project Bullet," Glenn had, in July 1957, set a trans-American speed record flying cross-country in a Vought F8U-1P Crusader fighter jet in just over three hours and twenty-three minutes. His average speed was more than 725 miles an hour.

Three months later, the same day *Sputnik* was launched, Glenn turned up on the network television game show *Name That Tune* in his US Marine Corps dress blues and teamed with the child star Eddie Hodges. Glenn wowed the audience with his intelligence and mastery of the new medium of television. NASA officials quickly realized that the self-promoting yet ascetic Glenn was the best of a very talented bunch, referring to him as "Mr. Straight." Glenn, a World War II fighter pilot from Ohio, would be the oldest of the Mercury Seven and would outlive all six of his brothers and rivals.

Donlan recalled Glenn showing up at his Langley office for a technical interview with a copy of the results of his centrifuge runs at the navy facility in Johnsville, Pennsylvania. At the end of the interview, Glenn asked if he could return that evening to look at drawings of the Mercury capsule. "Now those are the kind of things you look for when you evaluate a man's suitability for a job like that," Donlan stressed.[16]

By contrast, the other top candidates for Project Mercury were viewed as "typical fly-boys" who were nevertheless outstanding test pilots.[17] That assessment certainly applied to hotshots like Gordon Cooper and the cool, shrewd Alan Shepard, but the other finalists also were dedicated flyers who had spent years honing their skills. Malcolm Scott Carpenter, one heat-transfer course shy of the engineering degree required to be a candidate (NASA made an exception) was perhaps the least likely of the group expected to make the final cut since he spent the least amount of time flying advanced aircraft. Carpenter nevertheless impressed the NASA selection committee with his scientific curiosity, world-class conditioning, and the fact that he carried himself in a way it was thought an astronaut candidate should, acting responsibly, asking probing questions, dedicating himself to the task at hand—beating the Russians into space. It did not hurt that the chiseled Carpenter looked the part of an American hero.

Like Grissom, Slayton was a no-nonsense, nose-to-the-grindstone pilot and World War II veteran looking for a way to move up the test pilot hierarchy. Another midwesterner from the southern Wisconsin farming community of Sparta, Slayton's nickname, "Deke," told most people all they needed to know about him. When the time came to do something difficult, Slayton frequently faced the challenge by muttering "Let's get on with it."

Slayton dismissed the rigors of the astronaut testing at Wright Field as a waste of time. Being baked in a heat chamber at 130 degrees was pointless for a combat veteran who had graduated from test pilot school at Edwards, Slayton reasoned. At least he could catch a nap in the isolation chamber. The doctors "had a captive group, and they exploited it," Slayton concluded.[18]

Schirra, soon to become Grissom's neighbor in Virginia, seemed destined to fly in space—both of his parents were flyers, his mother an aerial acrobat, a "wing walker"—despite a rebellious nature that was offset by a precise engineering approach to flying.

Shepard, like Glenn, a fearless and distinguished aviator, brought a midshipman's spit and polish, as well as an innate understanding of his time and place in history. He also was widely viewed as the "shrewdest of the bunch." Soon, those traits would make Shepard the first American in space and eventually a wealthy businessman. His Mercury colleagues initially viewed Shepard as "complicated . . . cold and standoffish."[19]

Surrounded by extremely able men, Grissom proceeded through the Lovelace trial by fire, impressed by the competition but determined to keep pace. Working in his favor was the fact that he was compact (he would fit like a glove into the Mercury spacecraft), he had combat experience, and, most important, he was naturally competitive. Grissom respected his competitors, and they quickly respected him.

There was no complaining on Grissom's part about the tortuous physical exams, only regret over his performance on the treadmill test when his heart rate reached two hundred beats per minute. "I thought I should have done better."[20] Perhaps it was a result of growing up at sea level. The Coloradan Scott Carpenter, by far the best conditioned of the candidates, had grown up hiking, skiing, and lumberjacking at ten thousand feet.[21]

Grissom also could have done better protecting his urine jug. Carpenter recalled an evening at a Mexican restaurant as one group of Lovelace finalists welcomed the next: "At the feet of some of the outgoing candidates was a jug of urine, which they had been obliged to lug around all week in the interest of space medicine. Gus Grissom had yet to hand his over to the medics. Suddenly the most alarming expression transformed Gus's face. He glanced under the table, and soon guys downslope were shifting in their chairs and lifting their feet off the floor. Gus had knocked over his urine jug." More beers were ordered and everyone present helped refill Gus's jug. "They had it topped off before the check arrived," according to Carpenter.[22] So much for the scientific precision of the Lovelace medical testing.

There was one additional cliff-hanger during the medical marathon: the Lovelace doctors, looking for any reason to disqualify a candidate, discovered while probing his respiratory system that Grissom suffered from hay fever. Digging in his heels, the candidate reminded the doctors: "There won't be any ragweed pollen in space."[23] In his own way, Grissom had shown the doctors and shrinks how logical he could be in a crisis, albeit a crisis that only threatened his own career. Seeing this, the doctors relented and the tests continued.

While Grissom and the others were challenged by tests like the "Complex Behavior Simulator" (variously referred to as the "Idiot Box" or "Panic Box") designed to gauge a candidate's reaction times under pressure, others, like a heat chamber test, were trivial. Most of the candidates figured out the trick in the hot box involved remaining perfectly still, perhaps catching a nap, and then waiting patiently for the pointless test to end.

As much as anything, the psychological testing forced the flyers to devise coping strategies that would make it appear they were cooperating without giving away details they preferred to keep to themselves. "I tried not to give the headshrinkers anything more than they were actually asking for," Grissom admitted.[24] Others, like the highly motivated Carpenter, took a decidedly more intellectual approach that made him more of a participant in aerospace research than a mere test subject.

There was of course another point to this physical and mental stress. An individual's willingness to tolerate physical discomfort and endless questioning about matters test pilots preferred not to discuss was a way of gauging motivation, maturity, and the ability to tolerate frustration.[25] "If the other guys can take it, so can I" seemed to be the finalists' modus operandi.

Whether it was cold water squirted into their ears to detect involuntary eye movement (called nystagmus), muscles pierced by electrodes to gauge the response to nerve stimulation, barium enemas, pounding away on the treadmill, or dunking feet in a bucket of ice water—all were preferable to answering questions like, "Who am I?" Testing one's physical endurance against the best pilots in the world was one thing; reflecting on one's innermost feelings to the note-scribbling doctors was quite another. Moreover, the inquisitors seldom reacted to the candidates' responses. To some of the men, this was unnerving.

The attitude of the frustrated, ticked off, decidedly sore candidates was best summarized by the naval aviator Charles "Pete" Conrad, known to the Lovelace doctors as "examinee number eight." Largely due to his unwillingness to play along with the doctors, Conrad would not be accepted into Project Mercury. He would join the second astronaut class, the "New Nine," selected in September 1962. Seven years later, Conrad would walk on the moon after executing a pinpoint landing within sight of another manmade object—an unmanned lunar lander called *Surveyor*. After Conrad provided the shrinks a suggestive and detailed description of a Rorschach card, the psychiatrist held up a blank white card and again asked the wiseacre candidate to tell him what he saw. "I'm sorry, Doc. I can't," Conrad said. "Oh? And why can't you?" the doctor replied. "Because you've got it upside down."[26]

Voas, referred to by the Mercury astronauts as "our official headshrinker,"[27] described what the space agency ultimately sought: "Intelligence without genius, knowledge without inflexibility, a high degree of skill without over-training, fear but not cowardice, bravery without foolhardiness, self-confidence without egotism, physical fitness without being muscle-bound, a preference for participatory over spectator sports, frankness without blabber mouthing, enjoyment of life without excess, humor without disproportion, and fast reflexes without panic in a crisis."[28]

Along with the inkblots, the candidates took several widely used psychological tests requiring them to answer "yes" or "no" to questions like, "My father was a good man" and "Strangers keep trying to hurt me." Along with these personality and motivation tests, they also took a battery of aptitude and intelligence tests, including the air force officer and navy aviation qualification tests. For good measure, the candidates were quizzed on mechanical and spatial skills, tests that mechanical engineer Grissom likely aced.[29]

Grissom next reported on March 8, 1959, to the Aero Medical Laboratory at the Wright Air Development Center back in Ohio, his home base the previous two years. This would be the final phase of astronaut candidate evaluation.[30] Grissom was in the fourth group to come through the lab. Among the other members was navy Lieutenant Jim Lovell, who quickly would be eliminated from Project Mercury for a slightly elevated level of bilirubin, a natural liver pigment. The doctors were now looking for any reason to eliminate a candidate. Lovell too would join the second group of astronauts in 1962, fly twice to the moon, and become one of the American space program's most articulate ambassadors.

The roster of candidates was reduced to thirty-one as the "stress testing" began in earnest at Wright-Patterson. That number would be reduced further to eighteen by the end of March. The survivors were clearly the "cream of the crop," recalled Walter B. "Sully" Sullivan Jr., who as an air force first lieutenant served as the astronaut candidate's liaison officer at the Wright Aeromedical Laboratory. Sullivan had seen a lot of test pilots come through Wright-Patterson, including U-2 and X-series pilots.

The astronaut candidates were the "most wonderful group of men I ever met," Sullivan said a few months before his death in December 2012. Any of the remaining candidates could have qualified for Project Mercury, he reckoned.

Sullivan was assigned to meet the candidates at the airport in Dayton and make sure they got to the base without being noticed by reporters. "I'd hang out by the airline check-in desk and wait for the guys with 'white sidewall' haircuts to walk up to the ticket agent," Sullivan told author Colin Burgess. "You could tell them from a mile off." War stories about the ordeal at Lovelace were swapped on the ride to the air force base. "Little did they know of the 'torture' that awaited them, beginning Monday morning," Sullivan recalled.[31]

Sullivan and others at the base kept a "side list" of the best candidates. He refused in an interview to reveal who was on his final list but heaped praise on Grissom, whom Sullivan had come to know while the astronaut candidate was stationed at Patterson Field as a test pilot. Sullivan said he long ago decided to keep his memories of Grissom to himself, saying only: "The rest of the astronauts thought the world of him."

So too did the NASA doctors, who would later come to fear him. Grissom was a grinder. As an astronaut candidate, he applied the same determination that had gotten him through engineering school, qualified him as a fighter pilot in Korea, and propelled his rise through the ranks to become one of the military's best test pilots. What he lacked in polish, Grissom more than made up for in native intelligence, technical skills, and a willingness, like his colleagues, to devote his life to a risky, utterly new endeavor.

In the midst of astronaut selection, NASA awarded its first major Project Mercury contract to McDonnell Aircraft Corporation, which had been selected over Grumman Aircraft Engineering. The St. Louis aerospace company would build and equip the Mercury space *capsule*, the term used before the astronauts insisted it be called a *spacecraft*. McDonnell and Grumman were deemed by NASA procurement officials to be technically equal with sound management. The deciding factor, according to NASA's first administrator, T. Keith Glennan, was that Grumman was "heavily loaded with Navy projects in the conceptual stage."[32]

McDonnell Aircraft had something else going for it: an agile management structure that would eventually allow the Mercury astronauts to go to the top of the company, to James Smith McDonnell, the inestimable "Mr. Mac," to force changes in the Mercury design. The astronauts wanted a window and an exploding hatch that operated like an ejection seat on a fighter jet. If it made sense to him, Mr. Mac made sure the astronauts got what they wanted. By the time McDonnell won the contract for the next American spacecraft, the two-man Gemini, Grissom would be camping out at the company's facility in St. Louis.

With the psychological and stress tests completed at Wright-Patterson, the candidates drifted back to their duty stations to sweat out the final cut. Some of the candidates had picked up hints before departing that NASA was very interested in them. Schirra noted later that the doctors examining a polyp on his larynx were in a big hurry to have it removed. The attending physician, unnerved by the rush, remarked before the procedure: "From all the fuss they're making over you, you must be getting ready to go to the moon or something." Schirra took this as a sign that his chances of joining Project Mercury were excellent.[33]

Given his duty station at Wright-Patterson, Grissom too might have heard scuttlebutt that he was still in the running. At about this time, Grissom's school mate Bill Head told anyone who would listen in Mitchell that "I can tell you one [candidate] that's gonna be in" Project Mercury. "Whatever they announce, it's gonna be Grissom," he insisted. "I was sure he was gonna be [selected] from just things that I heard from him," Head recalled. "That's how he made it."[34]

The names of the eighteen finalists were recommended to NASA without medical reservations at the end of March. Donlan later claimed the ordeal of the medical and psychological testing actually had little to do with the final group of candidates he submitted to his boss, Robert Gilruth. "Those tests, per se, had little to do with their actual selection," Donlan told an interviewer in 1998, "because the only questions I ever asked finally was: 'Are there any physical or mental reasons any of these candidates should be dismissed?' If the answer to that was 'No,' they were on a list."[35]

It turned out that a critical consideration was gauging the candidates' reaction to viewing drawings of the Mercury capsule during technical interviews. "We would spread the drawings out and acquaint them with what at that time was the situation, and ask them if they thought there was any legitimate role for the test pilot experience," Donlan recalled nearly four decades later. "A lot depended on how they answered that question. Some would look at it and say, 'Uh, I guess not.' Well, others would say, 'My God, this is a pioneering venture. Of course.'"[36]

Donlan could be excused for conflating a key theme of the coming Kennedy administration with Eisenhower's hesitant but geopolitically expedient foray into manned spaceflight. Grissom was certainly among the astronaut candidates who expressed enthusiasm about the Mercury concept. Indeed, he eventually would help oversee development of the spacecraft manual and automatic controls that would make the early astronauts something more than just "spam in a can."

Carpenter's recollection of his first glimpse at the Mercury specifications sheds light on how critical the technical interviews were for the finalists. Carpenter, who would orbit Earth three times in May 1962, noticed that Donlan sat up in his chair when the navy test pilot mentioned a camera installed on a photo-reconnaissance fighter, the F-9F-8P, which he had flown at the Patuxent Naval Air Station. The camera gave the aviator a view of the ground.

Donlan's interest was piqued because the Mercury designers were contemplating a periscope-like device that would give the astronauts a view that could be used for navigation purposes. Carpenter's experience with the camera, along with his strong background in celestial navigation and communications while flying larger navy aircraft, made a favorable impression on Donlan. It was seemingly inconsequential incidents like this that greatly influenced the selection of the seven Mercury astronauts.[37]

Getting his first look at the spacecraft schematics, Grissom undoubtedly realized he was glimpsing the future of flight. "I knew instantly that this was for me," he wrote later. "This is where the future of test piloting lay."[38] Spaceships, not rocket planes, were going to take humans into space, and Grissom the test pilot instinctively understood Mercury was the best way to go faster and higher.

The selection committee settled on seven "premium" men at the beginning of April 1959. Gilruth signed off on the selections, and Donlan began notifying the chosen on Friday, April 2. "You've been selected to join us, if you're still interested" was about all Donlan said. Each candidate immediately accepted.

Before beginning his nearly seven-year career as an astronaut, Grissom had been rated as a "senior pilot" at the Wright Air Development Center. He was at the top of his profession. His decision to put his test pilot career on hold and accept NASA's invitation to try out for the astronaut corps was risky, since no one in the late 1950s was sure what would happen after the completion of the Project Mercury program. Would there be a follow-up manned effort? What about a space station? Early in the space competition with the Soviet Union, only Wernher von Braun and his US Army rocketeers were thinking seriously about a trip to the moon. The true intentions of the Soviets and von Braun's Russian counterpart, Sergei Korolev, remained unknown.

On April 13, 1959, "CAPT VIRGIL L. GRISSOM"[39] received special orders from Wright-Patterson Air Force Base, relieving him from his assignment at the Directorate of Flight and All-Weather Testing. He would be assigned until at least early 1962 to US Air Force Headquarters in Washington, DC, with a permanent duty station at Langley Research Center in Virginia, the home of NASA's Space Task Group.[40] The order noted only parenthetically that Grissom was now part of Project Mercury.

At age thirty-three, the second youngest member of the Mercury Seven after Cooper was instructed to report no later than April 27 to Warren North, a well-known NACA test pilot and a member of the astronaut selection committee, as well as chief of manned spaceflight for the Space Task Group. Grissom was ordered to personally carry his pressure suit and parachute with him to Langley Field.

A small-town striver from southern Indiana had made the final cut. Cold War necessity and the arc of aviation history had swept up Gus Grissom and his six colleagues. Some had seen combat, been shot at, and fired at faceless adversaries in the sky, sending them circling to their deaths. There also was a parallel group of less skilled but equally fearless fighter pilots gathering at a place called Star City in the Soviet Union. The astronauts, most of them top-notch test pilots, and Soviet flyers training to be cosmonauts prepared to duel in space. Grissom was now among them.

The Mercury Seven were brothers, and, like siblings, they would fight like hell to be first.

Four days before Grissom's new orders arrived, on April 9, 1959, an extraordinary event took place in the auditorium of NASA's temporary headquarters at Dolley Madison House in Lafayette Park adjacent to the White House. It was the long-awaited NASA press conference introducing the nation's new Mercury astronauts: Lieutenant Malcolm Scott Carpenter, along with Lieutenant Commanders Walter Marty Schirra Jr. and Alan Bartlett Shepard of the US Navy; Captains Leroy Gordon Cooper, Virgil Ivan Grissom, and Donald Kent Slayton of the US Air Force; and Lieutenant Colonel John Herschel Glenn of the US Marine Corps. Their names would become mythic, their faces forming the Mount Rushmore of American space explorers.

The press conference, memorable even by Washington, DC, standards, was the first time all seven astronauts appeared together in public. They had probably met in passing in a cafeteria or a restaurant during the testing ordeal. Now they were joined at the hips.

The seven were dumbfounded by the public reaction to their introduction, particularly since each understood he had done nothing to deserve the adulation. "I've never seen anything like it, before or since," Slayton wrote, recalling the media "frenzy."[41]

At 10 a.m. sharp, the NASA spokesman proclaimed to the breathless reporters and news photographers elbowing for a position: "Ladies and gentlemen, the astronaut volunteers." The seven men dressed in suits with skinny ties—Glenn and Slayton in bowties—were arranged at a long table in alphabetical order, meaning the reticent Grissom frequently had to follow the loquacious Glenn in responding to reporters' questions. The answers initially were clipped and perfunctory, until Glenn got ahold of a question and ran with it. Glenn "ate this stuff up," Slayton recalled.

Responding to a query about whether their wives supported their decision to fly in space, Glenn delivered a tour de force, aw-shucks reply that the newspapermen could not resist. "A damned speech about God and family and destiny," Slayton insisted.

Then it was Grissom's turn to reply. As always, he was matter-of-fact, sounding like the family man he was, even though he was not home much and his absences would now grow longer. "Well, my wife feels the same way [as Glenn's wife] or of course I couldn't be here," he began, pausing as Glenn and Schirra laughed. "She's with me all the way. The boys are a little too young to realize what's going on yet, but I'm sure they'll feel the same way."

Not bad for a reserved Hoosier with a deer-in-the-headlights expression on his face. Glenn was polished, sincere. Grissom was an everyman placed in an awkward situation, doing the best he could with little or no preparation. "We were all as green as grass," Slayton admitted.[42] The seven test pilots with little or no experience with the press were making it up as they went along.

The reporter's question about the wives' attitudes turned out to be perceptive. NASA psychiatrists had pointedly asked each astronaut candidate whether his spouse was opposed to him participating in the space program. Those who answered in the affirmative were rejected.

Grissom reluctantly learned how to deal with reporters and photographers, later saying the hardest part of a mission for him was the preflight press conference. Others like Glenn and Shepard quickly embraced their celebrity status; Grissom and the rest would take longer to adjust to the press scrutiny, the invasion of privacy, and the uncomfortable feeling of being marketed like soap. Upholding the image of the All-American astronaut also put a crimp in Grissom's by-now-established pattern of partying as hard as he worked, meaning he would have to be more discrete in his off-hours carousing.

Back in Mitchell, the Grissom family was divided over what to make of the eldest son's accomplishment. "My dad was really enthused about it. He thought it was something really wonderful," brother Lowell recalled. "My mom wasn't quite that excited about it. She'd heard too many stories like coming back into the atmosphere on a tail of fire so she was not that enthused about it."[43]

The new astronauts dined with the top air force and navy brass on the evening of April 9, and then made their way south to settle in at work in their cramped office with seven desks and a secretary in a building at Langley Field in Virginia. In the interim, they had signed a lucrative deal giving *Life* magazine exclusive rights to their stories. Before the deal was finalized in early August, the astronauts were still dealing with press queries while acclimating themselves to NASA's operations as officers on loan from their respective service branches.

With the astronauts' arrival at Langley Field in late April, the American manned space program was now gathering steam. "All of a sudden, we had money," said Jerome "Jerry" Hammack, a Mercury-Redstone project engineer at NASA Langley, who eventually moved into a house across the street from the Grissoms's in the Houston subdivision of Timber Cove. "Oh man, we were going!"

When the astronauts reported for duty at Langley Field in the spring of 1959, Hammack and others decided to head over to the cafeteria to meet them. Mercury had been a test program up to that point, and here were the astronauts, "flesh and blood," Hammack recalled.[44]

The Langley engineers immediately began working closely with the astronauts on the design of the spacecraft. Gilruth welcomed their participation in the design process. "I gravitated toward Gus," Hammack said. "He'd come over and bug me" about something. Scott and Mark Grissom were the same age as the Hammacks's two sons. "We got to be good friends." Indeed, Betty Grissom and Hammack's wife, Adelin, would become lifelong friends.

As the Redstone rocket and Mercury capsule began to take shape, Grissom and Hammack would frequently fly together to both McDonnell Aircraft in St. Louis, where the spacecraft was being built, and Huntsville, Alabama, to check on the Redstone rockets. At this point, Grissom did not know which booster he would be riding, but each of the astronauts became immersed in all aspects of the Mercury program.

About the time Grissom was selected as an astronaut, Sam Beddingfield, his flying buddy from Wright-Patterson, retired from the air force and took up farming back in North Carolina. It took Beddingfield about three days to realize he was not cut out to till the soil. He'd heard that NASA, just two hours up the road, was doing some new kinds of flight testing. On a whim, Beddingfield hopped into his car to see if he could get a job as an aeronautical engineer working on aircraft testing. That section at Langley wasn't hiring, so Beddingfield was sent to the other side of the runway to talk to the new "rocket people." The first person he ran into was Grissom. "What are you doing here?" the surprised astronaut asked Beddingfield. Sam told Gus he was looking for a job but knew nothing about rockets. The astronaut told him not to worry, "They don't have anybody who does."[45]

Indeed, the Mercury engineers at Langley and the contractors at McDonnell Aircraft were making things up as they went along. No one really knew how to go about flying in space. Lowell Grissom had started working at the McDonnell plant in St. Louis shortly after his brother was selected as an astronaut. "Those were exciting times," he said. "When I first started work there they had molded the couches for Mercury and they had them setting up on a wall with the individual names on them." Lowell continued, "Right across from my office is where they were building the heat shield for the Mercury spacecraft. . . . Those guys [at McDonnell], they really didn't know what they were doing. Everything was brand new. I remember talking to them about the heat shield, and one guy said, 'Well, we think it has to be this thick, so we're making it just a little bit thicker.'[46] Cecile Grissom's concerns about her son riding a tail of fire during a Mercury reentry were not unfounded.

Back at Langley, Beddingfield explained to Grissom that he had left the air force. "That's perfect," Grissom replied. "If you don't like it, you can just get up and leave."[47]

Ten days after being hired by NASA in September 1959, Beddingfield was reassigned to Cape Canaveral to work on Project Mercury. Perhaps Grissom had put in a word for him, but Beddingfield possessed practical engineering experience, and the new space agency needed every qualified engineer it could find. Beddingfield would retire from NASA in 1985 as deputy director of the US Space Shuttle Program. He was among the most able of the engineers who worked at NASA in the glory days of manned spaceflight. He and Grissom would work closely together for the next eight years. On Grissom's first flight, Beddingfield watched over his spaceship when it arrived at the Cape and was responsible for the "weight and balance" of the vehicle, along with the escape and retrorockets, the parachutes and the pyrotechnics, including those used to blow the hatch off Grissom's spacecraft.

Without engineers like Beddingfield, the United States would not have walked on the moon or flown the shuttle. Beddingfield, a country boy at heart, retired up the road from the Cape in Titusville, Florida, where he died on June 23, 2012. He and Grissom had made history together, and Beddingfield was determined to make sure no one forgot his air force buddy and what together they had done for the nation.

In August 1959, the Project Mercury astronauts signed an exclusive contract with *Time-Life* for theirs and their families' personal stories. The astronauts received $500,000 to be divided equally. The stories would appear in *Life* magazine under their own bylines, and the astronauts and their wives would have final approval on anything that was published. The controversial deal was designed in part to preclude a bidding war for individual story rights. The rest of the press corps was furious; the astronauts and their families tasted the first fruits of astronaut celebrity driven by the public's firm belief that at least some of them would go up in flames.

While the others made separate living arrangements, Grissom, Schirra, and Slayton began looking for a place to live near Langley Field. They ended up moving "off-base" into a housing development just up the peninsula from Langley near Newport News. The Grissoms and Slaytons were next-door neighbors, with the Schirras a few doors down. The three commuted to Langley while their wives unpacked and got the kids settled in new schools. Scott Grissom was now eight, a second grader. Mark was five.

Betty had been running a temperature of 102 the night before the NASA press conference in Washington when Gus called her back in Ohio to warn her about what he suspected would be a press onslaught once the news broke. Betty proceeded to straighten up the house and made a doctor's appointment for the next morning, where she received a penicillin shot. Stopping at the grocery store on her way home, Betty was approached by reporters from *Life*. She invited them home. Soon the place was crawling with journalists and photographers all wanting to know if Betty was proud of her husband, the new astronaut who, they assumed, would probably die in a fireball. The mob left behind a trail of trash, spent flashbulbs, and ashtrays full of cigarette butts.

When it was over, the *Life* reporters took Betty and the boys to dinner. Their heads were still spinning. NASA had let the wives fend for themselves. Betty would not forget.

It soon became evident that Betty simply was not cut out for this sort of thing. Unlike some of the other astronaut wives like Rene Carpenter, who appreciated the historic significance behind Project Mercury, small-town Gus and Betty never really understood why anyone would be interested to know how they lived their lives. Like the other wives, Betty would back her husband's decision to ride a rocket but keep her reservations to herself.

Two years later, when it was her husband's turn to be launched into space, Betty struggled mightily to hold it together as the press again laid siege to her home. Under the *Life* contract, the magazine's reporters had access to the Grissom home on the day of Gus's flight. Each family had their own access rules for the press, and Betty's were particularly stringent.

No one would be allowed in her house. "Look at them out on my lawn," she barked, veering between revulsion and a desire to support her husband by being available to answer the usual postflight questions. Rene was with Betty all that day and wrote out a statement for her to use. Betty glared at the draft and said, "What a bunch of lies!" Observing Betty throughout launch day and noticing the chip already forming on her shoulder, Rene concluded, "It was difficult."[48]

After the Project Mercury astronauts were introduced to the nation, Betty immediately began packing while Gus looked for a place to live in Virginia. Not fully grasping the extent to which their lives were about to change, Betty convinced herself that Langley was just another move to another duty station. The next thing she knew, Gus and his colleagues were appearing before Congress in May. The congressmen wanted to see the new heroes with their own eyes and be seen with them.

The furniture soon arrived from Ohio, banged up by the movers. The homebuilder had installed the wrong color tile in the bathroom. They wouldn't paint the outside trim the color Betty wanted. The roof leaked. However, it was easier for Betty to deal with these household matters and getting the boys situated in school than sitting around contemplating the family's new celebrity status and what it might mean. "I'm too busy with the house right now to worry about it," she claimed. "Maybe later I'll start to worry."[49]

Deskbound, the astronauts fretted about maintaining their flight proficiency along with the extra flight pay that came with it. On loan to NASA, they were no longer collecting badly needed per diem. NASA finally relented and provided the astronauts with access to T-33s, the training version of the F-80 Shooting Star.

Grissom and Slayton were so close by the time they moved to Virginia that they would head over to Langley Air Force Base on weekends, jump into the two-seat trainer, and fly cross-country and back just to squeeze in the flight hours needed to earn extra pay—in the case of air force captains, an extra $190 a month. The two midwesterners said little to each other on these flights. Glenn joked that it was "East Coast to West Coast in ten words or less."[50] Grissom and Slayton would show up at Langley Field on Saturdays and "just take off, flying the plane cross-country until our fannies were tired," Slayton said.[51] When they weren't flying across the continent, the test pilots–turned-astronauts were out hunting in the Virginia countryside. Betty and the boys waited at home.

Most of the future astronauts had at least one brush with death during their flying careers. After all, one reason they were selected for the Mercury program was their ability to find a way out of a tight spot.

Grissom came as close as any of the astronauts to "buying the farm" during a flight test of the unreliable Mercury Atlas rocket that would eventually take Americans into orbit. Grissom and Cooper had been assigned to fly "chase" on launch day, April 25, 1961. Grissom, flying a delta wing F-106A fighter, would approach the rocket dubbed MA-3 at about one thousand feet, ignite his afterburner, and climb alongside the Atlas to observe the early phase of the flight. Cooper would take over at 25,000 feet. "No sweat," Grissom said, describing the incident later. "Ignition and lift-off were bang on schedule, and I was congratulating myself on having the finest possible view of an ascending rocket."[52]

Grissom had maneuvered his aircraft alongside the Atlas and was observing the escape tower pulling the unmanned Mercury capsule away when, as described by the pilot not given to exaggeration—"*Kablooie!*" Forty seconds after liftoff, the spacecraft having separated from the booster, the NASA range safety officer destroyed the Atlas. However, the safety officer apparently had failed to note the position of the chase planes when he hit the self-destruct button. The exploding booster produced the largest fireball Grissom had ever seen, undoubtedly because he was practically inside it. Acting on instinct after hundreds of hours flying jet fighters, Grissom immediately pulled up and over and "went away from that place fast."[53] A friend in Cocoa Beach watching the launch turned to his wife and advised, "Well, now there are only six astronauts."[54]

Knowing the NASA engineers would want a report on how the spacecraft fared as it floated on its parachute to the ocean, Grissom headed down to find it. Suddenly, he noticed what he thought were "big seagulls" around his plane. They turned out to be large chunks of the exploded rocket raining down around him. Luckily, none hit his plane.

The test was considered a failure. The unmanned spacecraft splashed down just over seven minutes after launch. The exploding Atlas "was quite a spectacle, but never again, thanks," Grissom realized.[55] Luck and piloting skills had again saved his hide.

Amid their training, the Mercury astronauts were now required under their lucrative *Life* contract[56] to sit still for interviews. Early in the program, Grissom talked with space writer Loudon Wainwright for about forty-five minutes, the reporter's tape recorder apparently running. "Before that bright and laconic man left, I tried to play back the tape and found we'd recorded nothing. When Gus heard that, he stared hard at me for a moment, then sat down and said: 'Let's do it again.'"[57]

The astronauts also were busy focusing on various areas of specialization in early 1961 as NASA began sending chimps up on Mercury test flights. Each astronaut was assigned a component of the spacecraft or the two rockets they would fly, the suborbital Redstone and the Atlas, an intercontinental ballistic missile modified to send humans into Earth orbit. Grissom's assignment was the manual and automatic controls on the Mercury spacecraft.

Once the ship separated from its booster, Grissom explained a year before his suborbital flight, the automatic pilot would take over to position it properly in orbit, or what the astronauts considered a "bullet facing backwards."[58]

The autopilot then controlled the spacecraft "in its attitude as it orbits around the earth," Grissom continued, including the sensors used to pinpoint the earth's horizon as a navigation reference to control spacecraft attitude. The reaction controls used to change yaw (side-to-side), pitch (up and down), and roll were operated by a "hand controller which the pilot can use at his option to control the attitude of the capsule himself," particularly if the autopilot failed. In other words, Grissom emphasized, the pilot could fly the spacecraft by controlling its attitude. Beyond that, the Mercury flight path was unalterable.[59]

In the back of each astronaut's mind was the flight schedule and who would get the first mission, perhaps the first manned spaceflight in history. Each was absolutely convinced he was qualified. The process used to select the first American in space turned out to be somewhat arbitrary and more than a little political. Grissom, Shepard, and Glenn had appeared on the cover of *Life* in March 1961 under the headline: "Astronaut First Team."

Grissom, the press believed, remained in the running to be first right up until the day in May when a Redstone booster lofted the first American into space—three weeks *after* Russian pilot and cosmonaut Yuri Alekseyevich Gagarin became the first human being to orbit Earth.

7

EXTRACURRICULAR ACTIVITIES

*I deem as heroic those who have the harder task, face it
unflinchingly and live. In this world women do that.*
—*James Salter*

He move in space with minimum waste, maximum joy.
—*"Smooth Operator," music and lyrics by Sade Adu and Raymond St. John*

"The pressure to perform was nonstop. We needed to let off a little steam. We weren't going to let the fact that we were astronauts keep us from having fun."

Those words were spoken by a narrator channeling Deke Slayton in a 1994 documentary about the race to the moon. Slayton's views on how to mix work and play were synched to footage of an animated Gus Grissom chatting up a young woman during a break in astronaut training. Grissom appears relaxed and jovial in the NASA promotional footage, looking as if he were accustomed, like the other Mercury astronauts, to schmoozing with attractive young women who were not their wives.

Yes, there were women, and Gus Grissom was likely near the front of the pack. A former McDonnell Douglas secretary confronted Betty Grissom during a party in the mid-1960s, asking indiscreetly, "Did Gus Grissom have a girlfriend?" Incensed, Betty attempted to turn the tables and put her inquisitor on the spot. The woman backed off. Betty wrote later: "Frankly I have no idea whether Gus had a girl friend or not. Sometimes a wife is the last to know."[1] Some of the astronaut wives concluded that Betty was "in denial."

Alan Shepard favored the euphemism "extracurricular activities." Shepard's exploits during his navy and astronaut days have been widely chronicled.[2] "Doesn't everyone have the right to do what they want to do?" Shepard famously asserted when pressed about his infidelities by John Glenn. Glenn's view was that the personal freedom of astronauts—the most public of public figures in the 1960s—was now circumscribed by the larger cause of sending Americans into space before the Russians. Grissom sided with Shepard.

Even for military men accustomed to being away from home and family for long stretches, the social standing of the Mercury astronauts was unprecedented. Everyone—politicians, celebrities, groupies (otherwise known as "Cape Cookies"), the media—wanted a piece of the Mercury Seven. Several astronauts were more than willing to oblige when it came to that group of ladies at the other end of the bar in Cocoa Beach, described by one beat writer as "a harlot of a town."

"With the astros the biggest problem was loose women," recalled Walt Cunningham, failing to acknowledge equally loose men. Recalling an orientation speech delivered by Wally Schirra after being selected in the third group of astronauts in October 1963, Cunningham wrote: "We were expected to tolerate a certain amount of freewheeling behavior on the part of our compadres."[3]

Seldom if ever in the accounts of astronaut escapades are names named or specific instances cited. The point was that most everyone was doing it, and everyone was supposed to remain discreet.

When the navy test pilot John Young, Grissom's good friend and crewmate on the first flight of the Gemini program, joined the astronaut corps in September 1962, he listened intently as Slayton advised the "New Nine" to "watch the perks" and follow the old test pilot's creed: "Anything you can eat, drink, or screw within twenty-four hours is acceptable, but beyond that, take a pass!"[4] "From the experiences of the Mercury astronauts, they knew what temptations were out there, and that, for some of us, they would be too juicy to pass up," Young recalled.[5]

Slayton was well versed on the subject. When his wife, Marge, a former government employee, laid down the law and demanded to know why the wives of the new astronauts were being denied access to NASA headquarters at Langley Air Force Base in Virginia, her otherwise hard-nosed husband relented and snuck her onto the base. "Tell them I'm coming to wash your damn Ban-Lon shirts . . . that I'm your girlfriend, *that* ought to do it!"[6]

Discretion was key, even among the reporters on the space beat. Al Worden, among the first in the astronaut corps to endure the ostracism associated with divorce (mainly from astronaut wives, especially Marge Slayton[7]), recounted how mostly married astronauts used his "bachelor pad" in Houston. "It was more of a community apartment for visiting friends and family members, plus a host of secrecy-minded married astronauts who sometimes asked to borrow the key," the *Apollo 15* command module pilot wrote in his 2011 memoir. Fellow astronauts "likely saw more action in my so-called bachelor pad than I ever did."[8]

Tales of infidelities sell books, but does the private life of a public figure engaged in an extremely risky profession matter to anyone but himself and his family? Most of the reporters covering the Mercury astronauts looked the other way. Some saved salacious, mostly unconfirmable gossip for their books on the Space Race.[9]

The attitude of the space reporters was in keeping with the tenure of the times. CBS News correspondent Roger Mudd wrote in his 2008 memoir, *The Place to Be*, that he was stuck in 1962 with the assignment of tailing a boat chartered by President Kennedy and his senate buddy from Florida, George Smathers. In a chapter titled "Wolves on the Prowl," Mudd recounted how he, the unfortunate press pool reporter that day, had to follow the presidential flotilla off the Florida coast. The reporter's view of who was climbing aboard the president's yacht was blocked by the Secret Service. "It was a joke," Mudd recalled, "our pretending to be covering the president." Mudd quickly figured out and dismissed the fact that JFK and Smathers were likely headed for a clandestine rendezvous.

"What would today be called the 'mainstream media' didn't and wouldn't touch that story," Mudd wrote. "We figured, who cares? Besides, we told ourselves, we were political reporters, not gossip columnists."[10]

A friend of Jack Kennedy's mistress and confidante, Mary Pinchot Meyer, came at the issue of infidelity from a completely different perspective, one colored by the war experiences of a generation of American men. "Many of us have been lonely too, deprived by our male peers of that sensitivity they had to brutalize out of themselves in order to undergo the Second World War," wrote the artist Anne Truitt. "Confronted by the probability of their own deaths, it seems to me that many of the most percipient men of my generation killed off those parts of themselves that were most vulnerable to pain, and thus lost forever a delicacy of feeling on which intimacy depends."[11]

At the head of that generation was the Allied commanding general Dwight D. Eisenhower. As president, "Ike" had set in motion the process by which test pilots were selected as astronauts. His successor would make the astronauts agents of his "New Frontier." Writing to a friend in 1954, then-Senator John Kennedy emphasized: "The war made us. It was and is our greatest single moment. The memory of the war is a key to our characters."[12] In JFK's case, the postwar enemy was often boredom, an affliction that prompted risky personal behavior and a likely addiction to constant excitement.

The taciturn John Young, among the greatest of the early astronauts, wrote affectionately about his colleague and mentor: "Old Gus was a really hard working fellow, but hard playing too. He was really a good man to work with. In terms of getting a job done, he knew what it took—even if we had stayed out kind of late the night before."

As they worked by day and played by night to prepare for their Gemini flight, Grissom became a big brother to Young, who lovingly referred to his crewmate as "that old rascal Gus." Grissom and Young had little to say on an open communication channel to Mission Control during their three-orbit flight in March 1965. Between themselves aboard the new spacecraft Grissom named the "Unsinkable Molly Brown," however, they yakked like schoolboys on a playground.

Preparing for the retrofire burn that would lower them out of Earth orbit, Big Brother Gus asked Young if his seat belt and shoulder harness were secured. Not wanting their brief flight to end, Young replied that he was ready for reentry, but added, "Can you take it around a couple more times?"[13]

Frozen in time, the appeal of the gruff, no-nonsense Grissom has persisted. "I just think he is such a handsome man. & his voice . . . very sexy voice!" a female admirer chirped on one of several social media sites dedicated to Grissom. Fifty years after his death, the pugnacious pilot with the deep baritone voice retains a loyal following, even among those born long after he was gone.

Lowell Grissom considered his oldest brother to be a "mild extrovert" with a deceptive and well-honed sense of humor as well as an appreciation for the absurdity of life. These traits tended to show up when least expected. The silent NASA footage showing Grissom suiting up for yet another in a seemingly endless string of Apollo spacecraft tests in 1966 and early 1967 show him laughing and joking with his crewmates and the suit technicians. By this time, he was completely accustomed to the cameramen and the attention. He paid it no heed. The commander was busy defusing the tension as his crew prepared for a mission all were worried about.

"Gus had a good time as an astronaut," said Lowell, wanting his brother to be remembered fifty years after his death as a lighthearted adventurer, not the "Gloomy Gus" often portrayed by the beat reporters. "He loved to go fast. He loved a good joke."[14] Like sex, humor and a never-ending series of pranks were among the antidotes to the unrelenting pressure to perform, to be perfect in a situation where one mistake meant death.

Mark Grissom emphasized something similar about his father: "Basically, he liked to go fast and go high, and that's what the space program offered him. He had an opportunity and he took it."[15]

When not flying, Grissom also went very fast in his Corvette, in his boats, and on water skis. The need for speed was often dictated by competition among his peers. Joyriding in the Corvette around Timber Cove, where the Grissoms and many astronaut families had settled near Houston, Mark would egg on his father: "Dad, do a hundred" miles per hour![16]

Gus and Gordo became business partners, and together they built a duplex in the Colorado Rockies where Gus taught Scott and Mark how to ski. It was one of several joint ventures between the air force buddies that included Indianapolis racecars, speedboats, and a failed boat repair and retail business near Houston. Each lost $16,000 on the venture.

A family ski trip to Crested Butte Peak would be one of the Grissom family's last outings together. Gus was named commander of *Apollo 1* in March 1966, and immediately he was swept up in the effort to ready a defective spacecraft for a difficult shakedown mission.

Years before, each of the Mercury astronauts handled their sudden and unexpected celebrity in different ways. The author Tom Wolfe likely came closest to the mark in describing Glenn and Carpenter as the Boy Scouts and the rest, including Grissom, as the playboys. "Deep into our cups" one night in a hotel bar in Hawaii during the Mercury program, the army flight surgeon Robert Moser asked Grissom how he was handling his celebrity astronaut status. "You know, Doc," Gus replied, "one day I'm just another aviator and then I got into the Mercury program and [next] day I was an astronaut and I was every woman's hero."[17]

The longer Grissom worked for NASA, the shorter and less frequent were his trips home. Still bitter about the postflight snubs in 1961, Betty was tiring of her husband's long absences. In a letter written in the fall of 1961, Grissom confided to his mother that his wife was "getting pretty fed up with [him] being gone so much."

The four-page letter, dated October 7, 1961, informed Cecile that he had just returned from Florida after helping to evaluate proposals for the future three-man Apollo spacecraft. He took the time to explain to Cecile, who undoubtedly passed along the details to Dennis Grissom, that the Apollo program would begin in earnest early the following year, "but it will be a good number of years before we fly it."

The guilty son then apologized for failing to write more often or call, hinting that he "had some news" but cautioned: "I don't think I should talk about it over the phone." Did Grissom think someone was listening to his calls?[18]

Halfway through the letter, Gus informed his mother that Betty, Scott, and Mark were after him to go bowling. He would finish the letter the next day. Making up for lost time, they would hit the bowling alley again the day after the letter to Cecile was posted. "Betty bowls on a ladies team one morning each week and seems to like it real well. She beat me one game last night. Scotty almost beat me too." Cecile's grandsons were doing okay in school, he continued, "but we never know until the grades come out."

In fact, Scott and Mark had taken some grief at school over the near-tragic end of their father's Mercury flight.

In 1962, the family was preparing to leave Virginia and move to steaming Houston, the new headquarters of the American space program. "Probably not until after school is out," Grissom informed his mother. "We have our house up for sale though and if it sells right away I guess Betty and boys will head on to Houston. I'm not looking forward to going to Texas again but I guess it's as good as Virginia. I've been loaned to NASA by the Air Force for another three years and I'll probably [be] with them longer than that."

Despite growing frustrations with the direction of the new Apollo program and a nagging sense that he should be flying in combat with his air force comrades over Vietnam, where the air war was heating up by the mid-1960s, Grissom would remain with NASA until the end.

After inquiring about his father's upcoming business trip to Chicago, there was one last thing to report before closing. It was about Betty and the astronaut wives. "Betty and the other girls are going to [word crossed out] Seattle, Washington, to help dedicate a building [word crossed out] or something for the worlds [*sic*] fair that will be held out there next year. It will be a good trip for her. I'll be glad for her to get out away from the home awhile. We didn't get any vacation this year." The eldest son was clearly proud to inform his mother that astronauts earned thirty days of vacation each year, but it was unlikely he and his competitors took much of it.

To Cecile, the celebrity astronaut Gus Grissom was someone other than her eldest son, Virgil. "Gus" existed in newspapers articles, television interviews, and spaceshots. What her son was doing at NASA must have seemed unfathomable to a housewife in a small Indiana town. Dennis and Cecile were understandably proud of their son, but for Cecile it was hard to understand what exactly it was her eldest son was pursuing and why. Later, she made a notation at the bottom of the letter that read "Virgil was at Bermuda" serving as capsule communicator for Glenn's orbital flight.

Lowell Grissom told a reporter that the letter to their mother revealed the intense competition among the Mercury Seven astronauts. Aside from the petty jealousy over Glenn securing the big prize, the first American orbital flight, the letter also reveals how Grissom was trying to reassure his mother that his marriage was stable and that his career was advancing.

It also may have been intended to assuage the fears of someone he loved and worried about that he was okay despite his recent brush with death. And Grissom certainly knew the contents of his letter to Cecile would be shared with his father and siblings.

The time spent at home and the rare moments available to an astronaut to gather his thoughts to write a letter to his mother were few and far between by the mid-1960s. With three separate American space efforts under way, on the drawing board, or preparing for launch, along with the move from Virginia to Houston, the astronauts were always on the move. And for the new celebrities looking to blow off some steam, the temptations were always there in every town.

Soon Grissom would be back at the Cape or at some remote NASA communications relay station. The long days of testing were followed by equally long nights of partying. Grissom would think nothing of hopping on a plane and flying to Cape Canaveral just so he could head over to Fat Boy's BBQ in Cocoa Beach for the ribs he loved. His picture and the images of other astronauts and movie stars filled the walls of the rib joint. In the 1960s, the beach town's Motel Row on Florida Highway A1A was filled with other astronaut watering holes, like the Mouse Trap and dives like the Booby Trap, a strip joint with a roof shaped like a woman's breasts.

The weeks away from home were taking a toll Gus and Betty's marriage. Had he lived, it's unlikely their marriage would have survived the strains and temptations of being an astronaut and a public figure.

According to several accounts, Grissom's girlfriend, his "sweetie," as one of the children of a Mercury astronaut called her, showed up at his funeral service at Arlington National Cemetery on January 31, 1967. She was kept at a distance from the grieving family. Some who knew Gus well, or claimed they did, believed he eventually would have divorced Betty. That will never be known. Grissom took these secrets with him to his grave.

Somewhere along the line, things did come apart for Betty and Gus. She tired of his "playing astronaut" all week while she ran the household and raised the children in Timber Cove. Perhaps Betty's mother was right to be suspicious of boys from town, "the wolves of Mitchell."[19] Perhaps, also, Betty really was in denial. But the stoic midwesterner took literally her mother's admonition: "If you have any fights, don't come home."[20]

The *Life* photographer Ralph Morse had snapped a publicity shot of Betty and Gus together at the Cape in the early 1960s, just before Gus's first flight. The strain on their faces is evident. Betty's expression as she gazes at her husband seems to be saying, "What are you thinking?" or "Help me get through this, Gus." Her husband stares into the ground, resigned, as if to say, "Let's get this over with."

In the end, Betty was alone. After the lawsuit filed against the manufacturer of the Apollo spacecraft, she had few friends left among the astronauts, their wives, or the space groupies who privately criticized her for suing North American Aviation. To survive, Betty developed a suit of emotional armor and cared not a lick what anyone thought of her. What choice did she have? She had to soldier on even though she said, "I hate it that Gus is gone, even though I guess the [space] program was worth it."[21] In the end, it was just her and Mark. They are estranged from Scott.

Paradoxically, Americans may not have reached the moon before the Soviets without the *Apollo 1* fire that killed Gus Grissom, Ed White, and Roger Chaffee. In the end, Grissom's family and the families of White and Chaffee were the ultimate victims of what came to be known in the mid-1960s as "Go Fever," the relentless push to beat the Soviets to the moon.

Restless Gus Grissom seemed always to be going somewhere. Whether it was joining the US Army Air Corps to escape Mitchell, picking up and moving to West Lafayette after the war to earn an engineering degree, or later rejoining the new military branch and entering pilot school before shipping out to Korea, he was in constant motion. As an astronaut, he spent most of his time flying between Cape Canaveral, Langley, Houston, St. Louis, and the headquarters of other NASA contractors. He was seldom home and may have preferred it that way.

Betty had long ago figured out where her husband's heart was. Those fighter jets back at Williams Air Force Base had indeed been "the true love of his life," she understood, along with the risk, the excitement, and the freedom from entanglements all these things had come to represent. It is undeniable that Gus Grissom had a mistress. It was flight.

8

THE FLIGHT OF *LIBERTY BELL 7*

This I did not do.
—*Gus Grissom's reply to the allegation that he intentionally*
blew Liberty Bell 7*'s escape hatch[1]*

I n a pivotal scene from the 1944 film *Thirty Seconds Over Tokyo*, Lieutenant Ted Lawson, portrayed by the matinee idol Van Johnson, stares out from a rain-swept beach at his lost B-25 Mitchell medium bomber, the aircraft used to great effect in Lieutenant Colonel James H. Doolittle's famous 1942 raid on Tokyo.[2] Lawson's bomber ran out of gas before it could reach the Chinese mainland and safety. Through the downpour, Lawson sees only the tail of his beloved *Ruptured Duck* visible in the shallows after an emergency crash landing. "I lost my ship," the inconsolable Lawson says to no one, repeating, "I *lost* my ship."

The second American manned space flight came to a similar, unexpected climax on July 21, 1961, when Captain Virgil I. Grissom's ship vanished beneath the waves minutes after splashdown. His flight aboard the Mercury spacecraft *Liberty Bell 7* was a fifteen-minute cannon shot from Cape Canaveral, peaking at 118 miles over the Atlantic Ocean, covering a distance of 302 miles before landing in the sea. The mission had gone almost exactly as planned. The pilot was calmly recording switch positions on his main instrument panel, loosening his harnesses, disconnecting his pressure suit from the ship's oxygen supply, and stowing equipment in preparation for being picked up by recovery forces.

The astronaut was in good shape, ahead of schedule. As his spacecraft bobbed in the ocean, he unrolled a "neck dam," a kind of turtleneck diaphragm designed to keep water from seeping into his pressure suit. Later, he recalled it was the best thing he had done all day.[3] The recovery procedure called for Grissom to blow the escape hatch, exit the spacecraft, and then grab a "horse collar" that would be lowered from a waiting helicopter. The astronaut's sealed pressure suit would be inflated, allowing him to float in the unlikely event he ended up in the water.

"His [neck ring] had been stowed in the [same] position so long that it didn't really get tight," noted Wayne Koons, who assisted with recovery operations at Cape Canaveral. "So when he went in the water, it was leaking, and he was taking water in through his neck dam."[4] The Mercury recovery procedures looked OK on paper. Then all hell broke loose.

As Grissom lay on his couch waiting for word that the recovery helicopter had latched onto his ship and the horse collar had been lowered, the hatch suddenly blew. The sill of the spacecraft was below the water line allowing the ocean to pour in. The short, athletic pilot, who had earlier disconnected his suit from his ship and undone his harnesses, managed somehow to get out.[5] Grissom had just flown a ballistic trajectory and survived. He sure as hell was not going to drown, and he fought until the end to save his ship. The next thing he knew, he was in the water struggling to stay afloat. Minutes later, *Liberty Bell 7* sank in more than three miles of water, 15,600 feet, deeper than the *Titanic*.[6]

The combat veteran and accomplished test pilot had always brought his aircraft back in one piece, had never before lost a ship. It had been a textbook mission, but the pilot ended up treading water for more than four minutes, nearly drowning, before he was finally plucked from the sea.

Grissom was shattered, acknowledging in his official account of the mission: "The loss of the spacecraft was a great blow to me, but I felt that I had completed the flight and recovery with no ill effects."[7] His otherwise successful suborbital flight was overshadowed by controversy over how the exploding hatch had prematurely detonated after splashdown. The hatch incident and the loss of his ship would dog Grissom for the rest of his life. The recovery procedures for Grissom's mission were never used again, a tacit admission by NASA that they were flawed.

The flight of *Liberty Bell 7*, wedged between two historic US space-flights by Alan Shepard and John Glenn, had been the kind of nut-and-bolts engineering mission for which Grissom came to be known. Despite nearly drowning and enduring years of second-guessing, he had accomplished nearly all the goals of his mission, paving the way for Glenn's historic orbital flight seven months later. Down through the decades, however, all anyone seemed to remember about the flight of *Liberty Bell 7* was that the pilot had lost his ship.

Grissom's ship came in on March 7, 1961. Mercury Spacecraft Number 11, assembled ten months earlier by prime contractor McDonnell Douglas of St. Louis, was delivered to Cape Canaveral Air Station's Hangar S for initial checkout. Once there, Grissom seldom let the spacecraft out of his sight. Technicians immediately started removing instrumentation, communications, and other equipment for testing over the next thirty-three days. The astronaut pleaded with them to stop tinkering with the machine.

Robert Gilruth had informed Grissom in January that he would likely pilot the Mercury-Redstone 4, or MR-4, with Glenn as backup pilot. During the late winter and spring of 1961, after the Americans had launched the chimp named "Ham" into space, Grissom was busy serving as Alan Shepard's backup, practicing on mission and centrifuge trainers. He again rode the centrifuge at the US Navy's Aviation Medical Acceleration Laboratory in Johnsville, Pennsylvania, in early April. Eight days later, on April 12, 1961, as the Americans continued to train, the Soviets shocked the world by launching cosmonaut Yuri Gagarin into space for one circuit of the earth.

The Americans were suddenly behind in the first quarter of the Space Race.

After Shepard's successful suborbital flight on May 5 and the cele-brations that followed, Grissom resumed training in Hangar S at Cape Canaveral in preparation for his own flight scheduled for mid-July. A lengthy series of spacecraft systems checks began sixty days before his flight, including simulated high-altitude tests in a pressure chamber. The tests provided the pilot one of his few chances to test spacecraft systems under simulated flight conditions.[8]

Spacecraft Number 11 was mated to Mercury-Redstone booster Number 8 on July 1, about three weeks after its delivery to Cape Canaveral. It was agreed that each manned Mercury spacecraft should recognize the original seven astronauts. Given the ship's bell-like shape, Grissom settled on *Liberty Bell 7*. An engineer suggested painting a white crack on the side of the ship to complete the historical allusion. No one gave the symbolism a second thought.

The pilot spent much of his time during the next three weeks at Launch Complex 5 poring over every spacecraft component while imploring engineers to stop fiddling with his ship. A launch escape system that would pull the spacecraft to safety if his booster failed was installed on July 5. (The day before, Grissom and Shepard had traveled "incognito" sixty miles north to the Daytona International Speedway to attend the annual *Firecracker 250* stock car race.[9]) By mid-July, MR-4 was pronounced ready for flight. Grissom's two years of intensive training was about to pay off.

The MR-4 launch was originally scheduled for July 18, 1961. In the days before the flight, Grissom came down with a sore throat. Remembering the doctors at Lovelace Clinic who had threatened his chances of becoming an astronaut when they discovered his hay fever symptoms, and acutely aware he could be grounded, he said nothing to the NASA flight surgeons.

A medical issue also would arise prior to Grissom's Gemini flight in 1965. He would again remain silent until after the three-orbit mission. As NASA physician Fred Kelly later told colleagues after a Gemini flight simulation involving a sick crew, "It'll be a cold day in hell when Gus Grissom asks to talk to a flight surgeon."[10]

Later, after many drinks at Louie's Bar in the old Kauai Surf Hotel in Hawaii, Grissom explained to army flight surgeon Robert Moser why flyers hated doctors: "I'll tell you, Doc. When you walk into the flight surgeon's office you *have* your ticket. When you walk out, you might *not*."[11]

Moser got to know Grissom well as they prepared to man a tracking station for Wally Schirra's orbital flight in October 1962. Another evening at the bar, Moser asked: "Gus, if you were sitting on that big firecracker and the countdown got to about [T] minus seven and suddenly you felt the worst pain imaginable in your mid chest and radiate down inside of your left arm, what would you do? Would you let us know?" Grissom stared a long time at the bottom of his glass. "Honestly? Only if I thought I was going to die."[12]

While Grissom's mission would be a repeat of Shepard's *Freedom 7* flight in May 1961, *Liberty Bell 7* would be equipped with a new centerline window and manual hand controls that were the equivalent of power steering in a car. The trapezoidal window would provide Grissom with a 30-degree vertical by 33-degree horizontal view of the earth, an eight-hundred-mile arc at peak altitude. In early June, the pilot got his first chance to test-drive the control stick.

The astronauts had lobbied for an explosive hatch that operated much like an airplane canopy blowing off when a pilot ejected from an aircraft. *Liberty Bell 7*'s twenty-three-pound escape hatch was much lighter than the mechanically operated side hatch flown on Shepard's mission. Seventy quarter-inch titanium bolts secured the explosive hatch to the spacecraft. A small hole was drilled into each bolt to provide a weak point. A mild detonating fuse was installed in the channel between the outer and inner hatch seal. To blow the hatch, Grissom would remove a protective cap on the detonator, pull a steel cotter safety pin, and push a plunger with a force of at least five pounds to activate a firing pin. The weakened bolts would then fail, blowing the hatch clear of the spacecraft after a recovery helicopter had hooked onto the spacecraft and lifted its sill above the water line. The new hatch could also be activated via an external lanyard that required at least forty pounds of pressure to shear the safety pin.

In the months before his flight, Grissom observed tests of the new exploding hatch designed by Honeywell to give Mercury pilots a quick exit in an emergency. NASA film footage shows Grissom inspecting the hatch on a test stand just before it was detonated. The pilot can be seen questioning test engineers while inspecting one of the titanium bolts. Everyone seemed satisfied the device would work.

However, there had been no additional "egress training" on how to activate the hatch after April 1961. The emphasis was on familiarizing the pilot with every spacecraft component and system and flying the mission; few considered the possibility of a problem after the spacecraft splashed down.

Rather than exiting, the overriding concern was shoehorning the astronaut into the cramped spacecraft and getting him safely off the launchpad. Grissom began practicing "spacecraft insertion" procedures on July 6, including a simulated countdown to T minus forty-five minutes. The simulation also was intended to collect physiological data. Additionally, the pilot practiced an emergency evacuation that included boarding an armored vehicle parked near the pad.

As launch day approached, the recovery forces also practiced. It was routine at the height of the Cold War to spot Russian surveillance ships off Cape Canaveral. "We would always find a Russian trawler and fly by it at deck height and take pictures and they were taking pictures of us," Jim Lewis, pilot of the prime recovery helicopter, recalled 50 years later.[13]

In the months before launch, Grissom had flown 120 simulations of his flight profile in the Mercury procedures trainer. The simulations also included six additional practice flights involving flight controllers and capsule communicator Shepard. With testing and one last mission simulation completed in the spacecraft, the launch date was at last set for Tuesday, July 18.

In the run-up to the Mercury launches, the astronauts and pad engineers could not resist stashing mementos in their spacecraft. These would become "flown" items that could be distributed later as gifts. Decades later, they would be sold at auction, often for large sums. Unforeseen before his launch, the rolls of souvenir "Liberty" dimes and other mementos Grissom stuffed in the leg pocket of his pressure suit would act like a sea anchor at the end of his flight.

Procedures on launch day were timed to the minute. Thirty minutes for breakfast, a half hour for the final physical exam. To save time on the eve of a launch, the astronaut would shower and shave before retiring in the crew quarters on the balcony of Hangar S. Grissom was asleep by 5 p.m. on Monday, July 17. The first launch attempt was cancelled later that night when clouds moved in. The pilot was informed, and he yawned and went back to sleep.[14]

The second attempt on July 19 was scrubbed at T minus ten minutes. Grissom spent four hours in the spacecraft before the launch was postponed. Despite the delays—sweating out the countdown with the booster tanked up and pressurized, the hatch sealed—this was as close to the real thing as Grissom had yet experienced.

Recycling for another launch attempt required another forty-eight hours. Grissom used the delay to run with Glenn on the beach and to study maps of the expected view from his new window. These navigation points would be used during later orbital flights. With little else to do but wait, Grissom grabbed a fishing pole, headed to the beach, landed a four-pound bass, and released it.[15]

Grissom watched a TV western before turning in at about 9 p.m. He "slept like a brick" until the wee hours of July 21, woke up wondering about the time and the weather, and then was roused by the astronauts' doctor, William Douglas. While he slept, flight directors had decided to beat the weather moving across the Gulf of Mexico by moving up the launch one hour to 7 a.m. No one told the cook, and Grissom's breakfast was not ready at the appointed time. Instead, a physical exam was completed while Grissom's steak and eggs were prepared.

Grissom suited up, a procedure that included attaching biomedical sensors to measure heart rate, respiration, and body temperature, among other vital signs. (These sensors picked up no abnormalities during the flight.) Among the lessons learned from Shepard's flight was the undeniable fact that when you "had to go," you went. Therefore, Grissom's preparations included donning a makeshift urine collection contraption hastily rigged before the launch. It consisted of a panty girdle purchased in Cocoa Beach by NASA nurse Dee O'Hara and fitted out with a condom. Primitive, uncomfortable, but effective, the relieved pilot decided.

Grissom's pressure suit also included several other modifications, including new glove connections and a convex mirror worn on the astronaut's chest like a "heroes medal" that allowed a spacecraft camera to record instrument readings. New noise-filtering microphones also were inserted into Grissom's helmet along with additional foam padding on the contour couch headrest. The padding along with a redesigned fairing for the spacecraft adapter clamp that connected the ship to the booster would help dampen the vibrations that had blurred Shepard's vision.

Suited up and wired by the flight surgeons, Grissom boarded a van to Pad 5 at 4:15 a.m. As he walked to the elevator, the engineers applauded.

They understood what Grissom was about to undertake. "This choked me up a little," Grissom recalled later, knowing that "[he] had all those people pulling for [him]."[16] The skies began to clear as he rode the gantry elevator up to the spacecraft. Grissom again was crammed into the space-craft. The hatch was sealed. The countdown was held for half an hour at T minus forty-five minutes to inspect a misaligned hatch bolt. (McDonnell and NASA engineers decided sixty-nine bolts were sufficient to secure the hatch and didn't replace the misaligned bolt.) Another short hold was required to turn off pad lights to avoid interference with launch telemetry.

During the long delays, Grissom worked crossword puzzles. The puzzle book was Sam Beddingfield's idea: he wanted to keep the pilot focused during the lengthy launch countdown.

With the fickle Florida weather finally cooperating, the countdown resumed at T minus fifteen minutes. Nine minutes before launch, the gantry was moved away from the spacecraft. Grissom reported later that the movement of the service structure away from the Redstone produced the illusion of falling. Thirty-five seconds before liftoff, the power and communications umbilical was jettisoned from the spacecraft and the peri-scope retracted.

The countdown moved backward to zero. This was it. The eighty-three-foot-high rocket and spacecraft weighing 65,940 pounds stood alone on the concrete Pad 5, the booster's super-cold alcohol and liquid oxygen propellants hissing and steaming in the July humidity. By today's standards, the snake-infested launchpad was surprisingly Spartan.

The final seconds of the countdown continued uninterrupted. Grissom's heartbeat had always been higher than the other astronauts. If anything, it meant he was ready. The pilot's pulse rose during the spacecraft oxygen purge, a procedure Grissom's future copilot John Young later admitted made his knees shake. At last, after two launch scrubs: ignition! The pilot's pulse doubled. At 7:20 a.m. eastern daylight time, the Redstone's engine lit, eventually generating more than 78,000 pounds of thrust as *Liberty Bell 7* rose quickly on a thin stream of alcohol rocket exhaust.

Back in Virginia, Betty Grissom nearly missed her husband's launch while preparing breakfast for a houseful of guests that included Rene Carpenter, Jo Schirra, and Marge Slayton. Marge's husband, Deke, communicating with the astronaut from the blockhouse during the final two minutes of the countdown, confirmed liftoff. "Roger," replied Grissom, "this is *Liberty Bell 7*, the [mission elapsed time] clock is operating."[17]

Referencing the astronauts' sidekick, the comedian Bill Dana of *José Jiménez* fame, capsule communicator Shepard immediately chimed in, "Loud and clear, Jose! Don't cry too much."

"Ok-ey doke," replied Grissom, as if expecting the quip from his buddy and rival. The booster accelerated.

"OK, it's a nice ride up to now," the pilot reported eighteen seconds into the flight. Passing through a thin layer of broken clouds, MR-4 pitched over at a programmed rate of about one degree per second. A contrail soon appeared over the Florida skies behind the streaking rocket as G forces began to build. The view of the vehicle was growing smaller by the second. A vapor trail hung over the beach like a sign for about a minute. *Liberty Bell 7* eventually reached a maximum velocity of 5,134 miles per hour. None of the test pilots back at Edwards Air Force Base had flown this fast. Despite losing a carbon vane used to steer the booster during its ascent, the NASA television feed reported, "Straight as an arrow." The ride was much smoother than expected.

Two minutes into the flight, at an altitude of about eighteen miles, the pilot reported spotting a star as the sky turned pitch black. Grissom thought he had just won a bet with Glenn, but the star turned out to be Venus. His eyes back on the instrument panel, the pilot reported that his cabin pressure was holding at 5.5 pounds per square inch and his suit pressure was good. The Redstone's spent Rocketdyne engine shut down at two minutes and twenty-three seconds, and the escape tower was jettisoned with a loud bang. Grissom suddenly went from high Gs to weightlessness— the sensation was akin to the driver of a speeding car going over a rise, except in space one does not come down. The tumbling sensation was momentarily unsettling.

Ten seconds after engine shutdown, the spacecraft separated from the booster and began turning blunt-end forward. In the eerie, silent blackness of space with its blinding sunlight, the weightless astronaut reported, "There's a lot of stuff floating around up here," including loose wires. He had left the earth.

For the Mercury astronauts, test pilots accustomed to mostly level flight, the sensation of the "wild blue yonder" abruptly turning pitch black was, to say the least, arresting. Malcolm Scott Carpenter, the second American to orbit the earth, provided perhaps the most vivid description of leaving the gravitational bonds of the planet. The astronauts would "see the altimeter reach seventy, eighty, then ninety thousand feet and yet know that [they were] still going straight up," Carpenter recalled while riding an Atlas rocket into orbit aboard his *Aurora 7* spacecraft in May 1962.[18]

As *Liberty Bell 7* turned around, Grissom reported: "The sun is really bright." For a few seconds, the hard-nosed test pilot was swept up by the wonder of spaceflight. "Oh boy!" the astronaut exclaimed while gazing out the spacecraft's big window.

Capcom Shepard, whose view had been limited to a periscope and two ten-inch side portholes, was one of only two human beings who could appreciate what Grissom was describing. "*I* understand," Shepard replied.

During approximately five minutes of weightlessness at the top of the spacecraft's arc, Grissom's checklist called for him to test a new manual controller used to adjust the ship's attitude. The hand controller incorporated a rate stabilization system, a kind of power steering used to control spacecraft attitude by twisting a joystick. It also served as another way to control pitch, roll, and yaw thrusters.

Shepard's checklist had been overloaded. Grissom's was pared down to allow him more time to test the hand controller and make observations from his new window, including identifying landmarks for navigation references. The pilot steered his space ship. "I'm trying the yaw maneuver and I'm on the window" as a navigational reference point. Observing the stark beauty out the window, it was hard to concentrate. This was something that could never be simulated in the months of training. "It's such a fascinating view out the window [and] you just can't help but look out that way." Grissom found the manual controls balky; the new rate command controller was more precise but consumed more fuel.

Grissom later told reporters, "I could see the sun shining through the window and I was so fascinated by this view out the window that I had difficulty concentrating on the instruments; I kept wanting to peek out the window."[19]

The spacecraft lacked the velocity required to reach orbit, and Grissom soon had to set up his spacecraft for reentry and splashdown. "The spacecraft turnaround to retrofire attitude [roughly at apogee] is quite a weird maneuver to ride through," he recalled. "At first, I thought the spacecraft might be tumbling out of control," but instruments verified otherwise.[20] To the pilot, the maneuver felt as if his backward flight had been reversed and he was now flying nose first. Roll attitude was balky and behind schedule (off by about fifteen degrees prior to retrofire attitude). As the turnaround started and the spacecraft pitched down for reentry, Grissom tried to spot stars out his window but feared being blinded by the brightest sun he'd ever seen.

Given *Liberty Bell 7*'s ballistic flight path ("what goes up must come down" still applied), the firing of the reentry rockets was designed to test their performance for the benefit of later orbital flights. After completing the retrofire sequence and observing two spent retrorockets pass his periscope view, Grissom took another quick peek out the window and spotted Cape Canaveral. "Now I can see the Cape and, oh boy, that is some sight!"

Liberty Bell 7 was now descending, and the ride was becoming loud and bumpy. "Gs are starting to build," Grissom reported, the strain of the building gravitational forces of reentry evident in the astronaut's baritone voice. As instructed, Grissom kept relaying the mounting G forces to ground controllers so NASA flight surgeons could gauge how he was coping. "Gs are building. We're up to six, there's nine, there's . . . about . . . ten." The growing pressure on Grissom's body was evident in the transmissions as the ship oscillated while plunging through the upper atmosphere. He had experienced worse, though, "pulling more Gs" during training runs on the Johnstown centrifuge.

At 65,000 feet and dropping like a rock, *Liberty Bell 7* plunged back into the atmosphere. Condensation, smoke, and debris from its heat shield streamed by Grissom's window. The spacecraft began to roar as the heat shield dug into the upper atmosphere. On schedule, a small drogue parachute deployed at 21,000 feet caused some pulsating motion. Finally, "There's the main [parachute], it's reefed. Main chute is good," he reported. "Rate of descent is coming down to, there's forty feet per second."

After the main parachute deployed at 12,300 feet, Grissom radioed: "You might make a note that there is one small hole in my chute. It looks like it's about six inches by six inches—it's sort of a—actually it's a triangular rip, I guess." The pilot kept an eye on the tear, but his rate of descent continued to slow satisfactorily to about twenty-eight feet per second. He began dumping his unused peroxide fuel prior to splashdown.

At about six thousand feet, he opened the faceplate on his helmet and attempted to install the lanyard pins that would keep his hatch from flying away when detonated. "I can't get one door pin back in," he reported at five thousand feet. "I've tried and tried and can't get it back in."

He then inquired about the location of the recovery forces. "Getting ready for impact here, you can see the water coming right on up." Despite the small parachute tear, all was going exactly according to plan. The landing bag designed to cushion splashdown deployed with a *clunk*. The pilot removed his oxygen hose but left his suit ventilation hose attached. All the while he was relaying readings on the spacecraft panels. There was not a trace of concern in his voice; Gus Grissom sounded exactly like the test pilot he was.

Liberty Bell 7 hit the water "with a good bump" fifteen minutes and thirty-seven seconds after launch, at 7:35 a.m. EST. The impact was milder than expected. The spacecraft immediately tipped over, prompting the pilot now lying on his left side to release the main parachute that was dragging him across the surface. Upright again, he jettisoned the reserve parachute and activated rescue aids that included a green dye canister and a beacon that would help recovery forces get a fix on his location. A telescoping high-frequency communications antenna deployed automatically. The "whip" antenna would provide a link between the astronaut and the recovery helicopters.

Seconds after splashdown, one of the helicopters codenamed *Card File 9* radioed it had spotted *Liberty Bell 7* bobbing and rolling in the Atlantic swells. It would be over the ship in about thirty seconds. *Liberty Bell 7*'s reentry attitude was off target, coming in long and little north of the intended landing spot, about six miles from the recovery ship, the USS *Randolph*.

The main recovery helicopter, *Hunt Club 1*, piloted by Marine Lieutenant Jim Lewis and copilot Lieutenant John Reinhard, had begun moving into position, radioing Grissom to ask if he was ready to be picked up. Grissom instructed the crew: "latch on then give me a call and I'll power down and blow the hatch, OK?"

As he readied himself and his spacecraft for recovery, Grissom could clearly see the water line was above *Liberty Bell 7*'s hatch sill. Despite hearing what he thought was a "gurgling noise" in the cabin, as had Shepard, Grissom found no signs of a water leak. There was no reason Grissom would have deliberately blown the hatch before *Hunt Club 1* was over him.

Before arming the hatch, Grissom was to record spacecraft switch positions. That done, he checked his pressure suit and noted the lack of a snug seal on the neck dam, the result of having been stowed too long. Nevertheless, Grissom felt he was now in "very good shape."[21] Indeed, he was ahead of his closeout schedule. He was determined to be ready for pickup. The astronaut again opened his faceplate and disconnected the oxygen hose from his helmet, then unfastened it from his pressure suit and released his chest strap, lap belt, shoulder harness, knee straps, and his medical sensors. He checked his suit one last time but neglected to close its suit oxygen hose inlet.

In his desire to be ready for "egress" and recovery, Grissom decided to arm the explosive side hatch. To do this, he had to reach up, to his right and behind his helmet—a distance of between six and eight inches—to remove the protective cover and steel cotter safety pin from the hatch detonator.[22] A knurled knob had to be turned and removed to uncover the plunger used to detonate the hatch. Once the pin was out, the hatch was armed and the plunger could be pushed. Five pounds of pressure was required to blow the hatch from inside the spacecraft, and the plunger had a nasty kick. It would leave powder burns on whoever hit it.

The decades-old controversy over whether Grissom accidently blew the hatch comes down to this: "The plunger that detonates the [explosive] bolts is so far out of the way that I would have to reach for it on purpose to hit it," Grissom insisted. "This I did not do."[23]

Eleven days before his flight, Grissom had observed a demonstration of the explosive hatch. The test went off without a hitch. The astronaut and the engineers were confident the hatch would work as advertised. Moreover, they were far more concerned about what was only the second American manned spaceflight than any problems after splashdown. Still, this would be the first time the hatch was used, and the recovery procedures were less rigorous— they had been rehearsed fewer times—than other phases of the mission.

It has since been asserted with the benefit of hindsight that Grissom got "out of sequence" on his checklist by removing the detonator cover and safety pin before the recovery helicopter hooked onto the spacecraft. But the reality in July 1961 was that practically no one was concerned about these final steps on the checklist, and everyone figured the hatch would blow off only when Grissom hit the plunger—on purpose.

As the astronaut insisted, and all later efforts to simulate the hatch incident showed, it was physically impossible to have accidently blown the hatch. But something did, something that was never duplicated in the later reenactments.

The hatch now armed and a Randall survival knife attached to the hatch removed and stowed as a souvenir,[24] the astronaut prepared for Lewis and Reinhard to hover over the spacecraft. "When you blow the hatch, the collar will already be down there waiting for you," Lewis radioed. "Ah, roger," acknowledged Grissom in his last transmission from the spacecraft.[25]

Once over the ship, Reinhard, at the side door of *Hunt Club 1*, reached down with a long pole to cut the spacecraft's 13.7-foot communications antenna deployed at splashdown. The whip antenna had to be cut to avoid contact with the recovery helicopter's main rotor. A "cookie cutter" device used to snip the antenna was equipped with the equivalent of pruning shears. Once in place, it used a miniature explosive called a squib to sever the antenna. A "shepherd's hook" would then be used to latch onto a strong Dacron loop on top of the bobbing spacecraft. Lewis would rev his engines to hoist the spacecraft until the hatch sill was above the water line. Then, and only then, Grissom would hit the plunger and blow the hatch. Just as Reinhard reached down to sever the whip antenna, *Liberty Bell 7*'s hatch unexpectedly blew off—and with it, Grissom's hard-earned reputation as an unflappable test pilot.

The controversy over precisely what happened after *Liberty Bell 7* hit the Atlantic Ocean has lingered for decades. "The persistent myth about the hatch can be viewed in epidemiological terms," observed Kris Stoever, space historian and daughter of Mercury astronaut Scott Carpenter. "It's a kind of disinformation virus, resistant to vaccines." The controversy was revived in 1979 with the publication of Tom Wolfe's *The Right Stuff*, which contained a fictionalized account of Grissom's flight.[26] Besides pilot error, other possible explanations ranged from a faulty hatch design to landing bag straps catching the exterior lanyard designed to blow the hatch from the outside. The official NASA account of the incident concluded that *Liberty Bell 7* sank "after a faulty circuit blew the hatch before help arrived." But a faulty circuit appears to be only one of several possible causes.

Some of Wolfe's astronaut sources concluded that Grissom had "screwed the pooch" when he lost his ship. A few spacecraft engineers thought Grissom, moving around in his bulky spacesuit in the cramped cabin bobbing in the ocean, accidently bumped the plunger mechanism. That scenario could not be duplicated in reenactments. Grissom later said he believed the loose exterior lanyard caused the premature hatch explosion if it caught in the landing bag straps, perhaps creating enough force to shear the firing pin and blow the hatch from the outside.

According to a postflight NASA investigation, other potential causes included the omission of an O-ring seal on the detonator plunger. This would have reduced the amount of pressure needed to fire the hatch. Another possibility was a vacuum, or "differential pressure," in the plunger mechanism that could have allowed it to move by itself and blow the hatch after Grissom removed the cover and pulled the safety pin. Also considered by investigators were the chemical interactions of seawater on the hatch explosives and galvanic voltages generated when seawater came into contact with different metals used to construct the Mercury spacecraft.

Another electrical anomaly, electrostatic discharge between the Marine Corps Sikorsky HUS-1 *Seahorse* recovery helicopter and Grissom's spacecraft, was considered as a cause by investigators.[27] However, that scenario seems not to have been pursued very far. NASA investigators claimed they could not duplicate the hatch malfunction in dozens of postflight reenactments. Neither could they duplicate the exact weather conditions on the hot, humid morning of July 21, 1961 (Atlantic Ocean surface temperatures at the location where *Liberty Bell 7* splashed down averaged at least 80 degrees Fahrenheit during the month of July in 1961). One unexamined possibility is that "prop wash" from the recovery helicopter hovering over the warm Atlantic generated sufficient static electric discharge to work its way down the "cookie cutter" attached to the pole used to sever the antenna. The static discharge may very well have detonated the armed hatch. That is what Lieutenant John Reinhard, the eyewitness closest to the spacecraft when the hatch detonated, believed.

Immediately after splashdown, Grissom radioed: "I have actuated the rescue aids, the reserve [reentry] chute has jettisoned . . . and the whip antenna should be up." After *Hunt Club 1* moved into position over the spacecraft, the copilot reached down to cut the antenna. Reinhard later told researcher Rick Boos that electrostatic discharge from *Hunt Club 1*'s rotor wash while flying over warm ocean water generated an "arc" that could have blown the hatch prematurely. Indeed, the conditions on July 21, 1961, were ideal for generating electrostatic discharge in the vortex of humid ocean air.

Hovering over the spacecraft that sticky July morning, the recovery helicopter's prop wash was "supercharged." Reinhard was approximately five feet above the spacecraft when the hatch suddenly blew. "When I touched the antenna [with the squib-actuated cutter], there was an arc," Reinhard told Boos.[28] The cutter's primary and secondary squibs went off simultaneously. Static electricity generated by helicopter prop wash surged down the pole to the ungrounded spacecraft, likely detonating the hatch.

Reinhard told NASA investigators he was "preparing to cut the antenna whip (according to the new procedure) with a squib-actuated cutter at the end of a pole, when he saw the hatch cover fly off, strike the water at a distance of about five feet from the hatch, and then go skipping over the waves."[29] NASA footage of the recovery also shows the prime recovery helicopter hovering close to the *Liberty Bell 7*'s antenna, perhaps even touching it.[30]

The dangers posed by electrostatic discharge during helicopter water rescues are well understood. US Coast Guard procedures for dealing with electrostatic discharge, for example, state: "During helicopter hoist [operations], static electricity discharge is a common phenomenon between the surface (water, ground, or vessel) and the hoisting device. Over open water, this boundary layer tends to be more conducive to static discharge release than over land." Coast guard helicopter rescue procedures are unambiguous: "Do not touch the rescue device as it is being lowered! Allow it to touch the vessel first! STATIC ELECTRICITY."[31]

Similarly, US Navy guidelines dictate: "The helicopter cable or cargo hook must be grounded to discharge this electricity." It continues, a "grounding wand is designed to protect ground personnel from static electrical shock when working with all helicopters."[32]

In the instant Reinhard made contact with the antenna, *Liberty Bell 7*'s hatch blew off and shot across the water. Still photos from NASA recovery films confirm Reinhard's account. The hatch blows as the antenna cutter contacts the spacecraft and before Lewis could pull its windowsill above the water line. The next thing Reinhard saw was Grissom's head as the astronaut bolted through the narrow hatch into the water.

An untried and perhaps faulty hatch design, inadequate egress training, and Reinhard's eyewitness account of what happened during the recovery attempt, an account confirmed by NASA footage of the recovery, points to electrostatic discharge as the likely cause of the premature hatch explosion. The astronaut was lying on his couch awaiting pickup as disaster struck.

His ship now flooding, Grissom somehow managed to toss his helmet out and disconnect his pressure suit from the spacecraft before wedging his way through the narrow hatch into the water. It all happened so quickly, the astronaut said later, that he could not remember exactly how he got out. Had he not undone his harnesses and other restraints, it is likely Grissom would have gone down with his ship. In his extreme haste, Grissom never had a chance to close his suit's oxygen inlet valve. The resulting loss of buoyancy from the valve and a leaky neck dam added to the swamped astronaut's struggles to stay afloat for nearly five minutes. Once in the water, Lewis and Reinhard focused on salvaging the spacecraft, unaware that Grissom was sinking. The rolls of "Liberty" dimes and other souvenirs in his pocket now weighed him down.

The pilot remembered "the only two moves I remember making were tossing my helmet off and grabbing the, eh, [right side of the] instrument panel and pulling myself out. I only remember grabbing the instrument panel; I don't even remember going out the door."[33] Once in the water, Grissom battled the rotor wash generated by four helicopters, two marine recovery ships, and two navy choppers photographing the recovery.

After the hatch blew, Reinhard grabbed the "shepherd's hook" and succeeded at the last possible moment in making the connection to the loop on top of the spacecraft, which was now underwater. Lewis immediately attempted to drain the landing bag in hopes of reducing the spacecraft's weight. The flooded ship now weighed about five thousand pounds, a thousand pounds beyond the helicopter's lifting capacity. If the landing bag could be emptied, there was still a chance *Liberty Bell 7* could be retrieved and carried back to the *Randolph*.

Just then, the "chip detector light" flashed on Lewis's panel, indicating—erroneously, it turned out—there was metal in the helicopter engine's oil sump. "That's not a good thing for engines," Lewis observed.[34] The light meant he had about five minutes of power remaining before "things [would] really start to go bad."

Lewis said he maintained maximum power for about four minutes and forty-five seconds, with oil pressure dropping and the cylinder head temperature rising. He finally ordered Reinhard to cut *Liberty Bell 7* loose. He then radioed the backup helicopter: "Come and get Gus, I've got a sick bird!"

In those four and a half minutes, which seemed like an eternity, Grissom was fighting the prop wash while doing all he could to help save his ship. Recovery footage shows the astronaut swimming toward—not away from—the swamped spacecraft, guiding Reinhard as he struggled to latch onto it. The footage shows Grissom bobbing in the swells while guiding Reinhard's efforts to secure the spacecraft. Grissom confirmed that the recovery line had hooked on to the sinking spacecraft. He then signaled with a "double thumbs up" that Reinhard had succeeded as the spacecraft sank below the water line. All this time, Grissom managed to stay afloat as air was seeping from his pressure suit through the open oxygen inlet and his neck dam. Grissom was soon fighting to keep his head above water. Engaged in a tug-of-war with the sinking ship, Lewis was too preoccupied to notice Grissom's plight.

After nearly five minutes and warning lights flashing, Lewis ended the tug-of-war. He radioed for backup and instructed Reinhard not to lower a horse collar. Both believed Grissom's pressure suit would keep him afloat; neither realized air was leaking from it and the astronaut was in serious trouble. With no rescue sling in sight, the exhausted astronaut was getting angry.

The recovery line was cut and *Liberty Bell 7* sank. Lewis pulled away and made for the *Randolph*. Another recovery helicopter moved in and at last lowered a horse collar. After being dunked twice more, Grissom was plucked from the ocean. He slipped on the collar backward. By now, he was utterly unconcerned with procedures or appearances. Aboard the backup recovery helicopter, the waterlogged astronaut immediately donned a life vest and asked for something to blow his nose with. Nearly drowned, his only concern now was reaching the primary recovery ship.

Grissom had managed somehow to keep his nose above water; NASA had survived its first emergency in manned spaceflight. Spacecraft recovery procedures were quickly revised. Future Mercury astronauts detonated their spacecraft hatches from the safety of a carrier deck. John Glenn and Wally Schirra both sustained minor hand injuries from the recoil of the hatch detonator. Grissom sustained no such injury, indicating that he never touched the plunger.

Contrary to popular accounts of Grissom's suborbital flight, most notably *The Right Stuff* and the cartoonish 1983 film version of the book, those who knew the pilot and his spacecraft understood that the pilot had not panicked nor had he intentionally pushed the plunger that detonated *Liberty Bell 7*'s hatch. Having just flown a 302-mile ballistic arc, pulling more than eleven Gs in a fiery descent and splashdown, safely back on the earth, the astronaut was, if anything, exhilarated, not panicked, as he sat on his couch waiting to be picked up. None of his transmissions after splashdown indicated panic. The only doubt in the astronaut's mind was whether to stow his survival knife as a souvenir.

The hatch incident unfairly tagged the second American in space as a screw up. Despite overwhelming evidence to the contrary, the "hatch crap" would dog Grissom for the rest of his life.[35] The second-guessing that followed would steel him in his dealings with NASA managers, the media, and his fellow astronauts in the coming competitions to command orbital flights and the first moon landing.

During a humiliating postflight press conference on July 22 at the Starlite Motel in Cocoa Beach, Grissom provided skeptical reporters with his version of what had happened: "I was just [lying] there minding my own business, and POW! the hatch went. I looked up and I saw nothing but blue sky and water starting to come in over the sill. So I tossed my helmet off and my first thought was, 'Get out!' The capsule actually sank and went below the water . . . and so I was getting water in the suit and getting lower and lower in the water all the time, and having to fight quite hard to stay afloat."[36]

As always, Grissom was straightforward while masking his growing anger at the doubters in the press corps. Keenly aware that the hatch controversy could damage his future flying prospects, the astronaut was direct and succinct with the reporters, calmly describing his actions in the split seconds after the hatch blew. He had been operating on instinct, and the objective was to survive, keep his head above water, and avoid drowning in front of the entire world.

In his detailed account of the mission for the record, Grissom recalled pondering whether to take the survival knife as a souvenir when "[he] heard the hatch blow—the noise was a dull thud." Remembering the egress procedures, he continued, "I lifted the helmet from my head and dropped it, reached for the right side of the instrument panel, and pulled myself through the hatch."[37]

Near the end of the postflight press conference, a reporter asked: "Did you feel you were in danger at any time?" Without hesitation Grissom replied, "Well, I was scared a good portion of the time. I guess that's a pretty good indication." "You were *what?*" the reporter persisted. "Scared. OK?" Grissom shot back, turning to NASA boss Robert Gilruth on his right as they both nervously laughed. But the astronaut was seething inside while being skewered by the reporters.

A NASA photo shows a grim Betty Grissom and her sons in the audience observing helplessly. What should have been a joyous recounting of an otherwise successful spaceflight instead turned out to be another in a series of postflight ordeals for the astronaut and his family. The expression on Betty's face seems to be saying to NASA officials on stage "You owe me."

Surviving America's first space emergency was one thing. The indignity of having to defend his actions with little or no backing from his NASA superiors was another, a reality that would color Grissom's view of the press, and perhaps his NASA bosses, for the remainder of his life.

As network news anchor Walter Cronkite noted later, the reticent astronaut faced the mandatory news conferences "with considerable more trepidation than the flights themselves, and his response to questions was cryptic and laconic. It was this that undoubtedly contributed to considerable misunderstanding between the press and Gus which followed the loss of Grissom's Mercury capsule after the second successful suborbital flight."[38]

Grissom's fellow astronauts rushed to his defense. They and several NASA engineers insisted that he was further exonerated by the fact that his hand had not been bruised by the plunger's recoil, as was Schirra's when he blew the hatch aboard the recovery ship after his *Sigma 7* flight in October 1962. "Every time the astronaut hit that damned plunger he got a wound on his wrist. Gus did *not* have a wound on his wrist," Flight Director Christopher Columbus Kraft repeated in a 1999 interview.[39]

"The recoil on that plunger cut through the glove of my spacesuit and cut into my hand," added Schirra. When Grissom met Schirra after his orbital flight, "he had the biggest smile on his face when [he] showed him this cut hand because there was not a mark on his body after his problem with his hatch. So he couldn't have hit it with an elbow or a leg or something. He would have had a terrible bruise. "I said, 'Gus, look at my hand, it really kind of hurts.' He knew exactly what I was telling him."

Robert Thompson, the Project Mercury recovery chief, insisted the absence of a wound proved nothing. "That makes a good story but that's really a bunch of nonsense," Thompson asserted fifty years after Grissom's flight. "It's kind of like you're shooting a shotgun. You shoot a shotgun and put it against your eye, the side of your head, pull the trigger, it'll cut you. And, yes, any time you shoot a shotgun you should have a bloody eye. But if you put the shotgun against the fat of your arm and shoot it you won't have a bloody eye."

Nevertheless, Grissom and the engineers with a thorough understanding of his Mercury spacecraft believed the most likely explanation for the premature hatch release was the exterior lanyard designed to blow the hatch from the outside. Few considered static electricity a likely cause, except for Reinhard, the person closest to the spacecraft when the hatch blew. Reinhard was convinced the arc created when his cookie cutter device touched the spacecraft had blown the hatch.

Indeed, NASA had experienced catastrophic accidents involving static electricity in the earliest days of spaceflight, at a time when engineers frequently operated blind. According to McDonnell Aircraft engineer and Project Mercury "Pad Fuehrer" Guenter Wendt:[40]

> We did many things right, but we also goofed many things. The biggest scare I had was what we call the spin test facility where one satellite [undergoing testing] blew up and killed four people. What made it blow up turned out to be static electricity from the plastic the thing was covered with. And when I heard that, I found out what plastic it was. It was exactly the same plastic we covered our escape rockets with. So, you see, we didn't know that a little static, a spark from the static, can set off an igniter. That's a thing that you learned, plus the fact, in the very early days when we started running Mercury the facilities were rather primitive.[41]

Then there was Grissom's state of mind at the end of his flight. Wolfe implied that Grissom's elevated heart and respiratory rates indicated panic that somehow led the astronaut to blow the hatch too soon. (It should be noted that Grissom, broiling and seasick, his faceplate punctured after a rough reentry and splashdown at the end of his Gemini mission in March 1965, refused to open the hatches until navy frogmen had attached a floatation device.)

Robert Moser, a NASA flight surgeon on loan from the army during the Mercury and Gemini programs, worked closely with Grissom at the NASA tracking station in Hawaii. "I never believed that Gus panicked and hit the chicken switch," Moser wrote in a 2002 memoir. "He was just too cool for such foolishness."[42]

The proof of Moser's assertion is that Grissom survived a potentially deadly sequence of events that no one had anticipated. Having somehow squeezed out of the spacecraft as seawater poured in, Grissom barely had a chance to roll up the neck ring on his suit designed to keep him dry and buoyant. Normally, this and the fact that the Mercury pressure suit contained enough oxygen for buoyancy would have been sufficient to keep an astronaut comfortably afloat in the ocean. But Grissom either forgot or never had a chance to close an oxygen valve that also allowed air to escape.

Grissom finally was plucked from the sea by a backup recovery helicopter responding to Lewis's distress call. During his initial debriefing with Thompson and Koons, the astronaut remembered looking up and seeing recovery helicopter copilot George Cox: "That was really comforting because George and I had done most of the training for this." Among the most enduring images of the flight of *Liberty Bell 7* was the silhouette of a sodden Grissom hanging backward in the horse collar as Cox hauled him aboard the backup recovery helicopter. The image would later be used to great effect in the film version of Wolfe's book.

A mere thirty-five minutes had elapsed from liftoff until the moment Grissom was at last safely aboard the *Randolph*. Back at the Cape, Gilruth asked Recovery Chief Thompson what the hell had happened after splashdown. Thompson said he didn't know but would leave immediately for the Grand Bahamas where Grissom was taken for debriefing, find out, and report back.

Five decades after the flight of *Liberty Bell 7*, Thompson remembered it this way. Arriving at the barracks where Grissom would be debriefed:

I said, "Gus, come with me," and we went into a building there that had a little side room, it had two twin beds in it. Gus sat down on one bed and I sat down on the other. And he took his boot off and poured some water out.

I said, "Gus, tell me now step by step what went on out there." He said, "Well everything was going fine, the flight went well, parachute opened, I was in the water. I decided to get everything ready so I could be sure I had everything on time. So I took my helmet off and then put it back on, then I took the cap off the door activation mechanism and pulled the pin but I didn't push the plunger in."[43]

Thompson asked Grissom to repeat what happened: "He said, 'I just wanted to be ready. I took the cap off, pulled the retaining pin, but I didn't push the plunger.' I said, 'OK Gus, that's fine.'"

Thompson also spoke with Lewis and Reinhard before returning to the Cape about 10 p.m. By then, he knew the postflight celebrations would be under way, and the biggest party would be at the Starlite Motel with its distinctive roadside sign that included a soaring rocket. Thompson found Gilruth at the bar.

In the parking lot, Thompson told the NASA director:

Bob, it's pretty clear to me that Gus got ahead of the checklist. He took the cap off [the detonator] and pulled the retaining pin before the helicopter got hooked on and got everything stable. And, no, he didn't push the plunger in but he's sitting in a small capsule, the plunger is right at his shoulder, it's blowing and rocking around . . . easiest thing in the world for him to touch that thing and push it in—I'm not even sure he even had to push it in because once you took the cap off and pull the safety pin, the only thing that held the rod that went in and out were two O-rings. So I'm not even sure that the bobbing of the capsule wouldn't have ultimately worked that plunger in toward that firing pin.

In retrospect, Thompson emphasized: "Our training program was not as solid back then as it should have been. The checklist was not as disciplined as it should have been. And Gus was just trying to do a good job and be ready. And he didn't quite understand enough about the mechanism. Otherwise he would never have taken the cap off and never pulled that pin until we were ready for the [hatch] to blow. . . . He was just trying to do a good job."[44]

Gilruth immediately decided to have spacecraft manufacturer McDonnell Aircraft conduct tests to eliminate a "sneak circuit" in the firing mechanism, that is, an unexpected electrical pathway that could have caused the blown hatch. Soon to be named the first director of the Manned Spacecraft Center in Houston, Gilruth was looking for a way to quickly resolve the hatch issue so he could move to the next step: John Glenn's orbital flight.

Satisfied that Grissom hadn't intentionally hit the plunger, investigators then turned to the question of how exactly the armed hatch detonated. There were several possible explanations, including Thompson's assertion that waves tossing the spacecraft alone could have activated the detonator.

Sam Beddingfield, a NASA engineer and Grissom's buddy from the astronaut's test pilot days at Wright-Patterson Air Force Base in Ohio, worked the hardest to find the cause. Grissom participated in tests in which he intentionally bumped the plunger, failing to blow the hatch.

After studying the parachutes, the engineers' focus turned to the external release lanyard. It was held in place by a small shingle secured by a single screw and two clips. During the harsh reentry, the screw may have popped loose, causing both clips to let go. The suspicion was the shingle had flown off the hatch handle and ripped the chute, causing the small tear Grissom reported during his descent. After splashdown, the exterior hatch handle extended by a cable assembly may have caught in the landing bag straps. As the spacecraft moved up and down in the swells, the cord could have pulled against the handle with sufficient force to detonate the explosive hatch, Beddingfield concluded.

During their initial debriefing in the Grand Bahamas, Koons said he and Thompson decided to reverse the order of their questions. Koons and Thompson asked the exhausted, dispirited astronaut—"he was pretty tired and pretty uncomfortable"—to begin the debriefing at the end of the flight. NASA engineers used cue cards and a tape recorder during debriefings to help the amped-up astronauts collect their thoughts. "Gus, help us out here," Thompson recalled asking. "Would you mind doing the last card first?"

Grissom explained again that after splashdown he was "moving around, getting things stowed and getting ready to get out." He then removed the cover on the primer and pulled the safety pin.

"The way that thing's configured, there's a ring around that button, and it just doesn't seem possible that he made contact with that," Koons concluded. "Certainly, based on his debrief, he certainly didn't do it deliberately, and it's hard to see how he could have possibly done it accidentally, because the way that button is down inside a ring, a cylindrical protector, you have to be very deliberate about it to make that thing go off."[45]

Others, including Maxime Faget, the chief designer of the Mercury spacecraft, nevertheless clung to the belief that Grissom had indeed blown the hatch. Perhaps it was unintentional. Schirra, Carpenter, and Grissom's friends at the Cape, such as Wendt and Beddingfield, defended him to the hilt.

The veteran *Life* magazine photographer Ralph Morse, who earned the Mercury astronauts' trust through his sheer tenacity, was among those who also defended Grissom. The hatch incident "hurt him very, very much. It's easy to blame the astronaut, but that wasn't Gus. Gus was much too great an engineer, and too serious a pilot," Morse concluded after observing his subject in ways few had.[46]

Later, too late for Grissom to undo the damage to his reputation, it became clear that the Mercury hatch was poorly designed and not sufficiently tested. Robert Voas, a navy psychologist and member of NASA's first Space Task Group, described the hatch incident as a "human engineering failure." The escape hatch had been developed too late for Shepard's flight and, it turned out, was not yet fully wrung out for Grissom's.

The hatch "had been developed so rapidly that there had not been much time to train on it or to test it," Voas concluded. "So from the human engineering standpoint, we had a not optimally designed hatch, and the result was that Gus hit it inadvertently and it blew when it wasn't supposed to, and we lost that spacecraft."[47]

Stephen Clemmons, a North American Aviation technician who would play a central role in the *Apollo 1* fire in January 1967, explained: "There was a major design change on the emergency hatch system before the flight of John Glenn. I talked to one of the McDonnell engineers on Mercury and he admitted that it was a defective design. A new fail safe system was incorporated that would only fire when the astronaut really meant for it to happen."[48] He added, "We now know that the system on Mercury had a flaw and if it hadn't happened with Gus, it would have happened sooner or later, and later would have been disastrous."[49] Regardless, Grissom had to deal with the consequences, much like any captain who had lost his ship. The recovery fiasco would shape the public's perception of the second American in space, particularly given the avalanche of press coverage the incident received, including the astronaut's denial on the front page of the *New York Times*.[50] What is seldom remembered is that Grissom otherwise flew a flawless mission. His flight showed that the Mercury capsule was indeed space-worthy and that an astronaut could fly the spacecraft—he was more than just a passenger.

Grissom's near drowning also highlighted shortcomings in the Mercury training program, particularly during the recovery phase. Those training mistakes would be fixed, just as the tragic lessons of the *Apollo 1* fire six-and-a-half years later would put the lunar landing program back on track.

The flight of *Liberty Bell 7* ultimately illustrated Grissom's notion of the test pilot–turned-astronaut's role in the early days of the Space Race. The Mercury spacecraft may have been "man-rated," but it still needed to be wrung out in flight. This Grissom did do, thereby laying the foundation for future US space successes. Shepard and Glenn, the other members of the "Astronaut First Team," would be celebrated. Grissom would spend the rest of his life burying the myth that he was the "hard luck" astronaut.

Those who knew astronaut Grissom best understood immediately that, having just ridden a rocket into space and descended at supersonic speed to the ocean, it made no sense that he would suddenly panic at the end of a successful mission. "Some people are concerned about getting the hatch and proving one way or another what made it blow," Mercury astronaut Scott Carpenter observed after *Liberty Bell 7* was recovered in 1999. "It isn't important to me. I'm convinced that Gus was not responsible."[51]

Others who worked with Grissom and had less reason to circle the wagons in his defense said much the same. "Occasionally, maybe two or three times, I went down [from the mountain in Hawaii] with him and we went to the bar . . . and we'd have a few drinks and sit around and chat. I got to know him pretty well and I really got to like him," recalled Moser, the army flight surgeon. Moser remembered "a regular guy. He worked hard and he played hard."

To Moser, Grissom was unflappable. "When you got to know him, you realized [the prospect of Grissom panicking] was all baloney. He was just a cool guy. . . . He was not the kind of guy who would panic."[52]

Aboard the *Randolph*, a World War II carrier that had launched air raids against Tokyo, the waterlogged astronaut spoke briefly by radiophone with President Kennedy. Seeking to highlight another American space success, Kennedy called from the Oval Office and finally reached Grissom over a poor ship-to-shore connection. It is unclear exactly what the president knew that morning about Grissom's near drowning. "Captain, I want to congratulate you," Kennedy declared after both men could finally hear each other. "I've been watching your flight on TV here and I'm delighted that you got through alright." Grissom immediately downplayed his rescue, reminding the president of the fact that "we lost the capsule" and that, according to a hard-to-decipher audio tape of the conversation, "I'm shattered a bit."

Grissom later wrote about the botched recovery: "[It] was especially hard for me, as a professional pilot. In all of my years of flying—including combat in Korea—this was the first time that my aircraft and I had not come back together. In my entire career as a pilot, *Liberty Bell* was the first thing I had ever lost."[53] Kennedy would have none of it, again emphasizing: "It was a wonderful job and we really are delighted that it worked out well for you."

Grateful for the encouraging words and happy to be alive, Grissom told the president he hoped his flight would provide the administration another boost in its effort to sell the space program: "I hope it does something for you, like Commander Shepard said." This was a reference to the domestic political opening Shepard's successful flight in May had provided, allowing Kennedy to press Congress to fund a manned lunar landing "before this decade is out."

"Oh, well, it's a big help, I'll tell you that," the president responded before signaling the end of the call.

Kennedy closed with a vague promise of "seeing you sometime soon." But there would be no White House ceremony for the Grissom family, no private audience for Betty with the first lady, none of the VIP treatment Shepard and Glenn received after their flights. Grissom would not see the president again until after Glenn's historic orbital flight in February 1962. "Good luck, captain," Kennedy said before signing off. The congratulatory call lasted less than a minute.[54]

Later that day, Kennedy signed into law a NASA budget bill that would significantly expand the space agency's spending authority, and with it the American space effort. In brief remarks before signing the measure, Kennedy praised Grissom's courage and noted that his flight was conducted, unlike the Russians, in full view of the world.

The legislation would boost NASA's budget for research and development along with funding the construction of the Apollo infrastructure in Houston and Cape Canaveral. Kennedy claimed there was now "overwhelming support" in Congress for the American manned space program, "committed as we all are to seeing to it that the United States occupies an important position in the race into the far reaches of space." The political reality was that the administration had won a round in the budget skirmish, but congressional support would remain something less than "overwhelming."[55]

Kennedy went on to say, "It is especially fitting that this bill should be signed on the day that our second astronaut, Captain Virgil Grissom, who I spoke to this morning after he had made his successful flight—I think it is most important that we should have once again this emphasis on the leadership which our fellow Americans are showing in this field, their courage and also the strong scientific support that they've received from the entire American scientific community."[56] The president made no direct reference in his signing statement to the fact that Grissom's ship had been lost, instead stressing that his flight had been "made before the eyes of the watching world with all the hazards that that entails."

Whenever the Mercury astronauts gathered at the White House for later postflight celebrations, photos showed most of the astronauts standing up front, next to President Kennedy. Perhaps because he was the shortest of the group, Grissom often is hard to spot in films and photos. He was hanging back, staying as far from the limelight as possible. "I didn't give a good god*damn* about the White House," he said in the weeks before his death. "But my boys did. Betty did."[57] These images became a metaphor for Grissom's entire career as an astronaut. He was an engineer, a test pilot. Public relations were a chore, something to be endured.

Grissom was now also an explorer, making the first true Earth observations of the Mercury program. Little could be seen through the spacecraft periscope, but when the horizon came into view through a relatively large centerline window, "the sight was truly breathtaking," he remembered, particularly since he could detect the curvature of the earth.[58] "I could make out brilliant gradations of color, the blue of the water, the white of the beaches and the brown of the land."[59] Indeed, the coastline looked just like the maps.

Grissom spent much of the rest of 1961 licking his wounds, indulging in a bout of self-pity in the aftermath of his flight and "all that investigation bullshit" he was forced to endure over the blown hatch.[60] Still, he was now an authentic "astronaut," a test pilot who had climbed on top of a rocket, rode it into space, and survived. Grissom would emerge from the hatch ordeal tougher, wiser, and utterly single-minded. Glenn orbited the earth three times in February 1962, instantly becoming an American hero. Project Mercury would end in May 1963. A new batch of nine astronauts was introduced the previous fall, all hotshot test pilots, most with engineering degrees. There would be a scramble for missions to fly a new two-man spacecraft called Gemini. The Americans would use this new ship to catch and surpass the daring Russians. Emerging from his funk, Grissom threw himself into the design, the guts of the new machine.

His fortune would soon change. More hard work and circumstances would combine to hand Grissom command of the maiden flight of a new and splendid ship. This one he would not lose.

9

DOWN A PEG

Poor Gus . . . when things went wrong [the astronauts] would tend to get blamed.
—Robert Voas, NASA psychologist

Dating from the creation of NASA in October 1958 through to the
end of the Apollo program, there were periodic, intense power struggles within the space agency, pitting the celebrity astronauts seeking
to exercise their perceived prerogatives against increasingly bureaucratic
and cautious NASA managers. It soon fell to Donald "Deke" Slayton, the
head of the Astronaut Office after being grounded in 1962 with an irreg-
ular heartbeat,[1] to shield his colleagues to the extent possible from their
bosses. For astronauts who failed to play ball with NASA managers like
Christopher C. Kraft, there would be no more spaceflights. In the case of
a future Apollo astronaut, there would be disgrace and expulsion from the
astronaut corps. Gus Grissom, the dedicated pilot and engineer striving
to "do good work," was among the first of the American astronauts to be
taken down a peg.

In the formative years of NASA's Space Task Group, headed by the
visionary Robert Gilruth, it was unnecessary for the new astronauts to
wrest power from their managers. Rather, Gilruth handed the power to
them. The working premise of the Space Task Group as established by
Gilruth was that the new astronauts "would be happy with the spacecraft
before they flew," that no one "would push them into anything," and that
they were considered to be "precious human cargo."[2]

The astronauts were the direct beneficiaries of what came to be known as the "Gilruth System," or what others correctly called "management by respect."[3] This meant the Mercury astronauts, the ones assuming most of the risk in a deadly enterprise, initially got most of what they wanted in the spacecraft's design phase: a ship with rudimentary controls, a window from which to observe and navigate, and eventually an escape hatch that provided a quick exit much like a fighter jet ejection seat. Beyond the spacecraft, there was the lucrative *Life* magazine deal that would bring each astronaut and his family financial stability, the beach house at the Cape paid for by the magazine, the cut-rate Corvettes, and all of the other perks and adulation that came with instant celebrity.

The downside to the Mercury astronauts' notoriety was that any mistake, whether real or perceived, would be magnified by intense press scrutiny. For Grissom, the blanket coverage translated into second-guessing and unflattering front-page headlines. The upshot was that some senior NASA managers and several incoming Kennedy administration officials concluded the astronauts, pumped up by an adoring press corps, were getting mighty full of themselves.

After his paper-thin victory over Vice President Richard Nixon in the 1960 presidential election, John Kennedy's science advisors took a dim view of the manned spaceflight program reluctantly launched by JFK's predecessor. To them, it was a stunt and an unwarranted use of scarce funds for scientific research. Gilruth later described how White House science advisor Jerome Wiesner, the eminent electrical engineer, former MIT president, and a strident critic of manned spaceflight, quickly moved to create a "select committee on space." Gilruth considered the panel to be "highly political in nature." Wiesner's committee soon produced a white paper published during the presidential transition and intended to blunt efforts to send an American into orbit. According to Gilruth: "One of the items about which they were critical was the amount of publicity that manned space flight seemed to get. I believe they assumed that this was our own doing rather than just the general interest of the public. Of course, they soon found when they became part of the new administration that manned space flight got even more publicity because it then got into the active phase of flying."[4]

The nonstop publicity was a direct consequence of the fact that the Americans, unlike the Soviets, were operating in the open. The space program in general and the Space Race in particular made good copy. It sold newspapers and magazines. The American public cared about these men whom many believed were almost certainly destined to die a fiery death, perhaps on live television. If a rocket blew up on the pad, the failure was there for all to see. It was painfully apparent when Grissom nearly drowned in the Atlantic at the end of his suborbital flight in July 1961. He was held accountable for the loss of his spacecraft, and that shattering loss shaped everything he did in the last five-and-a-half years of his life.

Feeling that his hard-earned reputation as a first-rate test pilot was at stake, Grissom admitted the following in a letter to his mother in the fall of 1961: "I've been feeling pretty low for the past few days." The funk was partially attributable to a postflight letdown and the beating he had taken in the press. "Grissom Insists the Hatch Was Blown by Accident," the *New York Times* front-page headline declared two days after his flight under a picture of the astronaut and Mark, age seven, greeting the crowd at Patrick Air Force Base on his return to Florida.[5] The other reason he was down in the dumps, the son revealed to Cecile King Grissom in a handwritten note dated October 7, 1961, was that "the flight crew for the orbital missions [had] been picked and [he wasn't] on it." He continued: "Neither Al [Shepard] nor I get one of the first two orbital shots. [John] Glenn gets the first one [words crossed out] and Deke Slayton gets the second one. Al is to be the controller for John's shot and I'm to be Deke's controller. It's not a job I want. I have to do a great deal of the work. I'll be gone from home a lot and I don't get any of the credit, but if anything goes wrong I'll get a good deal of the blame."[6] (The self-pitying remark was largely unfounded since it was extremely unlikely a capsule communicator would be held responsible for a mission failure.)

According to Scott Carpenter, it was Grissom who broke the silence at Langley on the morning of October 4, 1961, when Gilruth announced the assignments for the first orbital flights: Glenn first, backed up by Carpenter; Slayton for the second flight, backed up by Schirra. At that point, Gordon Cooper was the odd man out. "Well, I guess a handshake is in order for John," Grissom piped up. Handshakes and back slaps were exchanged—stiff upper lips all around. Shepard passed out drinks.[7]

"All of us are mad because Glenn was picked," Grissom groused in the letter to Cecile, exaggerating the anger directed at Glenn. For instance, Carpenter, who was widely viewed at this point as Glenn's sidekick (some even referred to him as "Tonto"), was undoubtedly pleased with Glenn's selection. The letter to Cecile continued, "We expressed our views prior to the selection so there isn't much we can do about it but support the flight and the program." Grissom then asked his mother to keep the news "under [her] hat," adding that he was telling her to "ease [her] mind a bit" so she would not have to worry about another flight—at least not for a while.

The hatch incident, the ensuing press furor over the lost spacecraft, and official uncertainty over Grissom's actions provided one of several pretexts for bringing the high-flying astronauts back down to Earth. The doubts about precisely what had happened at the end of Grissom's flight were fueled by NASA officials who publicly did little to clarify matters, thereby leaving the unmistakable impression that Grissom, not a faulty hatch design, was at fault. Or as one of Grissom's colleagues speculated later: "Among all the good, earnest people working in good faith to understand a mechanical malfunction, some dark soul in CYA mode is insinuating a feckless astronaut was to blame." Whether that was the case, the wounded Grissom complained for the rest of his life that Kraft and others had "tried to hang [him] with the 'hatch' crap."[8]

In the early 1960s, the astronauts were a new kind of technology worker with their own set of newfound prerogatives. The astronauts possessed a unique set of skills but lacked the clout necessary to move the bureaucracy of which they were a critical component. NASA managers, increasingly fed up with hotshot test pilots and their many perks, began to exercise what they considered to be their own prerogatives in order to reassert authority over the entire manned space enterprise.

Despite the fact that it was their hides on the line, the Mercury Seven had managed to make enemies among the NASA technocrats. Few within NASA, beyond his fellow astronauts, came to Grissom's defense after his flight. This occurred despite the fact that some in a position to know understood the hatch had been poorly designed, had not been adequately tested, and that the recovery phase of Grissom's training regimen fell far short of what was required.

Robert Voas, the Space Task Group psychologist who had played a key role in astronaut selection, understood this institutional tension better than most. In hindsight, he acknowledged the following regarding the hatch incident: "[It] was tending to revolve back on Gus, even though I think that there were several elements of that that illustrated that we had been pushing hard and been trying to do things maybe a little too rapidly and that we had not applied some of what we should have from a human engineering standpoint." Voas continued, "Poor Gus, I think, got blamed partly for that, and that was another potential problem for the astronauts [because] when things went wrong, they would tend to get blamed."[9] Hence, there was growing friction among the ground controllers and flight surgeons on the one hand and the tight-knit astronaut corps on the other.

In the aftermath of his Mercury flight, Grissom found himself effectively out of the flight rotation for the remainder of the program. As the other Mercury astronauts received their flight assignments, Grissom traveled to Hawaii to support Schirra's *Sigma 7* orbital mission in October 1962, and then to Mexico for the final flight in the Mercury series, Cooper's twenty-two-orbit flight aboard *Faith 7* in May 1963.

NASA had announced that a successful orbital flight by Cooper would end the Mercury program. It was time to move on to the next step, the ambitious Gemini program that would provide a bridge to the main event: the Apollo moon landings. When it became clear that the Mercury program was winding down, Shepard, Cooper's backup, put his considerable influence behind a lobbying campaign to proceed with a three-day orbital flight aboard a long-duration spacecraft designated Mercury Mark II. NASA administrator James Webb refused, even though Shepard had the backing of Gilruth and his deputy, Walt Williams. The headstrong Shepard then went over Webb's head, appealing directly to the president, who also refused to sign off on the flight.

Shepard's self-serving campaign also included threats to go public. Rumors of the gambit delighted the press, fascinated as they were by the internal power struggles within the space agency. It also alienated Shepard's NASA bosses, who now viewed his actions as "insubordination." NASA associate administrator Robert Seamans ended the dispute before Shepard could air the space agency's dirty laundry. There would be no additional Mercury flights for Shepard or anyone else, end of discussion.

As it turned out, Shepard would be grounded in early 1964 with Ménière's disease, an inner ear disorder that causes spontaneous episodes of vertigo, hearing loss, ringing in the ears, and the accompanying symptoms of nausea and vomiting. In the mid-1960s, there was no known cure for Ménière's disease. It looked as if the first American in space was finished as an astronaut. Shepard eventually became Slayton's assistant in the Astronaut Office. The direct beneficiary of Shepard's grounding turned out to be Grissom, who would be selected to command the first two-man Gemini mission originally scheduled for the end of 1964.

Shepard's campaign to get an orbital flight also represented an indirect attempt to set NASA policy on manned spaceflight, and "the astronauts had overreached their authority," concluded the space historian Matthew Hersch. "The controversy over Shepard's abortive second flight eventually established the upper bound of the astronauts' authority: they could manipulate hardware and influence training, but they had no power to alter strategy, except through success or failure," Hersch observed.[10]

Unlike Grissom, however, Shepard had not been scapegoated by the NASA brass, had not been left to twist in the wind as Gus had been after the inconclusive *Liberty Bell 7* investigation. Despite the efforts of NASA technicians like Sam Beddingfield, who knew the Mercury spacecraft inside and out, the exact cause of the premature hatch explosion could not be found. Grissom concluded that the lingering doubts about the "success or failure" of his mission played into the hands of bosses like Kraft and others intent on reining in the flyboys.

After the astronauts had moved to NASA's sprawling new headquarters in Houston, Grissom would reveal to Carpenter's wife, Rene, the hard lesson of *Liberty Bell 7*: "I just close my eyes and kiss his ass," he told her during a pool party, referring to flight director Kraft.[11]

Schirra, who was becoming Grissom's most trusted ally among the astronauts, understood better than most the reasons why his old Langley neighbor was "disheartened" about losing his ship. Aiming to get back in the flight rotations, Schirra said Grissom "almost moved to [McDonnell Aircraft in] St. Louis to work on Gemini."

Schirra had similar views on the power struggles within the space agency. His attitude toward his NASA bosses was typical of the early astronauts, especially the navy aviators. "I was trained to be a commanding officer, and NASA never understood what a commanding officer was," Schirra told an interviewer in 1998.[12] During his *Apollo 7* flight, Schirra staged a near-mutiny in space when an overloaded mission checklist and a zero-gravity head cold frayed the nerves of the crew and ground controllers in Houston. Kraft was furious. Schirra retired from NASA after the October 1968 flight, the only astronaut to fly the Mercury, Gemini, and Apollo spacecraft.

Even the saintly John Glenn felt the sting of the managerial backlash. Shortly after reaching orbit, an indicator alerted Mercury controllers that the heat shield on Glenn's *Friendship 7* might be loose, meaning the pilot would be incinerated during the fiery orbital reentry. Flight controller Kraft unilaterally decided not to tell Glenn, claiming the astronaut had more than enough to do already. When instructed not to jettison the reentry rockets mounted on the blunt end of his spacecraft as a way to keep the heat shield in place, Glenn knew something was wrong. "This is *Friendship 7*. What is the reason for this?" he asked. Kraft's reply amounted to, "Because we said so."

The indicator light was faulty, the heat shield held, and Glenn became an instant American hero. Kraft was wrong. The pilot needed all the information he could get about his ship, especially on the first American orbital mission. Glenn had trained relentlessly for his flight and could have handled the heat shield emergency and anything else thrown at him during his three orbits.

After Glenn resigned from the astronaut corps, "Kraft crapped his pants worrying Kennedy'd hand NASA to John," Grissom insisted. "John was bigger than Jesus!"[13] The other astronauts clearly were not.

Between the flights of *Liberty Bell 7* in July 1961 and Glenn's *Friendship 7* orbital flight in February 1962, the astronauts and the rest of the space agency began working simultaneously on the two-man Gemini and Apollo moon-landing programs. It was the beginning of a period of unprecedented technological effort: three concurrent manned programs were under way as NASA was in the process of picking up and moving from Langley to the new Manned Spacecraft Center in Houston.

In the midst of this heavy lifting, Grissom began maneuvering to get his next flight. In September 1962, a month before the Cuban Missile

Crisis, President Kennedy visited the assembly line in St. Louis where Mercury prime contractor McDonnell Aircraft was manufacturing the new Gemini spacecraft. The two-seater would turn out to be one of the most reliable ships ever to fly in space. The president was impressed with what he saw, praising the engineers and other workers "who perform the vital functions which make it possible to put one man or two men first in orbit around the earth, and then in orbit around the moon, and then on the moon, and then come back."[14]

Among the engineers that day in St. Louis was Grissom, who served as the president's tour guide as he inspected the Gemini spacecraft that would eventually be known as the "Gus Mobile." There was a good reason NASA selected Grissom to show off the new spacecraft: he had played an integral role in designing it, ensuring greater use of new features like modular components that could be removed without tearing the spacecraft interior apart to make repairs.

"He was angry [after *Liberty Bell 7*] about being blamed for his spacecraft having sunk, and he was fighting to come back out of the pack," Schirra recalled in his 1988 memoir. "Gus was a tiger. He wanted the first Gemini flight, and by god he got it."[15]

Amid the blowback generated by the hatch debacle, Grissom's anger was directed at his NASA bosses who had provided the television networks with only heavily edited footage of his rescue at sea. While some of the Mercury astronaut wives were visiting Cape Canaveral for the first time in the fall of 1961, Gus and Betty tracked down Rene Carpenter poolside at the Cocoa Beach Holiday Inn. Rene had helped Betty get through the launch day media frenzy and had felt her revulsion. "C'mon Rene, I want you to see something," Gus instructed. Passing through the security gate at the Cape, the astronaut snapped at the guards, "They're with me." Waved though, he then took Betty and Rene to view the unedited version of his recovery.[16] Much of that footage would not emerge for decades until researchers like Mark Gray and Rick Boos discovered different camera angles showing what actually happened. The harrowing footage showed the returning astronaut jump out of his spacecraft, and then fight to keep his head above water as helicopter prop wash repeatedly pushed him underwater. Contrary to earlier accounts that had Grissom swimming away from his ship, the footage clearly shows the struggling astronaut aiding the recovery forces, even helping helicopter crew member John Reinhard latch on to his sinking ship. Little wonder Grissom seethed throughout the rest of 1961. A year after Grissom's flight, Carpenter would suffer a worse fate for failing to strictly adhere to his mission checklist: he would never fly in space again.

Unlike Grissom, Carpenter was unable to stage a comeback. It also is unclear whether he ever sought one. Carpenter piloted his *Aurora 7* spacecraft around the planet three times in May 1962 and brought it back despite serious defects in his ship's maneuvering and guidance systems. While orbiting Earth, Carpenter had the good sense to take in as much of the experience as possible. He was arguably the first scientific observer to fly in space; however, his lack of attention to the piloting aspects of this mission violated the unspoken code of sticking to the checklist and the macho requirement to bring the spacecraft back as close to the recovery ship as possible. Like Grissom's mission, the aftermath of *Aurora 7* was another opportunity to rein in the astronauts. Carpenter's considerable contributions to manned spaceflight would go largely unappreciated. For Kraft, it was another act of insubordination. He made sure Carpenter was permanently grounded.

A decade later, NASA would again make an example of an astronaut, this time Alfred Merrill Worden, command module pilot on the *Apollo 15* lunar mission. US Air Force Colonel Al Worden, a West Point graduate, would become the first human being to float outside his spacecraft in the vast emptiness between the earth and the moon—cislunar space. A farm boy from Michigan who worked his tail off to become a test pilot and an astronaut, Worden would be swept up in a souvenir scandal after returning from arguably the greatest of the six American lunar landings in 1971. Specially designed souvenir envelopes known as first-day covers had been taken by the crew on the flight to the moon and eventually sold. The resulting scandal brought discredit to NASA, and someone had to take the blame. The scapegoat was Worden, who had profited not one penny from the scheme. His distinguished career as a test pilot and astronaut was ruined.

After the scandal surfaced in the press, the predictable self-righteous outrage of the politicians was followed by the obligatory spectacle of congressional hearings. Worden was expendable. One day he was circling the moon, walking in space, and the next day he was on the outside looking in. His treatment at the hands of his NASA bosses was shameful. "I felt I had paid a bigger price than my actions deserved," Worden wrote years later. He had kept quiet for decades before finally deciding to tell his side of the story. NASA "was very quick to throw us under the bus," Worden told an interviewer forty years later. "They made an example of us."[17] NASA's shabby treatment of Worden can be traced directly back to the ordeals of Grissom and Carpenter in the early days of the space program. Only Grissom was in a position to fight back—and he did.

In early 1962, the Mercury program was headed for its climax. An Atlas rocket designated Mercury-Atlas 6 would catapult the first American into orbit around the earth. Grissom served as Bermuda capsule communicator during Glenn's historic flight on February 20, 1962. At the beginning of Glenn's third orbit, Grissom informed Glenn he was "in good shape." There was no hint of animosity in the exchange, and Glenn even managed to pay a compliment to his predecessor in space:

Glenn: This is *Friendship 7*, have the Cape in sight down there. It looks real fine from up here . . .

Grissom: Rog', rog'.

Glenn: . . . as *you* know.

Grissom: Yea, verily, Sonny!

Without a backup assignment and effectively shut out of the Mercury program, Grissom focused all his attention on Gemini. "Gus got the Gemini concept going very well," according to Schirra. "Everyone thought Gus was the smallest guy. He was the *shortest* guy, but not the smallest. He had the longest torso length."[18] Grissom left room in the Gemini cabin design for taller astronauts like rookie Thomas Stafford.

Beginning in early 1962, NASA started testing a contraption called a Rogallo wing, or the Parasev (for "Paraglider Research Vehicle"), in hopes of developing the capability to bring spacecraft back to Earth on land. The problem was the ungainly thing looked like a good way for a test pilot to break his neck. Perhaps thinking he needed to stick his own neck out to stand out from the crowd, Grissom volunteered to test the Parasev. "When it came to designing the new spacecraft, Grissom was very intense," Schirra recalled. "His intent was to get things done right."[19]

Returning to his experimental test pilot roots in the early days of the Gemini program, the undaunted Grissom attempted to fly the towed vehicle that looked like a hang glider with an inflatable wing. The test flights would simulate a desert landing at what was then NASA's Dryden Flight Research Center (it has since been renamed for Neil Armstrong, who died in 2012) adjacent to Edwards Air Force Base in the windswept California desert. "He was trying to fly a vehicle that would come down on a little parachute like a hang glider, and he almost didn't live through it," Schirra recalled.

The other astronauts wanted nothing to do with the Parasev concept, even though a Langley aeronautical engineer, Francis Rogallo, had come up with the idea in the late 1940s and later became known as the father of modern hang gliding. Speaking for the rest of the astronauts, Schirra told Grissom flat out during a meeting about the landing concept: "We're not going to do that." "Anybody else have an opinion?" replied Grissom, surveying the room. "Nope. That's our opinion," Schirra repeated. That was the end of the Parasev experiment; Gemini would land in the ocean.

In the fall of 1962, immersed in every detail of the new Gemini spacecraft, Grissom faced his peers for the first time since his Mercury flight during a meeting of the Society of Experimental Test Pilots. The assemblage included many who along with the sound barrier–breaker Chuck Yeager considered Mercury to be "spam in a can." Grissom had come to the meeting to disabuse his test pilot brethren of this notion. He had thrown himself into Gemini, putting all he had learned over the previous three years into the new craft.

Grissom acknowledged in his address to the Society that the Mercury astronauts were largely along for the ride. The point had been to show that humans could function in weightlessness and survive the blazing reentry. Gemini was different, he continued. "The most important difference is the amount of control the pilot exercises over all functions." Gemini, Grissom asserted, "is the first true pilot's spacecraft." The two-man ship would be an "operational spacecraft, not just a research and development vehicle." The new American spacecraft was a means to an end: sending humans to the moon.[20]

It was too soon to know whether Grissom had convinced the skeptics that astronauts, former test pilots, could become "the explorer[s] of space."[21] Determined to make a comeback, the astronaut would work tirelessly over the next twenty-two months to ensure the success of a machine that would come to symbolize his unwavering commitment to space exploration. Grissom would literally "write the book" on Gemini; that effort along with the Apollo program that followed would eventually consume Grissom.

A front-page story in the *New York Times* published on November 17, 1963, reported that President Kennedy had the previous day, a Saturday, toured Cape Canaveral, where he observed firsthand the mighty Saturn rocket that promised to outdo the Soviets: "Mr. Kennedy was briefed every step of the way by space experts, including two of the original seven astronauts, Maj. Virgil I. Grissom, who made a sub-orbital flight in July 1961; and Maj. L. Gordon Cooper Jr., who orbited the earth 22 times on the final Mercury flight last May."[22]

Standing directly under the more than two-hundred-foot-high colossus, JFK expressed his complete satisfaction with the machine capable of generating 1.5 million pounds of thrust to loft payloads up to 19,000 pounds, 4,000 more than the Soviets. Kennedy declared to Grissom, Cooper, and their NASA bosses: "When this goes up we'll be ahead of the Russians."[23]

In the months before his last visit to Florida, Kennedy was having second thoughts about the space race. He was coming to the realization that the cost of being first in any technological endeavor, especially a manned lunar landing, would be high, even if one of the dividends were international prestige. In the presence of Soviet Ambassador to the US Anatoly Dobrynin, the president suggested that the US and Russian spaceshots were fast becoming "three-day wonders" and that any prestige associated with them was fleeting.

On a parallel track, JFK quietly was seeking rapprochement with the Soviets in the aftermath of the October 1962 Cuban Missile Crisis. He had recently proposed a joint lunar expedition as a way to defuse tensions and avoid costly duplication of research.

Kennedy seemed to again reverse course during his November 16, 1963, visit to the Cape. After seeing for himself the impressive technological sights at Cape Canaveral, with its new moonport rising from the scrub of Merritt Island, its gigantic new Vehicle Assembly Building piercing the sky, the powerful new Saturn rocket, and the can-do attitudes of Grissom and Cooper—all of this seemed to reinvigorate his competitive juices.[24] Now he was thinking about returning to the Cape to view the upcoming Saturn launch.

The following week, during the first stop on a political visit to Texas, the president again emphasized his renewed support of the American manned space program, telling a crowd at the Brooks Aerospace Medical Center that a US lunar landing mission—not a joint US-Soviet effort—would be pursued "with safety and speed."

Like the astronauts, Kennedy showed a willingness to take a calculated risk, this one political, by traveling to Dallas despite dire warnings from advisors, law enforcement officials, and fellow politicians to skip the city and its right-wing threats during his two-day Texas tour. Not only would Kennedy ride through the streets of Dallas in a long motorcade, he would instruct the Secret Service not to use the bulletproof bubble roof used to cover the presidential limousine. "They put me in a bubble top thing and I can't get to the people. . . . I belong to them and they belong to me," insisted the president.[25] Both JFK and Grissom embraced risk with eyes wide open. One paid with his life in November 1963; the other would follow four years later.

Once it was clear that the manned space program would continue and thrive under President Lyndon B. Johnson, NASA was determined to meet the slain president's goal of "landing a man on the moon and returning him safely to the earth" before the end of the decade. Space agency managers would take literally JFK's admonition in San Antonio to proceed "with safety and speed." Ultimately, they would emphasize speed over safety.

In the period between the end of Mercury and the beginning of the Gemini program, Grissom likely had time to reflect on that sunny day at Cape Canaveral when he escorted the young president on his final tour of the American space complex. Kennedy had decided the day before his murder that he would attend the launch of the new rocket scheduled for December 1963. Perhaps the memory of JFK's visit also had given Grissom pause to reflect on the deadly business of spaceflight, even the fleeting nature of existence.

Either way, Grissom's own competitive juices were again stirring as never before. The dispirited, humiliated astronaut had weathered the worst storm of his flying career and was now poised to make a comeback that would catapult him to the top of the astronaut pyramid. His colleagues, NASA engineers, technicians, and even his bosses now would think twice before crossing swords with the commander of the first flight of the Gemini program.

10

APOGEE

She flew like a queen, did our unsinkable Molly.
—Gus Grissom

Six days before the launch of America's first two-man crew aboard the new Gemini spacecraft, March 18, 1965, the Soviet Union staged one of the great feats in the history of manned spaceflight: Cosmonaut Alexei Leonov emerged from his orbiting *Voskhod 2* spacecraft to become the first human to float in space. The ten-minute spacewalk ended with a desperate effort by the exhausted Leonov to somehow squeeze himself and his bulky pressure suit through a makeshift airlock leading back to the spacecraft cabin. Leonov barely made it back inside—only by bleeding pressure from his ballooning space suit.

The next day, Leonov and mission commander Pavel Belyayev overshot their landing site, ending up in a stand of fir trees two thousand kilometers off target, their spacecraft buried in deep snow. In the early days of manned spaceflight, recovery operations were primitive. Leonov and Belyayev spent a freezing night in the snowbound capsule, wolves howling in the distance.[1] Again, the Americans had been upstaged.

Walking in space was a key step toward reaching the moon. So too was the ability to maneuver an orbiting spaceship. So far, neither the United States nor the Soviet Union had launched a maneuverable spacecraft capable of other critical tasks like rendezvous and docking. Verifying the ability of a spacecraft to change its flight path in orbit was the goal of the first manned Gemini flight to be commanded by US Air Force Major Gus Grissom.

The Mercury program had ended in May 1963 with a successful twenty-two-and-a-half-orbit flight by Gordon Cooper. Somewhat erratic on the ground, Cooper had proven himself steady in space as one system after another failed during his thirty-four-hour flight.

During 1963, the Americans had three separate manned programs operating concurrently. As Gemini moved into its testing phase, work on the first three-man Apollo spacecraft began in August 1964. By December, the Americans were sweating out an unmanned test flight of the Gemini spacecraft designed to carry two astronauts into Earth orbit. Grissom quaintly described the agonizing months of delay before the test flight as a "real hard-luck Nelly."[2] "This flight was desperately important to us," the commander recalled.[3] One delay followed another. The downcast Grissom reflected the growing concern that the audacious Soviets were again stealing a march. Grissom fretted that "Gemini would probably still be on the pad when the Russians were launching commuter rockets to Mars."[4]

The hard-nosed reporters in Florida offered condolences after the unmanned Gemini launch failure in late 1964, but Grissom "wasn't looking for the crying towel." Despite the failure, the test showed the booster's Malfunction Detection System (MDS) had worked as designed, pinpointing a drop in hydraulic pressure in the number two engine thrust-vector actuator. The MDS monitored the performance of all spacecraft subsystems and displayed a cockpit warning if it detected a problem. It also illustrated a maturing US spacecraft design that emphasized crew safety. Skeptics thought the system was unnecessary extra weight on the *Titan II* rocket, a converted intercontinental ballistic missile. "They felt this was taking caution a step too far," Grissom wrote in his account of the Gemini program. "But then these critics had the refreshing knowledge they wouldn't be up there in the Gemini spacecraft." In a retort to the doubters in the press, Grissom added, "That helps a whole heap when you're criticizing."[5]

Grissom also addressed those who thought the American space program was a waste of resources. Without Gemini, without Apollo, "we would be handing [over] to the next generation a universe dominated by other powers, a world controlled from space, whether we liked it or not." At the height of the Cold War, it was difficult to envision any international cooperation in space.

Historians generally agree that geopolitical goals drove the race to the moon.[6] It was primarily about Cold War supremacy and international prestige, prestige that extends to the present day. One need only observe the steady stream of visitors each day to the Smithsonian National Air and Space Museum in Washington, DC, one of the most visited museums in the world, where foreign tourists marvel at the achievements of the American space pioneers. Grissom had a much more visceral goal than international prestige while contemplating the very real possibility of losing the race to the moon in the mid-1960s: "I don't want my two sons to inherit that kind of a world," he declared.[7] They did not, but the world Scott and Mark Grissom did inherent would be far more complicated than the relatively straightforward geopolitical rivalries of the Cold War.

The unmanned Gemini spacecraft eventually made it into orbit in January 1965. A few months later, in March 1965, Grissom and his copilot, US Navy Lieutenant Commander John Young, would prove the skeptics in the press wrong during the first manned space flight in which the occupants actually flew their spacecraft. Grissom and Young lobbied for a longer mission, but their flight lasted only three orbits. They were overruled by cautious space agency managers who did not want to push their luck on the maiden flight of a new spacecraft that would be controlled by an untested ground network. Those three orbits, just under five hours in space, were the only ones Grissom would ever fly.

The story of how Young came to be Grissom's copilot is a classic example of NASA's byzantine crew selection process. Thomas Stafford, a member of the second astronaut class who would fly twice during the Gemini program and once to the moon with Young, explained it this way: "In crew assignment, you assign a commander. It was Deke [Slayton] and Al [Alan B.] Shepard getting together, really. The commander had his, I guess, first right of refusal. They wouldn't make anybody fly with the commander if the commander didn't want."[8]

The respected air force test pilot Frank Borman, another member of the second group of astronauts, was originally assigned to fly with Grissom. It was a plum assignment, placing the rookie Borman nearly on par with the Mercury veterans. The problem was the new spacecraft was not large enough for the two pilots and their egos. According to Young, Borman let it be known that he simply could not work with Grissom.[9]

Not surprisingly, Borman had his own version: "I was told that I was going to be a—fly with Gus on the first flight of Gemini," Borman said in a 1999 interview. "I went over to his house to talk to him about it. And we had a long talk, and [laughs] after that I was scrubbed from the flight. So I guess that I didn't pass the test with Grissom."[10]

Borman, who went on to command *Gemini 7* and *Apollo 8*, mankind's first flight to the moon, said he quickly moved on. "I never asked. Could [*sic*] have cared less." When asked how he shrugged it off so quickly, Borman replied: "Well, you know, if they didn't want me, I didn't want to be there." Grissom apparently felt the same, and Young replaced Borman.

Judging from their résumés, the casual observer might have considered Grissom and Borman a good match. The rookie was a fellow Hoosier, born two years after Grissom in Gary. Both were air force test pilots. But Borman, a West Point graduate who had worked for Chuck Yeager at the test pilot school, may have rubbed the self-made enlistee Grissom the wrong way. Grissom and Borman turned out to be as different as the two halves of their native state. The veteran was a lone wolf; the new guy did things by the book. Ultimately, their clashing egos and Grissom's initial reluctance to give the new astronauts the time of day settled the matter. Forced to choose, he preferred to fly with the easygoing Young, becoming the equivalent of a big brother. Young went on to fly six times in space, including two trips to the moon. After Grissom died, Young made sure that his mentor and his deeds were not forgotten.

In February 1967, Borman would be assigned to help lead the investigation into the cause of the *Apollo 1* fire, overseeing the complex technical issues that got the moon program back on track while deftly handling delicate post-fire politics. After retiring from NASA, Borman worked for the Nixon administration but was appalled by the Watergate scandal. He later headed Eastern Airlines.

Grissom and Borman mixed like oil and water, but the crew of the first manned Gemini flight got along famously. Young and the other members of the second group of astronauts, "The New Nine," were introduced in September 1962. Grissom and Young had first worked together during survival training "up a creek" in the Panama Canal Zone. Growing up in Florida, Young knew his way around a swamp, how to survive in the jungle by cutting out hearts of palm and catching fish with worms and a safety-pin hook. "Eat anything that doesn't eat you first," a Panamanian guide told the astronauts. They did, developing a taste for delicacies like iguana steaks. "Gus and I got along well," Young remarked.[11]

Grissom and Young dove headfirst into the Gemini training. First, there were the endless mission planning sessions, and then centrifuge training in Pennsylvania, followed by spacesuit checks, physical examinations, and preparations for flight experiments. "The days just seemed to have 48 hours, the weeks 14 days, and still there was never enough time," the commander recalled later. "We saw our families just enough to reassure our youngsters they still had fathers."[12]

Grissom had by then essentially moved to St. Louis, where McDonnell Aircraft was building and testing the new spacecraft, and then to the renamed Cape Kennedy once the mission simulator was up and running in October 1964. He would eventually log more than seventy-seven hours in the Gemini simulator, rehearsing every detail of the five-hour mission. As launch day approached, Grissom had sat through more than two hundred abort scenarios.

During their training in St. Louis, Grissom and Young began considering a name for their ship, a tradition carried over from the Mercury program. Deciding what to call the first manned Gemini spacecraft proved almost as complicated as selecting Grissom's copilot. It would also be the last time a spaceship was named until the first flights of the Apollo lunar lander that required designations for two spacecraft. Grissom considered his options, including several Indiana references. He and Young were especially fond of *Wapasha*, a reference to the Mdewakanton Dakota chief and the nation for whom the Wabash River was likely named. Either way, it was "a truly American name," the commander decided; however, the name *Wapasha* did not fly with the NASA brass.

At that time, the Broadway musical *The Unsinkable Molly Brown* was closing to rave reviews. In an early example of branding, Grissom changed his mind and proposed *Molly Brown* as the name of his ship. *Molly Brown* would serve, Grissom reckoned in hopes of sticking it to his critics, as the perfect antidote to the sinking of *Liberty Bell 7* two years earlier. NASA managers objected. Grissom countered, "OK, how about the *Titanic*?" Management relented and the name *Molly Brown* stuck, at least informally.

While the *Titan II* rocket had its share of teething problems, the Gemini spacecraft looked and performed like a sports car. The two-seater handled like a dream, helping the United States in twenty short months take the lead in manned space exploration, a lead it would not relinquish. What she lacked in legroom, the spacecraft made up for in performance and reliability.

Grissom had a hand in nearly every aspect of the Gemini spacecraft's design. Realizing that the Mercury program was for him a dead end, he moved quickly to immerse himself in the innards of the next American spacecraft. In so doing, he was quickly heading to the top of the astronaut pecking order. Within the growing fraternity of the mid-1960s, few dared to cross Grissom, who was widely viewed as "tough, intense . . . , the kind of guy who didn't care if the sun came out or not."[13]

Eugene Cernan, another rookie from the third group of astronauts announced in October 1963, found it hard to fathom that he was working with some of the most competitive human beings on Earth. "I found myself walking the halls with the likes of Al Shepard, John Glenn, Wally Schirra, Gus Grissom, Slayton, the others. Sometimes I had to ask myself, 'What I was doing here among these guys?'"[14] Grissom, Cernan remembered, "was always sort of aloof. It was almost as if Gus didn't have time for the new kids on the block. Gus was too busy heading back into space." When a group of astronauts from Purdue attended the 1967 Rose Bowl, which pitted the Boilermakers against the University of Southern California, it was Cernan, the low man on the totem pole, who handled the arrangements on behalf of Grissom and Neil Armstrong.

Some believed Grissom had been given a pass to continue flying despite losing his Mercury spacecraft. Tom Wolfe, the chronicler of *The Right Stuff*, was among the doubters based on what his sources within the ranks of the astronauts told him. One gets the distinct impression reading Wolfe's best-selling account of Project Mercury that the author had a vendetta against the Grissoms and their "unsophisticated Hoosier grit."[15]

A decidedly different view came from NASA program managers who were more interested in putting incidents like the loss of *Liberty Bell 7* behind them, fixing problems, and getting on to the next flight. Hence, according to Robert Thompson, who headed NASA recovery operations through the Apollo program, "Gus was one of the better people we had, and I think that that whole incident allowed the program to move on and not damage that individual, which was the right thing to do."[16] So Grissom ignored the naysayers and moved on, immediately jockeying to command an early Gemini flight.

Alan Shepard had been in line to command the first Gemini mission, but his grounding with Ménière's disease fundamentally altered the crew assignments, which were announced in April 1964. Having secured the first flight and in the midst of intensive training, Young asked Grissom when he thought they would fly. Based on his thorough knowledge of the spacecraft, the performance of the *Titan II*, and the amount of testing needed to prepare for the flight, Grissom correctly estimated March 1965.

Indeed, March 23, 1965, turned out to be the high point of Grissom's flying career. The flight of *Gemini 3*, the venerable *Molly Brown*, resulted in a string of historic firsts. Astronauts for the first time piloted their space-craft, changing their orbital path around the earth while attempting to steer their ship to a designated landing point in the Atlantic Ocean. These and other maneuvers were key steps to a lunar landing. Commander Grissom also became the first human to fly twice in space. At last, he could claim a first in the history of manned spaceflight and human exploration. In the homespun mythology of Kennedy's New Frontier, Grissom consid-ered himself as much a pioneer as those who had settled the West. In the context of the Cold War, he was doing something the Russians with their big rockets and their many space firsts had yet to accomplish.

For the astronaut, his wife, and sons, the flight of *Molly Brown* was to be their crowning achievement, the payoff for Betty's more than twenty-five years of sacrifice, the endless moves from one base to the next, the lengthy absences. Betty recalled that Gemini was the project that gave her husband the most satisfaction. Appropriately, *Molly Brown* would eventually serve as the main attraction at the Virgil I. Grissom Memorial Museum at Spring Mill State Park outside Mitchell.

Grissom piloted his ship for three eventful orbits, pushing his total time in space to five hours and seven minutes. He and Young made the most of those three orbits by shaking down the two-man ship that would serve as the platform for perfecting the techniques needed to go to the moon.

Grissom's intimate involvement in nearly every aspect of the spacecraft design and layout earned the ship another nickname, the "Gus Mobile." Indeed, he would literally write the book on the Gemini spacecraft, collaborating with Macmillan editor Jacob Hay on a first-person account of the Gemini program, published posthumously in 1968. The volume would be Grissom's only chance to provide his version of the Space Race.

Gemini's objective was to "advance the state of the art," Grissom declared. NASA's specific goals for the program were "clear cut":

- Subject man and equipment to space flight up to two weeks in duration;

- rendezvous and dock with orbiting vehicles and maneuver the docked combination using the target vehicle's propulsion system; and

- perfect methods of entering the atmosphere and landing at a preselected point on land.[17]

The first two goals were met in spectacular fashion. A proposed ground landing, a concept personally tested by Grissom, was shelved in 1964. The ship would land in the ocean, testing reentry techniques that would be needed to return crews from the moon.

Gemini was the essential bridge between launching humans into space in a primitive spacecraft and actually leaving the earth for the moon aboard the three-man Apollo with its spindly lunar module. During the eventful months between March 1965 and December 1966, nearly every concept required to fly to the moon was proven.

It all began on a sunny morning in late winter in the middle of the 1960s, a month short of Grissom's thirty-ninth birthday, with the launch of the first manned Gemini flight. *Molly Brown*'s commander and Young, the quiet but cocksure navy aviator, accomplished nearly every task on their mission checklist—and some that were not present—despite an early, serious problem with the ship's environmental control system and a harrowing reentry.

Grissom and Young had been trained to a fine edge. The goal of the mission was to demonstrate that the Gemini spacecraft could be maneuvered in space. Grissom, heading into orbit for the first (and as it turned out, the only) time, was primed to show that it could be done. This would be a textbook operational flight that would set the stage for a series of space firsts.

The evening before the launch, Grissom and Young dined in the astronaut quarters at Cape Canaveral with their backup crew, the jovial Schirra and the rookie Tom Stafford, along with Alan Shepard, Deke Slayton, and the crew of the next Gemini flight, James McDivitt and Ed White. Also at the dinner table was Leo DeOrsey, the Washington tax lawyer who had brokered the Mercury astronauts' deal with *Life* magazine.

As the crew slept, Titan contractor Martin Marietta Company loaded the liquid-fueled rocket with propellant. On launch day, the crew was awakened at 4:40 a.m. Cape time. The traditional preflight breakfast of steak and eggs was attended by Shepard, Slayton, Robert Gilruth, flight director Christopher Kraft, flight surgeon Charles Berry, and Gemini program manager Charles Mathews. Also in attendance was James McDonnell, "Mr. Mac" of spacecraft manufacturer McDonnell Aircraft, as well as other NASA officials and contractors. Breakfast with the prime crew was a perk for those who had made the flight possible.

As the booster was being fueled, Schirra and Stafford had spent the night sleeping near Pad 19 and awoke early to prepare the spacecraft for launch, checking and setting switches. After breakfast, about 6 a.m., the crew of *Molly Brown* drove to a van parked at an adjoining pad where they donned their pressure suits. The incorrigible prankster Schirra was waiting for them wearing a beat up Mercury pressure suit "just in case," he jested, "you two chicken out."[18] Schirra's stunt, undoubtedly an attempt to defuse the launch-day tension, was a prelude to another prank, a Schirra "gotcha" that would be sprung during the flight.

The flight surgeons attached biomedical sensors to Grissom and Young before technicians helped them into their suits. The prelaunch procedure then required the astronauts to close the faceplates on their helmets and begin breathing pure oxygen. This would purge nitrogen from their bloodstream to avoid decompression sickness in space. Sealed in their suits, the crew then embarked for Pad 19 carrying portable ventilators until they could connect their suits to the spacecraft's environmental control system.

The crew, along with Schirra and Stafford, left for Pad 19 just after 7 a.m., traveling directly along a new road that had mysteriously appeared in the days before the scheduled launch. The crew had complained about the roundabout route between the two pads. Suited up for preflight tests, the long ride was "pretty uncomfortable," Grissom informed his bosses. There was no money in NASA's budget for a new road, they were told. Then, days before the launch, "a straight-as-an-arrow road suddenly appeared between Pad 16 and Pad 19," the commander recounted in awe. A resourceful air force warrant officer known around the Cape as "Gunner" Barton had somehow come up with the materials and labor needed to build the direct route, reducing the ride from the medical trailer to Pad 19 by nearly a mile. No one knew where Barton—the Cape's version of Sergeant Bilko, the scam artist played by Phil Silvers in the 1950s television comedy—had found the money to build the road. It was immediately dubbed the "Barton FREEway."[19]

Schirra and Stafford looked on with mischievous grins as pad leader Guenter Wendt loaded the crew into their spacecraft. Unbeknown to Grissom, the backup crew had slipped a surprise package to Young that would not appear until the crew was in orbit, testing its new "space food." As Wendt buttoned up the spacecraft, Schirra left for Gemini control, the old Mercury control center that was being used for the last time. All subsequent missions would be controlled from the new NASA Manned Spacecraft Center in Houston. Stafford retreated to a blockhouse near the launchpad to serve as "Stoney," the astronaut who monitored the fueled, pressurized launch vehicle and communicated with the crew on the pad until the end of the countdown. It was "Stoney"—no one knows the origin of the moniker—who counted backward from ten and provided visual confirmation to the crew that they had left the ground.

With *Molly Brown*'s swing-open hatches sealed, Grissom and Young were reclined in their seats about 135 feet above the ground on top of a two-stage rocket capable of generating about 435,000 pounds of thrust.

Between them and the *Titan II*'s second stage was a two-part spacecraft adapter section immediately behind the crew cabin. This was another Gemini innovation: the adapter remained with the spacecraft until reentry, and the rear section of the adapter carried equipment and fuel for the propulsion systems. On later flights, it would carry fuel cells that would replace some of the batteries used to power *Molly Brown*'s systems. The forward adapter section carried the braking rockets that would slow the spacecraft for its reentry. Both adapter sections would be jettisoned just before reentry. Together, the booster and the modular spacecraft made Gemini the first real flying machine of the Space Age.

Partly thanks to the "Barton FREEway" shortcut, the countdown was ahead of schedule when low overcast shrouded the Cape. The skies eventually cleared. Then, a leak was detected in a first-stage fuel line thirty-eight minutes before the scheduled liftoff at 9 a.m. local time. A hold in the countdown was declared at T minus thirty-five minutes. A technician went out on the launchpad, tightened a loose nut "with just one turn of a wrench on a valve to stop the leak," and the countdown resumed.[20]

The big, orange spacecraft erector was slowly lowered, and the crew began switching to internal power. As the countdown neared zero, *Titan II* started to come alive. "Check Stage One prevalves open," the commander confirmed. That meant the booster's hypergolic fuels that would ignite on contact were about to mix.

"T minus zero! Stage One ignition," came the call from the ground. The vehicle was no longer attached to the earth. Grissom described the moment of liftoff as "a distant, muffled thunder ninety feet below our heavily insulated cabin." He kept his gloved hand on the D-ring between his knees that would eject the crew if the booster's Malfunction Detection System sensed a problem with the engines or flight path. Three seconds after the *Titan II* engines ignited, belching their distinctive billowing orange exhaust, *Molly Brown* lifted off at precisely 9:24 a.m. local time.

The commander radioed that the mission clock had started, and then he noticed that the sky had begun to tilt in his window as the preplanned spacecraft roll program was initiated, followed by a pitch-over maneuver as the vehicle accelerated to the eventual 17,500-mile-per-hour escape velocity needed to reach Earth orbit.

"You're on your way, *Molly Brown!*" Cape Capcom Gordon Cooper intoned, and so too was the revived American space program. The liftoff of the converted ICBM was smoother than anticipated, much smoother than Grissom had experienced with the Mercury-Redstone rocket nearly four years earlier. "Yea, man!" Grissom replied as he began relaying the booster's performance to ground controllers.[21]

Up and out over the Atlantic, the vehicle quickly went supersonic. About eighty seconds into the ascent, passing through forty thousand feet, the crew felt the rattling of "Max Q," or maximum dynamic pressure on the launch vehicle. As soon as the rattling started, however, it abruptly ended. "It just got quiet," Grissom reported. The first-stage engines shut down after firing for about two and half minutes. *Molly Brown*'s flight path was "a little bit high," Cooper radioed, but not a problem. Grissom would correct the flight path at the end of the first orbit. About three minutes into the flight, the booster's first stage separated with a loud bang, and the second stage engine ignited, creating what the astronauts referred to as "fire in the hole" as they thrust away from the spent first stage. "Oh, man! Look at that horizon," Grissom told Young. "We're moving right along that horizon." The *Titan II*'s second stage boosted *Molly Brown* into Earth orbit. "Steering right down the old line," Cooper called.

Five and a half minutes into the flight, the second-stage engine cut off early; thirty seconds later, it separated with another surprisingly loud bang that drew the attention of both astronauts. Then, there was the eerie silence of the vacuum of space. Grissom used his spacecraft thrusters to first put some distance between his spacecraft and the burnt-out second stage, and then nudged his ship the rest of the way into orbit. It was not perfect, but they had made it: America's first two-man crew was now circling Earth with an initial low point, or perigee, of 87 miles and a high point, or apogee, of 125 miles. The path would be circularized over Texas at the end of *Molly Brown*'s first orbit using a series of maneuvering thrusters that made Gemini different from any previous flying machine: the Orbit Attitude and Maneuvering System, or OAMS.

OAMS consisted of a series of rocket motors of varying sizes arrayed around the Gemini spacecraft, providing either one hundred, eighty-five, or twenty-five pounds of thrust. Four big "translational" thrusters were used both to separate the spacecraft from the second stage of the Titan rocket and for vertical or lateral maneuvers. The medium thrusters were used for forward or rearward maneuvers. The small, twenty-five-pounders controlled spacecraft pitch (up and down), yaw (side to side), and roll.

Once in orbit, the crew raised the visors on their helmets and immediately noticed debris drifting around the cabin. "There's all kinds of junk floating around in here," Grissom informed Young. "Look at that thing. I don't know what we can do with any of this stuff floating around." They worked around it.

Cooper, who had logged thirty-four hours in space, took a moment before losing radio contact with his air force buddy to inquire about the view from orbit compared with his *Liberty Bell 7* ballistic flight. Grissom couldn't hear the question, and then the spacecraft began losing contact with the Cape as it headed out over the Atlantic toward the African coast. "How *do* it look?" Cooper repeated.

"It look great!" replied Grissom, who in fifteen minutes had already doubled his spaceflight experience. Nearly four years after the disastrous end to his first flight, the Gemini commander was back where he always wanted to be: flying higher and faster than anyone else in a ship he had helped design. But ever mindful of the consequences of his first flight, especially the press criticism, he would say little to the ground that could be misconstrued later by reporters.

The crew soon connected with the next communications link in a global tracking network in the Canary Islands. The Worldwide Tracking Network, used for the Gemini flights, consisted of a series of ground and "gap-filling," ship-based communications relays. The network also was being tested for the first time, and it was the primary reason Grissom's second flight was limited to three orbits. The crew had lobbied for a longer flight; the Astronaut Office wanted an open-ended mission at least as long as Cooper's twenty-two-and-half-orbit marathon. Conservative Gemini program managers ruled against a longer mission. They knew that after three orbits the earth's rotation would foul up the alignment needed for continuous tracking of *Molly Brown*. Grissom and Young would come down after three orbits, cautious senior NASA officials decreed.[22]

Grissom soon noticed they were over Africa and asked Young for the camera. In case they had to come down early, Grissom wanted to bring back at least a few pictures from orbit.

Mission tasks quickly stacked up, and the crew had little time to enjoy the view out the spacecraft's truncated half-moon windows.[23] What Grissom really wanted to do was fly *Molly Brown*. "Let's get lined up here," he told Young as he stabilized the spacecraft's orientation, its attitude, relative to the planet. This was the first time such orbital maneuvers were being made with any degree of accuracy because Grissom was piloting his spacecraft, not just riding along. The days of "spam in a can" were over. Grissom asked Young how it looked from his right-hand seat: "I'd say I was aligned pretty good, wouldn't you?" Young agreed.

Just after the crew made contact with the Canary Island station, the commander noticed that the OAMS thrusters were somehow causing an unwanted drift, a yaw, or twist, slightly to the left. Armed with a thorough knowledge of his spacecraft systems, Grissom quickly diagnosed a problem with the thrusters: "We must have a leak." The troublesome thruster could be periodically corrected during the flight while the McDonnell engineers on the ground worked the problem. Grissom would have to keep an eye on fuel consumption.

A far more serious malfunction soon emerged: Young noticed his oxygen pressure gauge had fallen abruptly, indicating an immediate hazard if the cause could not be quickly diagnosed. "As we passed the Canary Islands, all hell broke loose," Grissom recalled later.[24] "Look at the cabin pressure!" Young declared at twenty-four minutes into the flight. "Lost a primary converter." Having just settled in, the commander was caught off guard by a potentially serious problem. "Really?" he asked.

Like Grissom, Young knew the spacecraft systems for which he was responsible inside and out. It took Young, himself an engineering test pilot, less than a minute to figure out that a primary DC-to-DC converter that supplied power to the instrument had probably failed. Young switched to a backup power supply, and the gauge returned to normal.

Informed of the falling oxygen pressure, Grissom instinctively closed the visor on his helmet to seal his suit. He immediately realized this was pointless: if the spacecraft environment control system's oxygen pressure was dropping, his suit also was connected to it. "It won't make any difference; you've already had it," he realized. Embarrassed, he raised his visor. "John was smarter than I was," Grissom admitted later. Young let it slide.

Problem solved, Grissom informed Cooper via a relay station in Nigeria of the power converter failure. The capsule communicator then passed along some suggestions from the engineers on the ground about what to do next about the thruster problem. Ground controllers were concerned that pulsing the attitude thrusters to correct yaw drift would drain the fuel supply. Indeed, preserving propellant was a priority on practically every Gemini flight.

As the mission checklist required, the crew radioed that they had dutifully activated a science experiment to test how sea urchin eggs fertilized in space would react in zero gravity. Grissom considered the experiment a needless pain in the neck, especially on an engineering test flight. He managed to get other planned experiments dropped from the mission, but he was unable to keep the sea urchin eggs off his ship. While he told ground controllers the experiment was under way, he did not report that he had broken a knob that activated the experiment. (A scientist duplicating the experiment on the ground had done the same.[25])

Molly Brown soon crossed the evening terminator into darkness over East Africa. The crew soon began seeing lightning flashes in the night sky. "Hey! We're coming in on the night side. Look at that night come up," the commander declared. "There is lightning out there. Look at that stuff going by. Oh boy! Really does sparkle, doesn't it?" Young agreed but was more interested in stargazing as they headed out in darkness over the Indian Ocean, later spotting the Southern Cross, Alpha Centuri, and Beta Centuri: "Look at that! It's beautiful!" the rookie marveled. Grissom registered his surprise at not seeing as many stars as they expected. Still, he noted, "It's really black out there."[26]

The flight surgeons were soon pestering Gemini Flight Director Christopher Kraft for a medical update on the astronauts. Hence, Young was momentarily preoccupied with checking his blood pressure and temperature so the NASA doctors could determine how they were adapting to weightlessness. Grissom had trouble getting a special blood pressure bulb attached to his suit and relayed little or no medical data during the flight.

As the next relay station came into range, the crew returned to the problem of fixing the spacecraft's leftward drift. Grissom continued to use his hand controller to correct the unwanted motion. Later during the first ninety-minute orbit, Grissom stole another moment to look out his window, telling capsule communicator Pete Conrad, stationed in Carnarvon, Australia: "I can see very clearly the lights of Perth." Cooper, who two years earlier had had plenty of time to appreciate the view from orbit, mentioned later to Grissom, "Pretty spectacular up there, huh?" Grissom replied, "Yea, it really is, it really is." Grissom took in the view for a few seconds, and then continued, "We didn't get to see much of the States though."

The crew volunteered precious little information about their impressions to ground controllers, who, according to the *New York Times* account of this flight, "found it hard to prod Major Grissom into conversation." Indeed, Cooper, Conrad, and other capsule communicators had to continually prompt the crew to talk to controllers. Evert Clark, the *New York Times* reporter covering the flight, noted in his dispatch that one reason for the radio silence "was that both men had full work programs. Another was that test pilots are not given to talkativeness in flight, and Major Grissom is one of the best examples of that."[27]

The constant back and forth between Grissom and Young as captured by the onboard voice recorders gave a much more vivid impression of what it was like to fly in space. "You can really tell you're moving on. You know that?" Grissom noted. As they flew backward, or blunt-end forward, Young replied, "Never a doubt."

The impatient Kraft instructed Cooper to draw out of Grissom the commander's overall impressions of the Gemini control system. Kraft was also fending off the flight surgeons, who were clamoring for more blood pressure readings. Young dutifully recorded his and reported that they could not get a reading from Grissom's cuff. When Conrad relayed a request from the flight surgeons for an evaluation on prepared foods, the commander shot back: "No time! We'll see them when we get back."

"John and I weren't quite as fascinated with sea urchins and space food as we were by the chance to carry out some real space 'firsts,'" Grissom wrote later, understating his utter distain for science experiments and flight surgeons during what he viewed as an shakedown mission.[28]

Conrad soon passed along the news Grissom and Young wanted to hear: they were a "go" for a second orbit. That meant they would be able to perform the first real space maneuvers of the Space Age. With most of the spacecraft systems operating nominally, the crew now prepared for what came to be known as the "Texas burn," a thruster firing over the Lone Star State that would circularize *Molly Brown*'s orbit. The maneuver was one of several planned "burns" using the OAMS thrusters that were critical steps toward reaching the moon and coming back.

Despite their many space firsts, culminating in Leonov's spacewalk, the Soviets had only demonstrated the capability of launching spacecraft that could do little more than carry cosmonauts into space and return them. Before Gemini, it was the same for the Americans. "You've got to remember, Mercury was not a maneuverable vehicle," Kraft noted years later. "It could go up and come down, and that's all. It had no maneuvering capability."[29] By contrast, the eighteen-and-half-foot-long Gemini spacecraft, with its thrusters and other systems, was three times more complex than Mercury.

At the end of the first orbit, one hour and thirty-two minutes into the flight of *Molly Brown*, Grissom cancelled the yaw drift with the maneuvering thrusters to hold the forward-facing spacecraft steady. He was then ready to perform a "translational" maneuver over Texas that would roughly circularize his spacecraft's orbit at 98 miles at its low point by a maximum of 106 miles. The seventy-three-second burn slowed the spacecraft by forty-eight feet per second, thereby lowering its orbit.

Timing the burn, Grissom reported, "Mark!" as he ignited the forward-firing thrusters. Young reported they were functioning properly, oddly making no noise, but he could see them firing. Grissom had manually entered the desired velocity change into the spacecraft's speedometer, the Incremental Velocity Indicator. "Thrusting complete," he reported when the indicator reached zero. The capsule communicator over Texas was Roger Chaffee, a Purdue alumnus and future member of Grissom's *Apollo 1* crew.

With the new orbit confirmed, Grissom had become the first space-man to change his path through the heavens. "The longer we flew, the more jubilant we felt," he recalled after the flight.

In darkness over the Indian Ocean, Grissom performed the second of three OAMS burns, a "translational maneuver" increasing the spacecraft's velocity by about ten feet per second. The twelve-second burn pushed *Molly Brown's* flight path about a mile and a half from its original course. He then fired several short bursts to turn the spacecraft onto a course roughly par-allel to its original one. The spacecraft's inclination relative to the equator had been altered by two-hundredths of a degree to the north.

Today, such a maneuver would be considered routine. In March 1965, it represented a breakthrough in the history of manned space-flight: at two hours and seventeen minutes into the flight of *Gemini 3*, astronauts replaced Sir Isaac Newton in the driver's seat and changed the orbital path of their spacecraft. With Grissom at the controls of a ship he had been instrumental in designing, the first major step in getting to the moon, the rudimentary maneuvers needed to rendezvous with another spacecraft were accomplished.

Just over one hour and forty-four minutes into the first manned Gemini flight, another controlled experiment on the mission checklist was designed to test space food. Along with prepared meals in squeeze tubes and small food packets that included hot dogs, chicken legs, brownies, and applesauce, the copilot had brought along one other item.

The first orbital maneuver complete, Grissom asked Young: "Let's see, do you want your meal?" as he hustled to stay on the mission timeline. "Hot dog! Good old food," the copilot replied. Grissom asked for some juice, and then turned his attention to other chores such as recording a time check from ground controllers.

Then, at one hour and fifty-two minutes mission elapsed time, the offi-cial NASA transcript records the surprised commander of the spaceship *Molly Brown* asking: "What is it?" One could almost imagine Grissom's eyes widening. "You care for a corned beef sandwich, skipper?" the puckish

Southern Indiana, just beyond the city limits of Mitchell, Gus Grissom's home-town. Young Virgil likely took in similar rural scenes as he peddled his bicycle out to the country home of his high school sweetheart and future wife Betty Moore. (George Leopold)

Virgil Grissom's boyhood home at 715 Baker Street (later renamed West Grissom Avenue), a few blocks south of Mitchell's Main Street. Dennis and Cecile Grissom raised four children in the modest but comfortable wood-frame home. (George Leopold)

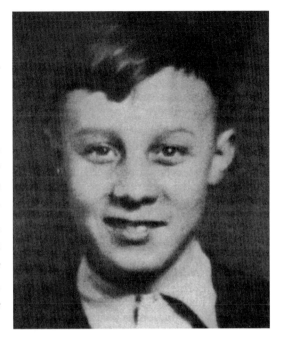

Virgil Grissom, class picture, 1939. The town librarian recalled that Dennis Grissom's eldest son possessed his father's demeanor, unassuming but with a "sparkle" that somehow made them both stand out. (Mitchell, Indiana, Junior High School)

Newlyweds Virgil and Betty Grissom before setting off for a brief honeymoon in Indianapolis in July 1945 while Virgil was on leave from the US Army Air Corps. (Erma Massey Thompson Family)

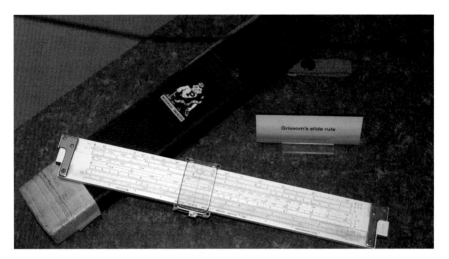

The Purdue engineering student's well-worn slide rule. (George Leopold)

"Mars here we come." Grissom with fellow air cadet Joe Dreyer at Randolph Air Force Base in 1950. The roommates joked that the headgear and goggles worn during flight training made them look like "men from space," recalled Dreyer. "It was a little prophetic." (Alfred Joe Dreyer)

Air cadet Grissom at the controls of a T-6 *Texan* trainer, a demanding aircraft that took a while for him to master. (Alfred Joe Dreyer)

Captain James Horowitz, the West Point graduate who drank beer and played softball with Gus Grissom at stateside air bases and in Korea. The air war over Korea forged the novelist, James Salter, Horowitz's pen name. Grissom's Apollo crewmate Ed White was under Salter's command in Europe. Horowitz/Salter walked away from a promising Air Force career to produce the finest writing about pilots and airplanes since the French aviation pioneer Antoine de Saint-Exupéry. (US Air Force)

Pilot Grissom in Korea in 1952. Jeep bears the logo of Grissom's unit, the 334th Fighter Squadron. The "Fighting Eagles" were among the most aggressive and decorated outfits of the Korean War. (Rex Anderson via Sun Newspapers)

Air cadet Grissom, Randolph Air Force Base, May 1950. (Alfred Joe Dreyer)

The flight line at Kimpo Air Base, better known as K-14. Wingman Gus Grissom was shot at by MiG pilots and occasionally had an opportunity to shoot back. Unlike some of his future astronaut colleagues, Grissom never recorded a kill. The intense feeling of being in the crosshairs nevertheless proved unforgettable. (US Air Force)

Lieutenant Grissom, November 1954, the Korean War veteran with 132 combat hours under his belt accumulated during 100 missions. Grissom volunteered for 25 more, but the Air Force sent him home to be a flight instructor. Training new pilots often proved as dangerous as combat. A year later, Captain Grissom would head back to school to study aeronautical engineering. (US Air Force)

GRISSOM
VIRGIL I
22450 A

Class 56D graduated from the US Air Force Experimental Test Flight School in April 1957. Gus Grissom is front row, center, in a class picture taken on the flight line at Edwards Air Force Base in California. Fellow astronaut Leroy Gordon Cooper is far left, first row. (Air Force Test Center History Office)

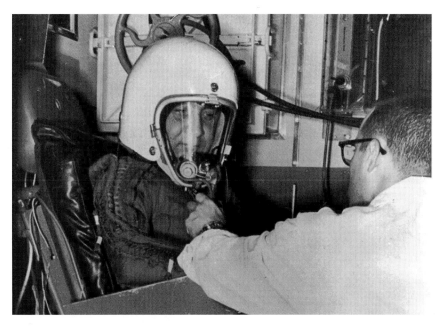

The test pilot checks out an early Air Force pressure suit. (Air Force Test Center History Office)

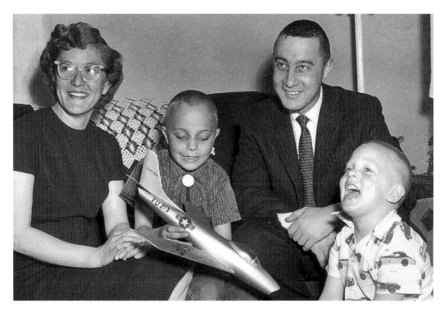

The Grissoms shortly after Gus was selected as a Mercury astronaut. Scotty holds a model of his father's F-86 as Mark mugs for the cameras. (NASA)

The second American in space prepares to fly. (NASA)

John Glenn helps Grissom wedge into *Liberty Bell 7* in July 1961. After splashdown, Grissom would somehow thrust his body through the narrow opening when the hatch blew and the cockpit filled with water and sank. (NASA)

The pilot of *Liberty Bell 7* reviews his checklist before the hatch is sealed. (NASA)

Mercury-Redstone 4 finally lifts off from Pad 5 at Cape Canaveral on the morning of July 21, 1961. (NASA)

Liberty Bell 7 climbs off the launchpad. (NASA)

Lieutenant John Reinhard, copilot of the prime recovery helicopter, lowers a recovery line to the struggling astronaut after managing to snag the spacecraft. The closest witness, Reinhard believed electrostatic discharge from the helicopter caused Grissom's hatch to blow prematurely. (NASA)

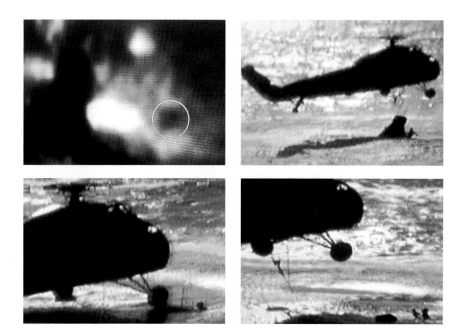

Extreme close-ups of NASA recovery footage showing the precise instant *Liberty Bell 7*'s hatch unexpectedly blew off (circle indicates hatch), forcing astronaut Grissom to scramble through the narrow hatch opening and into the Atlantic Ocean. Once in the water, Grissom assisted the recovery crew in latching onto the swamped spacecraft while simultaneously fighting to stay afloat. Finally hooked, Grissom signals the recovery crew with a "thumbs-up" to hoist his ship from the ocean. The astronaut fought the swells for nearly five minutes before a second helicopter moved in to finally pluck him from the water. Despite Grissom's efforts, his spacecraft sank and the astronaut suffered the consequences of losing his ship. (Rick Boos/NASA)

The recovery helicopter attempts to salvage the waterlogged *Liberty Bell 7* as the swamped pilot struggles to stay afloat. Grissom would eventually be flown to the USS *Randolph*, left, for debriefing. (NASA)

The humiliating end to the otherwise successful flight of *Liberty Bell 7*. The astronaut is hoisted aboard a backup recovery helicopter as his ship sinks in sixteen thousand feet of ocean. The botched recovery was the defining event of Gus Grissom's flying career. (NASA)

The exhausted, angry astronaut is escorted to a debriefing aboard the recovery ship USS *Randolph*. (NASA)

Back at Cape Canaveral, the astronaut and his family face the reporters probing to find out what happened at the end of his flight. Grissom answered all their questions, paying a steep price for his candor. NASA administrator James Webb observes the proceedings. (NASA)

Betty and Scott endure the formal postflight press conference in Cocoa Beach during which Gus acknowledges he was "scared." The reporters and a future writer misinterpreted the admission: Grissom feared drowning as his pressure suit lost buoyancy, taking on water as he fought to stay afloat. Had he feared flying—particularly the ballistic trajectory he had just survived—Grissom never would have volunteered for the astronaut corps. (NASA)

Grissom understood the public relations demands placed on him as an astronaut/celebrity but could not resist the temptation to crudely vent his true feelings toward the media in a photograph taken after the second astronaut group was selected in September 1962. Gordon Cooper drives through the security gate at Cape Canaveral. Seated in the front passenger seat is astronaut Elliot See; a mildly amused Neil Armstrong is next to Grissom. (Imgur)

The five-foot, seven-inch Grissom, wearing headgear fashioned by the training instructor, far right, strikes a Napoleonic pose during jungle survival training in 1963. Grissom possessed a mischievous sense of humor and loved a good joke. He immediately hit it off with his future Gemini crewmate John Young, second from right. Project Mercury veterans Gordon Cooper and Wally Schirra (with camera) observe the proceedings along with Ed White, third from right, who would die with Grissom aboard *Apollo 1* three-and-a-half years later. (NASA)

President John F. Kennedy tours the new Moonport at Cape Canaveral with astronauts Cooper and Grissom one week before his assassination in Dallas. (John F. Kennedy Presidential Library)

Grissom and NASA test pilot Milt Thompson pose with the Parasev 1-A prototype at the NASA Flight Research Center in the California desert, October 1962. Charting a comeback, Grissom returned to his test pilot roots to wring out the contraption as a replacement for parachute landings. His astronaut colleagues shot down the idea. (NASA)

The command pilot for the first two-man Gemini mission prepares for a communications test in early 1965 on the spacecraft widely known as the "Gus Mobile." (NASA)

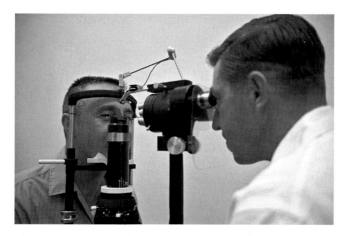

Grissom submits to an eye test during the run-up to his Gemini mission in March 1965. Like most of the astronauts, he instinctively distrusted the flight surgeons who had grounded his close friends Alan Shepard and Deke Slayton. "It'll be a cold day in hell when Gus Grissom calls for a doctor," one flight surgeon noted. (NASA)

Grissom (in raft) and John Young practice recovery procedures for their Gemini flight. (NASA)

The incomparable John Young, the only astronaut to fly in space with Gus Grissom, made certain no one forgot his mentor's contributions to the Space Race. Young would fly twice during Gemini, twice more to the moon on Apollo, and twice again on the space shuttle, including the extremely risky maiden flight. (NASA)

Grissom and Young prepare for the liftoff of the first American two-man space-craft in March 1965. Grissom would become the first human to fly twice in space. Young would fly five more times, including two trips to the moon. (NASA)

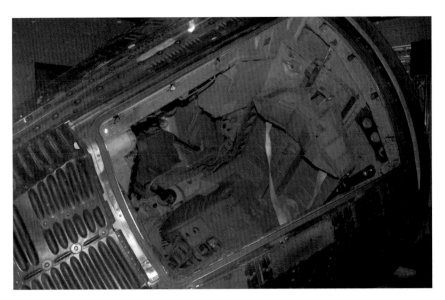

The cockpit of Grissom's *Gemini 3* spacecraft, *Molly Brown*, is currently displayed at the Virgil I. "Gus" Grissom Memorial Museum near Mitchell, Indiana. Grissom fired thrusters using the center control stick to become the first spacefarer to change his orbital path through space. The first human to fly twice in space also is credited with overseeing the design of Gemini's modular components. (George Leopold)

The crew of *Apollo 1* inspects their ship, Spacecraft 012, on the assembly floor at the North American Aviation plant in Downey, California. The Block I Apollo spacecraft would be shipped to Cape Canaveral in mid-1966 despite a long list of teething problems. It was then up to Commander Grissom to find a way to make it flightworthy. (NASA)

Gallows humor as the crew of *Apollo 1* posed for a preflight publicity picture. By the end of 1966, Grissom and his crew understood they had a deeply flawed machine on their hands. Still, a groupthink mentality known as "Go Fever" pervaded the entire Apollo program. The crew gambled they could engineer the flaws out of their ship despite fatal design decisions made at the beginning of the decade. (NASA)

Commander Grissom, his crew, and technicians walk across the Pad 34 service tower support arm to the Apollo spacecraft for the fateful plugs-out test with hatches sealed on January 27, 1967. (NASA)

The incinerated cockpit of *Apollo 1* in a photo taken after the crew was removed and before the command module was detached from its booster for inspection by investigators. The white hoses are ruptured oxygen lines that were connected to the astronauts' pressure suits during a launchpad dress rehearsal. Gus Grissom was seated on the left side, Ed White in the center coach, and Roger Chaffee on the right. (NASA)

A NASA investigator examines the inner (right) and outer (left) hatches of the *Apollo 1* spacecraft. Before succumbing to dense, toxic smoke and blowtorch-like flames, White and Grissom actually made progress retracting the dogleg locking bars seen at the top of the inverted inner hatch. The outer, or ablative, hatch bore scorch marks on both sides indicating the inner hatch seal was likely broken, allowing hot gases to escape. Grissom and his crew fought to the end to get out. (NASA)

Gus Grissom's casket borne by military honor guard to a waiting hearse on January 29, 1967. The bodies of the *Apollo 1* crew were later flown by air force transport for the burials at Arlington National Cemetery. Ed White was buried at West Point after astronaut Frank Borman intervened on behalf of White's family. (US Air Force)

The end of everything: Betty Grissom seethes as the burial detail folds the American flag over her husband's coffin during the military funeral at Arlington National Cemetery in January 1967. (*Life*)

President Lyndon B. Johnson offers condolences to Dennis Grissom at the conclusion of the burial ceremony at Arlington. Betty, left, holds the flag from her husband's coffin. Cecile Grissom, seated on the right, later said her son gave his life so mankind could reach the moon. (NASA)

Betty and Mark Grissom at the Virgil I. Grissom Memorial Museum in July 2011. The *Gemini 3* spacecraft is in the background. (George Leopold)

Betty and Mark during an *Apollo 1* memorial service at Cape Canaveral's abandoned Pad 34 in January 2014. (Lloyd Behrendt)

Young shot back. "Where did *that* come from?" the puzzled but mildly amused commander inquired, adding later, "If I could have fallen out of my couch, I would have." "I brought it with me," the pilot deadpanned, not mentioning for the record that he had smuggled the sandwich aboard in the pocket of his space suit with the help of backup crew members Schirra and Stafford. "Let's see how it tastes," Young urged. "Smells, doesn't it?"

Grissom took a bite out of the corned beef on rye. Crumbs immediately began floating around the cramped cabin, which was beginning to smell like the kitchen at Wolfie's, a delicatessen on North Atlantic Avenue in Cocoa Beach, the source of what came to be known as the "non-man-rated" sandwich.

Grissom played along with Schirra's "gotcha" for about ten seconds, and then decided, "It's breaking up. I'm going to stick it in my pocket." The prank ended. "It was a thought, anyway. Not a very good one," acknowledged Young. "Pretty good, though, if it would just hold together," allowed Grissom. The lunch conversation high over the Atlantic next turned to Young's noisy eating and the quality of the applesauce. "If we had some pork chops to go with it, we'd be all right."

The two astronauts who got along famously throughout months of intense training and the four-hour-and-fifty-three-minute flight of *Molly Brown* would catch hell later for the prank. NASA officials were livid when the unscheduled lunch was disclosed. Tom Stafford recalled that NASA administrator James Webb was "pissed" because, after word of the prank spread, angry lawmakers did not complain first to him but had instead questioned NASA officials in Florida.[30] How could these guys have smuggled a corned beef on rye sandwich aboard a spaceship on its maiden flight? Young would be reprimanded; Grissom laughed it off as an innocent prank.

Eventually, the crew was flabbergasted over the fuss being made about the space sandwich. Besides, Young joked years later, he hadn't even brought along mustard and a pickle! In fact, this was not the first snack smuggled aboard an American spacecraft: Schirra had left a surprise care package in Cooper's Mercury ship. "I didn't think it was any big deal," Young recalled. But once the press got a "whiff of the corned beef," the angry congressman thought the astronauts had failed in their duty to test expensive space food. Moreover, Young recalled, "The politicians saw [the incident] as a symbol of guys doing something that the big bosses [like Webb] didn't know they were doing, and they wondered what else was going on in the space program that they didn't know about."[31]

Before the crew knew it, *Molly Brown*'s journey was coming to a bumpy climax. Near the end of their last pass over Carnarvon, Conrad inquired: "Okay, Gus. I have only one question for you before you go out of range. How's the flying up there?" Without hesitating, Grissom replied, "Great!"

The crew had earlier slowed their spacecraft to ensure they would return to Earth in case *Molly Brown*'s braking rockets failed. As they prepared for retrofire and reentry, Grissom asked Young if he had his seat belt and shoulder harness secured. Not wanting to come down, Young replied, "Can you take it around a couple more times?" Later, Young told President Johnson during a congratulatory phone call between the White House and the recovery ship: "Oh boy! The only thing wrong with [the flight was] it didn't last long enough."[32]

While setting up the retrofire sequence that would slow the spacecraft for its fiery return, Grissom initially had trouble finding the horizon so he could line up his ship at the proper attitude. Finally, at four hours and fifteen minutes mission elapsed time: "Man! There's the horizon and it is beautiful."

Seventeen minutes later, Grissom released the adapter sections prior to the start of reentry. This was another new step in the return to Earth. The commander noted that the crew could really feel the explosive bolts that separated the adaptor section from the crew cabin.

Over California, Grissom fired the spacecraft's four braking rockets for 109 seconds to reduce its altitude to about fifty miles. "An automatic superfine retrofire down the line," Young confirmed.

Grissom jettisoned the spacecraft's retrorocket section and prepared to attempt another first: a controlled reentry of a spacecraft using Gemini's lifting capability. The spacecraft's center of gravity had been offset, allowing the pilot to bank during reentry to give the spacecraft a small amount of aerodynamic lift. This made it possible to steer the returning spacecraft to its splashdown target. Grissom began using bank angle commands from his onboard computer to bring *Molly Brown* down in the Atlantic as close as possible to the recovery forces. He was using his thrusters to bank left, and then right, later reversing the angles to adjust the craft's "lift vector" and steer toward the target, the USS *Intrepid*, stationed in the Atlantic off the Grand Turk Islands in the Bahamas.

On the ground, Cooper was also attempting to pass along reverse bank angles as the spacecraft was entering the atmosphere, but communications were poor. What Grissom and Young did not know at the time was the wind tunnel tests on the lifting capacity of the descending spacecraft had been overestimated by the spacecraft designers. Grissom and Young would splashdown sixty miles from their intended target.

Young said they found out later: "We had a thirty percent reduction in the lift-to-drag ratio which is why we landed sixty miles short of the target. We would have landed during reentry a hundred and ninety miles short, but Gus made up one hundred and thirty miles of it."

Young later admitted that "reentry could have gone a little better" but noted the crew was allotted only two weeks to train using the best NASA estimate of the lift-to-drag ratio, something that made a Gemini reentry a "brand-new thing." The goal was to show Gemini's capacity for a "lifting reentry," Young said. "We proved that."[33]

The copilot was understandably defensive about overshooting the recovery zone since some contemporaneous reports and official summaries of the mission left the strong impression the off-target landing was Grissom's fault. "All primary objectives were achieved except the controlled reentry objective was only partially achieved," a NASA mission summary states. "The angle of attack during reentry was lower than expected." But the mission summaries failed to note that the spacecraft test engineers had literally given the crew a "bum steer."[34] After all, the crew was testing a new spacecraft, and the point was to uncover any engineering miscalculation that would be corrected on future flights.

Along with the sea urchin eggs experiment and another testing the combined effects of weightlessness and radiation on human blood, Young now began a third experiment: he would squirt small amounts of water into the plasma of ionized air surrounding the reentering spacecraft. The intent was to determine if water had any beneficial effect on communications, which are lost for several minutes as spacecraft crash into Earth's atmosphere. The test proved inconclusive.

As Grissom maneuvered the spacecraft, the expected reentry communications blackout began, lasting for several minutes. Back in contact
with the ground and about seven minutes from splashdown at eighty thousand feet, Grissom radioed, erroneously, it turned out: "My needles show
us about 25 miles short" of the intended splashdown target. The drogue
parachutes that would begin slowing the spacecraft descent opened on
schedule. Then, the recovery forces aboard the USS *Intrepid*[35] informed the
crew they would land "five miles ahead" of the recovery ship. The result was
general confusion about precisely where *Molly Brown* would come down.
The spacecraft eventually splashed down east of Bermuda.

As *Molly Brown* plunged through the atmosphere, it began "really
oscillating" through forty thousand feet, the crew reported. Just under five
minutes from hitting the water, the main parachutes opened on schedule
and the crew shortly received an unexpected jolt. The chutes were designed
with a two-point suspension system so that the spacecraft would snap from
a nose-up to a forty-five-degree landing attitude when the chutes filled. "It
snapped all right," Grissom reported.

"Oh man!" both astronauts exclaimed as they were pitched forward
against the windows as if the spacecraft had just hit a tree. "That was the
roughest one of the whole bunch, wasn't it?" the momentarily stunned
commander observed. Grissom hit so hard that his helmet visor cracked.
Young's was scratched when it struck a protruding bracket extension.
Despite the hundreds of simulations, no one had thought to test what
would happen to the crew when the landing attitude system was activated. Later Gemini crews tightened their seatbelts in advance of
the violent pitch forward.

After regaining their equilibrium, Young asked Grissom if he had
maintained his grip on the D-ring that would activate the ejection system
in case the main chutes did not open. "You better believe it!" Grissom
replied.

The smell of smoking thrusters and reentry system fuel began to seep
into the cabin, prompting the crew to close what was left of their faceplates. Grissom told Young to be "ready to hit" the water. *Molly Brown*
splashed down at 2:18 p.m. eastern time. Virgil I. Grissom would never
fly again in space.

The commander faced one more challenge, the last echo of misfortune from the end of his Mercury flight: The landing parachutes had caught in the wind and dragged the spacecraft underwater. Instead of blue sky, Grissom was looking at water. "In all honesty," he reflected, "my first thought was, 'Oh my God, here we go again!'" Then, gathering himself, trusting in the spacecraft that he had helped shape, Grissom realized he had not cut loose the parachute that was dragging them below the surface like a submarine. He reached out and activated the release that would right the spacecraft: "Remembering that prematurely blown hatch on my *Liberty Bell 7*, it took all the nerve I could muster to reach out and trigger the parachute-release mechanism."[36] With the chutes free, the ship bobbed to the surface like a cork.

Pitching and rolling in the Atlantic, the cabin now hot as hell, the commander lost his lunch before the recovery forces arrived. With his sea legs and a cast iron stomach, Young barely held onto his.[37]

Finally, the commander broadcast, "This is *Molly Brown* in the water. Anyone read?" Mindful no doubt of what had happened on his first flight, he added, "We're floating well in the water." Their landing point was fifty-eight miles northwest of the recovery ship.

It was a triumphant return to the carrier USS *Intrepid* about an hour after *Molly Brown*'s splashdown. The recovery helicopter delivered the crew to the flight deck at 3:30 p.m. eastern time, their spacesuits removed in the hot spacecraft and winched up in their long johns. Grissom and Young wore navy-issue blue bathrobes and walked across the deck in their stocking feet. The returning heroes looked like convalescing hospital patients as they emerged from the helicopter to greet the captain and crew. No matter. Gus Grissom, now the first human being to fly twice in space, was beaming in his bathrobe.

Changed into his blue NASA flight suit, the commander later inspected *Molly Brown* in the carrier hangar. He looked pleased with himself and relieved to see his spacecraft safely aboard. It was a good day's work, the best day of Grissom's flying career.

The front page of the next day's edition of the *New York Times* carried a banner headline that was the exact opposite in tone of the one that had followed Gus Grissom's Mercury flight nearly four years before: "Grissom Maneuvers the Gemini as He and Young Make 3 Orbits in Test for a Space Rendezvous." The four-column photo under the headline showed a jubilant Grissom on the deck of the recovery ship. "The *Gemini 3* opened a new era in man's use of space, as Major Grissom flew it with its nose forward and backward and upside down and changed its flight path in three different ways on a three-orbit journey," the newspaper reported. Another front-page story quoted President Johnson as greeting the commander during a congratulatory phone call: "Gus? How are you?" Farther down the front page was a related item that illustrated the growing momentum of the American space program: "Ranger 9 to Hit the Moon Today."[38]

From March 1965 through December 1966, NASA launched ten Gemini flights, each building on the success of the previous mission. The result was a string of space spectaculars that vaulted the United States into an insurmountable lead in the race to the moon. Soviet cosmonaut Leonov performed the world's first spacewalk in March 1965, but America's spacewalk was far more ambitious, with the joyful Ed White tethered outside his *Gemini 4* spacecraft for twenty-three minutes. Capcom Grissom at the new Manned Spaceflight Center in Houston had to help coax his future crewmate back inside.

Next came a long-duration flight by Gordon Cooper and rookie Pete Conrad that tested fuel cells and the crew's ability to sit in the phone booth–like cabin for more than a week. Grissom again served as capcom, this time at the renamed Cape Kennedy. After *Gemini 5*, Grissom and Young remained in the crew rotation as backups on the next two-man flight, but by then Grissom understood he would not get another Gemini flight. Crew assignments were precious, and new astronaut classes needed flight experience. As with Project Mercury before, Grissom now turned his full attention to Project Apollo.

The first launch attempt of the *Gemini 6* almost ended in disaster. Its *Titan II* booster shut down a split second after the engines ignited, the consequence of the premature separation of an electrical umbilical cord. The engines roared, orange exhaust billowing, then shut down a second later. Everyone held their breath. Commander Wally Schirra, the coolest of customers, sat tight rather than pulling the D-ring that would have ejected him and Stafford. "We're just sitting here breathing," he finally told mission controllers when the abort was confirmed.

The mission goal was a "closed-loop" rendezvous with an unmanned Agena target vehicle that failed to reach orbit. There were further launch delays and no time to prepare another rendezvous target. Rather than scrapping the mission, Gemini managers decided to launch the next mission in the series and use *Gemini 7* as Schirra's rendezvous target.

The out-of-sequence launches of *Gemini 7* and the renamed *6-A* mission ended with the world's first meet-up in space. Schirra and Stafford tracked down and flew in formation for several hours with the *Gemini 7* crew, Frank Borman and Jim Lovell. Borman had gained a command after being bumped from Grissom's crew. Their rendezvous mission accomplished, Schirra and Stafford headed home while Borman and Lovell remained in orbit, breaking an endurance record on a flight that Lovell described as akin to "two weeks in the Men's Room."

A respected NASA test pilot and former navy aviator named Neil Armstrong and his air force copilot David Scott would become the first crew to rendezvous and dock with another spacecraft, an unmanned Agena, during the harrowing flight of *Gemini 8* in March 1966. After docking, the crew immediately ran into serious problems when a stuck thruster spun them end over end at a rate that eventually reached one revolution per second. Nearly blacking out, Armstrong undocked, which only increased the spacecraft's rotation, eventually using his reentry thrusters to regain control. By mission rules, the stopgap maneuver effectively ended the flight. Armstrong and Scott splashed down at the first available location near Okinawa, far from their intended landing point. But they managed to survive the first real crisis in space. Armstrong's coolness under pressure would not go unnoticed in Houston, although some of his astronaut colleagues whispered behind his back that he had screwed up.

Armstrong had served as capcom in Hawaii during the flight of *Molly Brown*. Grissom took time during the hectic reentry maneuvers to relay information to his friend Armstrong, whom he referred to during the air-to-ground conversations as "Neil" rather than "Hawaii Capcom." Little did the two Purdue graduates know that years later, the university's engineering buildings would bear their names.

Copilot Scott never got to make his scheduled spacewalk, but more "extravehicular activities" followed as NASA looked for ways to work in space. Space walkers Eugene Cernan (*Gemini 9*), Michael Collins (who flew with Young on *Gemini 10*), and Richard Gordon (*Gemini 11*) struggled mightily to develop the techniques needed to work in space. Cernan and Gordon quickly exhausted themselves, eventually being commanded back into their cabins. By contrast, Collins's tethered walk in space went off more or less as planned. He was able to retrieve an instrument from the unmanned Agena with which Young had docked. Unlike the spectacular footage of White's spacewalk, there is no photographic record of Collins floating in space; his camera drifted away before he could retrieve it.

The takeaway from these initial excursions outside the spacecraft underscored the reality that NASA still did not understand how to work in space. A team worked out space-walking techniques that were practiced by an air force colonel working at a NASA training facility complete with a huge swimming pool called a neutral buoyancy tank. Edwin "Buzz" Aldrin spent months in the tank developing the foot and handholds astronauts would need to accomplish meaningful work in space. His nearly two-hour *Gemini 12* spacewalk in November 1966 aboard a ship commanded by Lovell showed that astronauts could function efficiently while tethered to the spacecraft if they carefully planned each task, using foot and hand restraints to counteract the effects of weightlessness.

Aldrin, derisively known as "Doctor Rendezvous" for his obsession with orbital mechanics as a doctoral candidate at the Massachusetts Institute of Technology, would eventually be named to an Apollo backup crew and was perfectly positioned in Deke Slayton's crew rotation schedule to be one of the first astronauts to land on the moon. Aldrin and Grissom had both flown F-86s in combat during the Korean War. Aldrin seldom passed up an opportunity to mention his two MiG "kills" in aerial combat.

During the astronaut candidate's initial NASA interviews, Grissom told Aldrin he needed no résumé. He was wearing all of his aeronautical accomplishments on his air force uniform.

Grissom, unfairly perceived as a screwup after his first spaceflight, was hailed as a hero after his second. The astronaut and his family at last received the recognition that Betty, and perhaps Gus, yearned for: a call from President Johnson, a rain-soaked parade in New York City with Vice President Hubert Humphrey, and accolades for Grissom and Young, now the seventh American to fly in space. Once the cheering died down, Young would be reprimanded for the corned beef sandwich prank.

The postflight victory lap continued on to Washington, where politicians anxious to be seen with the new space heroes courted Grissom and Young. Among them was Lee Hamilton, a newly elected Indiana representative whose district included Mitchell and Lawrence County. Hamilton recalled a fellow Hoosier at the top of his game after the historic Gemini flight. Grissom "radiated competence," recalled Hamilton, who had witnessed the *Gemini 3* launch. "Obviously he was very good at what he did."[39]

Grissom was now the hottest ticket in the capital. As a result, Hamilton never got the chance to sit down with the astronaut to talk at length about his Purdue days (Hamilton was an Indiana University graduate) or the future of the American space program. To the young congressman, it seemed as if everyone was now behind the American space effort.

"I met him several times," Hamilton remembered from his office at the Indiana University campus in Bloomington, "although never for what I would call extended conversations and never alone, always in a group, sometimes a large group. I did have an opportunity on several occasions to chat with him briefly. My impressions were, first of all, that he was not a big man, he was very compact and strong. He was very, very pleasant, he [was] very *down to earth*."

Who among the larger-than-life astronauts could claim that, particularly the first one to fly twice in space? "I had enormous admiration for Gus," the retired statesman continued. "I was captivated by the excitement of the space program. All Hoosiers were very proud of their contributions to the space program and still are, I believe."

Hamilton also sensed the enormous pressure the astronauts were under, particularly the Mercury Seven. "It was a very different time then; there was great enthusiasm for the space program, great attention upon it," Hamilton reflected. "Rarely did you hear criticisms of it. It was a popular program, a very visible program; the astronauts were national heroes. All of that has changed over the years of course as it's lost some of its visibility."[40]

After ten successful Gemini missions, space flight now seemed routine. *Titan II* rockets, with their distinctive orange clouds of smoke and thrust, were hurtling astronauts into orbit every six weeks or so. NASA was on a roll, leaving the Soviets in its wake. After a precision docking with their Agena target vehicle on the first orbit of the *Gemini 11* mission, Conrad and Gordon used the spacecraft's engine to boost their orbit to a record-breaking altitude of over 850 miles. NASA was literally reaching new heights with every mission.

But something else was happening. Hubris was slowly seeping into the ranks of the space agency and its growing list of contractors as they scrambled to complete one manned program while getting the final act, Apollo, off the ground. Earth orbit was one thing, but going to the moon was an order of magnitude riskier and dangerous. It meant humans would for the first time leave the planet for another object in the sky. Something called "Go Fever" began to permeate the ranks of astronauts, technocrats, and engineers. From Wernher von Braun down to the lowliest technician, everyone wanted to get to the moon before President Kennedy's end-of-the-decade deadline.

The Apollo program, which had been gearing up since the fateful engineering decisions of the early 1960s, was next. Apollo prime contractor North American Aviation was starting to deliver early Apollo spacecraft designated Block I. Fabrication commenced in August 1965 on the first manned Apollo command module, designated Spacecraft 012. A year later, it was hastily shipped to the Kennedy Space Center. The spacecraft was a tangled mess when it arrived for testing. The list of fixes and modifications to the three-man ship grew by the day. Repair kits had to be prepared and shipped to the Cape in order to fix problems. Pressed to stay on schedule, NASA managers allowed North American Aviation to deliver a vehicle that was not flightworthy.

Nearly everyone working on Apollo was now in what Christopher Kraft later described as a "goddamned hurry," including Grissom, the commander of the first Apollo mission scheduled for early 1967. Corners were being cut, test results overlooked. Death was lurking, but no one bothered to notice.

In the afterglow of Gemini, things began moving very fast on Apollo, so fast that the NASA and North American Aviation engineers were having difficulty finding the time to sift through reams of test data, if they found the time at all. Had they stopped to take the time, future Apollo flight controller Gene Kranz acknowledged later, they would have reached the conclusion that NASA had no business putting three men on the first Apollo spacecraft. It was a fatal mistake that would take three lives, haunt three families, destroy many careers, and force a national reassessment of whether the risks inherent in sending humans into space were worth the terrible price.

Almost exactly one year after *Molly Brown* splashed down in the Atlantic Ocean, Grissom was introduced, on March 21, 1966, as the commander of the first Apollo flight. The plum assignment was perhaps the crowning achievement of Grissom's flying career. His crew included spacewalker Ed White and rookie astronaut and naval aviator Roger Chaffee.[41]

The maiden voyage of any ship is risky. So too is the prestige conferred on those who assume the risk and fly the ship. Grissom and his crew would soon discover they had a mess on their hands, a spacecraft built by a new contractor supervised by a space agency that was putting schedule ahead of crew safety. Grissom, White, and Chaffee would pay the ultimate price for assuming those risks. Among them, only Grissom fully comprehended the stakes. He chose to continue.

11

RISK AND REWARD

*I had come very close to achieving the self that is based on the risking of every-
thing, going where others would not go, giving what they would not give.*
—James Salter[1]

*The rate of progress is proportional to the risk encountered . . . but to
limit the progress in the name of eliminating risk is no virtue.*
—Neil Armstrong

The object of taking a risk, of being audacious, is to gain, to advance, to
progress. Gus Grissom risked everything and lost. Humankind benefited immeasurably. Grissom's family and the families of his crew were
left to deal with the consequences.

Failure in a risky endeavor exacts a steep price. Through the sacrifice
of Grissom, White, and Chaffee, we all gained. Humans reached another
world, an inevitable step in human history though not necessary for our survival. It was there, so we went. What mattered in the end was that human
beings gazed out the windows of their small spacecraft, awed by what they
saw. Then, they aimed their cameras back at Earth to show humanity for the
first time what our precious home looked like suspended in the firmament.
It was America's greatest technological achievement. It would not have
happened without the sacrifice of Virgil Ivan Grissom and his crewmates.

The reward for Grissom's calculated risk was a gift to humanity like no other in our history: the chance to see the whole circle of the earth, to at last appreciate all that we have here on the third planet from the sun.

Risks can be great or small. When Americans became the first from our planet to step foot on the lunar surface, the meticulous and supremely competent commander of *Apollo 11* decided then and there—238,000 miles from home—to depart from his detailed mission checklist to inspect a nearby crater. He recognized there was indeed "new knowledge to be gained," just as a young president had said seven years earlier.[2] "I candidly admit that I knowingly and deliberately left the planned working area out of TV coverage to examine and photograph the interior crater walls for possible bedrock exposure or other useful information. I felt the potential gain was worth the risk."[3]

Neil Armstrong, the utterly conservative midwestern engineer trained at the most traditional of engineering schools, Purdue University, fully appreciated the risks of walking on the lunar surface enclosed in an untried spacesuit in the vacuum of space. Nearing the end of mankind's first exploration of the lunar surface, the explorer remembered spotting Little West Crater during the final, hair-raising moments of the *Apollo 11* lunar descent, a landing perhaps only he could have pulled off. Standing on the ancient lava flows of the Sea of Tranquility, Armstrong decided that the crater beyond the view of mission controllers was undoubtedly worth examining.

Armstrong sauntered over for a look, snapped some pictures to document the area around the eighty-foot-diameter crater, and then retrieved a bit of the regolith, the lunar soil for which he and Aldrin had come. With the pressure of the mission checklist unrelenting, he hustled back to his lander. It was said later that Armstrong had brought back one of the most scientifically valuable collections of lunar material of any of the moonwalkers.

Armstrong's excursion to a small impact crater in the moon's surface seems trivial today. Not so at the time. The considerable risks embraced during the previous eight years, including the deaths of twelve astronauts and cosmonauts, had delivered Armstrong and Buzz Aldrin to the Sea of Tranquility in that magical summer of 1969. Armstrong, finding himself at what today we call the "network edge," independently decided to mosey over to the biggest crater near his landing site, an area about the size of a city block, to discover what geological secrets it held. It was the same impulse that sends a youngster deeper into the woods to find out what's over the next hill. The difference was that the explorer was walking on another world.

Armstrong understood at that instant of command prerogative and minor rebellion that examining Little West Crater about two hundred feet east of the *Apollo 11* lunar lander *Eagle* was the reason he had risked his neck to come all that way, unsure whether the machine that delivered him would also return him to Earth. Calculation made, he reckoned the brief excursion in the near perfect and deadly vacuum of the lunar surface, with its temperature swings of two hundred degrees Fahrenheit, was unquestionably worth the gamble.

Eighteen months later, during the third successful lunar landing, Gus Grissom's Mercury rival and buddy Alan Shepard would be hitting golf balls in the Fra Mauro highlands west of Tranquility Base. Walking on the moon had become routine despite the incalculable dangers.

The approach of the American space program in the 1960s to risk and reward is scarce today. It has become far easier to play it safe. The brokers on Wall Street tend only to take risks with other peoples' money. This aversion to risk has stifled innovation, and with it, human progress.

Apollo was a "time when we made bold moves," two-time lunar explorer Jim Lovell has noted. Astronaut Lovell was referring to the decision a year and a half after the deaths of the *Apollo 1* crew to circumnavigate the moon aboard a gigantic rocket no human had yet flown. In many ways, the flight of *Apollo 8* was a stunt, albeit an extremely risky one. It nevertheless provided humanity with its first Kodachrome view of what our home really looked like hanging by a thread in the blackness of space.

The images captured by Lovell and his crewmates forever changed our perspective on Earth's place in the universe. The explorers had for the first time in human history *left* the Earth. Leaving was what Apollo was about. The blue marble called Earth was alone in an unimaginably vast, blacker-than-black universe. Lovell's crewmate Bill Anders realized as he gazed out his spacecraft window that he was looking at roughly half the known universe, and there was no frame around what he was trying to take in.[4] It was Anders who snapped the iconic earthrise picture that became the "whole earth" metaphor for human space exploration.

The Apollo explorers stood on the shoulders of the early astronauts and cosmonauts who summoned the courage to climb atop unpredictable rockets and ride them into space. Approaching the eighty-three-foot-high Redstone rocket, complete with a Mercury spacecraft erected in front of the Kennedy Space Center press center at Cape Canaveral, one cannot help but realize that climbing on top of the hissing machine took guts.

The Mercury Seven astronauts had taken their cue from President John F. Kennedy. The president's declaration shortly after Alan Shepard's successful suborbital flight to send men to the moon and return them safely to Earth by the end of the decade represented one of the great political risks of the twentieth century. In his special message to a Joint Session of Congress on May 25, 1961, twenty days after Shepard's fifteen-minute suborbital hop, Kennedy acknowledged the stakes: "We take an additional risk by making [spaceflights] in full view of the world, but as shown by the feat of Astronaut Shepard, this very risk enhances our stature when we are successful."

JFK was legendary for his risky personal behavior, but his willingness to roll the dice extended well beyond his public life to include confronting and managing his own fragile health. Against the stern advice of his father, Ambassador Joseph P. Kennedy, Massachusetts Senator John Kennedy decided in 1954 to undergo extremely risky spinal fusion surgery to relieve unrelenting chronic back pain caused by collapsed vertebrae. The procedure was deemed all the more risky because Kennedy was suffering from Addison's disease. Combined with the long-term effects of corticosteroid treatments that were effectively collapsing his back through osteoporosis, JFK's immune system was suppressed. That left him prone to infection after the delicate surgery. Faced with the prospect of a life in extreme pain and the certainty that he would eventually become incapacitated, Kennedy resisted the advice of his iron-willed father and went ahead with the spinal fusion surgery.

Despite expected complications like severe infections and an adverse reaction to a transfusion that laid him up for months, the surgery enabled

Kennedy to continue his career in the Senate, run a nonstop presidential campaign in the late 1950s and early 1960s, and maintain an unrelenting presidential schedule through the darkest days of the Cold War.

A key battleground of that "long twilight struggle" was the contest to conquer space. "Surely the opening vistas of space promise high costs and hardships, as well as high reward," JFK told the spellbound crowd at Rice University Stadium on a sweltering September morning in 1962, enumerating in stirring imagery how and why humans should go to the moon.

JFK's character traits, among them fierce independence, stoic suffering, supreme self-confidence, and a willingness to take personal and political risks, were not lost on the new astronauts. Nor were the consequences, which culminated in Kennedy's assassination while riding in an open car through an American city that was clearly hostile to the president of the United States.

The American space program and a race to the moon also fit nicely with Kennedy's passion for manly pursuits and risk taking. The president was said to be fascinated with counterinsurgency and the Green Berets. He also appeared during his brief presidency to have been intensely interested in the progress of Wernher von Braun's rocketeers working first at Huntsville, Alabama, and later at Cape Canaveral. Kennedy was keenly aware that the Soviets possessed powerful rockets and that the United States would remain behind in the space race unless and until von Braun's team could build, test, and launch something bigger than the Atlas rockets used in the Mercury program.

Unlike today, taking risks at the dawn of the 1960s was widely seen as the best way to move the nation forward into what Kennedy called the "New Frontier." A critical component of this preassassination vision of the future was "the uncharted areas of science and space." This was to become the underlying narrative of the American space program.

JFK was a risk taker, often reckless, and he was endlessly fascinated with the seven charismatic astronauts who embodied his approach to life: pushing the envelope, and then bringing your ship back in one piece.

A photograph of JFK, Gus Grissom, and Gordon Cooper at Cape Canaveral a week before the assassination in Dallas illustrated how the lives of the astronauts were intertwined with the president who had elevated them to the status of national heroes. Indeed, Grissom and the president were linked in the sense that death was stalking both men. Just over three years after Kennedy was killed, Grissom and his crewmates would die in the *Apollo 1* fire. Like Kennedy, the astronauts had weighed the odds, decided they could beat them, but lost.

A few days after the launchpad fire, the bugler would again play "Taps" at Arlington National Cemetery as the "missing man" formation of jets roared overhead. Like JFK, Gus Grissom would be martyred.

Of the original Mercury astronauts, the future US Senator John Glenn was closest to the Kennedy clan. Glenn, who was portrayed in a March 1961 *Life* magazine article as "an unswerving and self-denying man," articulated his reasons for risking "hat, tail and gas mask on something like this."

"With risks you gain," *Life* writer Loudon Wainwright quoted Glenn as saying. "I've got a theory about this. People are afraid of the future, of the unknown. If a man faces up to it and takes the dare of the future, he can have some control over his destiny. That's an exciting idea to me, better than waiting with everybody else to see what's going to happen."[5]

The *Life* article also tagged Glenn, Shepard, and Grissom as the "Astronaut First Team," the New Frontiersmen anointed to lead the US comeback in space against the Soviets. The magazine's editors did not yet know in late winter of 1961 that Shepard had already been selected to fly the first Mercury mission. A month before the stunning, historic flight of Soviet cosmonaut Yuri Gagarin, Shepard's mission remained a good bet to be the first time a human would fly in space.

It was Grissom, of course, who was inextricably linked with the notion that the benefits of manned space exploration were "worth the risk." Grissom's high school and college buddy Bill Head paused years later to remember the *Apollo 1* fire, sighed, and concluded, "It was a shock in one sense. And in another sense, he knew the risk. He knew it."[6] Indeed, Grissom was keenly aware that the longer he remained on the "flight line," the greater the odds he would "buy the farm." This was especially true for a Korean War veteran, Air Force flight instructor, and test pilot who would become the first man to fly twice in space.

In his 1956 Korean War novel, *The Hunters*, novelist and former Air Force fighter pilot James Salter's alter ego, Captain Cleve Connell, recalls a member of his squadron shot down in a dog fight with Soviet MiGs, and then contemplates the nearness of violent death: "Death could be slighted or even ignored close by; but when the time came to meet it unexpectedly, no man could find it in himself not to cry silently or aloud for just one more reprieve to keep the world from ending."[7] The desperate cries of the doomed *Apollo 1* astronauts yelling "Fire!" and "We're burning up!" on the evening of January 27, 1967, lend credence to Salter's grim observation.

The years of nonstop training were meant to reduce risk, "to keep the world from ending." To narrow the chances of an accident, test pilots seek to limit the number of things that could go wrong, to gain some sort of advantage in an inherently dicey enterprise, to manage risk. These traits were identified and highlighted by those who selected the Mercury astronauts in 1959. "Danger is admitted, but de-emphasized—most feel nothing will happen to them," Air Force doctors concluded in their final report to the new space agency on the Mercury candidates. "But this seems to be less a wishful fantasy than a conviction that accidents can be avoided by knowledge and caution. They believe that risks are minimized [through] thorough planning and conservatism. Very few fit the popular concept of the daredevil test pilot."[8]

Recalling what it felt like sitting on top of the Saturn V moon rocket loaded with 5.6 million pounds of highly explosive propellant (or 960,000 gallons), *Apollo 12* command module pilot Richard Gordon emphasized: "Here we are, we spend all our lives in a risk environment. You acknowledge that fact going in and you don't dwell on it, you don't let it bother you. If the damned thing blows up you're gonna be dead. That's the least of the consequences, I'd rather do that than get smashed up and spend the rest of my life as an invalid."[9] Gordon's crewmate, Alan Bean, added: "If you are not willing to take some risks as an astronaut, you're in the wrong business."

During the Gemini program, Grissom had been intimately involved in nearly every aspect of spacecraft design and testing. Equally important, he had the ear of prime contractor McDonnell Aircraft's senior management, including "Mr. Mac," company founder James S. McDonnell. "On Mercury or Gemini, if there was a problem, he'd go right to Mr. Mac and it got fixed," recalled Lowell Grissom, who worked at McDonnell Aircraft as a junior systems analyst—"way down on the totem pole." At the beginning of the Apollo program, Lowell noted: "There wasn't that kind of a relationship at [spacecraft prime contractor] North American. It was so fragmented, so many people thought they were in charge, I guess, and there was nobody to go to. There were a lot of problems."[10]

By 1966, Gus Grissom found himself in unfamiliar territory in his career-long duel with risk. With the entire Apollo program now firmly in the grip of "Go Fever" even as the list of problems with his spacecraft grew longer by the day, Grissom was being forced to accept far more uncertainty than at any time as a fighter pilot, an experimental test pilot, or as an astronaut. He nevertheless tried in television network interviews before the scheduled flight of *Apollo 1* in February 1967 to downplay those risks, telling ABC science reporter Jules Bergman:

Oh, I doubt that I have any philosophy towards the danger. I recognize that, that there is some risk, but, uh, we just try to take as much out as we can during the pre-testing to make sure the systems are good. We recognize that there are unknowns, and things can happen that we haven't planned for. But I try to take care of this by leaving an open mind and trying not to let the fellas [White and Chaffee] get stereotyped in malfunction procedures and the way we do things, and make sure that, at least try to make sure, that they don't do anything impulsively. If we get a noise or something happens, why, "Take a check," take time to see what we're doing and make sure that every time they move a switch or push a button that they look, they have the right one, you know, that there is none of this blindfold cockpit business.[11]

Many of the beat reporters at the Cape understood that Grissom was deeply concerned about the condition of his Apollo spacecraft, among the first off the production line at North American Aviation. When asked again about the dangers associated with the upcoming Apollo mission, Grissom told Nelson Benton of CBS: "You sort of have to put that out of your mind. There's always a possibility that you can have a catastrophic failure, of course; this can happen on any flight; it can happen on the last one as well as the first one. So, you just plan as best you can to take care of all these eventualities, and you get a well-trained crew and you go fly."[12]

Among the reasons for what was increasingly sounding like resignation on the part of the Apollo crew was the fact that many key design decisions for the Apollo spacecraft, most notably the inward-opening hatch and the use of a pure oxygen atmosphere in the cabin, were made long before Grissom was assigned in March 1966 to command the first Apollo flight. For the first Apollo crew, the order-of-magnitude increase in technological complexity and inherent risks associated with the original, or Block I, Apollo spacecraft turned out to be much greater than anything Grissom had encountered during his air force test pilot days. Those risks, and the unrelenting pace of the Apollo schedule, would ultimately prove deadly. They would also confirm Grissom's grim prediction about what could happen to an astronaut who rolled the dice once too often. After all, recalled Bean, some astronauts simply quit, not wanting to push their luck. (Bean's *Apollo 12* commander Pete Conrad argued you couldn't quit until surviving your second flight to avoid the second guessers: "If you quit after the first one, they'll say it scared you to death, and you didn't want to go back. So you have to make a second flight."[13])

"We were willing to risk our lives to do that," the astronaut-turned-artist Bean explained during a 2009 exhibit of his Apollo paintings at the National Air and Space Museum in Washington, DC. During the opening of the exhibit, Bean turned and looked up at a self-portrait on the lunar surface as he recalled his walk on the moon. "We knew if the little old ladies who sewed that suit up, and I met them up in Delaware at the suit place, if they didn't sew those suits right and glue 'em, we were dead," pointing toward the sky. "So everybody that went out in space in that little spaceship, 240,000 miles away, knew our neck was out a long way. But we thought the game was worth the risk."[14]

In the late 1950s when NASA summoned 110 American test pilots to the Pentagon to discuss something called Project Mercury, most of the candidates and certainly the seven men ultimately selected understood the dangers. For them, the risk wasn't necessarily a rocket blowing up. Advanced fighter jets could be just as lethal as riding a rocket into space. All the candidates were used to that kind of danger and most embraced it. Rather, the risk perceived by the astronaut candidates standing at the threshold of the Space Age was whether it was worth endangering military careers to pursue some ill-defined scheme to send Americans into Earth orbit and beyond. Alan Shepard was on the fast track to becoming an admiral. Grissom, Schirra, and other candidates were hotshot test pilots climbing to the top of the "Right Stuff" pyramid. The naval aviators among the candidates gathered in a hotel room after the secret NASA briefing to consider the risks to their military careers. It took only a few hours and a couple of stiff drinks for all of them to decide they wanted to be part of Project Mercury.

In the earliest days of the Space Race, the Mercury program managers struggled to come up with a meaningful assessment of the risks associated with flying in space. They had little to nothing on which to base their judgments. Robert Gilruth, the head of the new Space Task Group, had a saying, according to his deputy Charles Donlan: "'We try and plan for the unknowns. It's the unknown unknowns that you have concerns about.' And that's what you're talking about, when you're talking about risk assessment."[15]

Grissom claimed later that he knew instantly that the Mercury program "was for [him]" and that space represented the future of test piloting.[16] But he had earlier acknowledged skepticism about the program. "A lot of people—including me—thought the project sounded a little too much like a stunt instead of a serious research program." If Mercury did not pan out as planned, the up-and-coming test pilot worried that he might return to the Air Force a few years later as a "green hand," back at the end of the line.[17]

Grissom later came around to the view that "the best way to face an unknown is to find out all you can about it in advance."[18] Those words appeared under Grissom's byline in an admiring 1961 book copublished by *Life* magazine. The statement was surely wordsmithed by *Life* ghostwriter Loudon Wainwright, who had unparalleled access to the Mercury astronauts thanks to the magazine's exclusive publishing deal with NASA. As we shall see, other remarks attributed to Grissom after his death—particularly lofty statements about the nature of risk—may also have been embellished.

Still, that single sentence describing the rationale behind the Space Race also distilled Grissom's approach to human frailty, risk, and confronting the unknown. More than any of the Mercury astronauts, Grissom candidly discussed his fears and those of his Mercury teammates. After the loss of *Liberty Bell 7*, Grissom paid a steep price for his candor. That lesson shaped his relationship with the media and the public for the rest of his short life.

Having staked out his position on facing the unknown, Grissom continued: "That's what we're doing for the flights in space—studying, perfecting our equipment, learning all we possibly can about the [Mercury] mission before we embark on it."

General Chuck Yeager, the war hero and legendary test pilot who broke the sound barrier in 1947, had many opportunities to contemplate the consequences of risk. Yeager had preceded Grissom at Wright Field just after World War II. There, the fighter ace proved himself time and again to be not only a first-rate test pilot but an aircraft maintenance expert. Yeager instinctively understood how flying machines worked, and that test pilots could never "wing it." "All pilots take chances from time to time," he wrote in his 1985 autobiography, "but knowing—not guessing—about what you can risk is often the difference between getting away with it or drilling a fifty-foot hole in mother earth."[19]

In the earliest days of supersonic flight, there was another consideration. Preparing to fly the Bell X-1 rocket plane beyond the mythical speed of sound, Yeager was confronted by his commanding officer about an additional hazard in selecting a test pilot with a family. The young captain rolled the dice and challenged the formidable Air Force commander Colonel Albert Boyd, himself a first-rate test pilot.

"Don't you agree that the selection of a pilot who has a wife and children would be simply adding to the risk?" inquired Colonel Boyd, probing to gauge how Yeager would respond. Sitting across Boyd's desk with the colonel's deputy present, Yeager screwed up his courage and replied, "No, sir, I do not agree with that." Challenged again, Yeager fumbled for a response as he sought a way to hang onto his plum assignment flying the fastest aircraft in the sky. The impatient Colonel Boyd continued, "Why don't you agree that your having a family, Yeager, would add to this project's already considerable risk?"

Cornered, the West Virginia country boy somehow found a way to make his commander understand why the risk was acceptable: "My being married and having responsibility should be in my favor, sir," Yeager countered as if engaged in the verbal equivalent of aerial combat. "Having a wife and children has made me more careful as a pilot and not less."

Boyd shot a knowing look at his assistant. "There is an argument I hadn't thought of." Both were again reminded during the grilling that Yeager was the most qualified test pilot on Earth to fly the rocket plane beyond the sound barrier. Pushed to the brink, Yeager had managed to assure his superiors he understood the extreme risks involved.[20] It was the same brand of fighter pilot moxie Grissom displayed a decade later when the NASA flight surgeons diagnosed his hay fever. "There won't be any ragweed pollen in space," he informed the doctors, who quickly dropped their concerns.

On the morning of October 14, 1947, while Grissom had his nose in an engineering textbook at Purdue, Yeager took off on a B-29 bomber carrying his rocket plane. He climbed down into the rocket plane, released it from the bomb bay at 23,000 feet, switched on its four-chamber engine, and at last broke through the storied sound barrier. Bell XS-1 rocket plane Number 1 was named for his wife, "Glamorous Glennis." Yeager was surprised to discover that "punching a hole in the sky" was as "smooth as a baby's bottom."[21]

Yeager recalled decades later that at 10:23 a.m. local time, flying at more than 35,000 feet: "I thought I had broken the Machmeter as it was all screwy going off the scale, which only went to 1.05. I don't think they had a helluva lot of confidence in us. Instead, I broke the sound barrier. Flew past Mach One." His official speed was Mach 1.07, or seven hundred miles per hour.

Yeager had done the hard work, listened, asked questions, and turned the answers over in his head. He understood. He had tamed a beast of an aircraft and in so doing corralled the risk, thereby accomplishing what some believed impossible. It turned out he was also at the right place at the right time. The sonic boom from Yeager's rocket plane reverberated as a shock wave tore across the windy California desert, heralding the beginning of the Space Age. Time and space would never be the same.

Those who followed in Yeager's considerable wake, including the Apollo moonwalkers, agreed with Grissom that they had overcome fear of the unknown through unrelenting training. "The more you train for something and the more you know about it, the more comfortable you are doing it," observed the *Apollo 15* command module pilot Al Worden.

But training, testing, and actually digesting test results was wholly inadequate by the mid-1960s. By then, everyone in the American space agency was in a hurry, focused solely on beating the Soviets to the moon. Walt Cunningham, a member of the backup crew for the first Apollo flight, noted that no one in the Astronaut Office, NASA management, or North America Aviation was willing to be "caught holding the umbrella of delay."[22]

In the midst of training at Cape Canaveral, Grissom was regularly chewing out the engineer in charge of his spacecraft simulator, Riley McCafferty, who was losing the battle of keeping the machine up to date. The simulator, an absolutely vital training tool for a successful flight, frequently had more than one hundred modifications outstanding at any given time. McCafferty had fallen hopelessly behind, prompting Grissom to "tear [his] heart out," the engineer remembered, because he could not keep up with the constant changes to the early Apollo spacecraft.[23]

Reality and the mounting risks were beginning to sink in for the commander of the first Apollo flight. Departing for Cape Canaveral the last week of his life, the embittered, fatalistic Grissom grabbed a lemon off a tree in his yard in Timber Cove, later hanging it on the balky Apollo training simulator in the days before the *Apollo 1* fire. "Leave it there!" he ordered McCafferty.[24] Like the simulator, Grissom's spacecraft, according to Cunningham, was a "piece of junk." But the *Apollo 1* crew's "attitude— and we all shared it—could be characterized as, 'Blow the bolts and we'll do whatever the hell is necessary to make [the mission] a success after we get in the air.'"[25]

Despite the bravado and growing technological arrogance, there were aspects of space flight like the use of pure oxygen in the sealed spacecraft that continually made the astronauts nervous. John Young recalled sitting on Pad 19 on the morning of March 23, 1965, waiting along with Grissom for *Gemini 3* to lift off: "The cabin purge replacing air with pure O_2 made a loud flow noise. My knees started shaking: the use of pure oxygen always worried me," Young said.[26]

Moving in parallel with risk and reward, of course, are statistical probability, fate, chance, and—if it exists—dumb luck. Flight training designed to mitigate risk taught the astronauts not to rely on luck, or, as some call it, the intersection of preparation and opportunity. As he prepared for the April 1981 maiden flight of the space shuttle *Columbia*, a machine that had never been tested in powered flight before its first manned mission, copilot and space rookie Robert Crippen responded to a "good luck" wish for his upcoming flight with Young this way: "Luck has nothing to do with it!"[27]

Was it, as Grissom believed, "worth the risk?" It depends on whom you ask. For those who flew to the moon, undoubtedly it was. Even for the three astronauts killed in the *Apollo 1* death trap, the thought may have crossed their minds in the last few seconds of life that they had had a great ride, but the odds had finally caught up with them in a way they had never expected: a dress rehearsal spacecraft test on the launchpad that was considered routine.

Later, back in Indiana, the stoic Dennis and Cecile Grissom struggled to understand the seemingly unyielding forces that had propelled their eldest child into space yet killed him on, of all places, the launchpad. "My son had to give his life to make [the Apollo spacecraft] better," Cecile told an interviewer after two Apollo crews had landed on the moon and returned to Earth at the end of 1969. The interviewer, veteran war correspondent Robert Sherrod, sensed a "trace of bitterness" in Cecile's response. Summing up the New Year's Eve conversation with Gus's mother, Sherrod noted for the record: "She seemed to be totally mystified about the whole idea of my calling her, and didn't understand the purpose. I think I finally put over an explanation."[28] Perhaps, but the explanation did not change the fact that Cecile and Dennis Grissom had outlived their eldest son.[29]

NASA's attitude toward risk has evolved over more than half a century of human spaceflight. The fire that killed Grissom and his crew transformed the space agency and its contractors in ways they never expected, paradoxically paving the way for the first moon landings in the late 1960s. The exploding oxygen tank that almost doomed the crew of *Apollo 13* in 1970 forced another risk reassessment that, along with budget cuts, led to the cancellation of at least three lunar landing missions. NASA senior managers concluded that the space agency would be pushing its luck by continuing beyond the final lunar landing, *Apollo 17*, in December 1972.

A similar process took place after the space shuttle accidents in January 1986 and February 2003. Each accident was a stark reminder that sending humans into space is a dangerous, accident-prone endeavor.

The same calculations are being made today as NASA launches probes packed with scientific instruments costing billions of dollars. In February 2009, NASA attempted to launch a payload called the Orbiting Carbon Observatory. The satellite was lost when a payload fairing, the clamshell-shaped cover that protected delicate scientific instruments during launch, failed to separate. The mission was a failure, but out of that failure came an opportunity to reassess what had gone wrong and begin the painstaking process of mitigating the risks. Though no one died, the loss of the climate satellite was "heartbreaking," said Ralph Basilio, the NASA Jet Propulsion Laboratory's program manager for the mission. "I'm an engineer. I was trained to solve problems and we walked away with nothing to solve."

Thirteen months later, Basilio's team was back in business, and they began the process of managing the risks of a new mission dubbed Orbiting Carbon Observatory-2. OCO-2 now circles the earth in a polar orbit, measuring carbon in the planet's fragile atmosphere. "If you don't take a risk, you will not reap the rewards," Basilio said. "You may as well stay on the ground and not explore."[30]

That attitude is reminiscent of the thousands of engineers and technicians who helped explorers like Grissom get off the ground, men like Guenter Wendt, the legendary launchpad leader from the glory days of the Mercury program and the historic spaceflights that followed. Wendt, a former *Luftwaffe* technician hired after the war by McDonnell Aircraft, eventually oversaw all American spacecraft preparations on the launchpad. The pad leader is the last person to shake the astronauts' hands before sealing the spacecraft hatch. Then they are on their own.

A mechanical engineer by training—"I knew how things were put together"—Wendt moved steadily through the ranks at McDonnell Aircraft while taking night classes on rocketry and management. He was soon assigned to early rocket testing and eventually launchpad closeout activities at Cape Canaveral. Wendt understood better than most the risks involved in riding rockets. He brooked no interference in his launchpad domain, running a ship so tight that the World War II veteran John Glenn dubbed him "Pad Fuehrer." Wendt took a different view, in essence: "If you follow my rules to the letter, there will be no problems with your launch or your flight."

Remembering the early days of the American program, punctuated by frequent launch disasters, Wendt stressed: "You had to realize you're playing with things that can go wrong in a hurry. I spent many, many nights on the [Banana River] on my boat playing the 'what if' game because there were many, many things we didn't know, and we did dumb things."[31] The only way to reduce the risks was to test the machines, sift through the pieces after an accident, and fix the faulty systems before loading the spacecraft with Gilruth's "precious human cargo."

Before the flight of *Friendship 7*, Annie Glenn asked Wendt whether he could guarantee her husband's safe return: "Annie, anybody that would guarantee that is a liar because there are so many unknowns that nobody can really guarantee a safe return. The only guarantee I can give you is that at the time when I say it is 'Go' there is nothing that I know that could be detrimental to a safe return. Beyond that, I cannot give you any other guarantee."[32]

The contract to build the Apollo spacecraft was awarded to North American Aviation in December 1961, meaning Wendt's duties as McDonnell's pad leader at Cape Canaveral would end with the completion of the Gemini program in November 1966. After the *Apollo 1* fire, Deke Slayton moved immediately to bring back Wendt as a first step toward steadying the reeling space agency. Wendt told an interviewer in 1999: "The fire hit me very hard because when you know the individuals, you know you have horsed around with them, they are your friends." Slayton made sure that North American gave Wendt everything he needed while the Apollo spacecraft was being overhauled. Wendt later came to believe he had been "spared" the torment felt by others over the deaths of his friends, Grissom, White, and Chaffee.

In retirement, Wendt refused to answer the frequently asked question whether he could have prevented the *Apollo 1* disaster. The honest answer, which Wendt undoubtedly understood, was that the fire was perhaps inevitable given the engineering trade-offs about pure oxygen made years earlier. Everyone understood there would be risks, but no one expected a fire to erupt in Wendt's domain: on the launchpad. That they had unknowingly accepted such risks haunted Grissom's friends for the rest of their lives.

Wendt had learned in the earliest days of the Space Race the inherent risks of pure oxygen under pressure, warning his launchpad technicians during tests: "Hey, anybody on the pad, don't smoke for the next four hours because the oxygen saturates your clothes and polyester clothing goes up in flames."

Without the help of careful, meticulous men like Wendt, it was largely up to Grissom to look out for his crew, to enforce a modicum of crew safety, to do all he possibly could to mitigate the risks on his next mission. He tried. He tried his damnedest. In this, Grissom had become a sort of lone wolf. He could not avoid the consequences of bad design decisions made years before. The commander decided to play the hand he had been dealt. Grissom complained loudly about the shoddy Apollo flight simulator but privately told John Young he could do nothing about the spacecraft's miles of faulty wiring, the likely ignition source of the fire that killed him and his crewmates.

The senior American astronaut with visions of being the first man on the moon weighed the risks and decided to fly his deathtrap of a spacecraft. If, as the Apollo flight controller Gene Kranz famously asserted, failure was not an option, neither in early 1967 was delay. The fatalist resolved to make lemonade out of the lemon that was his ship.

Weighing the risks as well as the rewards, Gus Grissom chose to continue. He was backed into a corner. It proved to be the worst decision of his brief life.

12

HOW ASTRONAUTS TALK

Manned spaceflight has produced many memorable phrases since humans starting riding rockets in the early 1960s: "That's one small step for man, one giant leap for mankind"; "OK, Houston, we've had a problem!"; and "From the crew of *Apollo 8*, we close with good night, good luck, a Merry Christmas—and God bless all of you, all of you on the good Earth."

Nearly every historical account of the life and career of Virgil I. Grissom cites a three-sentence quotation nearly perfect in its symmetry and undeniable in its logic. The words are variously reported to have been spoken in the weeks either before the *Apollo 1* fire or, perhaps, during a preflight press conference before or shortly after his Gemini flight in March 1965. The words are universally cited as foreshowing the Apollo crew's demise. Indeed, nearly every account of the launchpad fire and Grissom's star-crossed career includes the following quote for the ages: "If we die, we want people to accept it. We're in a risky business, and we hope that if anything happens to us it will not delay the program. The conquest of space is worth the risk of life."

To this day, it remains unclear when, where, and to whom Gus Grissom spoke these inspiring words, if in fact he spoke them at all. On several occasions, Grissom expressed similar sentiments about the risks and rewards of manned spaceflight, in written and spoken form. But given that he is forever linked with this thirty-nine-word statement, one that has become Gus Grissom's epitaph, it is incumbent on anyone seeking to understand Grissom and his place in the history of human spaceflight to track down the origin of these words.

NASA's History Office in Washington, DC, has no record of the quote's origin. The History Office at NASA's Johnson Space Center in Houston cites journalist James Schefter's 1999 book, *The Race*, which attributes the Grissom quote to a 1966 interview with the Associated Press aerospace reporter Howard Benedict.[1] (Schefter died in 2001, Benedict in 2005.) The AP has no record of the quotation in Benedict's voluminous files on the early days of the US space program. The wire service also could find no stories by Benedict containing the quote. Some wonder whether Grissom actually spoke the words universally attributed to him. "That's not how astronauts talk," noted the moonwalker Alan Bean.[2]

Several veteran reporters who covered Apollo also expressed skepticism about the origins of the "worth the risk" quote attributed to Grissom but stop short of saying it was manufactured for public relations purposes. Paul Recer of the Associated Press and others noted that journalists in the heady days of Mercury, Gemini, and Apollo were not above sprucing up a disjointed remark to make it sound better to readers who couldn't get enough of the astronauts. While Grissom was certainly capable (on the rare occasions he had time to reflect) of turning a memorable phrase, there was another side of him the public rarely saw. This was the one-upmanship and verbal jousting among the astronauts, particularly among the "gotcha"-loving Mercury Seven.

Bean recalled a meeting shortly after being accepted into the astronaut corps in 1963, a period when he mostly kept his mouth shut, listened, and observed. Alan Shepard, then head of the Astronaut Office, opened the proceedings one morning by reading aloud a newspaper article referring to his fellow astronaut as the "monk-like Gus Grissom." Continuing the razzing of his friend and rival, Shepard pressed Grissom on why the newspapers insisted on always describing him this way. Not missing a beat, Grissom replied, "I think it's because I say 'goddamn' so much."

Unlike most of the sophomoric pranks the Mercury astronauts played on one another, a ritual Bean acknowledged he did not really understand, the future *Apollo 12* lunar module pilot remembered getting a kick out of Grissom's comeback to Shepard. "That was funny," Bean recalled.[3]

Funny, of course, because it revealed a sharp wit able to parry and thrust with the best of them, particularly when confronted by the surly Shepard, the first American in space, who was now grounded with an inner ear condition. Grissom would not call attention to himself; neither would he be anyone's fool, whether he was racing Corvettes down the main drag in Cocoa Beach or matching wits with Shepard in a conference room full of highly competitive astronauts.

During an *Apollo 1* preflight press conference in late 1966, the discussion turned to what would constitute a successful flight—three orbits, six, a day? After Deke Slayton punted on the question, telling reporters it was the Apollo program manager's call, Grissom chimed in: "As far as we're concerned, it's a success if all three of us get back."[4] The auditorium full of reporters erupted in laughter, but the astronaut was only half-joking. He also was sending a message about his deep dissatisfaction with his ship.

The remark reflected Grissom's attitude toward the risky first flight of a spacecraft plagued with problems. Around the same time, the AP's Benedict quoted Grissom as saying there was "a pretty slim chance" his spacecraft would last the maximum two weeks. "This is the first one we've flown," Grissom told Benedict. "We don't know exactly how to budget the consumables such as fuel."[5]

That was the way Grissom talked: no-nonsense, strictly matter-of-fact, nuts-and-bolts stuff. He was not trying for anything pithy or what today would be called a "sound bite." He simply didn't talk that way, on or off the record, which again raises doubts about whether he actually gave Benedict or anyone else the "worth the risk" quote.

So where did it come from? And does it matter if Grissom never actually spoke those thirty-nine iconic words? Perhaps not, but the quote has taken on a life of its own and is deeply rooted in the history of American manned spaceflight. That's why it's important to know how it came about.

Marcia Dunn, who succeeded Benedict as the AP reporter at Cape Canaveral in 1990, spent years poring through Benedict's voluminous files and folders at the AP office at the Kennedy Space Center. "I never spotted any transcribed notes of astronaut interviews, especially from the early days. And I never saw anything pertaining to that quote from Grissom," Dunn said.[6]

The rest of the AP files on the early days of manned space flight are archived at the wire service's headquarters in New York City. A search by archivists there also turned up nothing. Perhaps Benedict recorded Grissom's words in a notebook stored away in a box somewhere, but it has yet to surface.

Making it even harder to track down the origin of the quote, of course, was the fact that Grissom was among the least voluble of the Mercury astronauts. One reason was his service background. He, Deke Slayton, and Gordon Cooper spent many years on the flight line as test pilots. Like all test pilots, they had no use for small talk. It was far better to keep the communication channels open in case something important came up.

Meanwhile, Shepard and Schirra were being groomed as midshipmen at the US Naval Academy. Like the bow-tied John Glenn, both were articulate and, when circumstances called for it, outspoken. The same could be said for Scott Carpenter. Their air force brethren, by contrast, tended to be tight-lipped and circumspect.

"The Navy guys—Al, Wally, Scott, and John (the Marines are part of the Navy)—with their spit and polish and dress blues had a distinct advantage over us Air Force guys," observed Cooper. "Gus, Deke and I came into the program looking like we were straight off the flight line, knocking the desert sand off our old leather jackets and boots."[7]

The way astronauts actually spoke is best summed up by an impromptu pep talk Grissom was compelled to deliver in early 1960 at the General Dynamics Convair plant in San Diego, where the Atlas booster was being built. Eighteen thousand employees had gathered in front of an outdoor stage to see and hear the new astronauts. It is difficult to imagine today how these seven men had come to embody the hopes and fears of an entire nation. A Convair executive asked if one of the astronauts would address the workers. Grissom drew the short straw that day and found himself standing before the huge assemblage hanging on his every word. Abraham Lincoln had found time riding the train from Washington to Gettysburg to compose his immortal two-hundred-and-seventy-two-word address. Grissom had to come up with something between the instant he left his seat on the stage and the moment he reached the microphone.

Still, he managed to formulate in those few seconds what amounted to a call to action that would inspire the entire American space program. Nervously surveying the crowd, Grissom cleared his throat and finally spoke up in his distinctive baritone. "Well," he intoned, "do good work."

Having said what he meant to say, Grissom returned to his seat. His intent was that there would be no misunderstanding about what the astronauts required as they prepared to take on the Soviets for control of the heavens. Unspoken but understood by all was the admonition: It's our hide on the line, so make damned sure the Atlas rocket is tested, retested, and tested again. It must not fail.

Realizing Grissom was finished, his exhortation to "do good work" washed over the throng of aerospace workers. Instantly, eighteen thousand American workers realized this was all that needed to be said. The place erupted in cheers. Posters reproducing Grissom's entire "speech" soon filled the Convair plant. Good work *was* being done, and the Atlas carried four astronauts into orbit.

This was the way the Mercury astronauts really talked, and Grissom's plainspoken manner inspired the engineers and technicians who built the machines that allowed him and his fellow astronauts to begin exploring space. What they were making was no longer just an object. It was now a machine that stood in relation to the world. It would come to symbolize the hopes of an entire Cold War generation. It was a vehicle that would carry, as the astronauts' boss Robert Gilruth described them, "precious human cargo."[8]

Undoubtedly, the press played a central role in shaping—perhaps editing—the words that came out of astronauts' mouths. Recer of the AP confirmed what others later admitted—some of the beat reporters covering the American space program had become advocates, and they thought nothing of putting inspiring and fully formed sentences in the mouths of astronauts. After gaining exclusive rights to the Mercury astronauts' personal stories, veteran *Life* magazine writer Loudon Wainwright acknowledged: "We had virtually abdicated skepticism" in covering the astronauts/heroes.[9] Indeed, Wainwright admitted, *Life*'s editors had become "cheerleaders" for the US space program and its seven new heroes.

The Mercury astronauts were "at various times small-minded, vengeful, crude, boring or even stupid," noted Wainwright—in others words, just like other mortals, except they could land an airplane nearly anywhere.[10] Regardless of whether Grissom actually spoke the words attributed to him, tracing what journalists call "attribution" of the quote illustrates how it was amplified by successive generations of books about the Space Race. For example, the respected space historian Colin Burgess cited Andrew

Chaikin's seminal account titled *A Man on the Moon* as his source of the quote.[11] A check of Chaikin's footnotes attributes the Grissom quote to the *Apollo 11* crew's official account of the lunar landing program.[12] Others attributed it to an Associated Press memorial volume on the first lunar landing.[13]

The words attributed to Grissom did, however, ring true with some of his colleagues. Walt Cunningham dutifully cited them in his insider's account of the Apollo program, and then explained: "Gus was just expressing what we all felt. No other attitude would have been tolerable."[14]

The historical record remains unclear on the question of whether Grissom actually spoke the words that would be widely used to justify the enormous risks—calculated and embraced—at the core of the monumental human effort to leave the planet and explore another world. In the end, after Grissom and his crew had been laid to rest, it was for the living to decide whether they had died in vain. Most concluded they had not.

In his deeds more than his words did Gus Grissom give meaning to the central idea behind the American space effort: "The conquest of space is worth the risk of life."

13

FRONT OF THE LINE

Use me forever,
Use me for rocket fuel;
I'll be air,
I'll be fire.
—*"Engines," lyrics by Arjen Lucassen*

The astronaut and memoirist Walter Cunningham provided a cogent insight into Gus Grissom's work ethic and outlook on life. As the new Apollo spacecraft was being built in the mid-1960s at prime contractor North American Aviation's plant in Downey, California, the veteran and rookie astronauts alike would spend entire weeks on the factory floor monitoring the installation of equipment, often arguing with the engineers over changes they wanted. Cunningham and the other crew members, he recalled, were "engineers and managers without portfolio."[1] The hours were long, the work often monotonous.

Two rookie astronauts, the naval aviator Roger B. Chaffee and air force test pilot Donn F. Eisele, had originally been selected for Grissom's Apollo crew. (The Gemini veteran Edward H. White Jr. would replace Eisele after the rookie was injured in a training accident.) Grissom drove his crew hard but led by example. He was the meticulous engineering test pilot who again had been tapped to command the maiden flight of a new ship. Grissom's place at the top of the astronaut pecking order was not lost on the rest of the astronaut corps.

"You learn a good deal about the thresholds of men in tedious, demanding situations," observed Cunningham, who worked closely with Grissom as a member of what became his Apollo backup crew. Grissom "took his regular turn at both the good and the bad right along with everyone else. He was a hard liver and loved to party, but if Roger Chaffee, the youngest astronaut in the program, was pulling some notably boring duty, you were likely to find Gus sharing it with him."[2]

There had never been a spaceship as complex as Apollo nor one capable of so much. It was Grissom's job to find out if it could fly and bring its crew home. Hence, he seldom let the ship out of his sight. Similarly, Chaffee was known to confront the North American Aviation engineers on the California factory floor with design sketches for fixing a faulty system. Some, like Cunningham, thought these back-of-the-envelope solutions gave the contractor an out if the fix did not solve Chaffee's problem.[3]

It quickly dawned on Grissom that the Apollo prime contractor operated far differently from McDonnell Aircraft, where he could push through design changes by going all the way to the top. The chain of command was clear at McDonnell, which built the Mercury and Gemini spacecraft; at North American Aviation, everything was, according to Lowell Grissom, "fragmented." Lowell's assessment of company management certainly was colored by understandable loyalty to his former employer of twenty-five years, but his judgment also is supported by others as well as by the chain of events that eventually claimed his brother's life.

Gus "did say quite a bit [about the condition of his spacecraft but] North American, they're responsibilities were so fragmented, they just couldn't get things done. You know, there was no 'Mr. Mac' to go to."[4]

North American Aviation won the prime contract to design and manufacture the Apollo command and service modules back in 1961. The service module was a kind of space trailer that carried the propulsion systems and most of the consumables needed to get three astronauts to and from the moon. North American Aviation won the Apollo contract largely on the strength of its highly successful design for the X-15 rocket plane. Though competitors like McDonnell Aircraft and the Martin Company had more experience building spacecraft and rockets, the top brass at NASA were impressed with the legendary X-15, which had carried test pilots to the edge of space. North American Aviation also had excellent political connections in Washington, a fact that played a key role in its selection as Apollo prime contractor.[5]

After Eisele was bumped, the new prime crew for the first Apollo flight was introduced in Houston on March 21, 1966. Commander Gus Grissom's crew now included America's first spacewalker Ed White, who was designated as senior pilot, and rookie Roger Chaffee as pilot. (The astronaut corps frowned on the designation "copilot.") The backup crew assignment for the first Apollo flight was shuffled in December after Wally Schirra convinced his bosses that a repeat of Grissom's shakedown mission was a waste of his time. Schirra's backup crew consisted of Cunningham and Eisele.

Internally, the first flight was designated by NASA as AS-204, as in Apollo-Saturn 204, an Apollo spacecraft launched by an early Saturn rocket dubbed Saturn 1B, not the big moon rocket that was still being built. Grissom fully intended to ride the Saturn V rocket by the end of the decade. The contractor designated Grissom's ship, the first-generation (or Block I) Apollo command module, as Spacecraft 012. The new ship had a truncated cone shape that came to a distinctive point. (A mockup of the spacecraft is on display at the Neil Armstrong Hall of Engineering on the Purdue University campus.) This deeply flawed early version of the Apollo spacecraft would never make it off the ground.

The fundamental difference between the first version and the completely revamped spacecraft that emerged from the *Apollo 1* fire was a heavy, inward-opening hatch the astronauts hated, both because it was hard to crank open and because it eliminated any possibility of spacewalks.[6] A hinged-hatch design was in the works and would be incorporated into a later version of the Apollo command module. The Block I spacecraft was intended primarily to show the ship was flightworthy during long-duration shakedown missions in Earth orbit.

Later flights in a more advanced version of the Apollo spacecraft would be able to dock with a lunar lander, first in Earth orbital test flights and later in lunar orbit. The modular configuration was dictated by a 1962 decision, preceded by a contentious debate, to adopt a risky concept called lunar orbit rendezvous, or LOR, as the flight mode astronauts would use to reach the moon, land, and return home. Risky and controversial, the concept eventually won on the merits: LOR required astronauts to meet up and dock in lunar orbit, a capability NASA had yet to demonstrate, but it also saved money, time, and—most important of all—weight. The alternative to LOR was gigantic, budget-busting rockets. There would have been no moon landings without the modular concept.

These attributes were the currency of the early Apollo program that was moving at an increasingly rapid pace. The lunar rendezvous concept required a combined Apollo command and service modules to extract a lunar module from the Saturn V's third stage en route to the moon. The ships would then fly linked together to lunar orbit. After a moon landing, the lunar and service module would be jettisoned with only the command module carrying the crew back to Earth.

In the early 1960s, no one really knew how to get to the moon and back. Lunar orbit rendezvous was among the riskiest but most ingenious ideas in the history of manned spaceflight, a bold engineering gambit that eventually ensured that the Americans reached the moon by the end of the decade. The mighty Saturn V rocket was huge—363 feet high, as tall as a thirty-six-story building—but without LOR, it would have been much larger, more expensive, and impractical. John Houbolt, the aerospace engineer credited with conceiving the concept, was initially considered a crackpot. When Armstrong and Aldrin landed on the moon in July 1969, Wernher von Braun turned to Houbolt in Houston Mission Control and confessed that the United States would not have reached the moon without the audacious idea.

Deke Slayton, head of the Astronaut Office, and his boss, Robert Gilruth, agreed that a Mercury astronaut would have the first crack at a moon landing. In 1966, that remained wishful thinking: NASA had yet to demonstrate a long list of new capabilities required to get Apollo off the ground, into orbit, and headed to the moon. Grissom was among the early favorites to reach the moon, but many things would have to fall into place before he was in line for a lunar landing, much less the first. The first human to fly twice in space believed there was a chance—however slim—he could be first. This possibility drove his efforts for the remainder of his life.

The Apollo crew assignments were revealed within the Astronaut Office in January 1966. Commanding a crew was about seniority, and Gus Grissom was now the most experienced of the American astronauts. For test pilots, gaining the rare first flight of a new ship was a milestone. Apollo would be Grissom's second in two years. A month later, he was named chief of the Apollo Branch Office. He and his crew immediately began training for the mission that was logged into the flight manifest for the first quarter of 1967.[7] Given the complexity of the new Apollo spacecraft, the flight schedule was extremely demanding—certainly unrealistic. But everyone, including the Apollo commander, was in a hurry.

Grissom was working more closely with rookie Apollo astronauts and was proving easier to get along with than some of the other Mercury and Gemini veterans. Cunningham was pleasantly surprised to find that the Apollo commander was "a decisive guy, a team leader and an independent thinker" who encouraged the younger guys to speak up if they had an idea. However, the long hours and ongoing problems with his Apollo spacecraft and its faulty training simulator were making Grissom increasingly "cranky," Cunningham observed. Even so, the new guys were attracted to his work ethic, his intensity, and his ability to play as hard as he worked. They also noticed, Cunningham recalled, that Grissom "could sit at a bar for hours, and never failed to notice a pretty girl in the room." Grissom "went his own way. He wasn't a hanger-on," deduced Cunningham, who among the Apollo astronauts spent as much time working under Grissom as any of the rookies.[8] Among the newcomers was the US Navy lieutenant commander Roger Chaffee, holder of a bachelor of science degree in aeronautical engineering from Purdue University, class of 1957. Chaffee earned his pilot's license that same year as a naval ROTC air cadet. "It took me four years to learn how little I knew," he recalled after graduation, vowing that he would seize "every opportunity that comes along" to gain experience.[9] Chaffee would learn plenty working with the relentless Grissom.

Initially, his fellow astronauts tended to underestimate the unassuming Chaffee. That quickly changed when they saw him dive headfirst into engineering challenges, pressing the Apollo engineers to fix the communications and other systems he would be responsible for on the craft's maiden flight.

Chaffee and Grissom had much in common. Chaffee was from neighboring Michigan. Both had come from modest, middle-class backgrounds, grown up in small towns, and loved the outdoors and airplanes. Roger's father, Donald, was a barnstorming pilot in the 1930s. Father and son would spend "hours together at the dining room table building model planes and making sure they got each piece just right," Roger's sister, Donna, told an interviewer after Donald's death. "They were always talking aviation."[10]

After graduating from Purdue and flying navy reconnaissance aircraft, Chaffee followed Grissom to the Air Force Institute for Technology at Wright-Patterson to train as a test pilot. Both had two children, and like their crewmate, Ed White, Grissom and Chaffee were ambitious. Chaffee too had his eye on a lunar landing mission.

As he had with John Young during the Gemini program, Grissom would take Chaffee under his wing. The commander would be the first astronaut responsible for the lives of two other crew members. Chaffee had served as one of the capsule communicators during Grissom's Gemini flight. Hence, the Apollo commander knew something of Chaffee's capabilities.

Chaffee worked briefly at Douglas Aircraft in Los Angeles after graduating from Purdue before completing his naval training. In August 1957, the new navy ensign married the Purdue homecoming queen, Martha Horn of Oklahoma. The bride was nineteen, the groom was twenty-two. They had met two years earlier on a blind date. Chaffee characteristically wasted little time in proposing marriage. The new couple lived together briefly in Norfolk, Virginia, before Roger shipped out for flight training. A daughter, Sheryl, was born in November 1958; a son, Stephen, arrived in July 1961.

In 1960, Roger Chaffee was assigned to a photo reconnaissance squadron designated VAP-62. He was soon flying reconnaissance missions over Europe and the Mediterranean in the summer of 1961. During one flight, his aircraft engine began leaking hydraulic fluid. Spraying fluid ignited, but Chaffee was able to isolate the damage and bring his plane back. The aircraft was eventually repaired and returned to service. The aviator's number had come up, and he had walked away in one piece. Chaffee was well liked in his unit, taking some ribbing for his ambition. A unit history described him as "the Beaver," as in eager. He would soon be flying missions at the height of the Cold War. Returning stateside, the squadron's early assignments included aerial photography along the Florida coast from the squadron's base in Jacksonville south to the American base at Guantanamo Bay, Cuba. During one mission, Chaffee was assigned to fly along the Florida coast to make an aerial photo survey of Cape Canaveral. Chaffee's photography was eventually used to help lay out the launchpads used for the American moon landings, as well as Launch Complex 34, the place where Chaffee would be killed less than seven years later.[11]

After flying high-performance aircraft for several years, Roger and Martha began to appreciate the risks involved. "There's only room for one mistake," Donald Chaffee remembered his son saying. "You can buy the farm only once."[12]

The stakes grew more serious as Kennedy and Nikita Khrushchev sparred over Berlin and, by the fall of 1962, Cuba. With the fate of the planet hanging in the balance, Chaffee's squadron was assigned to fly daily reconnaissance missions over Fidel Castro's Cuba. Chaffee was credited with bringing back photographic evidence documenting suspected Soviet nuclear missile installations on the island just ninety miles from Florida.

Like most flyers, Chaffee had been closely monitoring the successes of the Mercury astronauts. Spaceflight was no longer a stunt, and he understood that the future of flight was in orbit and, ultimately, the moon. When asked at the end of each year about his career plans, Chaffee said he wished to train as a test pilot to qualify for astronaut status. At the end of 1962, he accepted an invitation to pursue a master's degree in engineering at the Air Force Institute of Technology at Wright-Patterson Air Force Base, the same school Gus Grissom had attended seven years earlier. The Chaffees moved to Dayton, and Roger became a candidate for astronaut testing. He survived an updated version of the humiliating medical tests the Mercury astronauts endured along with batteries of psychological testing. Outside of a relatively small lung capacity, he came through the testing with flying colors, and then sweated out the final selection process.

While on a brief hunting trip in Michigan, the call came from NASA. On October 18, 1963, Chaffee and thirteen other pilots were named to the third class of astronauts. "The Fourteen" were an outstanding if star-crossed group. Seven would fly to the moon, four would walk on it, and four would be killed in accidents.

Cunningham assessed Chaffee this way: "In the early days, some tended to underestimate Roger, perhaps because of his small stature. But he had the capacity to fill a room—any room. It was impossible to attend a meeting with Roger and not be aware of his presence. He had a fighter pilot attitude, even though [his] brief career was in multi-engine photoreconnaissance aircraft."[13]

When confronted with a problem, Cunningham continued, "Roger would bore right in—even if it was totally outside his expertise. One of the youngest of the third group, he was fearless, confident, bright, with the all-American-boy look and a beautiful wife to boot." Within the NASA hierarchy and the test pilot fraternity, Chaffee was considered a first-rate flyer and among the best in terms of flight preparation. He also possessed a reputation Grissom appreciated: Chaffee "was a real hard-ass," one former NASA flight controller recalled.

Martha Chaffee acknowledged the risk at the time her husband was selected to be an astronaut. "What's familiar doesn't frighten you, but it's only natural to be afraid of the unknown," she told a reporter.[14]

As with everything he undertook, Chaffee dove headfirst into his astronaut career, serving as capsule communicator in Texas during Grissom's Gemini flight. Chaffee and Grissom worked together on the next mission, Ed White's, in June 1965. Chaffee would be passed over during the Gemini program, prompting the Purdue alumnus Eugene Cernan, another member of the third astronaut class, to tag Chaffee as a "nugget," a rookie, who nevertheless "had so impressed our bosses that they assigned him a coveted spot on the first Apollo" mission.[15] While others in his astronaut class had flown on Gemini and walked in space, Chaffee was now in the flight rotation at a spot that could eventually place him on a lunar landing crew. All along, this is what Chaffee had his sights set on. Flying with Grissom could only increase his chances.

The crew selection process was widely considered a mystery to most of the astronauts. Several attempted to parse it in their memoirs. Some, like Gordon Cooper, who had an ax to grind against Alan Shepard and Deke Slayton, insisted that Apollo crews were selected based purely on astronaut office politics. (Shepard gave himself a lunar flight. "Devious Deke," as

Cernan called him, was part of the last crew to fly on Apollo. Cooper got nothing but backup commander assignments after his 120-orbit *Gemini 5* flight in August 1965. He quit NASA and retired from the air force in 1970.)

Grissom understood he had leverage with his air force buddy and hunting companion Slayton, who effectively had the final say on crew assignments. Grissom did not hesitate to use this leverage, just as he had unceremoniously dumped Frank Borman from his Gemini flight in favor of John Young.

With the possible exception of Schirra, who would be the only American astronaut to fly in Mercury, Gemini, and Apollo, all of the astronauts had their eye on a flight to the moon. "You'll be flying along some nights with a full moon," Chaffee told a reporter while training for his Apollo flight. "You're up at 45,000 feet. Up there you can see it like you can't see it down here. It's just the big, bright, clear moon. You look up there and just say to yourself: 'I've got to get up there. I've just got to get one of those flights.'"[16]

A 1966 photo shows Roger Chaffee surrounded by workers at the Grumman Corporation plant on Long Island, where the lunar module was being built. The astronaut asked the assistant plant manager to introduce him to every Grumman employee working to build the ship.

Despite his outward enthusiasm, Chaffee was profoundly aware of the risks inherent in the first flight of a spaceship of unprecedented complexity. During a family visit to the Cape in August 1966, Chaffee confided to his father his growing doubts. Donald Chaffee recalled: "We were walking on the beach, kicking sand, you might say, and Rog said, 'Dad, if anything happens and I buy the farm, I don't want you to be bitter. I want you to do what you can for the space program.'" Taken aback, Donald replied: "Hell Rog, things will go fine," gripping his son on the shoulder. "Everything will be all right; you're going to make it." "No dad," replied the son in earnest, "I'm serious. I want you to do what you can for the space program. I want your word on it." Donald remembered his surprise as Roger grabbed his arm, turned him around, and shook on the pledge. "That was it," the elder Chaffee recalled. "And I kept that promise. But at the time I thought, like everybody else, it was going to be okay."[17]

E d White landed on Grissom's crew after Donn Eisele underwent surgery for a dislocated shoulder suffered during weightlessness training aboard a NASA KC-135 aircraft affectionately known as the "Vomit Comet." White expressed nothing but enthusiasm for the upcoming flight, telling ABC News science correspondent Jules Bergman in the weeks before the scheduled launch: "I always look forward to flying, and I look forward to test flying." He told the *New York Times* that he felt a "deal of great pride" in making the first Apollo flight.

The preflight interview was intended for broadcast while the crew was in orbit. Instead, the interviews with ABC News and the other broadcast networks would serve as remembrances of the dead crew. Bergman introduced White as "afraid of no man . . . our first space walker, who believed so strongly you could feel it in his words."[18]

Indeed, it would be hard to exaggerate the bonds of affection that tied Edward Higgins White II to his family, friends, fellow pilots, and astronauts. The first American to walk in space and the astronaut in the center couch of the *Apollo 1* spacecraft was beloved by all who knew him. "No question, Ed White was as capable as they came," observed fellow astronaut John Young.[19]

The American novelist James Salter held the distinction of having flown with both Gus Grissom in Korea and Ed White in Germany after the Korean War.[20] "Ed White I knew better," Salter said.

He was in the 22nd Fighter Squadron at Bitburg, Germany, with me, 1954 to 1957. I was operations officer and my job was to know him, it was my responsibility to. We had an affinity because of West Point, and I liked his character. I liked him. He had some weaknesses as a pilot when he began in the squadron, but he was the kind of man who corrects them—he was weak in instrument flying, probably because of lack of experience, and there was a lot of bad weather in Germany during the winter especially. As I say, he completely overcame it. He was that very desirable thing, a man who could be relied upon—in every way. [White possessed] high standards and even temperament. They used to say, straight arrow.[21]

Several months after the *Apollo 1* disaster, Salter wrote the widow, Patricia Finnegan White, confiding that he had "dreamed of [Ed] many times," continuing, "he was precious to me. I believed in him. In him I saw myself, what I might have been."

Having known White made Salter "intimate with greatness," he told Pat. "We were convinced he was going to make his mark in history, not the history of his country or even of flight, but the history of mankind."[22]

White was the son of an aeronautics pioneer, US Air Force Major General Edward H. White of Fort Wayne, Indiana. The son followed his father to West Point, where he excelled in engineering and athletics. Ed White barely missed qualifying for the 1952 US Olympic track team.

Selected to the second group of astronauts in September 1962, White quickly became a household name after pushing himself out the narrow hatch of *Gemini 4* on June 3, 1965, three months after the flight of Grissom and Young. Thoroughly enjoying the view, White floated through space while traveling at 17,500 miles per hour. He was fearless, joyful, and extremely reluctant to return to the spacecraft as it passed into the planet's pitch-black shadow. The country was emerging from the horror of President Kennedy's assassination, and the renewed Space Race allowed Americans to again cheer for something. Star-spangled Ed White, floating in the blackness of space, helped his countrymen forget the sorrow of Dallas.

"I feel like a million dollars!" White declared as he floated above the earth, his gold-coated faceplate reflecting the stunning sunlight. White's twenty-one-minute walk was a tour de force, one of the highlights of manned spaceflight. It seemed White was born for this, that for Americans he could be the next John Glenn.

After splashing down, the Gemini explorers were plucked from the sea and delivered safely to the rusting recovery ship, the USS *Kearsage*. White and commander James McDivitt were steaming back to Cape Kennedy at "flank speed." Onboard, NASA flight surgeon Robert Moser couldn't hear a thing aboard the old ship and was having trouble taking blood samples from astronauts. Moser demanded that the ship's captain slow down for five minutes, eliciting looks of disbelief from crewmen. White intervened: "Give the Doc a break, he needs to do his stuff." Moser recalled:

"Magically, the giant bucket of bolts stopped rattling," prompting Moser to conclude that White possessed a rare quality: "Hero power."[23]

In the weeks before the Apollo fire, White told an interviewer: "People might look at our work as being perhaps dangerous, or risky of sorts, but I think we train in it and work in it so much and understand it well enough that we don't look at it from this viewpoint." Echoing Grissom, he continued: "We accept the risks, if there are, what risks there are, and the people we work with do everything that's humanly possible to reduce these risks to as small as possible. I believe very deeply in the people we work with and the crew, I certainly do."[24] There was little doubt that Ed White believed every word.

Of Grissom and White, James Salter observed: "To be killed flying had always been a possibility, but the two of them had somehow moved beyond that. They were already visible in the great photograph of our time, the one called celebrity. Still youthful and so far as I knew, unspoiled, they were like jockeys moving to the post for an event that would mark the century, the race to the moon."[25]

As a fighter pilot who had peered over the abyss and survived, Salter concluded: "The absolutely unforeseen had destroyed them." Grissom called his senior pilot "a real hard driver," adding: "I don't care what kind of job you give Ed, he's going to get it done; he's going to get it finished."[26]

Still, in the weeks before the scheduled launch there was friction between Grissom and his crew as the list of problems with the spacecraft grew ever longer. NASA investigators would acknowledge later that inattention to "mundane but equally vital questions of crew safety" was a root cause of the accident.[27] Indeed, the commander worried incessantly that these "mundane" details were being overlooked, that the crew and the spacecraft technicians were distracted and in too much of a hurry. He downplayed many of these concerns in network interviews, daring not to vent his frustrations in public since the network broadcasts were seen as critical to building public support for the space program. Grissom had long ago figured out how the public relations game was played, and he approached it on his own terms.

In the months before the Apollo fire, it was increasingly apparent to Grissom and other astronauts that many of the North American Aviation engineers and technicians seemed more interested in weekend camping trips in the mountains than making sure wire bundles were properly installed and insulated. Unlike Apollo contractors such as lunar module manufacturer Grumman Corporation, which installed wire bundles by hand, North American Aviation was machine bundling miles of spacecraft wiring in the Block I spacecraft. Machine bundling would save time and money, but those who understood the importance of spacecraft electrical systems could see its approach was slipshod and dangerous.[28]

John Young had learned plenty about aircraft electrical systems as a navy test pilot. He appreciated how carefully McDonnell Aircraft had been installing wiring in a Gemini spacecraft that would be filled just before liftoff with pure oxygen. "If anything set off even a tiny spark, the results would be fatal," Young understood.[29] He was justifiably worried about pure oxygen under pressure, so much so that the otherwise fearless astronaut admitted that the combination of live, hot spacecraft wiring and pure oxygen made his knees shake.

The Block I Apollo spacecraft contained an estimated twenty miles of wiring and no less than 640 switches, circuit breakers, event indicators, and computer controls. According to Young, their arrangement was "pretty darned arbitrary." During test runs in Downey on another Apollo command module, the crew had seen ethyl glycol coolant dripping into a puddle on the floor. Indeed, the Block I environment control system was a mess. The day before the Apollo fire, as another Apollo crew trained in the Downey spacecraft, crew member David Scott received a "pretty strong electrical shock" while wearing a suit pressurized with pure oxygen. Scott was "very lucky he didn't get electrocuted, burnt to death," Young noted.

Young and others had reached the same conclusion: the Apollo Block I spacecraft that would be pressurized with pure oxygen on the launchpad contained literally miles of potential short circuits. "I knew it when I saw it, and I saw it in spades in the Block I command module," Young revealed in his 2012 memoir. He observed big wire bundles resting up against aluminum stringers with no support. Despite the use of machine bundling, Young considered the Apollo wire bundles far larger than they should have been, and wiring insulation was often frayed.

Young has on numerous occasions recounted how he asked Gus Grissom in the weeks before the accident why he did not complain about the bad wiring, which was clearly deficient when compared to their Gemini spacecraft. "If I say anything about it, they'll fire me," Young claims Grissom replied. "That's what he told me," Young continued. "I couldn't believe it."[30]

In describing the conversation, Young has never fully explained precisely what he thought Grissom was driving at. Would Grissom, if he complained about the bad wiring, have lost his Apollo command and with it his shot at a lunar landing? Was it the macho test pilot code about remaining stoic in the face of adversity? Others suspected as much; Young did not elaborate on this critical point. Nevertheless, Grissom and his Apollo crew should never have been placed in such a dangerous position. Crew safety had been compromised.

While Grissom complained loud and long behind the scenes about many of the problems with his spacecraft, he likely tolerated the bad wiring because he, NASA, and its contractors were at that time firmly in the grip of a deadly malady called "Go Fever." "There was a lot of pressure within NASA to get off on time," backup crew member Cunningham recalled. Congress was increasingly in the mood to cut the space agency's budget, hence "time was money."[31] Grissom and his crew were gambling that the growing list of problems with the spacecraft would somehow be fixed in time for the February launch. That gamble would prove to be a fatal miscalculation.

Struggling to stay on schedule, NASA accepted Spacecraft 012 and allowed North American Aviation to ship it to Cape Kennedy in August 1966. The next five months would be spent fixing and reinstalling critical systems. The spacecraft simulator, a critical training tool for the shakedown mission, was falling hopelessly behind as the number of design changes mounted.

The Apollo cabin would be pressurized with pure oxygen at 16.7 pounds per square inch on the launchpad and five pounds per square inch in space. The overpressure would ensure that a heavy, inward-opening hatch would seal like a cork. This was necessary in part because Apollo planners had specified a shirtsleeve environment in the cabin so the crew could get out of their pressure suits and eventually fly the complex machine to the moon and back.

The Apollo hatch consisted of three parts, or what astronaut Jim Lovell described as a "three-layer sandwich":[32] the outermost or boost protective cover, which shielded the command module during launch before being jettisoned along with the Apollo escape system; a middle, or ablative, hatch, which became the outer hatch when the boost protective cover was jettisoned, providing thermal protection during reentry; and an inner hatch, which sealed the cabin's pressure vessel wall.

The inner hatch, variously described as "a monster," "pretty damned heavy," and "a brute of a thing,"[33] was held in place by multiple dog bolts that had to be hand-cranked to open. It also was awkwardly placed behind the center couch, where White would be sitting. Commander Grissom, in the left-hand seat, would have to help White open the hatch. A ratchet handle would be used to crank the hatch open in six different places. Then, it would have to be pulled inside the spacecraft. Under the best of circumstances, at least ninety seconds would be required to remove the inner hatch. Removal could not commence until the cabin pressure was equalized with outside pressure, so the seal could be broken. The ablative hatch was also opened from the inside, but its release was less complicated. The Block I hatch design was effectively a kluge, and nearly all the Apollo astronauts hated it.

Explosive bolts or an outward-opening hatch had been considered for the early Apollo design. Most accounts of how the Apollo command module hatch was designed note that Grissom opposed such a hatch in reaction to his ordeal on *Liberty Bell 7*. This was false. These accounts fail to note that Grissom harbored no such concerns in helping to design an outward-opening hatch for the Gemini spacecraft. Moreover, it is unclear whether he or other astronauts actually approved the hatch design that would be used on the first version of the Apollo command module. Grissom had bigger problems than the hatch design by the time he was named *Apollo 1* commander.

One former NASA official recalls that it was likely astronauts Gordon Cooper and Pete Conrad, not Grissom, who actually signed off on the early Apollo hatch design on behalf of the Astronaut Office, despite internal opposition.[34] "One of the things that we complained very bitterly about was the hatch," *Apollo 12* command module pilot Richard Gordon told an interviewer. "It was very difficult to open. It was dogged down from the inside. Took a long time to get it open. And it was not like the Gemini hatch, which opened outward very rapidly and very, very quickly."[35]

Once the hatch was sealed, the suited astronauts would be breathing pure oxygen. Oxygen under pressure combined with an ignition source and flammable material is deadly. At the time of the *Apollo 1* fire, NASA had logged more than twenty thousand hours of experience with pure oxygen in flight and in altitude chambers. By 1966, however, the space agency was pressing its luck.

From a physiological standpoint, there was little doubt that pure oxygen was preferable since it eliminated the possibility of "the bends" should there be a loss of cabin pressure in space. Then, there was the badly needed weight savings a single-gas system would provide over the extra plumbing, sensors, and controls required for an oxygen-nitrogen atmosphere. But simpler and lighter did not mean safer. As the engineering trade-offs were made during Apollo development, these additional risks were often overlooked in the race to get Apollo into orbit.

The dangers associated with pure oxygen under pressure were understood. A string of fires had broken out in test chambers filled with pure oxygen earlier in the decade. Several American test subjects had been killed largely because of pure oxygen, including two men in a spacecraft simulator at Brooks Air Force Base in Texas just four days after the Apollo fire.[36]

Of greatest concern to the Apollo managers in the months before the fire were recurring problems with the spacecraft's environmental control system that supplied oxygen, cooling, and air handling in the command module. The system, designed by a North American Aviation subcontractor, the AiResearch division of the Garrett Corporation, initially failed during an unmanned test in July 1964 when the insulation around a heater coil failed, causing an explosion in the test chamber.

Things went from bad to worse after the system was installed in the Block I spacecraft. A fire broke out nearly a day into another qualification test in April 1966 using pure oxygen at five pounds per square inch of pressure, the same atmosphere that would be used in space. The probable cause was traced to insulation used in a failed commercial heater.

Months before the Apollo fire, an accident board examining the cause of the April 1966 accident recommended eliminating all nonmetallic material in the spacecraft that could come in contact with wire bundles, indicating that investigators understood those wires were potential ignition sources. Spacecraft 012 was full of ignition sources.

Dr. Fred Kelly, an astronaut candidate, naval aviator, and NASA flight surgeon, oversaw the medical panel that investigated the Apollo fire. On the question of whether the fire could have been prevented, Kelly was unequivocal: "With 20/20 hindsight anyone off the street should see that a spacecraft with 72.5 pounds of flammable material, miles of unprotected wiring and 47 possible ignition points in an atmosphere of 100 percent oxygen at 16.7 psi was an accident waiting to happen."[37] Kelly noted that any atmosphere that supports life could fuel a fire. Still, as a member of the medical requirements office that was formed as Apollo was ramping up, Kelly coauthored a paper detailing the fire hazards of pure oxygen under partial pressure. Those warnings and others from North American Aviation went unheeded, and the Apollo cabin's pure oxygen atmosphere remained.[38]

By October 1966, senior Apollo managers had concluded that the AiResearch environmental control unit was in "serious trouble," threatening a "major delay in the first flight of Apollo." Samuel C. Phillips, the Apollo program director, warned Garrett executives that the "current difficulty is the latest in a long string of failures and problems associated with the AiResearch equipment." Phillips cited inadequate development testing and "poor workmanship."[39]

With the launch of Grissom's Apollo flight now scheduled for February 21, 1967, Phillips leaned on Garrett to fix the system, the sooner the better. Spacecraft 012's environmental control system had again been replaced when the ship was delivered to the Cape in August 1966, delaying testing of the spacecraft in a vacuum chamber. AiResearch shipped a new system from its West Coast plant to Cape Kennedy in November for installation and testing. That unit was again returned to California for further repairs. It was finally reinstalled in the spacecraft in mid-December.[40] By then, NASA was allowing for virtually no margin of error.

The environmental control unit and a system installed in another Block I command module in Downey continued to leak ethylene glycol up until the night of the Apollo fire. (The Apollo Block I command module used a coolant designated RS-89, a mixture of 62.5 percent ethylene glycol, 35.7 percent water, and 1.8 percent stabilizer and corrosion inhibitor.) Fluid leaks were acknowledged by the Apollo 204 Review Board to be "considerable fire hazards." Moreover, the inhibitor contained combustible salts that did not evaporate. The residue from spilled coolant could conduct electricity if it came in contact with wire that was not properly insulated.[41]

The list of serious problems with Grissom's spacecraft seemed insurmountable prior to the launchpad test of the command module internal power system, the plugs-out rehearsal consisting of a simulated launch countdown with the crew sealed in the cabin on top of an unfueled rocket. Weeks before, the spacecraft's service module, which included thrusters and its main engine, was damaged after being inserted into a vacuum chamber for testing. A light shattered and falling debris damaged several maneuvering thrusters. In October 1966, a separate service module at the North American Aviation plant that would be mated to another Block I spacecraft was damaged during routine pressure tests when the propellant tanks exploded.[42] It was increasingly apparent to anyone paying attention that Grissom had a lemon of a spacecraft on his hands. By December, he was telling reporters that a successful flight would be one in which he and his crew made it back alive. The reporters thought Grissom was joking. Indeed, he was dead serious and increasingly pessimistic that his ship could be made to fly. Grissom's intuition about the dangers of being the first to fly a new machine and remaining too long on the flight line were becoming his new reality as launch day drew closer. He grew more irritable by the day.

The combination of the Apollo designers' insistence on a pure oxygen cabin atmosphere and the inward-opening hatch posed a grave threat that no one, including Grissom, fully appreciated. These hazards were obvious in hindsight, but the level of risk being tolerated by program managers was arguably unprecedented in the history of the American space program.

Launch preparations continued even as the planned February launch date grew more unrealistic. Following a year-end round of press interviews in which Grissom was repeatedly asked about the dangers associated with the first Apollo flight, he, Betty, and Purdue's growing list of astronaut alumni traveled to Pasadena, California, to attend the Tournament of

Roses Parade and the Rose Bowl football game. The Boilermakers were representing the Big Ten Conference against the University of Southern California. Purdue quarterback Bob Griese, an All-American and future National Football League Hall of Famer, led the Boilermakers to a 14-13 victory. Purdue graduate and future spacewalker Jerry Ross helped tear down the goal posts.

The Rose Bowl victory lifted the Grissom family's spirits and perhaps steeled Gus for the difficult days ahead. American football, a game Grissom had been too slight to play, provided a brief respite from the unrelenting pressures of his upcoming mission and all the hazards it entailed. The trip also marked the last time Betty and Gus would relax together and, if only for a day, forget about the risky business of spaceflight.

Back in Timber Cove, Grissom was mostly absent, constantly shuttling between California, Florida, and Houston. (Ever the hotshot pilot and competitor, he had mastered a technique called "hot refueling"—connecting the hose and refueling the astronauts' T-38 aircraft while the engines were still running. Walt Cunningham claimed Grissom held the record for the fastest turnaround using the frowned-upon technique: "a flat five minutes."[43]) Mark Grissom calculated his father was home about six weeks in 1966. On the rare occasions when he was, the phone would ring off the hook, calls from the Cape or California about some new problem with the spacecraft. "They would be fussing about something," Betty remembered. This was not like Gus. He did not bring work home with him. "He would rather be messing around with the kids. But now he was uptight about it."[44]

The absentee father nevertheless cared deeply about his family and did not want his problems to become theirs. But the pressure was unceasing, and the commander was reluctantly playing the hand he had been dealt. The last weeks of Grissom's life were more than most humans could endure. There were "too many bosses" at North American Aviation. Committees were making decisions about what spacecraft fixes to make and when. The old, reliable way of doing things, the way McDonnell Aircraft had managed Mercury and Gemini, was no longer available. Apollo program managers were fixated on sticking to an impossible schedule. The careful test pilot who worked every day to mitigate risk was being painted into a corner.

Along with the Rose Bowl, a lemon tree in the Grissom's backyard would provide some inspiration and momentary relief from the unending pressure. The Apollo crew had been in California during late January. They were due back at the Cape on Monday, January 23. Gus, Ed, and Roger arrived home on Sunday to spend time with their families and catch up on mail before flying back to the Cape the next day. A critical launch countdown simulation of the spacecraft's internal power systems was scheduled for the end of the week. If successful, *Apollo 1* might actually get off the ground in February. Then the pressure would be off until the next flight.

Gus packed his bag that Monday morning and prepared to leave. Before departing, he sliced a hunk of cheese from a large block, a Christmas gift from a friend, and then stuffed the cheese in his bag. Before leaving, he suddenly turned, walked out into the courtyard, and pulled a Texas lemon as big as a grapefruit from the tree. Gus decided there and then to hang the lemon on the nearly useless Apollo simulator at the Cape, a final act of defiance that expressed his months of frustration and, for the first time in his astronaut career, his doubts about the upcoming flight of *Apollo 1*.

The husband briefly explained the lemon's purpose, kissed his wife of twenty-one years good-bye, and left. The years of struggle and sacrifice were about to end. Betty would never see Gus again.

14

DEATH AT 218 FEET

It was a bad day. Worst I ever had.
—Donald K. Slayton

Everything was wrong; everything was wrong.
—Walter M. Schirra

The plan was for the *Apollo 1* crew to fly back to Houston during the last weekend in January 1967 to attend a party for the astronauts and their wives on Saturday evening, January 28. Field Enterprises, the publisher that had also contracted for the astronauts' stories, was throwing the bash.[1] It would be a chance to blow off some steam after another trying week of launchpad simulations culminating on January 27 in a crucial plugs-out test of Spacecraft 012's internal power, communications, and environmental control systems. The countdown rehearsal would be among the last opportunities for Gus Grissom and his crew to get their flawed machine to work after five months of troubleshooting.

Gus had called Betty from the Cape the night before the Friday test to check in, see how the boys were doing, and let her know that a countdown simulation with the spacecraft plugged into external power went okay. Perhaps, at last, the *Apollo 1* mission would actually get off the ground as scheduled on February 21. For a while, then, the pressure would be off until Gus's next flight, he assumed, to the moon.

"We'll see you Saturday then," Betty said before signing off.[2] It had been just another day at the office. There would be another test tomorrow. No sweat. Foremost on Betty's mind was the phone call itself, the primary connection to her absentee husband, commander of the first Apollo flight. Together since high school, married for more than twenty-one years, it would be Gus and Betty's last phone call.

Despite a mounting list of unresolved technical problems, the Apollo command and service modules had been hoisted and stacked on top of its Saturn 1B booster at Pad 34 during the first week of January. The "uprated" rocket was a scaled-down version of the gigantic Saturn V moon rocket. Nevertheless, Wally Schirra referred to it as "the Big Maumoo" since it was at the time among the largest boosters designed to launch humans.[3] Once the vehicle was stacked, the command module and its launch escape tower were enclosed in a White Room at the eighth level, 218 feet high, near the top of the thirty-one-story orange service structure at Pad 34.[4] The movable tower along with the other launchpads and the gigantic new Vehicle Assembly Building now dominated the Florida coastline. From here, the Kennedy Space Center, humans would for the first time leave the earth to explore another world.

A team of North American Aviation technicians set up shop on Level 8A to support the launch simulations that would culminate in the plugs-out test designed to demonstrate that all spacecraft systems worked and that NASA's operational procedures were sound. The launch simulation would be as close to the actual flight configuration as possible on the pad, meaning the crew would be in pressure suits, the hatches sealed, and the spacecraft pressurized with pure oxygen.

In the weeks before the tests, Gus Grissom was becoming increasingly irritable, pessimistic—perhaps fatalistic—about the prospects of his next flight and the condition of his spacecraft and its all-important simulator. If Spacecraft 012 "had been a horse they would have shot it sometime in 1966, perhaps as early as 1965," observed Walt Williams, the aerospace pioneer and NASA's director of operations during the Mercury program. "Surely, no machine suffered so many ailments, not even one that was the first of its kind."[5]

"Grumpy" Gus Grissom, as Williams dubbed the *Apollo 1* commander, also concluded that the Apollo managers had lost control of the program. Williams, deeply concerned about crew safety and the unrelenting pace of the Apollo program, left NASA in 1964. Painted into a corner, Grissom was increasingly operating on his own initiative, driving his crew but not asking them to do anything he wouldn't undertake himself. "I feel like a wolf howling in the wilderness," NASA technicians recalled Grissom complaining in the weeks before the tests.[6]

Jay Barbree, NBC's reporter at Cape Kennedy, claimed decades later that Grissom had approached him in late 1966 at a Cocoa Beach watering hole to complain about the miserable condition of his spacecraft. Barbree asserted that Grissom pulled him aside, asked for his help, and described Spacecraft 012 as a "piece of crap." "You guys in the press, well, shit Jay, you guys have to help us. Apollo is not ready." Barbree's recollection was written some forty years after a nose-to-nose conversation with Grissom as they listened to a local folk singer referred to only as "Trish." (Barbree said Grissom enjoyed Trish's singing and her company, but there was nothing between them. "I knew she was involved with an astronaut, but it wasn't Gus Grissom," Barbree claimed.[7])

Given Grissom's adversarial relationship with the press, it seems a stretch to imagine he would enlist the help of Barbree or other journalists to help expose serious technical problems with his ship and inattentive management at NASA and North American Aviation. On the other hand, the "lone wolf" may have been sufficiently desperate for help from any source. Whatever he said to the reporter at the Cocoa Beach nightspot, it was clear that Grissom had profound misgivings about his ship and the preparations for his upcoming mission. Schirra was among the few involved who fully understood the hazards of a launchpad simulation conducted with sealed hatches in a pure oxygen atmosphere, "an environment that's not very forgiving," he said. "We didn't realize how unforgiving it was at that point." Schirra and his crew performed a "full-up system test" of the Apollo-Saturn 204, the spacecraft and the booster, using external power on Thursday, January 26. This was the test Gus and Betty had discussed during their final phone conversation. Spacecraft hatches were left open, and the crew breathed sea-level air. After the test, Schirra met with Grissom and Joe Shea, the Apollo program manager. The debriefing took place in the "ready room" of the crew quarters at Cape Kennedy. Schirra pulled no punches.

"Frankly, Gus, I don't like it," Schirra warned. "You're going to be in there with full oxygen tomorrow, and if you have the same feeling I do, I suggest you get out."[8] Named the backup commander in September 1966 after a reshuffling of crew assignments, Schirra described the fall of 1966 as a period of intense struggle to stay on schedule, akin to "riding a locomotive down a track with ten more locomotives bearing down [from] behind."[9]

Grissom duly noted Schirra's warning during the debriefing, but he appeared more concerned about the reliably unreliable spacecraft communications. He suggested that either Shea or Deke Slayton crawl into the spacecraft during the Friday test so they could hear for themselves just how bad the communications were between the spacecraft and the test conductors and ground controllers. The suggestion was considered but soon dropped as impractical. Slayton decided to observe the plugs-out test from the blockhouse. Shea planned to fly back to Houston the next day after finishing an interview with a *Time* magazine reporter for a cover story timed to coincide with the first Apollo mission. Both men, especially Shea, would be tormented for the rest of their lives, knowing they could have been inside the sealed spacecraft when the fire broke out.

The relentless schedule continued nonstop until the day of the plugs-out test. In between were rounds of network interviews and a press conference focused on the objectives and length of the first Apollo flight. Grissom was repeatedly asked in the weeks before the scheduled flight whether he had misgivings about the mission, particularly the dangers inherent in a maiden flight. Those questions undoubtedly stemmed from the knowledge that the command pilot was extremely unhappy, even resentful, about the mess he had inherited. Grissom mostly kept his worries to himself, assuring reporters he had things under control. The outwardly confident commander revealed his concerns only in an off-the-cuff remark during a preflight press conference. After Slayton punted a reporter's question about what constituted a successful first Apollo mission, Grissom chimed in, "As far as we're concerned, it's success if all three of us get back" alive.[10]

Nearly everyone thought he was joking. Rather, the commander was hinting that launch preparations were going badly and the prospects for a successful shakedown flight were slim. Grissom had concluded by the end of 1966 that he had a poorly designed, even dangerous spacecraft on his hands. But the arc of human space exploration had brought him to this time and place, and he was determined to play the hand he'd been dealt.

Dennis and Cecile Grissom visited their son at the Cape in the weeks before the scheduled launch. Gus "didn't have much faith in [the space-craft]," Cecile recalled. After her eldest son's death, Cecile nursed a grudge against NASA for awarding the Apollo contract to North American Aviation rather than sticking with McDonnell, where Lowell had worked during the Mercury program. NASA took manned spacecraft production "away from McDonnell and gave it to that plant in California." It was as if Cecile could not bring herself to utter the Apollo contractor's name.

The *Apollo 1* prime and backup crews along with Slayton met with reporters in Houston at the end of 1966, completing a series of year-end interviews. Seeking to put the best possible face on the crews' training and the condition of his ship, Grissom summarized the list of problems he was up against, highlighting the slow progress toward fixing the Spacecraft 012's environmental control system and the balky mission simulator.

Much of the crew training was taking place on a navigation and guidance "evaluator" in Downey, he acknowledged, concealing his anguish with the primary trainer at Cape Canaveral. Grissom insisted the Cape simulator was "getting in real good shape" and the prime crew would start using it "as our primary trainer after the first of the year." As the lemon-hanging incident illustrated, this was wishful thinking—and Grissom probably knew it.

Continuing problems with the spacecraft environmental controls were also acknowledged, but Grissom asserted they had at last been fixed. Altitude chamber testing would resume in January 1967. Yet, Grissom must have realized that retesting a critical spacecraft system so close to his scheduled February launch date was cutting it close.

The *Apollo 1* backup crews had been shuffled; Schirra was the new backup commander. The press conference also served as the introduction of Schirra's backup crew, which included Cunningham and Eisele. Rookie astronauts had been assigned "dog work" in support of the prime crew, Grissom added. He then narrated a short film showing the prime crew practicing its egress procedures, including White dealing with the heavy inner and outer hatches.[11]

Grissom would be more expansive in broadcast network interviews, particularly with Jules Bergman of ABC News, whom he trusted. Grissom also understood these tedious interviews were part of the NASA public relations drill. In this case, he also appreciated Bergman's reputation as a straight shooter. With others, he remained circumspect. When another TV reporter stuck a microphone in his face and asked Grissom about his Apollo prospects, he curtly replied, "I expect to be around for most of the Apollo program." How about a moon landing? "I'm planning on it." And that was the end of the interview.

Spacecraft 012 remained a mess at the beginning of 1967, as did overall management of the Apollo program. Technicians who worked on Pad 34 as launch day approached claimed quality control in the White Room was beyond lax. They recalled NASA and contractor brass bringing friends and girlfriends up to Level 8A to see—even climb into—the spacecraft. Each time this happened, the technicians had to interrupt their work until the tour ended. Among other things, each one of these lapses increased the chances that flammable contaminants were being introduced into the cabin that would be pressurized with pure oxygen.

There were other lapses, including some that occurred in the crews' presence. The North American Aviation engineer overseeing the crew compartment admitted later: "Lights would come on when they weren't supposed to." Worse, North American technicians twice dropped coins in the cabin, even though their pockets were supposed to be empty. After one incident, Grissom blew his stack when he and Roger Chaffee heard coins jingling in technicians' pockets.

"Ed White complained to me," the project engineer said. He took the matter all the way up the line to Harrison Storms, who was running the Apollo program for North American. Storms offered to fire the technician, but the Apollo cabin chief saved the worker's job. After the coin incident, North American assigned a Spacecraft 012 manager, Joseph Cuzzupoli, who later became program manager for the space shuttle orbiter project.

"I was in charge of checking [Spacecraft 012] out prior to shipping it" to Cape Kennedy, Cuzzupoli told an interviewer. "It was a tough job, again, because of the changes in the system, and we had a considerable amount of rework that we had to do to the vehicle. And we had a lot of pressure on this schedule, but it did not get us away from the fact that we didn't do a good quality job. But when the vehicle left Downey, California, it was not complete at all, and we shipped it under the understanding that it [would] be complete in the field. There was a considerable amount of changes yet to be done."[12]

The spacecraft unfit for flight was nevertheless shipped to Cape Kennedy in the hope that it could be fixed in time for the first Apollo mission. The schedule now took precedence over everything, apparently even crew safety. The machine was unmistakable evidence that NASA, after sixteen manned spaceflights with no loss of life, had lost its moorings.

In the months before the fire, an irresistible force had taken hold of Gus Grissom along with nearly all involved in the *Apollo 1* mission, obscuring the ample warnings of a potential disaster. North American Aviation manager John Moore remembered: "We were going very fast—NASA, we were behind schedule as always, and we were running tests without taking time to really look at the data."

The test data that no one had time to evaluate was telling the space agency that its prime contractor had built a deathtrap based on NASA's specifications. The embittered Schirra later defined "Go Fever" as "We've got to keep going, got to keep going, got to keep going!" The spacecraft should never have been shipped from the factory. "It was not finished," Schirra could see. "It was what they called a lot of uncompleted work or incomplete tests. . . . So it was shipped to the Cape with a bunch of spare parts and things to finish it out."[13]

Jim Lovell, who had just completed his second spaceflight in the run-up to the *Apollo 1* mission, later claimed he could see in hindsight what Grissom could not in early 1967: "Gus was a charger, he was a very macho type. He was really the typical test pilot. But he also had 'Go Fever,' you know, he wanted to get it going; he wanted to get up there and do the job."

Schirra's concerns about crew safety, the inability to fix problems, and the tight schedule were escalating into anger. "I was no longer annoyed, I was really pretty goddamn mad! There were glitches, electronic things that just didn't come out right. That evening I debriefed with Joe Shea and Gus, and I said: 'If there are any things that go wrong, like a glitch in the electronic circuits and bad sounds, scrub the test!'"[14] Schirra and those who bothered to pay attention could now see that Grissom, despite his complaints, had embraced a deadly form of "group think." There simply was no time to reflect, to take a step back and recognize the danger.

Apollo managers had fallen "into a pattern of group think, where the number of people involved in the decision-making process gets smaller and smaller, and they decide to perceive something in a certain way," Donn Eisele of the Apollo backup crew recalled years later. "From then on, all information that doesn't jibe with the mind-set of the group is rejected."[15] As for the rush to complete the plugs-out test, Schirra insisted Grissom "should have scrubbed. He didn't."[16]

Eisele agreed. "I asked the Apollo managers before the fire, 'What's the hurry?' We had until 1970 to land on the moon. They had it worked out that they were going to do it in 1968, two years early. The trouble was they were forcing the pace."[17]

Eisele died in December 1987 of a heart attack while on a business trip in Tokyo. The retired air force colonel who was assigned to the original *Apollo 1* crew before reinjuring his shoulder is buried at Arlington National Cemetery, a few plots away from Virgil I. Grissom and Roger B. Chaffee.

Eisele was correct. There was another glaring institutional problem compounding the myriad technical issues with the spacecraft: Joe Shea was not keeping his boss, Robert Gilruth, fully informed of the mounting problems with Spacecraft 012. Moreover, NASA administrator James Webb never saw scathing reports about North American Aviation's shoddy work on the command module. Flight Director Chris Kraft acknowledged later: "We were all getting too compartmentalized."[18]

Kraft remembered reports from Cape Canaveral that "described the quality of the hardware being delivered as a disaster waiting to happen." He continued, "I could see it myself, because I'd been spending some time at the contractor's in California." Still, no one at NASA in a position to do so was willing to stick his neck out to slow the program.

John Bailey, a trusted confidante of Gilruth and Kraft, was instead dispatched to the Cape after the spacecraft was shipped from California to keep an eye on things. In a memo to Gilruth distributed among senior management in Houston, Bailey warned: "This hardware is not very good. The people are really not very good at checking this thing out. They're not very good at trying to maintain some semblance of the fact that a human being is going to be in this machine. I'm telling you, it's not good."[19]

Nevertheless, Apollo program managers allowed the contractor to ship Spacecraft 012 to the Kennedy Space Center despite unresolved problems with the command module's electrical systems and a leaking environmental control unit. It arrived on August 26. Not only should the spacecraft never have been shipped to the Cape in that condition, NASA should never have accepted delivery. But it did. Now it was Gus Grissom's burden.

Slipshod engineering, distracted management, poor quality control, inattention to test data, the "Go Fever" schedule, and plain old hubris after the success of Gemini combined to create a lethal situation as the crew prepared for a full dress rehearsal three weeks before the scheduled launch on February 21, 1967. The Saturn rocket would not be fueled, and no pyrotechnics were installed—just a sealed spacecraft powered up for a simulated launch. As a result, NASA did not classify the test as hazardous. Schirra suspected "everything was wrong," but no one else seemed particularly worried about the test, including Grissom, who was now fixated on nonlethal but maddening communications problems.

The last day of the lives of Gus Grissom and his crew began as it would have on launch day: breakfast with Deke Slayton in the crew quarters. Shea had joined them. Grissom continued to lobby Shea to squeeze into the spacecraft that afternoon so he could observe firsthand just how bad the communications were and why spacecraft subsystems were not checking out. Over steak and eggs, Grissom pleaded his case to Shea: "It's really messy. We want you to go fix it."[20] The communications technicians shortly reported they could not rig another headset into the communications loop in time for the test. Shea ruled out observing the proceedings from the spacecraft's lower equipment bay, promising Grissom he would return the following Monday to run the test again, this time in the faulty Apollo simulator.

As the crew ate breakfast, the pad technicians were making the connections to power up the spacecraft for the plugs-out test. The pad technicians and the test conductors spent the next few hours running initial verification tests on the spacecraft to ensure it was ready for what was to follow. No one had any inkling of what was about to transpire.

Grissom, Chaffee, and White were fitted with biosensors and suited up at 10 a.m. Cape time. They appeared much more reserved than in previous NASA promotional films released to the press in the days before the critical test. Lola Morrow, the astronauts' secretary and "den mother"—who claimed to know Grissom's state of mind—felt the tension that Friday morning. "I don't [know] what it was that I sensed, but I picked up something from all three of them. There was a quietness about them, instead of being ready for a test where they usually just get up and bounce out the door, it was something they didn't want to do. Their attitude was one eighty [degrees] from anything I'd ever seen before."[21]

The consequences of the mounting problems with the spacecraft and the first mission were visibly weighing on the crew: it could now be seen in their body language. Friday, January 27, 1967, was going to be a long day. But as Grissom's fellow midwesterner, Slayton, remarked on such occasions: "Let's get on with it."

Despite the fact that the spacecraft hatches would be sealed, the air forced out, and the spacecraft pressurized with pure oxygen, few besides Schirra considered the plugs-out test to be dangerous. The rocket would not be fueled, and the exploding bolts used to separate the rocket stages were not yet installed. Hence, the test was officially considered "routine" despite a pure oxygen cabin environment, several score potential ignition points, and more than seventy pounds of flammable material sealed inside. "That's really hard to explain," concluded Dr. Fred Kelly, the NASA flight surgeon who helped investigate the fire.[22]

It was time to head out to the pad, ride the elevator to the White Room, climb into the spacecraft, seal the hatches, pump up the cabin pressure, and see what the spacecraft could and could not do. Or as Schirra observed, the six astronauts—his and Grissom's crews—had resolved to gang tackle the spacecraft's problems and "make [the] machine work."[23]

After donning their suits, the astronauts boarded a van to ride out to Pad 34 around midday, entering the spacecraft at approximately 1 p.m. local time. The appearance of the *Apollo 1* prime crew buttoned up in their pressure suits always drew the full attention of the pad workers, who dared not question the prerogatives of the spacecraft commander. The irascible Grissom maintained his commanding presence. There was no question as to who was in charge. Nevertheless, some of the workers appreciated what he was up against. The plugs-out test would be the closest thing to an actual launch the technicians would experience without actually lighting the new rocket's engines. Each worker was on his toes as the crew entered the cabin: Grissom first, and then Chaffee, and then White in the center couch last. It took more than an hour to get the two inner hatches closed and sealed. The heavy, inward-opening hatch was secured by a series of clamps. The NASA technician who installed the hatches that day, Charles Stevenson, recalled that one had to be pounded into place. Since this was a simulation, the boost protective cover that was part of the escape rocket system was not secured as it would be on launch day. Still, the launch escape system, which included solid rocket motors more powerful than the Mercury-Redstone Grissom had ridden into space in 1961, would pose a major hazard to the North American Aviation pad crew later in the day.

Grissom settled into his couch, connected his suit to the cabin oxygen supply, and immediately reported a sour milk odor in his suit loop. Donald Babbitt, the North American Aviation pad leader who arrived in the White Room for his normal shift about 3:30 p.m., later told investigators the smell "reminded [him] of a potting compound" used in spacecraft assemblies for waterproofing and to withstand shock and vibrations.[24]

An air sample was taken by the "watermelon gang," so named for the device they used to take samples through a port in the spacecraft. After talking it over with test conductors, Grissom decided to press on.

Soon, another problem surfaced with the troublesome environmental control system. A high oxygen flow indicator was periodically triggering a master alarm. There was more back and forth with technicians responsible for the system, but outside of concluding that the high flow was the result of crew movements, the problem was never resolved.

The test dragged along with the crew throwing switches and monitoring systems while straining to hear the test conductors' instructions. Persistent, maddening communications breakdowns between the spacecraft and test conductors plagued the entire simulation, just as Grissom had predicted during breakfast with Shea and Slayton. Some of the commander's last known words would bemoan the fact that the crew often could not hear the controllers and the controllers could not hear the crew.

Among the most graphic displays of the commander's seething anger came in the minutes before the first report of a fire as the crew struggled with yet another communications glitch between the spacecraft and the blockhouse. Initially, controllers believed the problem was solely between Grissom and the blockhouse. Later, it extended to communications between the blockhouse and the operations checkout building a few miles from the pad, where test conductors were monitoring spacecraft systems. The plugs-out test conductor later told investigators that the overall communications problems were so bad that his engineers could barely understand what the crew was saying.

At times, local air traffic control chatter could even be heard bleeding over to the same RF communications channel being used for the test. As the afternoon turned to evening, Grissom was fuming. His widely quoted remark "How are we going to get to the moon if we can't talk between three buildings?" was followed by an even more telling display of frayed nerves and absolute frustration.

White chimed in over the static that the test controllers, who had asked the commander if he wanted to use the phone to communicate, "can't hear a thing you're saying." Grissom shot back in a sarcastic tone reminiscent of a father scolding a wayward son, "Jee-sus Christ!" A less well-known act of defiance that also underscored growing frustration occurred several weeks earlier as the crew prepared for an altitude chamber test designed to check out the spacecraft in a simulated vacuum. The requirement for a pretest medical examination had somehow been omitted from the schedule. It mattered little since the bullheaded Grissom, never trusting the flight surgeons, adamantly refused to submit to the exam. It was determined that the chamber test could not begin without the flight surgeons' approval. A flurry of calls ensued as Grissom pleaded with Slayton to keep the doctors off his back.

"Deke and [NASA chief flight surgeon Dr. Charles Berry] would have to work it out at the directors' level before Gus would submit to a five-minute physical examination," recalled Fred Kelly, another NASA flight surgeon who had been summoned by Berry to help mediate the dispute. Kelly, an aviator and astronaut candidate, had earned the crew's respect despite his stethoscope. "I asked to speak with Gus in private and was able to restore some degree of peace," Kelly wrote decades later. "Gus could be reasonable if you used the right words."[25] Kelly, who several weeks later would be assigned to head the Apollo 204 Accident Review Board's medical panel, never revealed what words he used to convince Grissom to submit to the exam.

The *Apollo 1* crew, flight controllers, test conductors, and flight surgeons, all monitoring the plugs-out test, used multiple channels to communicate. As far as can be determined, only one channel has ever been released, and it contains the frustrating minutes and horrible last seconds of the lives of Gus Grissom, Ed White, and Roger Chaffee. The unexpected alerts of a fire in the spacecraft and the terrifying last shouts would drive some who worked on Apollo to nervous breakdowns or suicide.

At 6:28 p.m., two minutes and forty-three seconds before the first report of a fire, Grissom uttered a puzzling phrase that made little sense, particularly given the horrendous events that would soon follow. Only a fragment of what was said could be heard when the command pilot stated, "It's good for you." What Grissom meant, to what he was referring, remains a mystery. It is possible that he was speaking on a different communications channel used by the crew and that the transmission may have bled over from the adjacent channel. Whether other communications channels were being recorded on the night of the fire has never been revealed.

Things had been going from bad to worse when the countdown was held at T minus ten minutes beginning at 6:20 p.m. The crew and controllers continued to troubleshoot the nagging communications problems that stopped the simulated countdown at 5:40 p.m. The crew began swapping out communications equipment in an attempt to isolate the problems. The troubleshooting resulted in even more communications problems among ground controllers and the crew. At least part of the problem was eventually traced to a microphone somewhere in the faulty communications network stuck in the "on" position that the crew could not turn off. The final steps in the countdown designed to transfer the spacecraft to internal power, including a switch over to simulated fuel cell power, were completed before controllers held the count pending resolution of the communications problems. At T minus zero, the pad crew would pull the spacecraft umbilical just as it would be released during an actual launch.

As the plugs-out test dragged on into the evening, the hope was that the countdown could be resumed once the communications problems were either resolved or bypassed. After the power transfer was completed and the plugs-out test was finally over, Grissom wanted to test the Apollo emergency escape procedures. His old buddy Sam Beddingfield would serve as the supervising engineer. Beddingfield was just then returning to the Kennedy Space Center from dinner in Cocoa Beach to prepare for the test. Grissom knew he had to complete these steps if he was going to make his February 21 launch date. He was prepared to work himself, his crew, and the pad technicians all night if that was what it took to gain some peace of mind.

During the countdown hold, Grissom was changing a cable used to connect his suit to the communications loop. Motion and biosensors detected movement inside the cabin at least thirty seconds before the first report of a fire, maybe more if in fact Grissom had been out of his couch trying to change out his "cobra" communications cable. Scratching sounds could be heard over Grissom's open microphone, indicating movement. In the moments before the initial fire report, another possible explanation for the movement was that Grissom and White were attempting to trace the source of an acrid smell as a spark under Grissom's couch grew into a conflagration that would soon spread across the cabin.

Spacecraft 012 had been equipped with a gas chromatograph that could be used to monitor the cabin atmosphere for possible trace contaminants. The instrument was not installed on the day of the fatal test. When the gas chromatograph was disconnected, the unit unexpectedly acted as an antenna. The signal output from the gas chromatograph cable presently detected a variation in signal output about fourteen seconds before the first report of a fire. This indicated either voltage transients as equipment was switched off or, more likely, crew movement. These and other bits of hard engineering data such as the dropout of communications signals were, as one engineer graphically noted, indications that *Apollo 1* was "dutifully reporting its own demise."[26]

Some of the test conductors had pressed to scrub the launch simulation. They were overruled, and supervisors prepared to resume the countdown after a lengthy hold at T minus ten minutes. Grissom and the NASA managers decided to press on, to get the damned test out of the way before Beddingfield's team showed up to complete the emergency egress drill. Only then would the long day on Pad 34 be over.

At five seconds after 6:30 p.m., the commander of *Apollo 1* informed all who were listening of the inescapable fact that communications on a lunar mission would be impossible if the ground controllers could not figure out a way to "talk between two or three buildings." It was less than a minute before the first sign of an impending disaster. The crew was preoccupied for the next minute. There were indications that something was happening inside the spacecraft. A voltage surge was recorded at just before 6:31 p.m. Then, suddenly, something utterly unanticipated shattered the radio silence.

Voices from inside the spacecraft called out with desperate warnings that echo still across the decades. What transpired over the next five minutes would alter the course of the Space Race and the course of human space exploration. Those agonizing minutes would call into question the wisdom of attempting a crash program to send humans to another world. And it would devastate three families.

Four ticks past 6:31 p.m. EST on January 27, 1967, a voice that sounded like either Grissom's or Chaffee's pierced the scratchy radio silence over the otherwise unreliable VHF retransmission communication link designated Channel Black-3. "Hey!" a crewman shouted.[27] This was not something an experienced test pilot would shout over an open communications link. All who heard the exclamation—the test conductors, the ground controllers, the flight surgeons, the pad crew—immediately sensed that something lethal and completely unexpected was happening inside a spacecraft pumped full of pure oxygen. No one who heard the report initially considered the possibility of a fire.

The shocking alert coincided with motion in the spacecraft detected by sensitive gyroscopes. It was accompanied by a voltage surge in the spacecraft's electrical system and a spike in oxygen flow as well as crew heart rates. Grissom had spotted a fire under his couch where an electrical arc had probably jumped between two exposed segments of wiring.

Grissom had by now jumped back onto his couch, probably banging the back of his helmet on the instrument panel in his haste. He would next try as best he could to suppress the flames and then help open the hatches directly above the senior pilot's center couch.

One of the next transmissions came from Ed White approximately seven seconds later: "Fire! We've got a fire in the cockpit!" Time now slowed to a crawl as the enormity of that confirmation sunk in.

As White and Grissom struggled to open the hatches, Chaffee remained on his couch, switched on the cabin lights, and continued reporting to the test conductors and the blockhouse in an increasingly agitated voice: "We have a bad fire!" he reported thirteen seconds after the first alert.

With Grissom's help, the world-class athlete Ed White grabbed a torque wrench and commenced a death struggle to ratchet open the damned hatches, actually making progress toward retracting the dogleg locking bars that secured the inner hatch. Technology had catapulted humans into space. Its misapplication would now take the lives of three men who ultimately had no real chance of escape. Chaffee's last words, which sounded like "We're burning up!," came eighteen seconds after the initial report. The inferno was consuming the Raschel netting used to stow gear along with every other oxygen-soaked and flammable item in the cabin. Next came a shout. Then, as quickly as the catastrophe began, there was only deathly silence. No response to the frantic calls from the blockhouse and the operations center.

Apollo 1's pressure vessel had ruptured. Part of Grissom's suit was blown out of the spacecraft by the force of the explosion. Investigators later found a fragment of material from the command pilot's suit about five feet from the point of rupture, indicating that the suit had failed about fifteen seconds after the conflagration was first detected.

A fire likely touched off by an electrical arc in the miles of spacecraft wiring and fueled by pure oxygen had engulfed the spacecraft and its occupants, generating temperatures and pressures that would quickly breach the spacecraft's pressure vessel. It was later estimated that the fire lasted just over twenty-five seconds. The cabin rupture and explosion rapidly depleted the oxygen in the spacecraft, replacing flames and steel-melting heat with thick, black smoke and deadly concentrations of carbon monoxide that would ultimately claim the three astronauts' lives. In the seconds before being overcome, the crew fought a desperate but hopeless battle to get out. Commander, senior pilot, and pilot acted precisely as they were trained to do in an emergency. Their spacecraft was a death trap, and despite their heroic efforts there was never a realistic chance of escape or survival.

After years of playing with fire, NASA's luck—the nation's luck—had finally run out. The failure to comprehend the dangers of filling a spacecraft with pure oxygen and then sealing three men inside had at last caught up with the American space program. Just as he had told Betty—"If there ever is a serious accident in the space program, it's likely to be me"[28]—Gus Grissom had remained on the flight line long enough for past miscalculations and unnecessary risks to take his life and the lives of his crewmates.

Instead of blazing a trail to the moon, Grissom and his crew would ultimately serve as an inspirational kick in the pants to those who eventually left the earth. They and the technicians who fixed the moon machines dared not let down their dead colleagues. The lunar explorers would walk on the *Apollo 1* commander's shoulders. Virgil Ivan Grissom would serve as a martyr to the sacred cause of leaving the earth and exploring a new world.

Those monitoring the test in the concrete blockhouse and the operations building could not at first comprehend what they were hearing. "Did he say 'fire'?" an engineer asked the fellow at the next console, who replied that he had heard the same. "What the hell are they talking about?" they asked each other. A fire on the launchpad was the last thing anyone expected.

Indeed, no one foresaw the dangers of locking three astronauts inside a ship with miles of bad wiring, flammable material in abundance, corklike

hatches, and pressurized with pure oxygen. How could the Apollo designers have overlooked the obvious dangers? The consequences of a series of
engineering trade-offs made nearly six years earlier would effectively stop
the American manned space program in its tracks. Many feared the Apollo
program had died along with the astronauts on Pad 34. Those who had
warned against a "crash program" had been proven correct.

While all three astronauts suffered serious but likely survivable burns,
it was toxic smoke and carbon monoxide in the cabin and in the suit oxygen
loops of Grissom and Chaffee that killed them. White had managed to
disconnect his suit from the spacecraft oxygen supply and with his enormous lung capacity may have lived slightly longer. The official cause of
death was asphyxiation from smoke inhalation, carbon monoxide poison-
ing. A contributing cause, according to NASA flight surgeon Fred Kelly,
was hemorrhagic pulmonary edema—the astronauts' lungs filled with body
fluids and blood.[29] Fifty years after the tragedy, a detailed version of the
official autopsy reports has yet to be released.

Those closest to the spacecraft at the moment of maximum peril, the
pad crew, were as stunned by what was happening as the controllers in the
blockhouse and the operations building. It was relatively quiet in the White
Room as the final hold in the countdown dragged on. Just past 6:31 p.m.,
Pad 34 erupted in flames, smoke, and shouts. Was this a drill, some of the
technicians wondered?

All quickly realized this was no exercise when the spacecraft's pressure vessel ruptured, generating enough force to throw several workers
against the walls and door of the White Room enclosure. Pad Leader
Donald Babbitt was at his desk near the White Room waiting for the simulated countdown to resume as planned after 6:30 p.m. His crew would
pull the spacecraft connections at the end of the simulated countdown. In
the interim, the pad crew was talking among themselves and listening to
Grissom grouse as they waited for the countdown to resume.

"Gus was fussing a little bit," Stephen Clemmons, the North American
Aviation systems technician recalled. "Of course Gus always fussed.
Sometimes we'd call him 'The Nitpicker.' He probably had a right 'cause
he was very unhappy with the spacecraft and he didn't bother to conceal
his feelings on it."[30]

After hearing the initial report of a fire on Channel Black-3, Babbitt yelled to his lead mechanical technician, James Gleaves: "Get them out of there!" Babbitt ran to his left toward the pad communications box to notify controllers. He recalled the following: "Out of the corner of my eye, I saw flame come out from under the boost near the steam duct. I almost completed my turn when I was hit by a concussion or sheet of flame."[31]

The explosion knocked Babbitt against the communications box. His understandable reaction, he told investigators, was "to get out of there." (Babbitt was not alone; later reports had workers on Pad 34 scrambling down the service structure, mostly out of fear that the fire would set off the solid rocket motors on the Apollo Launch Escape System atop the command module.)

Babbitt recovered, ran across the Level A8 swing arm catwalk, and told the elevator operator who was wearing a headset to inform test supervisor Clarence "Skip" Chauvin of the fire and explosion. Babbitt also pleaded for firefighting equipment and ambulances. The only fire extinguishers available were all but useless for fighting an electrical fire. Babbitt, Gleaves, Clemmons, and another White Room technician, Jerry Hawkins, found the sole carbon dioxide bottle available on the A8 level of the service structure with which to fight the fire. They then made their way back to the cauldron that was now the White Room to begin removing the hatches. L. D. Reece, the quality control inspector, also heard the report of a fire and immediately threw his headset down to search for the lone functioning fire extinguisher. As the tragedy unfolded, there was but a sliver of hope the pad workers could somehow act quickly enough to save the crew. They failed, but not for lack of trying.

Clemmons had been monitoring the spacecraft panel that was feeding oxygen through a hose connected to an access port on the command module. It turned out he was the person closest to Spacecraft 012 when the fire erupted. That fact greatly complicated Clemmons's life for several days.

Recalling the nightmarish moments after the crew reported a fire, Clemmons observed the shocked expression on the face of Gleaves. Both men immediately understood the astronauts were probably doomed and the pad crew was in serious trouble. Like the astronauts, they did not abandon their stations. "Let's get them out," yelled Gleaves, who had been thrown against the swing arm door when the spacecraft ruptured. Gleaves realized he needed the T-handle Allen wrench used to open the hatches from the outside. The tool was inside Babbitt's desk. No one figured it would be needed immediately. Either Gleaves or Hawkins—the record is unclear—ducked under the thick smoke to Babbitt's scorched desk and began rifling through the drawers looking for the tool.

About thirty seconds after the first report of the fire, Babbitt and his crew were finally able to crawl to the smoldering spacecraft and begin working on the hatches in a swift succession of back-and-forth intervals, each lasting no more than two minutes. Using masks designed only to protect against noxious gas but useless against heavy smoke, they could hold their breath only so long. Gleaves eventually passed out and was ordered by Babbitt to stay out, but he soon returned. After repeated trips into the White Room and back out across the swing arm to gasp fresh air, Gleaves managed to remove the boost protective cover. He then gave the tool to Clemmons, Reece, or perhaps Hawkins, who together removed the outer, ablative hatch. The inner hatch was extremely hot to the touch when it was finally uncovered. The pad technicians could barely grab the heavy hatch by its handles.

"We attempted to both remove the inner hatch [and] lower the hatch down inside the command module," Babbitt later told investigators,[32] but they could only lower it partially into the spacecraft. The reason was the bodies of Grissom and White just below the foot of the hatch were blocking the way. Babbitt could make out the two crewmen but could not distinguish one from the other. "My observation at the time of hatch removal was that the flight crew were dead and that the destruction inside the command module was considerable."

It had taken Babbitt's crew about five minutes of herculean effort to remove the scorched hatches. Suffocating in the smoke and heat, a powerful escape rocket overhead, flames scorching the White Room ceiling, it was five minutes of maximum peril. There had been a desperate struggle on both sides of the hatches, but they could not be breached in time to save the crew.

It was quickly determined that saving the crew was impossible. Babbitt again walked across the swing arm at thirty seconds after 6:36 p.m. local time, found a working headset, and reported to test conductor Chauvin what he had seen amid the smoking ruins of the cockpit. The pad leader paused to consider all who were surely listening on the open communications line: "I can't tell you what I see" was all he revealed. Only then did everyone monitoring the countdown simulation grasp the unthinkable: The crew of *Apollo 1* was dead.

Grissom instinctively knew when the fire broke out that he had to dump the cabin pressure if there was any hope of extinguishing the flames. It required over a minute to release normal cabin pressure; the vent orifices in the relief valves were far too small for the enormous pressure building up in the spacecraft. Still, the commander understood this was his only option. There were no fire extinguishers aboard the spacecraft during the test. NASA had considered installing them prior to the launch but decided against it since they could only be used if the crew were in their pressure suits connected to a separate oxygen supply.

The likely ignition point was below Grissom's couch. Oxygen-fed flames raced over his station, up and over White's center couch, and around and under Chaffee's, incinerating everything in their path. As the heat and internal cabin pressure grew, the inner shell of the spacecraft, the pressure vessel, was giving way.

The official accident report and at least one congressional investigation of the Apollo 204 fire concluded that a device located to the left of Grissom's couch called a cabin pressure dump valve was "for reasons unknown" not activated to depressurize the cabin.[33] However, technicians who independently examined the dump valve actuators after the fire concluded that Grissom had partially succeeded in opening them. To do this, he had to reach his gloved hand through a wall of flame in an attempt to activate the valves that operated much like a gearshift. In his extreme haste to activate them, Grissom may have broken one or both of the valves. Rick Boos, the researcher who years later gained access to the burned out Apollo command module, believes Grissom at least made an attempt to open the valves. "Were they engaged enough to dump [cabin pressure]? I cannot answer that because the cabin ruptured at the same time. The main point is that Gus made the effort and was following emergency egress procedures," Boos concluded.[34]

Gleaves, the lead technician on Level A8, told investigators he heard a venting sound—the cabin relief valve opening and high-velocity gas escaping—as he ran to the White Room. "As we went up these two stairs we heard a loud *shooooo*, like maybe they had dumped cabin pressure," Gleaves testified.[35] Immediately after hearing the venting sound, the spacecraft heat shield ruptured under the tremendous internal pressure, covering Gleaves and Babbitt with flaming debris.

After reaching through the flames to activate the valves, emergency procedures required Grissom to help White open the hatches. This Grissom most certainly did. The commander removed the headrest on White's center couch so the senior pilot could grab a torque wrench used to ratchet open the clumsy inner hatch. But even the muscular White was no match for the heavy, corklike hatch held in place by enormous pressure. White and Grissom fought to the death trying to crank it open. Contrary to the official accident report, burn marks on the outer hatch indicated that White might have succeeded in at least breaking the seal on the inner hatch before succumbing to smoke and flames. Charles Stevenson, the NASA technician who had locked the hatches with difficulty at the beginning of the plugs-out test, claimed he observed what he later described as "claw marks" on the inside of the ablative hatch. White and Grissom likely made more progress opening the inner and outer hatches than officially acknowledged.

In the few seconds he had, White cranked away on the wrench to retract the six dogleg locking bars that held the inner hatch in place. Under normal circumstances, cabin pressure also would have to be purged before White could pull a release mechanism unlocking the outer hatch. The crew simply ran out of time and breathable air. Despite the ferocious fire, Grissom and his crew performed exactly as they were trained under unimaginable conditions. The spacecraft had become an inferno, eventually reaching temperatures well in excess of one thousand degrees Fahrenheit.[36] The astronauts were not incinerated; they were badly burned before flames consumed the spacecraft oxygen.

Throughout the death struggle, stunned controllers stared at their console screens as a video camera pointing at the hatch window showed flames engulfing the cockpit. The camera also showed White struggling with the hatch, and then another set of arms, Grissom's, helping to open it. (Whether a video recording of the fire ever existed remains a mystery.) Speaking figuratively, a former NASA official recalled: "The window went white and you watched the paint peel."

The fire raced across the cabin from Grissom's side to Chaffee's, likely penetrating Grissom's suit along with his and Chaffee's oxygen loops, filling them with toxic smoke and gases. As the temperature inside the cabin soared, cabin pressure split open the spacecraft seconds after the fire was first detected. The concussion knocked the pad workers off their feet and filled the immediate area of the White Room with dense, toxic smoke.

The precise time of death is unknown, and there were unsubstantiated claims that the crew may have remained alive and unconscious longer than what NASA has acknowledged. Doctors arrived at the White Room at 6:43 p.m.; by then, all three were certainly dead. What is known is that there were clear signs of a titanic struggle to get out, including White's handprints burned into the Teflon coating of the hatch and perhaps, according to the earliest press reports attributed to unnamed NASA sources, human skin found on the inner hatch.

NASA immediately insisted that a "flash fire" had killed the astronauts within seconds. Without the autopsy reports, it is impossible to say with any precision how long they lived. It was a terrible way to die. The one statement everyone agreed on from the accident investigation was that "three gallant men lost their lives in the line of duty."

What must be understood fifty years later is that the crew of *Apollo 1* acted precisely as they were trained to act in an emergency. After detecting flames, Grissom attempted to release cabin pressure despite flames originating on his side of the cramped cabin, perhaps hitting the valves so hard that, according to one NASA inspector, he broke them. The commander then helped remove White's headrest and assisted the senior pilot in the doomed effort to open the heavy inner hatch. Chaffee remained in his right-hand couch despite the terror of a fire fueled by pressurized oxygen, maintaining communications with the blockhouse before he too was overcome by smoke and toxic gases in his suit oxygen loop. Only eighteen seconds passed between the initial report of a fire and Chaffee's final shout. So much was happening so fast that no one could take it all in.

In the control room at the Operations and Checkout Building about five miles from the launchpad, spacecraft test conductor Skip Chauvin, the only person in the room authorized to speak to the astronauts, kept trying to raise the crew on Channel Black-3. The test conductors in the operations building and other controllers in the blockhouse sat stunned and confused when they heard the initial reports of a fire in the cockpit. Unable to raise the crew and realizing something extraordinary had occurred, the normally unflappable Chauvin yelled across the control room to personnel monitoring the spacecraft electrical systems to immediately power down the spacecraft. When that happened, it was clear to all in the room there was a serious problem with the spacecraft and the crew was in mortal danger.[37]

The Pad 34 blockhouse was located about five hundred yards from the launchpad. Rookie astronaut Stuart Roosa, who four years later would fly to the moon, was serving as "Stoney," the blockhouse Capcom. Deke Slayton was sitting next to Roosa at the Capcom's console. Despite the earlier debate over whether Slayton or Shea should climb into the spacecraft during the test to listen to the faulty communications for themselves, the plan was dismissed as impractical. Slayton monitored the test from the blockhouse. Shea cut short an interview in Cocoa Beach with a *Time* magazine reporter when informed of the fire and raced to the Kennedy Space Center.

After hearing the reports of a fire, Roosa and Chauvin both tried to contact the crew. Since no one considered the test dangerous, Roosa remembered thinking, "Chaffee is gonna hate to hear this tape in the morning." It soon dawned on Roosa, however, that a pure oxygen fire in a sealed spacecraft would be fatal.[38]

As Chauvin instructed his test conductors to power down the spacecraft, Roosa ran out of the blockhouse, straining to spot the command module through the service structure. After Slayton instructed emergency crews to get up to the A8 Level and contacted Houston to begin informing the families, he and Roosa headed for the launchpad. The hatches had been removed by the time they reached the White Room. The stench of death and an electrical fire permeated the enclosure. Slayton and Roosa looked inside the spacecraft and confirmed what the pad crew already knew: Grissom, White, and Chaffee were dead—asphyxiated and badly burned.

Like Pad Leader Babbitt, Slayton and Roosa also noted from the positions of the bodies that the crew had fought to open the hatches. All were unanimous that Grissom and White were found together, out of their couches, their melted pressure suits fused together at the base of the hatch.

Numerous accounts of the *Apollo 1* fire published over the intervening fifty years have misstated the positions of the bodies after the hatches were finally opened. Why does this matter? It is important because their location at the time of death bears directly on the crew's actions in the final seconds of their lives. In particular, the observations of those with the unenviable task of documenting the crew's positions when the hatches were finally pried open shows that Grissom did not panic, as NASA and others have suggested, attempting to escape the flames. Instead, the commander fought to the end to save his crew, battling the hatches alongside White. For Grissom, Apollo had been a long series of losing battles; the struggle to open the hatches was his last.

Erroneous accounts of the crew's actions asserted that Grissom's body was found with feet on his own couch and face up on the floor of the spacecraft, the implication being he had crawled there to escape the flames. These accounts have White strewn across the couches after failing to open the inner hatch. In fact, the last place Grissom would have retreated was the aft bulkhead, where a highly flammable foam pad was placed.[39] Given the path of the flames, the bulkhead would have been the most hellish spot in the cabin. In reality, the nylon pressure suits of White and Grissom were fused together by the intense cabin heat and pressure as they struggled to open the inner hatch.[40]

Likely the first NASA employee to inspect the gutted spacecraft and certainly the most senior official to view the carnage was Slayton. Grissom's weekend flying companion back at Langley Field in Virginia found himself in the horrendous position of having to peer into the smoldering cockpit to observe the dead astronauts and note their positions for the record.

What Slayton saw was surreal: small fluorescent cabin lights still flickering, gauges continuing to glow on the panels amid the acrid smoke and heat of the charred ruins of the cockpit. "It was a bad day," remembered Slayton. "Worst I ever had."[41]

Chaffee had remained in his right-hand seat throughout the horror of the fire. Grissom and White were found together at the base of the hatch, their faceplates blackened by the toxic smoke and fumes. Slayton told investigators he could not tell one from the other. It is likely, however, the command pilot was on top of the senior pilot.

In a statement to investigators on February 8, 1967, and later to a congressional committee, Slayton was unequivocal in stating that Grissom and White were "jumbled together" and Grissom was not, as the official version of events misstated, "lying supine on the aft bulkhead or floor of the command module."

"They were sort of jumbled together, and I couldn't really tell which head even belonged to which body at that point. I guess the only thing that was real obvious is that both bodies were at the lower edge of the hatch. They were not in the seats. They were almost completely clear of the seat areas."[42] The inference that Grissom had abandoned his post at the instant of maximum danger, shirking his sacred duty to protect his crew, that he instead had attempted to escape the flames, was a fiction.

NASA moved swiftly to seal off Pad 34 and the Kennedy Space Center in the hours after the hatches were opened and the astronauts' deaths confirmed. Several controllers managed to call home to inform their wives they would be working late. The phone lines were soon cut. Some of those wives called newspapers to find out what had happened at the Cape, tipping off editors and reporters that something was amiss on Pad 34 (no reporters had been allowed to observe the plugs-out test). NASA responded by circling the wagons, claiming nothing had happened in response to initial press queries, that there was nothing to report. It was a knee-jerk reaction and a futile attempt to control the flow of information, ostensibly as a way to shield the families of Grissom, White, and Chaffee.

Slayton and Jack King, the voice of NASA Mission Control, did not want the wives of the dead astronauts to find out what had happened in a radio or television news flash or a knock on the door from a reporter seeking comment. Slayton, the astronaut turned technocrat, was think-ing only of Betty Grissom, Pat White, and Martha Chaffee, not the First Amendment, in the agonizing minutes after the fire that killed one of his closest friends. It was wrong to suppress bad news, but Slayton did what he thought was right, and there would be no further discussion.

King, the former Associated Press space writer, understood the report-ers were doing their jobs by pursuing tips about something going wrong during the launchpad test. Still, King went along with the NASA brass. No one was prepared for what happened on January 27, 1967. NASA impro-vised, often badly.

The inferno on Pad 34 and the sudden deaths of the crew would ultimately send shock waves from the Kennedy Space Center to the Manned Spacecraft Center in Houston, on to North American Aviation in California and eventually back to the White House. "It hit you tre-mendously," recalled King, who was observing the plugs-out test from the blockhouse. "Of course there's no way to explain how you felt in the blockhouse at Pad 34. I went in there probably at one o'clock in the after-noon and I didn't get out there 'til about 12:30 the following morning."[43]

No one was permitted to leave until the Apollo escape rocket with its 155,000-pound thrust, solid-propellant motors was disarmed. "We were locked in for quite a while, and you had an awful lot to think about," King recalled.[44] "Of course I had to think about my responsibilities." Despite mounting pressure from the media for information, King made a deal with Slayton to withhold news of the tragedy until NASA had notified Betty Grissom, Pat White, and Martha Chaffee. He decided he "didn't want to spend the rest of [his] life knowing that Betty Grissom heard about [the fire and her husband's death] because of [his] announcement."

Back in Houston, Alan Bean was the sole astronaut on duty that evening when the call came in from the Cape. "We've lost the crew," Bean was told in the minutes after the fire. Bean initially thought the caller meant NASA couldn't locate Grissom, White, and Chaffee. How odd. Then it dawned on Bean, on station to take the call because he always arrived for work early and left late, that the caller meant something other than what Bean thought he had meant. The realization was sinking in: Grissom, the hard-nosed veteran; White, the all-American astronaut; and the rookie Chaffee were all gone. American astronauts had finally died, as many involved in the Apollo program privately expected. The odds of a fatal accident were better than even, but for Christ's sake, not on the launchpad! That was no way for astronauts to die.

Comprehending at last what the caller was telling him, Bean immediately began working the phones to track down Slayton and Alan Shepard, Slayton's assistant in the Astronaut Office, who was at the time of the fire delivering a speech in Dallas. Bean got through to both on the first try. The rookie was amazed the Mercury veterans instinctively knew what to do. Send someone—a wife, another astronaut, anyone connected with NASA—as fast as possible to the crew members' homes in Timber Cove. The knock on the door, the look in the neighbor's eyes would immediately convey the enormity of what had just happened. Your husband, the father of your children, is dead. You are on your own.

Gene Kranz, the legendary NASA flight director, called the fire "perhaps the defining moment in our race to get to the Moon. After this," Kranz observed, "nothing would be quite the same, ever again."[45] Kranz, dressing for dinner out that Friday evening, learned about the fire from his neighbor, a fellow flight director who banged on Kranz's door. When told that the crew was probably dead, Kranz figured the Saturn rocket had blown up.

When asked years later about the *Apollo 1* fire, the first man to walk on the moon recalled the trauma. "Oh yes, I remember it very well," Neil Armstrong told the historian Douglas Brinkley. "I'd known Gus for a long time. Ed White and I bought some property together and split it. I built my house on one half of it, and he built his house on the other. We were good friends, neighbors. Some very traumatic times. You know, I suppose you're much more likely to accept loss of a friend in flight, but it really hurt to lose them in a ground test." Armstrong continued, "That was an indictment of ourselves. . . . I mean, [it happened] because we didn't do the right thing somehow. That's doubly, doubly traumatic."

Contemporaneous press accounts before NASA's "flash fire" narrative took hold were graphic. A *New York Times* article on January 31 reported some of the first grim details about the seconds before and after the fire, attributing its report to "an engineer who spent most of the day listening to tape recordings of the fatal test and who heard reports from men on the launchpad at the time of the tragedy." According to the newspaper, "At the hatch the technicians found fingerprints and the skin of fingers that stuck there. The astronauts were almost completely destroyed by the fire. Little more than their bones remained."[46]

Despite these initial exaggerated reports, the reality was quickly sinking in that the decision to fill the Apollo spacecraft on the launchpad with pure oxygen at 16.7 pounds per square inch had been a fatal and unnecessary mistake. George Page, chief test conductor for Gemini and Apollo, told an interviewer decades later: "We put 100 percent oxygen into that vehicle and then pressurized it. Now we'd done that all through Gemini, all through Mercury. And we were doing that in Apollo. And nobody stood up and said, 'Hey, [do] you guys know what you got when you pressurize a hundred percent oxygen? You got a bomb sittin' there!'"

Across the swampy Florida peninsula, west beyond the Gulf of Mexico, far from the machinery of rockets and spaceships and launch simulations, it was the end of another week in the astronaut enclave of Timber Cove. Betty Grissom and sons Scott and Mark were looking forward to the weekend and seeing their husband and father for at least part of the weekend. They did not yet realize as the sun set over Houston that the husband and father was gone.

Betty was preparing dinner when the doorbell rang. It was her neighbor Adelin Hammack, the wife of Gus's NASA buddy Jerry, who went out hot-rodding with Gus and Mark in Gus's Corvette. It was Adelin who would help Betty through the hard months ahead. On the evening of the fire, Adelin was instructed without explanation to rush to the Grissom's house. Betty immediately suspected something had happened, probably something serious. She later remembered "a certain numbness" after Adelin arrived. Friends did not just turn up unannounced on a Friday evening just before dinner.

Betty held it together and invited Adelin in for a drink. Then the doorbell rang again. It was Jo Schirra, Wally's wife, the Grissoms's next-door neighbor. She had ducked through a hole cut in the fence between their yards to reach the Grissom threshold. Betty saw Jo's face and knew immediately it was bad. Jo told Betty there had been an accident and Gus had been injured, but she was not sure how badly.

Presently, the wife of Dr. Charles Berry, the astronauts' physician arrived, followed by the chief NASA flight surgeon himself. It was Dr. Berry who conveyed the news on behalf of NASA to Betty that her husband of twenty-one years was dead, killed in a cockpit fire along with his crew. It was a test on the launchpad. The Saturn rocket was not fueled. How, she must have thought, could such a thing happen?

Betty—the wife of a military test pilot, astronaut, and national hero who had spent the better part of the last decade on the flight line—immediately assumed the role of stoic NASA widow. She turned from Dr. Berry, walked to the back of the house, closed the bedroom door, and informed Scott and Mark their father was dead. The wide-eyed boys, inheritors of their parents' Indiana stoicism, did not cry at the news. Scott idolized his father; Mark hardly knew him.

It would not seem much different for a while because Gus was "gone most of the time anyway," Betty wrote in her recollection of the awful evening. "Now he was gone, period."[47] Among Betty's first realizations was that she would miss her husband's phone calls.

Wally Schirra arrived soon after the others. He would act as executor of Virgil I. Grissom's estate, helping to guide Betty, Scott, and Mark through the coming darkness. Schirra and his backup crew had hightailed it out of Cape Kennedy as the plugs-out test dragged on. What was the point of sitting around listening to Gus bellyache about his ship? He, Walt Cunningham, and Donn Eisele hopped into their T-38s and headed back to Houston for the weekend. As they taxied to a stop at Ellington Air Force Base near Houston, Bud Ream, with NASA flight operations, met them on the tarmac. The crew could tell by his presence on a Friday night and the grim expression on his face that something bad had happened. The prime crew of *Apollo 1* was dead, Ream informed the backup crew. "They're dead. All of them."[48]

Schirra raced down the Gulf Freeway to his next-door neighbor's home, thinking all the way from the airfield about his warning the day before to the Apollo commander to get out if the launch simulation was going badly. The plugs-out test exposed one problem after another, which is the primary purpose of such an exercise. Grissom had persevered, however, resisting the calls of some of the test conductors to call it off and start over the next day or the following week.

It was now painfully obvious Grissom should have taken Schirra's advice. Colleagues acknowledged later that Grissom should have known better. Al Worden, a member of the third group of astronauts, never worked on the Block I Apollo spacecraft, but he understood it was a dangerous ship. "A lot of things, a lot of things went wrong on *Apollo 1*. They were overpressurizing it with pure oxygen and all it took was a spark," Worden noted. "And [Grissom] should have known that, a lot of people should have known that."[49]

Meanwhile, Slayton's call to Houston had set in motion a well-established astronaut ritual designed to shield the families in the event of a tragedy. Slayton cared not a whit for the reporters or their queries about what happened that evening on Pad 34; his sole concern was making certain that NASA employees or their wives got to the homes of the dead astronauts before the reporters. Meanwhile, the ham-handed NASA public affairs apparatus initially responded to the disaster by telling reporters to "go on home, nothing has happened."

Stonewalling reporters doing their jobs was one thing. Purposely deceiving the press corps was another matter entirely. With the exception of Slayton, the NASA PR machine was utterly unprepared in the hours after the fire to deal with an unprecedented calamity.

And so the wake began. It fell to Betty to inform her in-laws in Mitchell that Gus was dead. Nearly simultaneously, the news of fatalities on Pad 34 arrived from the Kennedy Space Center over Dennis and Cecile's television. Gus's parents were home the entire evening, but Cecile recalled no one from NASA calling to notify them of their son's death.[50] The call from Betty was followed by a visit from the Grissoms's pastor. After calling their sons and daughter, Dennis and Cecile pulled down their window shades and turned out the lights of the same modest home on Baker Street where their dead son had grown up. Later, Cecile would tell an interviewer, "My son had to give his life to make [the Apollo spacecraft] better."[51]

owell Grissom was still at the office that Friday evening at the General Electric jet engine plant in Cincinnati. "My dad called and told me there had been an accident on the launchpad and they hadn't survived. It was before 7 o'clock" in the evening eastern time. "They wanted to make sure that we were called before it hit the news."

In Downey, where other Apollo crews had been training that day in another Block I spacecraft, it was late afternoon. Harrison Storms, president of North American Aviation's Space and Information Division, was in a conference room thinking about his youngest son's wedding rehearsal dinner that evening. He had promised to show up on time for a change despite the long technical meeting about the Apollo Block II spacecraft droning on in front of him. His secretary interrupted the meeting to inform Storms that someone from the Cape was on the phone and there had been a fire in the *Apollo 1* spacecraft.

Storms had the call transferred to the speakerphone, where all in the room heard the shocking report. "There is no hope now," an eyewitness told Storms and his stunned engineering staff.

Lee Atwood, Storms's boss, was in Washington at that moment about to sit down to dinner at the International Club with NASA administrator James Webb, Wernher von Braun, and Robert Gilruth. All had attended a White House ceremony earlier in the day commemorating the signing of the Outer Space Treaty. Atwood was paged. It was Storms on the other end of the line when Atwood picked up. "There has been a bad fire at the Cape," Storms reported. "How bad?" Atwood inquired. "All the astronauts are dead," Storms replied.

Dumbstruck, Atwood asked Storms to repeat what he had just reported. Atwood spotted Gilruth with a drink in his hand. Handing the phone to the director of the Manned Spacecraft Center, Atwood exclaimed: "Jesus, Bob, have you heard about this tragedy at the Cape?"[52]

The news was passed along to Webb, who immediately called the White House. Word soon spread around the dining room as dinner was being served. No one could eat.

When Rene Carpenter heard about the fire on the television, she raced through Glenn's backyard, past the Hammacks, and crossed Pine Shadows Drive. The Grissoms's front door at Number 211 was ajar. Rene entered and saw Betty already "stone-faced and composed."[53] The house on Pine Shadows was already full of NASA people when Rene arrived; Betty was putting on the brave face that was now her burden. Betty and Rene had been through much together, riding out Gus's first flight, agonizing over the disastrous recovery when Gus nearly drowned. On the night of the fire, Rene remembered that no one could bring himself to speak of the "cataclysmic folly" that had killed three men.

The old test pilot ritual had begun, a wake in which friends and colleagues brought food no one could eat, the booze flowed with little effect, and few if anyone knew what to say, simply because there was nothing to be said. "They didn't feel anything," Betty repeated throughout the grim evening. It was over in ten seconds. To believe otherwise would have been unbearable. One had to keep going no matter what the knock on the door brought.

Later, to get him out of the house, Rene took thirteen-year-old Mark to the feed store in Seabrook to pick up sweet feed for the Carpenter girls' horses. After a popsicle, they drove slowly back to Timber Cove. The bewildered boy returned to his home as the funeral arrangements were being made.

An Associated Press photographer camped out in front of the Grissom home snapped a series of pictures of the forlorn family hound, Sam, waiting on the front walk. Perhaps Sam was guarding the fort. The wire service decided Sam was "waiting for his master who will never return."

Early on the morning of January 28, 1967, the bodies of Air Force Lieutenant Colonel Virgil I. Grissom, age 40, Air Force Lieutenant Colonel Edward H. White Jr., age 36, and Navy Lieutenant Commander Roger B. Chaffee, just 31, were finally removed from their charred ship, the ill-fated Spacecraft 012. The bodies were transported by ambulance to nearby Patrick Air Force Base for an autopsy and preparation for burial.

The *Apollo 1* crew had been expected back in Houston that Saturday to continue flight preparations and presumably review the results of the plugs-out test. Then the Grissoms would head to the Field Enterprises bash that evening in Houston. The party was of course cancelled, the entire city now in mourning over the dead astronauts. Funeral arrangements had to be made, memorial services planned, the details of somehow coming to grips with the enormity of sudden and violent death worked out. All this took place in an atmosphere of shock and national grief on a scale not seen since JFK's assassination three years earlier. The nation cared deeply about these men, "pioneers," Schirra later told a reporter, "who put themselves out on a limb."[54]

Sam Beddingfield, who had joined NASA in 1959 at his buddy Gus Grissom's urging, summed up the space agency's failure to ensure the safety of the *Apollo 1* crew. Beddingfield grimly concluded after the fire: "You couldn't have built a better booby trap."[55]

15

ABANDON IN PLACE

This was Arlington and here they all lay, formed up for the last time.
—James Salter

Gus Grissom and the crew of *Apollo 1* were casualties of the Cold War, the ideological, technological, and military struggle between the United States and the Soviet Union. The decades-long competition came closer to destroying the planet at its zenith during the Cuban Missile Crisis of 1962 than any previous war.

The US-Soviet race in space helped redefine the goals of the Cold War. Grissom had been a different kind of Cold Warrior during one of its key flash points, the Korean War. Cold War tensions soared again with the 1957 launch of *Sputnik*, fueling fears of Soviet domination of space. The US space program was hastily established on the principle that America would respond to *Sputnik* and compete for the high ground. By the spring of 1961, two months before Grissom's first flight, the United States boldly declared it would land a man on the moon ahead of the Russians. For the winner, there would be international prestige, the opportunity to claim the superiority of its technology and—by extension—its political and economic systems. Grissom and his Mercury colleagues would serve as the vanguard of a new kind of Technological Cold Warrior competing in a new arena, one in which risk takers would seek to outdo each other in the deadly vacuum of space rather than over the contested skies of Central Europe or, later, Southeast Asia.

The Space Race, a competition cooked up in a matter of weeks, officially began on May 25, 1961, when a young president declared the United States would send men to the moon and return them safely home by the end of the decade. Stung by defeat and betrayal weeks earlier at the Bay of Pigs in Cuba, another flashpoint in the Cold War, President John F. Kennedy sought a way to change the subject while channeling the pent-up energy and innovation of the richest nation in the history of the world. JFK's trusted counselor, Theodore Sorensen, who helped lay the groundwork for Kennedy's moon-landing speech to a joint session of Congress, recalled the existential threat posed by Moscow's rocket capabilities and the very real prospect of Soviet military control of outer space. Kennedy and Sorensen quickly came around to the view that a manned lunar landing would help close the space gap while giving substance to the candidate's New Frontier campaign slogan. Grissom saw himself as a pioneer. Along with the other Mercury astronauts, he was more than willing to answer Kennedy's call. The costs would be high in lives and treasure.

Even politicians with the most to gain in terms of Cold War prestige understood that exploring space could quickly drain their coffers. In the late 1950s, the gulag survivor and Russian rocket designer Sergei Pavlovich Korolev informed Nikita Khrushchev that each Soviet R-7 rocket installation would cost half a billion rubles. "What will we do?" Khrushchev responded. "We'll be without our pants."[1]

By 1963, the economic realities of the Space Race also were closing in on the American president. Kennedy was utterly enamored by the danger, risk, and scientific prestige of manned space exploration. He eventually understood a race to the moon could break the bank. To the Soviet ambassador Anatoly Dobrynin, no less, he downplayed the importance of a series of Russian and American orbital missions, dismissing them as "three-day wonders" that were "not that important"[2] and too costly in the long run. His post–Cuban Missile Crisis policies now aimed at détente with the Soviet Union while reining in his own trigger-happy generals. Hence, Kennedy was proposing a joint lunar mission with the Russians by the fall of 1963.[3]

The president fully understood the importance of national prestige as a Cold War tenet but also was concluding in autumn 1963 that the United States could no longer afford to go to the moon alone. Hence, he was feeling out the Russians about a joint lunar mission. JFK was in the midst of a fundamental reassessment of US-Soviet relations, one that reevaluated the wisdom of a "crash" lunar program. A year later, Kennedy was dead and Soviet Premier Nikita Khrushchev was ousted from power.

In the last year of the Kennedy administration, the enormous costs of a manned lunar landing had finally hit home.[4] Politicians were only considering the financial costs. There would be other sacrifices, which few could foresee. In his haste to secure the next flight, it is unlikely Grissom considered those costs; he and the rest of the astronaut corps were now firmly in the grip of forces they could no longer control. All wanted to beat the Russians to the moon. Every Soviet space success was grudgingly acknowledged while firing the competitive drive of the growing astronaut corps.

A week before his assassination in Dallas, Kennedy again visited Cape Canaveral to see for himself the mighty new Saturn rocket developed by Wernher von Braun's team in Huntsville, Alabama. The Saturn rocket would at last give the Americans the lead in the Space Race. Accompanying the president on his tour of the Cape were Grissom and Gordon Cooper.

From the day of Kennedy's moon landing declaration to Congress in 1961, the clock began ticking on a crash program. Once started, Apollo gathered momentum and moved fast, much faster than other government-funded technology programs. In the political parlance of Washington, the Apollo program had "legs." The scale of development quickly outpaced the ability of engineers and managers to keep up with the details of arguably the largest technological endeavor since World War II.

The men and women of Apollo—overwhelmingly men—simply could not get their collective arms around all that they were undertaking, overlooking what the early, faulty machinery was revealing in the test data. The warnings signs were either overlooked or ignored. Apollo would become the very definition of a "crash" program. At the very top of this technological pyramid, hastily constructed on a foundation of sand, was Gus Grissom. NASA flight director Chris Kraft acknowledged the deadly consequences of "Go Fever," the hell-bent drive to beat the Russians to the moon: "We were willing to put up with a lot of poor hardware and poor preparation in order to try to get on with the job. And a lot of us knew that we were doing that."[5]

It is easy in hindsight to see the consequences of the technological train wreck[6] that was Apollo in the mid-1960s. The fact remains that those inside the program, responsible for the lives of the astronauts, had simply lost sight of crew safety. Later, too late, many acknowledged their failures, finally understanding that the astronauts' deaths were a direct result of their carelessness. Some never recovered.

A series of early US space successes bred complacency. Complacency kills. Grissom understood the risks. In return for embracing them, he had won the coveted slot as commander of the first Apollo mission. Had he decided against flying a flawed machine, Grissom understood others would quickly line up to replace him. Boxed in and blinded by the rewards, Grissom rolled the dice. He and the rest of the astronaut corps believed they could engineer the risks out of the faulty Apollo hardware. Grissom had inherited a mess but reckoned he could somehow beat the odds, even though he and his bosses were literally playing with fire.

The odds of failure in an all-out program like Apollo were high; the chances of an accident finally caught up with the American space program at a time and place no one could imagine: on the launchpad in a three-man spacecraft on top of an unfueled rocket during what was considered a routine test. The fire that killed Grissom, White, and Chaffee was a direct consequence of shortsighted engineering decisions made several years before: using a pure oxygen environment in a spaceship equipped with a heavy, inward-opening hatch and an outer hatch requiring at least ninety seconds to crank open.

Dedication, professionalism, and attention to every detail, especially crew safety, might have prevented a deadly fire, but human endeavors as complex as Apollo seldom work that way. Where technology is preeminent, lessons often must be learned the hard way. It turned out in January 1967 that the deaths of three astronauts were among the sacrifices required for humans to reach the moon.

After news of the disaster broke and the deaths of the astronauts spread like a shock wave across the nation, the NASA public affairs machine managed to release a terse three-paragraph statement confirming that Grissom, White, and Chaffee were "killed . . . in a flash fire." The news release inaccurately stated that the crew entered the spacecraft at 3 p.m. EST (they were in the couches shortly after 1 p.m.), the hatches had been sealed, and "emergency crews were hampered by dense smoke in removing the hatches." In reality, there were no "emergency crews" near the spacecraft, only pad technicians. And there was little or no effective fire-fighting equipment available. NASA's statement was at least accurate in two respects: the crew was dead and "all data [had] been impounded pending an investigation."

With that, any chance of an independent probe of what happened on Pad 34 was foreclosed as NASA management closed ranks in the hours after the tragedy. Little in the way of information was released beyond NASA Administrator James Webb's telling remark: "Although everyone realized that someday space pilots would die, who would have thought the first tragedy would be on the ground?"

With the assembled media at Cape Kennedy clamoring for details, NASA relented, allowing the experienced yet friendly journalist George Alexander, accompanied by a news photographer, to examine the charred cockpit. As "pool" reporters, they would share their observations with colleagues at Cape Canaveral. Alexander accurately described the spacecraft interior as looking "like the cockpit of an aircraft in World War II that took a direct hit."

NASA moved quickly to appoint an official board of inquiry chaired by Floyd Thompson, director of the Langley Research Center. The board consisted primarily of NASA, Air Force, and other government officials who quickly began interviewing witnesses and sifting through what was left of Grissom's spacecraft in search of clues. With the in-house inquiry under way, the space agency said little else in the days and weeks after the fire. The American space program was now dead in the water, a moon landing now farther away than ever.

D espite months of finger-pointing and blame-laying in reaction to the *Apollo 1* fire, most everyone at the space agency and its contractors understood immediately they dared not let down their fallen comrades. As Walter Cunningham of the backup crew wrote: "The accident would have been even more tragic if the work the crew started had not been allowed to continue and they had died for nothing." In the tragic aftermath, he observed: "At least the evidence was right in front of us—on Pad 34."

It was Cunningham who retrieved the Apollo commander's air force uniform, hopping on a NASA T-38 trainer and delivering it to Cape Kennedy after the astronauts' autopsy. Cunningham had earlier arrived at the Schirras's and slipped through the hole cut into the backyard fence to the Grissoms's. Schirra had removed Grissom's uniform from a bedroom closet and handed it to Cunningham through the back door, out of Betty's sight. It was the dress uniform in which Grissom would be buried.[7] Cunningham was grateful that grim weekend to have something useful to do.

The astronauts immediately understood a launchpad fire meant there existed at least a chance the cause could be traced and the utterly flawed Block I Apollo command module fixed. In the ensuing months, such a machine was built. The Block II Apollo spacecraft represented a complete overhaul of the ship that killed Grissom and his crew. It included a hinged, outward-swinging hatch that could be opened in three seconds, a two-gas cabin atmosphere in the cockpit, protective floorboards, and vastly improved wiring and fireproofing. It would eventually take twenty-four humans to the moon and return them safely. A great machine would be forged from the flames of *Apollo 1*.

The sixth man to walk on the moon, Edgar Mitchell, who was among the astronauts who flew the "Missing Man" formation honoring the lost crew during the weekend memorial services near Houston, recalled later that those charged with fixing Apollo "would make certain that Gus, Roger and Ed did not die in vain." The fire "would be transformed into a bitter blessing, a Pyrrhic victory that would one day quietly contribute to the success of the astronauts who followed."[8]

Articulating the meaning of Apollo, Mitchell continued: "NASA and its individual members were a part of the evolutionary process of humankind, a significant cog in the machine that would take us to other worlds. The people around me would be the first of our species to explore these new landscapes; Ed, Roger, and Gus were a part of the process as well, even in death."

Mitchell and the other astronauts realized and understood the following: "Our three compatriots would admonish us were we to abandon the larger project as a result of their death[s], because from the beginning it seemed unlikely that a project of this magnitude could be accomplished without loss of life."[9]

For all its horror, the fire on Pad 34 proved to be *the* decisive turning point in the Space Race. The United States would not have reached the moon by the end of the decade had *Apollo 1* not exploded. "I hesitate to say this, but I have to say it: I don't think that we would have gotten to the moon in the Sixties if we had not had the fire," said flight director Kraft, echoing the sentiments of many who worked on Apollo. "That's a terrible thing to say, but I think it is true."[10]

Other NASA veterans have over the decades expressed a decidedly different view, one that dismisses the notion that avoidable sacrifices teach valuable lessons. This interpretation of the fire on Pad 34 and fatal space shuttle accidents that followed instead stresses the visceral need to touch these tragedies, to imagine how the astronauts died, and to feel the inconsolable grief of parents, spouses, and children. Flight director Gene Kranz believed everyone at NASA needed to reexamine his or her role in Apollo and the fatal fire. Ultimately, each individual needed to take responsibility for what happened, acknowledge the consequences of creeping complacency and carelessness, and thereafter strive never again to repeat those deadly mistakes. All who worked on Apollo had to understand that lives were always at stake in human spaceflight, that no one in the space agency or its contractors could ever duck the "fearsome responsibility" described by the former NASA mission controller James Oberg: "We should have known already, and people should not have had to die to remind us." *Apollo 1*, *Challenger*, and *Columbia* were not accidents, Oberg insisted. "They were consequences of complacency and carelessness."[11]

Grissom understood better than most that risk played no favorites. He nevertheless decided it was worth taking. That decision turned out to be his undoing. It also was his greatest contribution to the history of human space exploration. All who followed owed a debt to Grissom and his crew.

However high-minded the sacrifice, the senseless tragedy was a direct result of negligence on the part of Grissom's bosses and the contractors NASA was obliged to oversee. Ultimately, NASA was culpable for the deaths of Grissom, White, and Chaffee after accepting delivery of a "dumb machine"[12] in the summer of 1966 that should never have left the factory.

Critics soon filled the void created by official silence in the aftermath of the fire. They had watched along with the rest of the nation the televised burials of the three astronauts. Paul Conrad, the Pulitzer Prize–winning editorial cartoonist of the *Los Angeles Times*, distilled the public's sense of revulsion in the tragedy's aftermath. About a week after the fire, as the Apollo review board's investigation was ramping up, Conrad depicted in a way no official report ever could the deadly element of risk that hung always over the Space Race. In Conrad's rendering, the specter of death is pictured in a spacesuit holding a Mercury spacecraft in one hand and a Gemini spacecraft in the other. Gus Grissom's smoldering Apollo spacecraft is seen in the background. Conrad's caption reads: "I thought you knew. I've been aboard on every flight."[13]

The fatal fire and NASA's knee-jerk response to it would signal a fundamental shift within the space agency and its army of contractors. The first sign was the predictable bureaucratic response in a crisis: circle the wagons and attempt to control the flow of information.[14] NASA officials moved swiftly to lock down the Kennedy Space Center and mission control in Houston. It took just over two months for a swift in-house investigation to conclude that faulty wiring was the likely cause of the fire. For the record, investigators said they could not pin down the exact location of the ignition source. Perhaps no investigation could have in a machine as complex and flawed as the Block I Apollo command module.

The harsh reality was that political and engineering trade-offs made years earlier became the foundation for an inherently risky enterprise on an extremely tight schedule that ended up killing three men. Grissom was caught up in these powerful forces and surely concluded in the months before his death that he had little choice but to play the hand he had been dealt.

nvestigators documented the spacecraft interior before the crew was removed early on the morning of January 28. Grissom's and White's nylon suits had been fused together by the tremendous heat. Following the military autopsies of Grissom, White, and Chaffee at Patrick Air Force Base just south of the Kennedy Space Center, their bodies were prepared for burial and transferred in civilian hearses with a military escort from the medical dispensary to the airfield. Their caskets were loaded onto military transports for a flight to Andrews Air Force Base outside Washington, DC. White's body would be transferred to New York for burial at the US Military Academy at West Point.[15]

As the bodies of the crew members were being prepared for burial, a series of hastily planned memorial services were being held during the last weekend of January 1967 in the Houston suburb of Seabrook and elsewhere. Betty Grissom, wearing a light-colored dress and gloves, is seen in newsreel footage being escorted into a chapel by Marge Slayton and Michael Collins. Collins was standing in for Deke Slayton, who was already swept up in the fire investigation. Wernher von Braun also attended the memorial service for Grissom. The first of several "Missing Man" formations flew over the mourners. Betty steeled herself to bury her husband back in Virginia, where Grissom's career as an astronaut began.

irgil Ivan Grissom and Roger Bruce Chaffee were buried side by side on a rise overlooking the Capitol from the Virginia side of the Potomac River on January 31, 1967, a sharply cold, clear day. The grave sites are tucked away deep within the hallowed grounds of Arlington National Cemetery in out-of-the-way Section 3 reserved for aviation pioneers.

US Army First Lieutenant Thomas Etholen Selfridge was among the first to be buried in Section 3, not far from the spot where a plane in which he was a passenger crashed at Fort Myer near the western end of the military cemetery. Selfridge, a West Point graduate and ardent aviation supporter, was an associate of Alexander Graham Bell, himself an airplane inventor and rival of the Wright brothers. Selfridge became the first military air casualty while aboard a plane piloted by one of the world's first two test pilots, Orville Wright. The younger of the Wright brothers had recently completed a series of record-setting endurance flights at Fort Myer. Selfridge had arranged to be assigned as a passenger on another of Orville's test flights. The strapping Selfridge weighed 175 pounds, more than any previous passenger. (Even then, weight was a critical factor in aviation.) The pair took off in the late afternoon of September 17, 1908. On the fourth pass over the field, Orville Wright heard "a light tapping" followed by "a terrible shaking."[16] A propeller blade cracked, and the propeller began to vibrate, tearing loose a stay wire that wrapped around the blade. The blade snapped off, and the out-of-control aircraft dropped like a rock, about seventy-five feet before crashing.[17] Selfridge died several hours later of a fractured skull at the age of twenty-six; Wright remained in critical condition for days with a fractured leg and hip and broken ribs. Selfridge was the first military casualty of powered flight, but he had at least gotten off the ground.

Grissom[18] and Chaffee were buried a short distance from Selfridge's grave. Other astronauts killed in plane crashes also were interred at Arlington, but Grissom and Chaffee were the first US astronauts killed in their spacecraft.

Grissom's casket was delivered to Arlington by hearse at 9 a.m. A six-man Air Force honor guard transferred the casket to a caisson. The Air Force band led the procession to the gravesite, which had been covered with fake grass that stood out against the drab winter landscape.

A long line of limousines waited behind as Grissom's flagged-draped coffin was transferred to the caisson drawn by a team of six horses, three riderless. Grissom's fellow Mercury astronauts and his Gemini crewmate John Young served as pallbearers, marching alongside the caisson in military cadence: Glenn, Cooper, and Young on one side, Shepard, Carpenter, and the retired air force officer Slayton in civilian clothes on the other. Wally Schirra escorted Betty, her two sons, and Gus's parents.

Behind the caisson walked Gilruth, Kraft, and other NASA administrators, who no doubt felt, Betty Grissom recalled, "the weight of diffused guilt and persistent self-questioning."[19] She also would remember hoof beats, the stiff caisson wheels creaking on the pavement, and the biting cold. The solemnity and formality of the military funeral summoned memories of JFK's burial at Arlington just over three years earlier.

Newsmen and photographers flanked the funeral procession, dodging rows of headstones as they ran. A large crowd of mourners and onlookers had already gathered at the gravesite. Soon, the procession arrived and the casket was placed on the catafalque. Betty, Scott, and Mark, along with Dennis and Cecile, facing west, filled the seats to the right of the casket. Gus Grissom was briefly eulogized as the Missing Man formation thundered overhead for the last time. A bugler played "Taps." After the flag on Grissom's coffin was presented to Betty, who betrayed no emotion, President Lyndon B. Johnson, the driving force behind the manned space program after *Sputnik*, rose to grasp and hold the silent widow's hand and offer condolences. Johnson then shook the hands of the two Grissom sons, who remained seated. Each was still trying to come to grips with the reality that their father was gone. Scott and Mark mostly stared at the ground, numbed by the events of the previous four days.

Unflinching, Betty glared at the honor guard as they folded the American flag over her husband's casket. The realization was sinking in that she and the boys were now truly on their own. A *Life* magazine photographer captured the image. The magazine's editors spread the photo over a page and a half of its funeral coverage.[20] Betty's expression—a combination of shock, pain, bitterness, and resignation—was among the earliest images to distill the human toll of risk taking during the Space Age. It was a reminder that death lingered always in the race to the moon. Betty, a widow at thirty-nine, would come to symbolize all the astronaut wives whose husbands were killed in training accidents during the 1960s and, eventually, the survivors of later space disasters.[21]

Finally, Dennis Grissom rose to accept the president's condolences. Johnson exchanged a few words with Virgil's parents. Cecile, in a beige cloth coat and white hat, remained seated as the president leaned over, held her hand, and whispered a few words. Johnson moved closer to hear Cecile's reply. The president patted the mother's hand one last time, straightened up, and walked back to the waiting presidential limousine. He would repeat these official duties several hours later at the same spot during the funeral of Roger Chaffee.

With that, the service ended. The mourners filed back to the waiting limousines, each filled with the emptiness and loss that accompanies tragedy. Only the January cold, the rustling of the oak trees, and the empty caisson remained. Betty, her sons, and the dead astronaut's parents departed, and the cemetery workers arrived. Gus Grissom had always wanted to be buried at Arlington, believing he had earned the honor to be interred there among the other pioneers of flight. Indeed, this was the least his country could do for him, for his family. The far corner of Arlington again fell silent, and the exploits of the fearless astronaut who had risked everything over the previous decade would soon be forgotten. Others riding giant rockets would be the first to truly leave the planet, to see the whole circle of Earth from their spaceships. Grissom was now consigned to the earth.

The Grissom family displayed characteristic Midwest stoicism after their son, husband, father, and brother was killed. So too had the Chaffees of Michigan. Roger's inconsolable mother, Blanche, summoned the strength and dignity to answer a reporter's question during a memorial service for her son. Through her tears, Blanche recalled: "Roger was so energetic, so enthusiastic about the whole program. We're sure that as long as he had to leave this world, he's happy in his spaceship anyway."

A reporter then asked Donald Chaffee if he harbored any ill will over his son's death. "None whatsoever," the father replied, recalling the promise he had made to his son on a Florida beach the previous summer. "The price of progress comes high at times."[22]

Chaffee, the rookie astronaut who carried himself with a "bantam-rooster air of confident competence,"[23] never got his chance to fly in space, to fulfill his dream of walking on the moon. Chaffee had been a perfectionist, a trait that would have consequences for his family after his death. "He ruled his household, wrote all the checks, made all the decisions," his friend, fellow astronaut, and Purdue graduate Eugene Cernan observed later. "Now that he was gone, his wife and children were adrift." Lieutenant Commander Roger Chaffee was just thirty-one years old when he perished in the flames.

West of the main campus, at the end of Airport Road and Aviation Drive, off the main runway at the Purdue University Airport, sits Chaffee Hall. The modest building situated among the fluid dynamics, combustion research, and high-pressure research laboratories is in the thick of things, just as its namesake was from his first days as an astronaut.

A s the crew of *Apollo 1* was being buried, NASA investigators were scrambling to determine how the disaster could have occurred during a supposedly "routine" test. Still in denial about the fundamentally flawed machine NASA had designed, investigators were initially convinced that Pad 34 was a crime scene and someone must have done something wrong to cause the fire. The space agency simply could not acknowledge that its own mismanagement had killed the crew.

In the frantic hours and days after the fire, investigators instead focused on several potential causes that included faulty wiring harnesses, an exploding battery, and a cockpit switch providing power to a backup spacecraft guidance system called a body-mounted attitude gyro, or BMAG. They also zeroed in on the actions of the pad technicians on duty the night of the fire, specifically, Stephen B. Clemmons.

Clemmons, the North American Aviation spacecraft mechanical technician, was monitoring the panel supplying pure oxygen to the spacecraft's environmental control system on the evening of the fire. "I had the misfortune of being next to *Apollo 1*, America's newest spacecraft built by North American Aviation, at the crucial moment when it burst into flames," Clemmons recalled decades later.[24] Haunted by the Apollo fire, Clemmons recalled the smoke and flames, the shouting astronauts, and his colleagues' shock on Pad 34 as they braved the inferno to open the hatches. Like the others, Clemmons had to live with the memory of the launchpad fire for the rest of his days, the toxic smoke perhaps shortening a life that ended on June 1, 2014.

Amid the flames, confusion, and the shouts for help, Clemmons immediately asked engineers in the blockhouse whether to stop the flow of oxygen that was surely fueling the fire. Or should he keep the oxygen flowing in case there was a slim chance the crew was still alive? Clemmons was driven from the White Room shortly after fire engulfed the spacecraft and, still waiting for instructions from the blockhouse, left the oxygen panel on. He then joined the perilous effort amid the "heavy biting black smoke" to open the heavy hatches. It took nearly five minutes; by then, the crew was dead.

Clemmons, the skilled technician who remained at his post throughout the minutes of maximum peril, was instead treated by investigators as a suspect. His boss informed him in the hours after the fire that he was a "person of interest" since he had been next to the spacecraft when the fire erupted. Clemmons was flabbergasted. Over the next few days, he was forced to go over his statement with investigators four more times before it became obvious that his actions were unrelated to the fire.

"NASA was determined that somebody had caused that fire," Clemmons told researcher Mark Gray in a 2007 documentary on the *Apollo 1* fire.[25] "They could not believe that the spacecraft could burn on its own." Investigators had looked at Clemmons "real heavy," he said. "So we just kind of stayed hidden 'til the investigation was over."

Clemmons claimed to his dying day that he was told by investigators to keep quiet. Four decades later, he decided it was time to reveal what he saw on the night of the launchpad fire that killed Grissom and his crew.

Clemmons and the other pad workers were wary of the Apollo commander, a man not to be trifled with. Few were willing to go toe-to-toe with the irascible Grissom on a technical issue. Clemmons first met Grissom in 1959 while working at the Convair plant in San Diego, where the "go-or-blow" Atlas booster was being built.[26] Clemmons's initial brush with the Mercury astronauts, by now national celebrities, left the distinct impression that they were a very "tight" group and never let outsiders get close. Grissom "was a very difficult person to understand," Clemmons recalled. There were always two camps: Grissom was viewed either as an arrogant son of a bitch or a respected, uncompromising engineer who wanted to get the job done. Either way, "he held everyone's nose to the grindstone," Clemmons said.

Not surprisingly, Clemmons sided with his employer, North American Aviation, when it came to assigning blame for the deadly spacecraft design. He insisted it was NASA that was cutting corners on Apollo, running a crash program that was bound to kill someone sooner rather than later. Grissom "was pushing in the wrong direction, the contractors," Clemmons argued. "He should have pushed against senior NASA officials," not North American Aviation, to fix his spacecraft.

It was the space agency, Clemmons insisted, that tolerated exposed wiring and leaking coolant lines in the Block I spacecraft. The space agency insisted it did not need new fire-resistant beta cloth in the cockpit or a quick-opening hatch. Quality control at the Cape was practically nonexistent prior to the fire, the technician asserted.

Perhaps, but the contractor that had built great machines, including the X-15 rocket plane and the T-6 Texan training aircraft Grissom had flown as a young air force cadet, ultimately delivered a deathtrap of a spacecraft. Amid the finger-pointing that followed the fire, investigators would acknowledge "sloppy planning and supervision" by NASA while stressing "shamefully inadequate" design and test work by North American.[27] There was, it turned out, more than enough blame to go around. But no one could fault the pad crew or their heroic actions on the night of the fire.

"After the fire, there was a big push from NASA to keep our mouths shut," Clemmons alleged. There were threats, he continued. "You will not talk. Period. Nothing. If you do, you will be fired."[28] Beyond their official statements to the Apollo review board, Clemmons and the others remained silent for decades about what happened on Pad 34. Clemmons stayed on after the fire, working to repair Pad 34 for the first Apollo flight in October 1968. He served as a pad worker through the ill-fated flight of *Apollo 13* in April 1970.

In the aftermath of the disaster on Pad 34, NASA's political decision to award the prime contract for the Apollo command module to North American Aviation looked like a tragic mistake. Even though Grissom had fallen in line to back the aerospace company over more experienced firms like McDonnell and Martin Company, it now looked as if Cecile Grissom's instincts were correct about what she called "that plant in California."

Doubts about North American's ability to deliver grew as the Apollo astronauts worked more closely with company engineers in Downey. While other NASA contractors, like lunar module manufacturer Grumman Corporation, seemed committed to quality, "North American was positively schizophrenic," Frank Borman noted. It was "populated by conscientious men who knew what they were doing and at least an equal number who didn't know their butts from third base."[29]

NASA eventually selected Borman to help oversee Apollo operations in Downey. Gilruth loyalist George Low in Houston replaced the broken Joseph Shea as Apollo program manager. Under intense pressure from NASA, North American brought in Bill Bergen from Martin, the runner-up for the Apollo contract, to straighten out the mess in Downey.[30] Among the first steps taken in direct response to the *Apollo 1* fire was replacing the plug-type door with a single, outward-opening hatch. The days of sacrificing crew safety to save weight were over: the new hatch could be opened in seconds but would add about fifteen hundred pounds to the command module design. The added weight would have to be shed elsewhere on the huge Saturn V rocket. It took the deaths of three men before NASA figured out that crew safety trumped all other design considerations.

Then there was the curious case of the BMAG switch. In addition to the spacecraft inertial measurement unit (IMU) used to control liftoff and provide navigation data to the guidance computer, the Apollo command module also was equipped with a backup navigation system, the BMAG. The Daven Hermetic Division of Thomas Edison Industries supplied the airtight switches that provided power to the gyros, spacecraft wiring harnesses, and batteries.

The IMU was the central element of one of the great machines invented for Apollo, the Primary Guidance, Navigation and Control System. While the IMU was installed on a rotating platform to provide its sensors with a fixed orientation in space, the "body-mounted" BMAG sensors rotated along with the Apollo spacecraft. Hence, these "rate gyros" served as another set of accelerometers used to measure how fast the spacecraft turned around its pitch, roll, and yaw axes. As such, the BMAG served as a backup to the IMU.

After the fire, investigators discovered that the BMAG switch on the cockpit panel was incorrectly set in the "off" position. In the rush to pinpoint the cause of the fire and assign blame, the sealed BMAG switch somehow became another prime suspect.

In the weeks before the fire, Grissom had complained about the operation of the BMAG switches. In a meeting with Deke Slayton and Herbert Kean, the division manager of the Edison Industries' switch unit, Grissom insisted that the turning torque on the switches be increased. "He wanted to be absolutely positive that they could not 'hang up' between positions," Kean remembered.[31] The meeting concerning a relatively minor issue also demonstrated how finicky Grissom could be on a technical point and the lengths to which he would go as the first Apollo commander to get what he wanted in his spacecraft.

To Kean, it did not matter. "If Grissom wanted [heavier torque], that was it. You didn't question it." The rub was that the plugs-out test was fast approaching and a switch retrofit would cause further delays. Grissom relented, and the decision was made to replace the BMAG switches after the plugs-out test.

Kean's assessment of Grissom in the tense weeks before the fire matched that of others who worked closely with the commander. "I respected him, even though he was a little grumpy towards me at that meeting," Kean recalled.[32]

Ultimately, the BMAG switch had nothing to do with the *Apollo 1* fire. But in the early days of the fire investigation, the fact that the cockpit switch had been turned to the "off" position was enough to arouse suspicion. As in the case of the pad worker Clemmons, investigators were grasping at straws in their haste to come up with a cause for the fire. Kean later suspected someone might have gotten wind of his meeting with Grissom and Slayton to discuss a switch retrofit. Because one of the original switches was not properly set in the "on" position, Kean was summoned to Cape Kennedy on the night of the fire to answer to investigators on behalf of his employer. He was filled with anxiety, especially when he found two security guards outside his hotel room as he departed for the Kennedy Space Center the morning after the fire.

Kean now thinks that a pad technician probably turned off the BMAG switch as part of an effort to power down the smoldering spacecraft. Nevertheless, he was called onto the carpet by investigators who were searching for anyone or anything they considered physical evidence of faulty design.

Others intimately familiar with the Apollo hardware wonder to this day why NASA investigators would have wasted their time on the BMAG switch as a possible ignition source. "As a hermetic switch it seems odd the component was chased as a cause of the fire at all," notes David Carey, a collector of Apollo hardware and professional engineer who tears apart and probes the innards of electronic devices for a living. "The hermeticity of the [BMAG] switch would imply to me that any arcing in the switch contacts would stay isolated from the oxygen atmosphere of the cabin and thus [would be] unable to spark the blaze."[33]

Indeed, Clemmons and Kean had done their jobs to the best of their abilities. When Grissom asked for something, they delivered. Still, NASA treated each like a criminal suspect in their failed attempts to deflect blame away from the space agency and its prime contractor. NASA's equivalent of Keystone Cops were not taken off the case until Floyd Thompson, director of the NASA Langley Research Center, was named chairman of the Apollo 204 Review Board, which was formed to probe the causes of the fire. It was not until Borman was appointed to effectively run the Apollo fire investigation that the real work of probing the actual causes of the fire began.

"Grumpy" Gus Grissom could surely be a pain in the neck to work with—surly, demanding, and detail oriented to a fault. But he also gained the respect of men like Clemmons and Kean, who understood what the Apollo commander was up against.

So, too, did Wally Schirra, the executor of Grissom's estate. At the time of the Apollo fire, Schirra also stood near the top of the astronaut pecking order. He had distinguished himself during the Mercury and Gemini programs, flying a textbook orbital mission on his first flight while surviving his own brush with death on the launchpad during his second. Once in orbit, Schirra executed the world's first rendezvous in space.

Apollo was different. The stakes were far higher; it was about life and death. "I was known as 'Jolly Wally' for a long time, until I got mad at

Apollo," Schirra admitted. "Why did I get mad? I lost my next-door neighbor, Gus Grissom, who was killed on the launchpad. And I didn't feel very good about that."[34]

Apollo 7, the October 1968 maiden flight of the overhauled command module, the mission that got the American space program back on track, was Schirra's last. The cranky commander with a head cold argued with ground controllers throughout the nearly eleven-day flight. Some thought Schirra insubordinate. He viewed the long, tedious shakedown mission as the flight his friend and neighbor was no longer around to fly. For Schirra, it was the end of the line. Only one Mercury astronaut, Alan Shepard, would make it to the moon.

Months before Schirra's flight, in the darkest days of Apollo, silent NASA footage shows spacecraft designer Maxime Faget, along with other NASA officials, picking over the carcass of the burnt-out *Apollo 1* spacecraft. One wonders whether Faget was having second thoughts about his central role nearly five years earlier in NASA's insistence on using pure oxygen in the Apollo spacecraft on the launchpad. Faget and the other spacecraft designers did have experience with pure oxygen under pressure,[35] thought they understood the dangers, and believed they could still ensure crew safety.

Others were not so sure. The outspoken John Young, Grissom's protégé, considered Faget a "brilliant NASA aerodynamicist" but also recalled that he and others eventually concluded the engineer's last name was an acronym for "Flat Ass Guess Every Time."[36] Ultimately, the Apollo designers had risked the lives of astronauts for the sole purpose of shaving a few pounds off the spacecraft.

Borman, Grissom's original Gemini copilot and commander of a later Gemini flight, was effectively in charge of investigating the Apollo fire. The fate of the lunar landing program was largely in the hands of Borman, whose ego would not fit in the same spacecraft with Grissom's. NASA film of the hangar where the spacecraft was disassembled shows the aggressive, by-the-book Borman grilling technicians and searching the gutted spacecraft for clues. "Hour after hour, I'd sit in the charred cabin—for a long time, I was the only one allowed to enter," Borman recalled.[37]

It did not take the intuitive Borman long to figure out that a basic design premise of the Apollo program was fatally flawed, namely the mistaken belief that 100 percent pure oxygen under pressure could be used safely in a sealed spacecraft. That deadly assumption when combined with carelessness and complacency meant the *Apollo 1* crew had been "sitting on a live bomb," he concluded. An ignition source, a "bright arc" below Grissom's couch, in the pure oxygen environment had consumed the flammable materials in the cabin, creating what Borman accurately described as "faucets of toxic fumes." With no chance of escape, the astronauts were doomed.

Borman summed up months of investigating and soul-searching this way: "Sloppy planning and supervision on NASA's part and some shamefully inadequate design and test work by North American" had killed the crew.[38] Before a congressional committee investigating the causes of the fire, he acknowledged what was now clear: "The space program had overlooked the obvious hazard of putting a 100 percent oxygen environment into a spacecraft pressurized to more than 20 psi."[39]

All involved were at fault—the engineers, the technicians, the paper pushers, senior managers—the astronauts themselves. Someone, anyone, needed to step forward and demand a pause as the crash program went off the rails. Not the least among them was the commander of *Apollo 1*. No one dared speak up, and Grissom understood there would be a long line of volunteers eager to replace him if he faltered. So he carried on.

Michael Collins and William Anders were among the astronauts scanning the remains of Spacecraft 012 for clues. (Less than two years later, Anders would accompany Borman on man's first flight to the moon.) Collins and Anders, both deeply involved in the Apollo design, arrived at the Cape Kennedy warehouse after the spacecraft was disassembled and made a beeline for the singed hatches. They understood far better than the engineers exactly what White and Grissom had been up against as the fire engulfed the cabin.

Recounting the disaster and the tumultuous early days of Apollo, Collins would later concede: "We were incredibly intelligent about some of the hazards we faced and we thought long and hard about them and we did everything we could to ward them off. But the business of a hundred percent oxygen environment inside the spacecraft, we really had not thought that through."[40]

The precise cause of the Apollo fire, the source of the spark that touched off the oxygen-fueled conflagration, was never officially determined and perhaps can never be known. But those closest to the investigation and the engineers who helped write the official history of the tragedy were convinced it started near a small door under Grissom's couch on the left side of the spacecraft. The door located in the equipment bay provided access to lithium hydroxide canisters used to scrub carbon dioxide from the cabin atmosphere. Wire bundles ran below the door, which was opened repeatedly during months of training. The door had a sharp edge.

Directly underneath the access door was a DC power cable. The large wire bundles that filled the cabin wedged this cable against the bottom of the access door. Investigators reckoned that every time the door was opened and closed, the edge scraped against the cable. Over time, they believed, the repeated abrasions wore through the insulation, exposing wire sections of the cable.

Borman and others, including Scott Simpkinson, who helped disassemble the Apollo 204 spacecraft and edited the final NASA report on the fire, were persuaded the exposed section likely caused a brief electrical arc between the exposed wires. In a pure oxygen atmosphere with plenty of flammable material, this would have been sufficient to ignite a fire that would engulf the cockpit in seconds.

Lending further credence to this explanation about the fire's source was a section of aluminum tubing just below the scuffed wiring that was bent at a ninety-degree angle. The joint, yet another example of shoddy engineering by North American Aviation that was tolerated by NASA, may have been leaking glycol coolant after repeated jostling. The liquid glycol was not flammable, but the fumes likely were.[41]

While NASA insisted the exact source of the fire was never found, Simpkinson and others believed the exposed wires under Grissom's couch were the most likely point of ignition—the inevitable result of a series of design risks and inferior workmanship overlooked during construction of the first manned Apollo spacecraft.[42] When investigators started digging, they soon discovered that Apollo had been moving so fast in the months before the fire that there was inadequate documentation about what had been installed in the spacecraft and when. Like the spacecraft testers who seldom found time to study the results of their simulations, the project engineers and spacecraft managers failed to adequately record the endless modifications to Grissom's ship. All this would change as a direct result of the fire.

As details of the fire investigation leaked out during the spring of 1967, the space agency came in for withering criticism from a growing chorus of congressional opponents.[43] Once the Apollo 204 Review Board released its findings and a series of embarrassing congressional hearings were staged to maximum effect, NASA began salvaging Apollo. Nearly 400,000 engineers and technicians would ensure Grissom, White, and Chaffee had not died in vain.

One of them, Jerry Goodman, an Apollo crew compartment project engineer, recalled the following after resumption of the Apollo program: "All of us were shocked with how easily things burned in oxygen, the high-pressure oxygen." Still reeling from the horror of the astronauts' deaths, the sleepless nights, and the agonizing realization that lives were at stake, Goodman pronounced himself rededicated. "I felt like a warrior. I think the team ended up like a lean and mean group of Trojan warriors."[44]

These words would have been music to the ears of the Cold Warrior Gus Grissom. This was precisely what the commander had been pushing for in the last, dispiriting days before the plugs-out test. Grissom's unflagging dedication ultimately inspired engineers like Goodman to slough off carelessness and complacency, to learn the hard lessons paid for with the lives of the Apollo astronauts, eventually ensuring that the sacrifice of Grissom and his crew would indeed be "worth the risk."

In the fire's aftermath, a scathing critique of NASA, the Space Race, and Apollo was published in 1968 under the misleading title *Murder on Pad 34*. The diatribe by Erik Bergaust, "one of America's foremost space age writers," was not the murder mystery suggested by its sensational title. Rather, the book was a polemic aimed squarely at NASA administrator James Webb and the space agency's senior management. NASA has long dismissed Bergaust's ad hominem attack. Indeed, most of the author's assertions about "the shocking story of the Apollo disaster—and why it may happen again"—proved unsettling but mostly unfounded. The book's title was a marketing ploy rather than an accurate description of the author's thesis.

Still, *Murder on Pad 34* forced NASA to confront its deadly miscalculations and justify the huge risks inherent in a crash program to land men on the moon. Bergaust's book also legitimized the views of critics like the atom bomb designer and eminent science advisor Vannevar Bush, who viewed Apollo as "folly, engendered by childish enthusiasm."[45] In a prescient letter published in the *New York Times* a week before JFK's assassination, Bush warned of an inevitable accident in space, predicting that "things will go wrong, and we will be unable to do anything to get them down out of space. It is not just that this sort of thing may happen; it is bound to happen, especially in a crash program."

Stung by its critics, NASA sought to pick up the pieces and move on. As the spacecraft was being fixed, the space agency shifted its focus to the gigantic rocket that would launch humans to the moon. Looking for a way to jumpstart Apollo, NASA embraced an aggressive approach called "all-up testing," which involved stacking and launching a complete Saturn V rocket in November 1967. Having learned the lessons of the fire, NASA and its army of contractors who had built the mighty vehicle would closely scrutinize all test results. Astronaut Collins marveled later that no Saturn V ever blew up, as had the gigantic Soviet N1 moon rocket. When the unmanned *Apollo 4* thundered off the pad and achieved orbit with barely a hiccup on November 9, 1967, NASA had at last emerged from the tragedy of *Apollo 1*. Twenty-one months after the fire, in October 1968, the American manned space program resumed, culminating in the first lunar landing on July 20, 1969. Among the many mementos left on the lunar surface was a plaque with the names of the fallen astronauts and cosmonauts. A crater on the far side of the moon is also named for Gus Grissom.[46]

Fifty years later, raw emotions persist over the circumstances surrounding the *Apollo 1* fire and the way in which NASA's handled the investigation. Even the question of how best to remember and honor Grissom, White, and Chaffee has divided families and former colleagues over the decades, prompting lawsuits, controversy, anguish—even conspiracy theories. The controversy begins and ends with the *Report of*

Apollo 204 Review Board to the Administrator of the National Aeronautics and Space Administration, released on April 5, 1967, about eight weeks after the *Apollo 1* fire.[47] Critics condemn the report as "a swift, in-house, self-serving investigation."[48] The increasingly bureaucratic space agency moved swiftly to head off an outside investigation, asserting control over all physical evidence on Pad 34. In the case of eyewitnesses like Clemmons and perhaps other pad technicians, statements for the record were "gone over" for days before submission to the review board. These and other missteps served to undermine public confidence in many of the board's conclusions. Still, the voluminous appendices to the review board's report are sufficiently detailed to determine the actions of Grissom and his crew immediately before and during the fire. This supporting evidence confirms that the crew acted in accordance with all emergency procedures. The fatal error, of course, was that no one involved with Apollo, including the crew, considered the plugs-out test dangerous. A launchpad fire was the furthest thing from anyone's mind in the headlong rush to beat the Russians to the moon.

The grim proceedings in the aftermath of the fire—the covering of backsides, the political posturing—obscured the reality that Betty Grissom and her sons had lost a husband and father. For Scott and Mark, the shock was leavened by a simple fact: "Dad was gone most of the time so, sad to say, [his death] wasn't that big of a change," Mark recalled a generation later. "I think that last year, 1966, he was home like fourteen, eighteen days that year."[49]

NASA would do little of substance to support the *Apollo 1* astronauts' families after the fire. The space agency was, after all, a goal-oriented technical agency seemingly insensitive to those who moved through it. Despite the frequent references to the "NASA family," it proved unfeeling despite occasional, ham-handed displays of sympathy toward the Grissom family. Ultimately, posthumous awards, lunar craters, and similar gestures rung hollow. By contrast, Purdue University moved swiftly to dedicate an engineering building in Grissom's name a year after the fire. It also arranged for Scott and Mark to attend their father's alma mater for free. Betty was moved by these acts of kindness from her friends back in Indiana, realizing that they were among the most fitting ways to preserve her husband's memory. Gus had been an eager, dedicated engineering student. Generations of Purdue engineering students would be inspired by his example.

The United States eventually sent twenty-four humans to the moon; twelve walked on its surface. It was a historic achievement, among the greatest feats of American ingenuity. Some moonwalkers wept when they gazed back at Earth. But as the lunar dust settled and the American moon landings faded from memory, so too did the sacrifice of the *Apollo 1* crew. The Grissom family struggled to find an appropriate way to remember Gus. It became—and remains to the present—an emotional, complicated affair, equal parts resentment, bruised feelings and egos, misunderstandings, and, in the troubling case of Scott Grissom, unfounded conspiracy theories about the circumstances of his father's death. Gus Grissom, the no-nonsense engineer, meticulous test pilot, and intrepid astronaut, could not have foreseen the bitter disputes over what he stood for, his place in the pantheon of space pioneers. He undoubtedly would have disapproved of all the fuss, preferring instead that everyone focus not on him but on pushing the bounds of space exploration.

A decision made eight years before his death to volunteer for a great human adventure had determined Grissom's fate and that of his family. Few could have predicted the outcome: humans exploring another world two short years after Grissom, White, and Chaffee were killed.

Betty Grissom mostly kept her pain and resentment to herself during the glory days of Apollo from 1969 to 1972. For her, Apollo had amounted to "a half ton of rocks."[50] Scott and Mark were still too young to cope with any additional publicity after their father's funeral. They spent their summers working as ball boys for the NFL Houston Oilers[51] and hanging out with racecar drivers who had befriended their father.[52] Pursuing legal action against North American Aviation remained out of the question. The success of the space program was paramount. Betty remained quiet. While Purdue had helped with her sons' educations, Betty continued to rely on the *Life* and Field Enterprise contracts to make ends meet. At the height of the Apollo program, the question arose: How long should the widows of astronauts killed during the race to the moon continue receiving a share of the "publication money"?

As the astronaut corps swelled and documentaries were planned about the lives of the moonwalkers and their families, the issue of how to divide the proceeds came to a head. Betty balked at a proposed contract for the astronauts' stories. Charles "Pete" Conrad, the *Apollo 12* commander, seeking to settle the matter, summarily informed Betty, according to her account: "The newer fellows won't want to share the money with the widows. They won't even know who Gus Grissom was." It was the last straw, the final insult. "If they don't know who Gus Grissom was," Betty shot back, "then they'd better find out."[53]

There and then, Betty resolved to take her own calculated risk, a gamble that would eventually alienate her from the few friends she had left in the air force, the astronaut ranks, and the rest of NASA. Betty would spend the remainder of her life in isolation, deeply suspicious of NASA, ostracized by those who saw her as the aggrieved widow of a dead astronaut—a test pilot who, they never failed to mention, had volunteered for a dangerous job.

Increasingly bitter over what she viewed as NASA's indifference, understandably resentful over North American Aviation's slipshod workmanship and program management that led directly to the fire, Betty Grissom defied the Test Pilot Code: she sued the Apollo contractor in 1971 for negligence in the manufacturing of her husband's spacecraft. The lawsuit alleged gross negligence on the part of North American Aviation in the design and manufacture of the Apollo spacecraft, resulting in the deaths of the *Apollo 1* crew. Betty's decision to sue was met with derision from most of her husband's colleagues.

A federal judge in Florida initially dismissed her lawsuit based on a two-year statute of limitations. Betty's attorney then asserted the children's rights under Texas law in California, where Spacecraft 012 had been built. A date was set for trial. The legal issue eventually came down to how much the heirs of Gus Grissom could be compensated by putting a price tag on fifteen seconds of human pain and suffering. As the trial neared, Betty's Houston attorney approached North American Aviation about an out-of-court settlement. After three days of negotiations, a settlement totaling $375,000 was reached. The American legal system had determined that the life of Virgil I. Grissom was worth about $25,000 for each second he struggled and suffered before losing consciousness and dying in his spacecraft. The widows of White and Chaffee declined to join Betty's lawsuit against North American Aviation. They later accepted settlements for the same amount.

Betty had gained a measure of justice. It came at a steep price; she was now isolated from the other astronaut wives, "Togethersville," as the support network had come to be known. The boys grew up and became pilots like their father, and Betty moved from the suburbs into Houston. Like her husband at the end of his life, Betty was now fending for herself.

A new way of describing events and interpreting their meaning emerged in the 1960s and flourished in the 1970s. It came to be called the New Journalism. Its earliest practitioner was the stylish writer with the nuanced ear, the provocateur Tom Wolfe. Among Wolfe's early subjects were the Mercury astronauts. He mostly got their stories right, telling them in a completely new and compelling way that dispensed with traditional journalism conventions. When it came to Grissom, however, the dandy from Richmond, Virginia, got it mostly wrong.

Wolfe's groundbreaking 1979 bestseller, *The Right Stuff*, managed to transform the competent engineer and fearless test pilot Gus Grissom into a cartoon character, all in the service of a New Journalism narrative. Wolfe's research for his book was exhaustive, his insights about the early American manned space program profound. However, Wolfe simply ignored or failed to understand the character of the second American in space. The compelling story of the early Space Race required a protagonist: Shepard and Glenn each fit the bill. Cooper played the role of a renegade. Wolfe understood that Grissom was a central player in the drama that was the Space Race. He would emerge as the foil in the author's *Right Stuff* narrative, contrasting with those who sought the limelight, those who did not lose their ships. Wolfe's subplot, focusing on the loss of *Liberty Bell 7*, served as a counterpoint to the heroic flights of test pilot Chuck Yeager and the historic missions of Shepard and Glenn.

The film version of Wolfe's book directed by Philip Kaufman and released in 1983 was worse, portraying Grissom as an inarticulate, boorish, beer-drinking fighter jock who "screwed the pooch," panicking at the end of his flight, blowing the hatch on his Mercury spacecraft, sending it to the bottom of the ocean. The fundamental problem with Wolfe's portrayal of

Grissom and Kaufman's schmaltzy film treatment is that it simply did not happen. So much for the New Journalism—a style of reporting that contributed to an era of profound narcissism in American culture. For all its flaws, however, *The Right Stuff* did rekindle appreciation for the exploits and sheer guts of the largely forgotten Mercury astronauts. Wolfe's intentions were admirable, but he could not resist embellishing to provoke. Mostly, he provoked the family of Gus Grissom.

Lowell Grissom is an even-tempered, thoughtful man who is as steady as a compass pointing north, but mention the name Tom Wolfe and he comes out swinging. Of *The Right Stuff*, Gus's younger brother declares: "I thought it was awful, I thought it was character assassination . . . so many things that were so wrong with it." He continues for some time in this vein, and then adds a phrase reminiscent of his pugnacious older brother: "It's a good thing I never met [Tom Wolfe]. He might have fallen down the stairs!"

Director Philip Kaufman has called Grissom "a fucking hero." It is hard to square that observation with what amounts to Kaufman's fictional account of Grissom panicking at the end of his Mercury flight. The essence of Hollywood's version of Project Mercury and Grissom's role in it was summed up best by the central character in Wolfe's book, Chuck Yeager. A member of Kaufman's film crew recalled movie consultant Yeager's comment about a planned scene: "Well, that's not exactly how it happened, but I know you fellas have to flower it up."[54]

And "flower it up" they did. The film's portrayal of the end of Grissom's Mercury flight simply does not square with the facts. Kaufman's film concludes with Grissom hanging from a horse collar, his shoelaces undone—something done completely for effect. Fred Ward, the actor who portrayed Grissom in the film, later said he felt a kinship with his character, Grissom as "almost totally defeated, like a dead fish on the end of a line, and then coming up toward the whirling helicopter blades, being pulled in."

Back at Edwards Air Force Base, the Chuck Yeager character played by Sam Shepard watches on television as Grissom is hauled up to a rescue helicopter. Yeager's bar mates have a good laugh at Gus's expense. Yeager reminds them of the guts required to climb on top of a rocket and ride it into space. As if to apologize for the phony portrayal of the second American in space, Yeager/Shepard declares: "Good ol' Gus. He did alright."

At least one film critic spotted the fraudulent depiction. "The movie's portrait of Grissom includes a scene showing the astronaut freaking out with claustrophobia after his capsule lands in the Pacific [*sic*]," observed movie reviewer Roger Ebert. "Kaufman cuts to an exterior shot to show the escape hatch being blown open with explosive bolts, but the implication is that Grissom panicked. Grissom always said the hatch blew on its own. Certainly the space program never lost confidence in him as one of their best men."[55] Ebert, like Yeager in the film, understood that Grissom had done far better than "alright."

On a steaming Saturday morning in July 2011, the citizens of Mitchell, Indiana, gathered outside Masonic Lodge Number 228 in the shadow of its limestone sculpture of the Titan II rocket to remember "Brother" Gus Grissom, the second American in space. A plaque installed by the local Masons declares: "ONE OF US: In grateful tribute to Virgil I. Grissom, Master Mason, Explorer and trailblazer in the best of American traditions." Amid buzzing cicadas, fussing children, and the clicks of the air force honor guards' heels and rifle bolts, Reverend Eric Kersey began by praising the town's hero whose "achievements literally stretch into space."

Kersey thanked the Almighty for Gus's "brave heart, whether in combat for his country or in our country's space program." All in attendance that day, fifty years after Grissom's first space flight, would give thanks "for his quick wit, his inquisitive and probing mind, his loyalty to the mission, his love of flight and sense of adventure and exploration, and his willingness to give himself to expand human knowledge and increase human achievement for all mankind."

Next to speak was Norman Grissom, a reserved man who unlike his siblings remained in Mitchell, was active in local politics, and edited the Mitchell newspaper. Norman described an older brother burning with ambition. "Growing up with brothers, as we all know, sometimes can be very contentious, with the usual squabbles and such. But it began to occur to me before too long that maybe the guy who was pulling weeds in the garden with me and mowing the yard and such was maybe somebody special. I think we all know that even back then I was right. . . . As he grew up and progressed [in] is career and took advantage of the things that were offered to him, he said, 'You have to be ready when the opportunity comes.' Gus was ready when his opportunity arrived."[56]

Norman had previously traveled to the space museum in Hutchinson, Kansas, to see his brother's restored *Liberty Bell 7*. Betty preferred the ship be left at the bottom of the ocean. But Norman and Lowell were by contrast pleased to see that the spacecraft in remarkably good condition had at last been displayed. Both want the nation to remember their brother's exploits.

Norman stared in silence at the restored ship for a long time, and then remarked: "I'm just imagining Gus sitting in there."[57]

Norman's words in Mitchell during the fiftieth anniversary of his brother's first space flight were the perfect expression of siblings' complicated love for one another. Norman's heartfelt recollections were juxtaposed with what followed: the next speaker was Scott Grissom, who has long alleged that NASA conspired to murder his father. Scott had come to Mitchell to repeat his conspiracy theories and demand a reopening of the Apollo fire investigation. Betty and Mark were not there to hear Scott's tirade; they are estranged from the eldest son. Gus's siblings cringed, suffering in silence.

Grissom's first son had his say. "My father and the crew of *Apollo 1* have never rested, their deaths have never received an independent investigation, their ship is still in disarray and was carried on a barge from Cape Canaveral to a resting hangar for permanent storage under a veil of secrecy. In fact, NASA and the US government have classified much of the materials that we have sought," Scott asserted.

The son then called for "an independent investigation and full access to NASA personnel and materials in the event that we discover espionage or sabotage. We intend to seek criminal prosecution. And finally, we want a professional and public display of the *Apollo 1* spacecraft." A few in the audience applauded Scott's remarks. Others were puzzled. His aunt and uncles were deeply dismayed.

Later, inside the Masonic Lodge, Scott distributed copies of his statement in hopes the local papers would reprint his allegations. Lowell advised the mayor of Mitchell to toss the statement in the trash. Informed of his allegations, Scott's peers, the children of the other Mercury astronauts, expressed sadness that a celebration of Grissom's life and career could be marred by the repetition of unfounded conspiracy claims. NASA's negligence certainly contributed to the fatal fire, and it had in fact moved to head off any outside investigations that might embarrass the American space program. The agency would do little of substance to help the dead astronaut's family, but surely it did not "murder" Gus Grissom.

Scott Grissom's troubling accusations succeeded in stirring painful memories while spoiling an otherwise dignified ceremony celebrating his father's accomplishments. The eldest son's quixotic attempt to reopen the *Apollo 1* fire investigation is at best highly unlikely.

The consequences of the catastrophe on Pad 34 reverberate still across the decades. Noting that Scott was sixteen years old when his father died, a former NASA official concedes, "I cut him a couple of light years of slack."

In contrast to the simple observance in Mitchell, NASA marked the historic flights of Alan Shepard and John Glenn fifty years earlier with great fanfare. NASA's administrator and his deputy both attended a two-day conference at Ohio State University in February 2012 celebrating Glenn's historic orbital flight. Each space pioneer was deserving of those honors. So, too, was Gus Grissom, but no one from NASA attended the fiftieth anniversary observance of the flight of *Liberty Bell 7* in Mitchell. Nor did the space agency send a congratulatory message to his family.

The monolithic concrete base of the launch structure, a steel ring it supports, and flame deflectors are all that remains of Pad 34 at Cape Canaveral Air Force Station in Florida. Until recently,[58] the Kennedy Space Center tour bus delivered sightseers to Pad 34. The overgrown remnants of the blockhouse remain off to one side of what is officially known as Launch Complex 34. Several private memorials have over the decades been placed at the site. Among them is one reminding visitors: *"Ad astra per aspera"* ("A rough road leads to the stars").

"Remember them not for how they died but for those ideals for which they lived," exhorts another.

For decades, the anniversary of the *Apollo 1* fire has been observed at this stark place—a concrete pedestal anchored in the coastal Florida scrub. What most visitors to the pad invariably notice are the ironic words stenciled on the massive base of the old launchpad: "ABANDON IN PLACE."

For the families of the dead astronauts, the bureaucratese serves as a painful, fitting metaphor for how Betty, Scott, and Mark Grissom feel about the treatment they have received at the hands of NASA in the fifty years since the fire. Resentment over the deaths of Gus Grissom and his crew lingers like a dark cloud over the question of how best to honor the crew of *Apollo 1*. Betty insists the space agency did little to help her family after her husband's death. The astronaut's wife eventually declined the many invitations to attend official NASA ceremonies. The medals she was to accept in her husband's name meant nothing.

One thing the government got right was loaning Grissom's Gemini spacecraft to a museum just outside Mitchell, Indiana. Two days before the *Liberty Bell 7* observances in the astronaut's hometown, admirers gathered at the Virgil I. "Gus" Grissom Memorial Museum at Spring Mill State Park to mark the fiftieth anniversary of Gus's suborbital flight. Betty and Mark were there to answer the same questions they have been asked for decades: What was Gus like? What made him want to fly? Did he think it was dangerous work? Why did he risk his life to fly in space? Betty dutifully provided the television crews with a guided tour of her husband's museum. Along with *Molly Brown*, the Gemini spacecraft Gus and John Young flew in March 1965, the museum collection includes mementoes from Gus's youth, his years at Purdue, and the air force throughout his career as an astronaut. A display case from his college days contains a leather case embossed with the Purdue logo: Gus Grissom's slide rule.

The local TV stations used footage of Betty's museum tour to set up an interview in which she vented about NASA, its failings, and the future of manned spaceflight. Betty is decidedly unenthusiastic. Things are different now, not like the supercharged days of the 1960s when anything was a possibility, when Grissom and the others risked everything. NASA is adrift, Betty insisted, and the American space program is a waste of money—money, she notes, we do not have. She may have harbored similar thoughts when her husband was at the top of the astronaut pyramid, but she held her tongue. A half a century later, unconstrained, she asserts the American space program is going nowhere.

After the TV interviews, Betty agreed to sit with Mark in a small conference room to answer a few written questions from admirers, the curious, fans of her husband, those with a vague idea of what the mother and son had endured. Betty and Mark submitted to this because they know Gus is beloved, that many still suspect he got the short end of the stick. Grissom, the icon, is to these admirers a kind of working-class hero, who if he had lived would have flown to the moon. Grissom risked everything, which is something rare, something to be honored. It was Mark's task to sort through the three-by-five cards, select questions, and read them aloud, Betty's hearing being not what it once was. Many of the queries were of the "What was it like?" variety.

What was it like to be married to a test pilot, an astronaut? "I didn't know anything else," Betty replied. Laughter. "He always had to have more flying hours, and I think he was very qualified to be an astronaut. Fifty years ago I think he felt that he was as well qualified as anybody. I think that somebody asked him that question and he said, 'No one knows anything' about spaceflight or how to get to the moon." This was true. Mark found it hard to remember much about his father: "He was always gone," he stated matter-of-factly.

Someone asked which NASA program Gus enjoyed the most. "Gemminy," Betty replied, the southern Indiana twang returning, her way of pronouncing the two-man spacecraft Gus had done so much to design, test, and fly: "The Gus Mobile." Exhausted after a long day, Betty's responses were increasingly laced with disdain for NASA. The decades of resentment over her husband's death simmered just below the surface in most of her responses.

Someone asked whether the space agency had supported the astronauts' families. This was the crux of the matter, the subtext of Betty's existence fifty years after her husband's first flight. Piqued, Betty's simple reply was, "No." She turned to Mark and asked, "You backing me up on that?" "Not in our day they didn't," the son agreed. "Do what you're told and other than that [NASA was] kind of 'out of sight, out of mind.'" The resentment spilled out amid the display cases filled with the remnants of Gus Grissom's life in Mitchell, his studies at Purdue, the Korean War, the rest of his air force career, and his two successful spaceflights.

Gus was long gone, taken from his family by the thing he cared most about. "I knew that he had always wanted to fly, and I was never going to disagree with anything," Betty told another questioner. "He knew he did not have to have my approval to do what he wanted to do, even though it was considered a very dangerous job. . . . I'm not so sure he really considered it dangerous."

It was indeed dangerous, among the riskiest of professions. Betty had little time to ponder her husband's death, to indulge in self-pity. "I had other things to think about, like raising a family."

It had been a long, sweltering day at Spring Mill, so hot that some of the *Liberty Bell 7* anniversary festivities scheduled for that weekend in Mitchell were canceled. Betty was weary and was having trouble hearing the questions Mark read off the cards. Both did their best to answer them all.

A question from a child was completely out of context, but it somehow brought to the surface a side of Gus Grissom's wife seldom if ever seen in public. Betty has many reasons to feel aggrieved. After all, she lost her husband and the father of her children in a tragedy, enduring the consequences in front of the entire nation.

Mark read the child's innocent query: "Do you like animals?" Betty was confused, so she asked Mark to repeat the question. A more experienced moderator would have set it aside and left it at that. "Do you like animals?" Mark repeated.

At last comprehending the child's meaning, Betty's entire demeanor suddenly changed, softened. *This* was a subject she cared deeply about. She loved animals, always had! Sam, the loyal family hound, had waited in vain for his master to return home in January 1967. Unlike most humans, animals are faithful. For a brief moment, Betty let down her guard. Fifty years of anger and grief melted away. "Do I like animals? I think so," Gus Grissom's wife replied. "I feed the birds every day, and *they miss me. They're waiting by the house.*"[59]

owell Grissom understands why his sister-in-law remains aggrieved fifty years after Gus was killed. "Betty has a big grudge against NASA, doesn't feel like she was ever treated properly. There's some validity to some of her feelings because when the accident first happened [NASA] didn't want to admit it at all, that there was anything wrong. It was years before they would even call [the mission] *Apollo 1.*" Betty "does have some valid points," he continued, "but I can't agree with all the stuff she's into and has done."

Betty's disillusionment began with the media spectacle she and her husband endured after his Mercury flight. A decade later, Betty concluded that NASA and the manufacturer of the Apollo spacecraft that killed her husband and his crew owed her. In fact, if not in law, they did. This time she exacted her pound of flesh. In poor health at the time of this writing, Betty struggles each year to attend the anniversary observance of the *Apollo 1* fire, seated next to Mark at what is left of Pad 34, below the stenciled words "ABANDON IN PLACE."

hat remains of Grissom's charred ship languishes in cold storage at the NASA Langley Research Center in Hampton, Virginia. For a time, it was sealed in an airtight container filled with nitrogen designed to preserve the spacecraft and its components. The use of a nitrogen atmosphere has long since ended. NASA announced in February 2007, forty years after the *Apollo 1* fire, that it was moving the spacecraft from the storage container[60] to an "environmentally controlled warehouse." The transfer was said to provide better protection for the spacecraft. Fifty years after the fire, Spacecraft 012 is slowly deteriorating, and NASA has so far resisted all attempts to display the spacecraft. "When the NASA Administrator was faced with making a decision about doing something with this spacecraft, his response was that he saw no way to avoid a difficult political situation should he choose either to place it on display, no matter the tastefulness of the exhibitry, or choose to entomb it anywhere," the National Air and Space Museum historian and curator Roger Launius has noted.[61]

Only a few private citizens, including Scott Grissom, have been permitted by NASA to examine the spacecraft since it was moved to Virginia from Cape Canaveral. In 1990, the space agency proposed burying it in an old missile silo at the Cape. NASA's plan to entomb the spacecraft was blocked by a group led by preservationist David Alberg, who later as a member of the National Marine Sanctuary Program helped raise and display the Civil War ironclad *Monitor*. Alberg cites the *Monitor* and the USS *Arizona* as examples of how a ship in which humans perished could be publicly displayed in a dignified, historically significant way. "How long was Ford's Theater closed?" Alberg correctly asks.

Just as the *Monitor* and the *Arizona* have been displayed with dignity, so too, Alberg insists, should Spacecraft 012. The other ships have brought the history of the American Civil War and World War II into stark relief. A public display of the *Apollo 1* command module "could help bring back to life the history of the glory days of Apollo," Alberg argues, as well as reminding us of the huge risks.

Indeed, a central premise of the American space program is that it should be conducted in full view of the world. That tenet applies to disasters as well as successes. Official reluctance to display Grissom's ship is part of a "cultural failure," the NASA veteran James Oberg observes. Rather than owning up to its failures, argues Oberg, NASA gives us phony official "remembrances." Four decades after the *Apollo 1* fire, Oberg wrote: "Space workers need to touch the wreckage of Apollo-204 and the lost shuttles, not have the fragments stashed away underground, out of sight and mind."[62]

The Grissom family is of several minds about how and where Gus's ship should be displayed. Before the thirtieth anniversary of the fire, Betty sought to have the spacecraft moved to the US Astronaut Hall of Fame in Florida. NASA administrator Daniel Goldin declined to release the ship, promised an alternate exhibit honoring the *Apollo 1* crew that never materialized, and then essentially waited for the political storm to fade. For Betty, it was just another in a long list of slights by NASA.

Lowell prefers that the ship be removed from cold storage and entombed at Pad 34. "I don't think it should be publicly displayed but I think it should be encapsulated some way and put in a place where people can pay their respects. And I can't think of a better place than Launch Pad 34."

It is probably true, as Lowell suspects, that Spacecraft 012 will remain locked away until the immediate families of the crew are gone. Presently, NASA continues to resist efforts to display the spacecraft, arguing it would tarnish the memory of the astronauts.

Someday, somewhere, Grissom's ship must be displayed if for no other reason than to confirm that those who insist we have mastered technology are mistaken. As Rudyard Kipling observed in his 1935 poem "Hymn of Breaking Strain":

We hold all Earth to plunder—
All Time and Space as well—
Too wonder-stale to wonder
At each new miracle;
Till, in the mid-illusion
Of Godhead 'neath our hand,
Falls multiple confusion
On all we did or planned—
The mighty works we planned.[63]

The controversy over whether and how to exhibit the gutted spacecraft along with the other indignities have only served to prolong the families' anguish. Lowell presses on, explaining that he supports any effort that will give meaning to his brother's life and sacrifice. "I've told [Betty] and Scott that if I can do something that honors Gus and keeps his memory alive, I'm going to do it." Lowell has served on the Astronaut Memorial Foundation board and remains a trustee. He has but one regret. "Unfortunately, I think, a lot of the things that I've done and am doing [for Gus], his boys should have done. It shouldn't have been me."[64]

Lowell was there again in 1999 when a salvage expert named Curt Newport figured out a way to recover Gus Grissom's Mercury spacecraft from the bottom of the Atlantic Ocean. Newport devoted a third of his life to studying every design detail of Grissom's ship, the ballistic trajectory of the astronaut's fifteen-minute suborbital flight, NASA and air force radar tracks, weather conditions on July 21, 1961, the sea state on the day of the launch—anything he could lay his hands on to help locate the sunken ship. Newport's obsession struck many as quixotic. However, the salvage expert pressed on, eventually coming up with the funds to hire an experienced crew, secure a recovery vessel, and obtain the latest sonar and submersible technologies. Thirty-eight years after the loss of *Liberty Bell 7*, these technologies along with Newport's intimate knowledge of Grissom's first flight would be applied in a search nearly three miles below the surface of the Atlantic.

Newport and his crew began a systematic survey of the ocean floor in the spring of 1999, documenting and logging a list of promising targets that had reflected his sonar pings. Deep-water salvage operations take time, planning, lots of money, and luck. Newport quickly ran out of each. Exhausting sponsorship funding from the Discovery Channel, Newport briefly considered abandoning his quest at the end of April 1999. He instead concluded it was time to narrow his search to the most promising sonar targets and make one last sweep.

By May 1, under growing pressure from his financial backers, Newport winnowed his list of targets to sixteen. Among them was a dark-colored object extending roughly nine feet above the ocean floor designated Target 71. It had previously been logged into Newport's contact list as a "hard target across ravine."[65] The metal object had reflected a sonar ping as a man-made object should.

The remaining targets were grouped in three areas. One contained six targets, including Target 71. They were clustered around tracking radar locations compiled on the day of Grissom's flight by NASA's Marshall Spaceflight Center, the builder of the Redstone booster. "Those six contacts were closest to my best guess as to where *Liberty Bell 7* now lay," Newport later wrote.[66]

Newport, a pioneer in the use of remotely operated vehicles, lowered his submersible nicknamed *Magellan* to the bottom of the Atlantic for the last time, telling the operator, "Let's start with this one, number 71."

In the pitch-black of the ocean floor, with water pressure in excess of 7,100 pounds per square inch, the robotic vehicle equipped with intensely bright lights and a video camera began making its way up a small rise.

Soon, a debris trail appeared. It was bright. Newport figured it might be crumpled aluminum or a wing from an aircraft known to have crashed north of the search area. Based on years of experience, Newport understood the first target seldom if ever panned out. He was prepared to cover all sixteen targets, hoping something might turn up, some clue as to where Grissom's ship had settled thirty-eight years before. If the salvage operation came up empty again, Newport would find new backers and keep trying, as he always had.

Then, just ahead in the inky blackness, a distinct tall shape came into the video camera's view. "It looked dark and ominous," Newport recalled.

On the flat ocean floor, Newport noticed the shape had "some height to it." To himself, he thought, the object was about the right size and shape as the object that had obsessed him for decades.

As the submersible slowly approached, Newport and his operator could clearly see a conical shape just ahead on the ocean floor. Finally, the bright lights of the submersible illuminated these words on one side of the object: "UNITED STATES." On the other: "LIBERTY BELL 7." Topside, Newport and his crew were stunned. "I don't believe it! The first target! This never happens!" At least not to Curt Newport.

After years of searching for the proverbial needle in a haystack, Newport had at long last found Grissom's spacecraft in 16,000 feet of water resting on a pile of disintegrated beryllium heat shield. Other than a missing hatch, *Liberty Bell 7* was in remarkably good condition.

There were back slaps and high fives all around as crew members stuck their heads into the control room to catch a glimpse of what they had sought. Then, celebration ended and the work resumed; Newport noted the coordinates. The euphoria was short-lived when the expensive submersible was lost after its cable snapped. Newport would again have to hustle to find another underwater robot that could be used to connect the spacecraft to the heavy cables that would lift it to the surface.

Ashore, Newport announced the find during a triumphant press conference at Port Canaveral. The press corps audibly gasped when it viewed the video of *Liberty Bell 7* suddenly appearing on the sea floor. The news of the discovery shot around the world. It was as if a part of Grissom had been recovered, his ship no longer lost, the myth of the "lost astronaut" at last vanquished. All that was left now was to find a way to pull *Liberty Bell 7* up from the bottom of the Atlantic. Newport understood the sea would not give up Grissom's spacecraft without a fight.

The salvage expert quickly set about acquiring a bigger, more stable ship, along with other equipment he would need to raise the fragile spacecraft. In studying *Liberty Bell 7*'s blueprints, Newport knew there were several strong structural points on the spacecraft's escape-tower mounting ring. These would serve as attachment points for a custom-made, clamp-style recovery tool. It would make the connection between the top of the spacecraft and the reinforced cables that would be used to winch it to the surface and onto the recovery ship.

When Newport returned in July 1999 to the spot about three hundred miles east of Cape Canaveral to haul *Liberty Bell 7* to the surface, he initially could not relocate it. He had been certain of the spacecraft's position, taking a satellite navigation fix before departing in May. Weeks later, Target 71 was nowhere to be found on the ocean floor.

Newport referred to his sonar records from the May recovery. The side-scan sonar used for the salvage operation painted a picture of the sea floor by measuring the strength of a return echo. Rocks and objects reflect more sound; sand less. Armed with the hard sonar data, Newport's crew eventually determined they were searching the Blake Basin five hundred meters to the east of the known location of Grissom's ship. Three days after arriving, Newport and his crew again found *Liberty Bell 7*. The delay had cost the salvage expert the slim chance of also locating the spacecraft's blown hatch, which may have provided valuable clues about why it prematurely exploded. To this day, the hatch remains somewhere at the bottom of the Atlantic.[67]

Next, Newport's team used a new robot to connect custom recovery tools to the spacecraft and then lowered 25,000 feet of three-eighths-inch Kevlar cable to the ocean floor. The line was attached to a three-point lifting sling. Once the submersible made the attachment, a nerve-racking three-mile lift began.

There was one final obstacle: the recovery ship's diesel engine, which powered the hydraulic winches, coughed and quit near the end of the lift. *Liberty Bell 7* was now hanging from a very long line more than a mile below the surface. The question now was whether the line would snap before the engine was restarted.

It held. At 2:10 a.m. on July 30, 1999, Newport's fourteen-year obsession ended when *Liberty Bell 7* was finally pulled from the Atlantic Ocean onto the wooden deck of his ship. McDonnell Douglas Capsule Number 11 had at last returned from the deep after nearly four decades. Demolition experts onboard cleared the decks and disarmed a sound fixing and ranging (SOFAR) bomb installed to fix the spacecraft's position during or after splashdown. Only then could Newport peer inside Grissom's ship, already pondering how it could be restored and properly displayed.

When *Liberty Bell 7* was delivered to Port Canaveral, Lowell Grissom was waiting to meet the triumphant recovery crew. The sea had given up something significant: Gus Grissom's ship. It was no longer lost, nor was its pilot.

When things looked bleakest, the indefatigable Newport had drawn inspiration from the example of the tenacious Grissom. *Liberty Bell 7* was faithfully restored and is displayed today at the Kansas Cosmosphere and Space Center in Kansas. Among the many items recovered from the ship is a reel of magnetic tape containing the recorded conversations between Grissom and recovery forces after splashdown. The tape may contain important clues as to precisely what occurred before the spacecraft hatch unexpectedly blew off, nearly drowning the astronaut. Estimates of the cost of restoring the tape run into the tens of thousands of dollars. Hence, the recording remains submerged in water at the Kansas space museum. Newport's expedition to locate and recover *Liberty Bell 7* remains among the deepest commercial salvage operations in history.

A mong the last known words of Gus Grissom's brief life was his stern admonition to the engineers and technocrats: How will we leave the earth and reach another world if we cannot make ourselves understood between a machine carrying three spacemen and those charged with monitoring its vital systems? How, indeed! The impatient, hard-nosed flyer from southern Indiana pushed with everything he had in his last days to solve this and all the other problems. The answer to Grissom's question, of course, was to roll up one's sleeves, redouble the effort, keep eyes on the ball, and—in hindsight—make damned sure you looked before you leapt, resisting the temptation to be in such a hell-bent hurry to reach the goal.

Given the opportunity, that is precisely what Grissom would have done. Circumstances, perhaps fate, the course of history itself, ensured he never got that chance. Once the American goal was achieved with the six manned lunar landings between July 1969 and December 1972, Grissom and his pioneering efforts to reach another world mostly faded from memory in the decade after Apollo. If remembered at all, he was the tight-lipped fellow with the buzz cut, the engineering test pilot who handled the unglamorous but essential tasks, flying the shakedown missions, shunning the limelight. The others—Shepard, Glenn, Armstrong—names we remember and cherish, would not have achieved the goals the nation set for itself without the selfless efforts of men like Grissom.

"We did what we said we were going to do," one of the moonwalkers noted with obvious pride decades later. It was a declaration made before the entire world. Men like Grissom turned mere words into deeds.

Grissom, a son of middle America, the striver who burned to break away, unwilling to sit still, yearning to go higher and faster—to go—was the authentic American risk taker who would put everything on the line for the cause of space exploration. Grissom believed the risks he embraced were fundamental to humanity's destiny. Despite the steep odds, he pressed on when others quit. Worker, engineer, test pilot, astronaut, pioneer, he spit in fate's eye and pushed ahead. Some thought him brash, boorish, enigmatic, thin-skinned, selfish, unfaithful. He was all of these things. He also was an original, a product of time and place, sufficiently bright and ambitious to recognize an opportunity and to seize it.

Some still view Grissom as the "hard luck" or "lost" astronaut. He was not lost. He knew exactly where he was going and how he would get there. He would do whatever was required to succeed. That commitment cost him his life and his family untold sorrow.

First and foremost, Grissom was a product of an unprecedented period of technological upheaval in American history, a small-town boy who came of age in the middle of the violent twentieth century. Everything was moving faster, beyond the speed of sound, fast enough to break the bonds of Earth itself. The sheer velocity of technological change engendered by global war would paradoxically provide the means by which a young man and his bride could escape a small Indiana town. Gus seized the opportunity to master engineering, and later flight, fighting in Korea and then realizing his dream of becoming a test pilot and ultimately riding rockets. Once in space, he marveled at the sight of a curving blue world from space. The astronaut gazed down at Earth and was amazed to see that it looked just like the maps he had studied as a boy in Mitchell.

Grissom, like his astronaut brethren, was determined to act while others stood passively on the sidelines and watched. The young man refused to settle for a life installing doors on school buses in the middle of nowhere. This was no way to live. There were opportunities if one worked hard, sacrificed, and in his case, hit the books while flipping burgers. Grissom's would be a life of action, of calculated risks, and, he fervently hoped, of reward—perhaps he would be his generation's Lindbergh! For better or worse, his uncomplaining family followed him to each new duty station. They too would be swept up in historic events they could not control, only endure.

In the end, the odds, such as they were, caught up with the risk taker, his wife, and their two sons. But better in the end to have embraced the risk, to know that one had lived, done something worthwhile, to have gone somewhere. To have advanced the human race in the short time each of us has. That is why we are here. And that is undoubtedly how Gus Grissom would have wished to be remembered.

NOTES

PREFACE

1.   Transcript of the *Apollo 11* postflight press conference, August 12, 1969, Manned Spacecraft Center, Houston, Texas.

INTRODUCTION

1.   Courtney Brooks, James Grimwood, and Loyd S. Swenson Jr., *Chariots for Apollo: A History of Manned Lunar Spacecraft* (Washington, DC: NASA History Series, 1979), chapter 7-2, http://www.hq.nasa.gov/pao/History/SP-4205/ch7-2.html.

2.   The roadway from the Vehicle Assembly Building to Pad 39, about the width of an eight-lane highway, was designed to carry a combined weight of about 18 million pounds. It was built in three layers with an average depth of seven feet. The base layer consisted of 2.5 feet of hydraulic fill, the middle made up of three feet of crushed rock, and the top layer about eight inches of river rock.

3.   *Moon Machines* (Silver Spring, MD: Discovery Channel, 2008). The Block II Apollo command module that flew to the moon nine times eventually weighed in at 13,000 pounds (crew included). See https://www.hq.nasa.gov/alsj /CSM06_Command_Module_Overview_pp39-52.pdf.

4.   BBC Archive, "Three Astronauts Die in Apollo 1 Tragedy," February 8, 1967. See also http://www.bbc.co.uk/news/science-environment-12804764.

5.   Mike Gray, *Angle of Attack: Harrison Storms and the Race to the Moon* (New York: Norton, 1992), 138.

6.   David J. Shayler, *Disasters and Accidents in Manned Spaceflight* (Chichester, UK: Springer-Praxis Books, 2000), 104.

7.   John Young and James Hansen, *Forever Young: A Life of Adventure in Air and Space* (Gainesville: University Press of Florida, 2012), 111.

8.   Ibid., 114.

9.   Geoffrey Little, "John Young, Spaceman," *Air and Space Magazine*, September 2005, p. 3, online edition. http://www.airspacemag.com/space /spaceman-7766826/?no-ist=&page=3; see also David Sington, *In the Shadow of the Moon* (New York: THINKFilm, 2008).

10.   Michael Collins, *Carrying the Fire: An Astronaut's Journeys* (New York: Farrar, Straus and Giroux, 1974), 270.

11.   Young and Hansen, *Forever Young*, 114.

12.   Curt Newport, *Lost Spacecraft: The Search for Liberty Bell 7* (Burlington, Ontario: Apogee Books, 2002), 185.

13.   According to Dr. Lawrence Lamb, an Air Force flight surgeon, "It was not possible to have the luxury of a two-gas system" in the American space-craft. See Lawrence E. Lamb, MD, *Inside the Space Race: A Space Surgeon's Diary* (Austin, TX: Synergy Books, 2006), 139.

14.   Thurston Clarke, *JFK's Last Hundred Days: The Transformation of a Man and the Emergence of a Great President* (New York: Penguin Press, 2013), 306–307.

15.   For a detailed discussion of the engineering trade-offs involved in the decision to use a pure oxygen atmosphere in the Block I Apollo spacecraft, see Erland A. Kennan and Edmund H. Harvey Jr., *Mission to the Moon: A Critical Examination of NASA and the Space Program* (New York: William Morrow and Co., 1969). See especially chapter 7, "Oxygen: The Most Dangerous Gas," 123–50. The authors refer to the use of a pure oxygen atmosphere in Apollo as "the better of several evils" (136).

16.   The Apollo Spacecraft—A Chronology, Volume 1, Part 3 (D), "Lunar Orbit Rendezvous: Mode and Module, July 1962 through September 1962"; Apollo Spacecraft Project Office, Manned Spacecraft Center, Weekly Activity Report, July 8–14, 1962; Apollo Quarterly Status Report No. 1, 13. See also http://www.hq.nasa.gov/office/pao/History/SP-4009/v1p3d.htm.

17.   North American Aviation had used a two-gas (oxygen and nitrogen) atmosphere in the X-15 cockpit specifically to reduce the fire hazard.

18.   Letter from Carl D. Sword, Manned Spacecraft Center, to North American Aviation, Space and Information Systems Division, "Contract Change Authorization No. 1," August 28, 1962.

1: 1926

1.   NASA Goddard Space Flight Center, "Dr. Robert H. Goddard, American Rocketry Pioneer," http://www.nasa.gov/centers/goddard/about/history/dr_goddard.html.

2.   Sington, *In the Shadow of the Moon*.

3.   Smithsonian Institution, National Air and Space Museum, "Goddard Rocket (1926)." http://airandspace.si.edu/exhibitions/milestones-of-flight/online /current-objects/1926.cfm.

4.   Neil Armstrong, "Armstrong Recalls History-Making Career" (John H. Glenn Lecture Series, National Air and Space Museum, Smithsonian Institution, Washington, DC, July 19, 2009).

5.   Carl L. Chappell, *Seven Minus One: The Story of Gus Grissom* (Madison, IN: Frontier Publishing, 1968), 1.

6.   Edgar Mitchell with Dwight Williams, *The Way of the Explorer: An Apollo Astronaut's Journey through the Material and Mystical Worlds* (Franklin Lakes, NJ: Career Press, 2008), 24–25.

7.   Ibid.

8.   Chappell, *Seven Minus One*, 13.

9.   "Bicycle mechanic" was a common occupation among the earliest American flyers, notably Orville and Wilbur Wright along with the aviation pioneer Glenn Curtiss. See David McCullough, *The Wright Brothers* (New York: Simon and Schuster, 2015), 239.

10.   Chappell, *Seven Minus One*, 13

11.   Jamie Doran and Piers Bizony, *Starman: The Truth Behind the Legend of Yuri Gagarin* (New York: Walker and Walker, 2011), 22; Wilfred Burchett and Anthony Purdy, *Cosmonaut Yuri Gagarin: First Man in Space* (London: Panther Books, 1961), 103.

12.   Chappell, *Seven Minus One*, 14.

13.   Origin of "Indiana: Indiana State Name Origin": http://www.state symbolsusa.org/symbol-official-item/indiana/state-name-origin/origin-indiana.

14.   King family history at: http://www.myrootsplace.com/familygroup.php ?familyID=F39723&tree=mrptree.

15.   Virgil "Gus" Grissom, *Gemini: A Personal Account of Man's Venture in Space* (New York: Macmillan, 1968), 17.

16.   Booth Tarkington, *Penrod and Sam* (New York: Grosset and Dunlap, 1916), 83, 118.

17.   Weeks before Gus Grissom's first space flight in July 1961, four workers were killed in a natural gas explosion at the Mitchell plant. See "Four Killed in Mitchell Plant Blast," *Daily Tribune*, Seymour, IN, June 22, 1961, 1.

18.   Chappell, *Seven Minus One*, 40.

19.   Dick Calkins, "Strange Adventures in the Spider Ship," *Buck Rogers 25th Century* (Chicago: Pleasure Books, 1935).

20.   Carpenter, M. Scott, L. Gordon Cooper Jr., John H. Glenn Jr., Virgil I. Grissom, Walter M. Schirra Jr., Alan B. Shepard Jr., and Donald K. Slayton, *We Seven* (New York: Simon and Schuster, 1962), 55.

21.   Russell Baker, *Growing Up* (New York: Signet, 1982), 207.

22.   Chappell, *Seven Minus One*, 17.

23.   Ibid., 27.

24.   Harrison Smith, "Test Pilot Made 2,407 Carrier Landings." *Washington Post*, February 23, 2016.

25.   Chappell, *Seven Minus One*, 19.

26.   Author's interview with Lowell Grissom, September 1, 2011. See also Francis French and Colin Burgess, *Into That Silent Sea: Trailblazers of the Space Era, 1961–1965* (Lincoln: University of Nebraska Press, 2007), 77.

27.   "The Three Degrees of Masonry: Master Mason Degree," at http://www .mastermason.com/jjcrowder/threedegrees/threedegrees.htm.

28.   See McCullough, *The Wright Brothers*.

29.   Al Worden and Francis French, *Falling to Earth: An Apollo 15 Astronaut's Journey to the Moon* (Washington, DC: Smithsonian Books, 2011), 8.

2: WORK

1.   Joseph Heller, *Now and Then: From Coney Island to Here* (New York: Vintage Books, 1998), 165.

2.   Chappell, *Seven Minus One*, 6.

3.   Indiana Historical Society, "Notable Hoosiers." http://www.indianahistory .org/our-collections/reference/notable-hoosiers/virgil-gus-grissom.

4.   Sington, *In the Shadow of the Moon*.

5.   Ray Boomhower, *Gus Grissom: The Lost Astronaut* (Indianapolis: Indiana Historical Society, 2004), 42.

6.   Ibid. See also "Hoosier Astronaut Traded BB Gun for 1st Air Jaunt," *Indianapolis Times*, April 12, 1959.

7.   Grissom, *Gemini*, 17–18.

8.   Indiana Historical Society, "Notable Hoosiers."

9.   Betty Grissom comments during fiftieth anniversary observance of the flight of *Liberty Bell 7*, Mitchell, IN, July 21, 2011.

10.   Ibid., 18.

11.   Chappell, *Seven Minus One*, 4.

12.   Author's interview with Jenny Leonard, July 23, 2011, Mitchell, IN.

13.   Indiana Historical Society, "Notable Hoosiers."

14.   Heller, *Now and Then*, 67.

15.   Grissom, *Gemini*, 18. The author's cousin, once removed, was advised in early 1943 to join the US Navy to avoid the "foul trenches" his father had endured in World War I. John H. "Doc" Bradley would later spend several weeks on a sulfurous Pacific island as a Navy corpsman. He is best known as one of the men who helped raise the American flag on Mount Suribachi during the Battle of Iwo Jima, the scene captured in AP photographer Joe Rosenthal's iconic photo. To his relatives, he was cousin "Jack," and he never, ever, talked about his war experiences, except to say: "The heroes are the guys who didn't come home." See also James Bradley and Ron Powers, *Flags of Our Fathers* (New York: Bantam Books, 2000), 83.

16.   NASA Johnson Manned Spacecraft Center oral history interview with George Page, June 25, 2001.

17.   US Department of Veterans Affairs, "Education and Training: History and Timeline," http://www.benefits.va.gov/gibill/history.asp.

18.   Application for Marriage License, Virgil I. Grissom and Betty Lavonne Moore, Lawrence County, State of Indiana, July 3, 1945. Reproduced at https://familysearch.org/pal:/MM9.3.1/TH-1951-21134-30835-29?cc=1410397.

19.   Betty Grissom and Henry Still, *Starfall* (New York: Thomas Y. Crowell Co., 1974), 19.

20.   John Norberg, *Wings of Their Dreams: Purdue in Flight* (West Lafayette, IN: Purdue University Press, 2007), 327.

3: PURDUE

1.   Carpenter et al., *We Seven*, 56.

2.   Author's interview with Bill Head, July 23, 2011, Mitchell, IN.

3.   Norberg, *Wings of Their Dreams*, 324.

4.   Grissom and Still, *Starfall*, 24–25.

5.   Grissom, *Gemini*, 76.

6. Norberg, *Wings of Their Dreams*, 324.

7. *Purdue Engineer*, February 1967, 24.

8. John Norberg, ed., *Full Steam Ahead: Purdue Mechanical Engineering Yesterday, Today and Tomorrow* (West Lafayette, IN: Purdue University Press, 2013), 42–43.

9. Carpenter et al., *We Seven*, 227.

10. In a video pitch for membership in the High Twelve International, the Academy Award–winning actor and World War II Navy veteran Ernest Borgnine insisted that members "seldom experience a bad meal or sit through a boring program." http://www.high12.org.

11. The house on Sylvia Street is long gone, having been razed to make room for a parking garage. The couple's last address in West Lafayette was 219½ Littleton Street, a few blocks east of campus toward the Wabash River.

12. Author's interview with Bill Head, July 23, 2011, Mitchell, IN.

13. Ibid.

14. Betty Grissom comments during fiftieth anniversary observance of the flight of *Liberty Bell 7*, Mitchell, IN, July 21, 2011.

15. Author's interview with Bill Head, July 23, 2011, Mitchell, IN.

16. Frederick L. Hovde Papers, Archives and Special Collections, Purdue University Libraries.

17. *Apollo 11* Commander Neil Armstrong and *Apollo 17* Commander Eugene Cernan.

18. Grissom, *Gemini*, 175–76.

19. Author's interview with Bill Head, July 23, 2011, Mitchell, IN.

20. US National Archives and Records Administration, National Personnel Records Center, St. Louis, "Records of Persons of Exceptional Prominence," Official Military Personnel Files, Virgil I. Grissom.

21. Grissom and Still, *Starfall*, 27–28.

22. Norberg, *Wings of Their Dreams*, 326.

23. Betty Grissom correspondence with Purdue University President Frederick L. Hovde, March 23, 1967, Purdue University Libraries Archives and Special Collections, Frederick L. Hovde Papers.

24. Frederick L. Hovde Papers, Archives and Special Collections, Purdue University Libraries.

25.   Timber Cove was the real estate development in Seabrook, Texas, where many of the early astronauts lived along with many NASA program managers.

26.   Frederick L. Hovde Papers, Archives and Special Collections, Purdue University Libraries.

4: WINGMAN

1.   James Salter, *Burning the Days: Recollection* (New York: Vintage, 1997), 135, 139.

2.   James Salter, *The Hunters* (New York: Vintage, 1997 edition), xiv.

3.   Ibid., 102.

4.   Salter, *Burning the Days*, 203.

5.   See, for example, I. F. Stone, *The Hidden History of the Korean War, 1950–1951: A Nonconformist History of Our Times* (New York: Monthly Review Press, 1952).

6.   The title "jet ace" was bestowed on pilots with five confirmed enemy kills. An "ace" stood above all other pilots in his unit.

7.   "The Last American Aces," Air and Space/Smithsonian, August 2015, 38.

8.   Richard Hallion, ed., *Silver Wings, Golden Valor: The USAF Remembers Korea* (Washington, DC: Air Force History and Museums Program, 2006), 54; Frederick C. Blesse, *Check Six: A Fighter Pilot Looks Back* (New York: Ivy Books, 1987), 71.

9.   James Salter, *Gods of Tin: The Flying Years* (Washington, DC: Shoemaker and Hoard, 2004), 45.

10.   James Salter, interviewed on the PBS Newshour, May 28, 2001. http://www.pbs.org/newshour/bb/entertainment-jan-june01-hunters_05-28/.

11.   Hallion, *Silver Wings, Golden Valor*, 29.

12.   Ibid., 29–30.

13.   Salter, *Gods of Tin*, 68.

14.   Ibid., 46.

15.   In October 1946, engineers at White Sands had launched a V-2 missile to an altitude of sixty-five miles where a small 35mm camera recorded the first pictures of Earth as seen from space. The camera was smashed, but the film canister survived the descent, bringing back with it the black-and-white images. See Tony Reichhardt, "The First Photo from Space," *Air and Space Magazine*, November 2006, http://www.airspacemag.com/space/the-first-photo-from-space-13721411/?no-ist.

16.   Robert G. Rogers, *Round Trip to the Morgue: Snapshots and Reflections of Colonel Robert G. Rogers* (Grand Prairie, TX: Semaphore Publishing House, 2006), 52.

17.   Ibid., 57.

18.   Grissom and Still, *Starfall*, 29.

19.   Rogers, *Roundtrip to the Morgue*, 55.

20.   Ibid., 61–62.

21.   Ibid., 30.

22.   Ibid., 31.

23.   Grissom and Still, *Starfall*, 31.

24.   Grissom, *Gemini*, 19.

25.   Rogers, *Round Trip to the Morgue*, 61.

26.   Grissom and Still, *Starfall*, 31.

27.   Salter, *Gods of Tin*, 48.

28.   Many of the American Korean War aces, fighter pilots who had shot down at least five enemy aircraft, were from the 4th Fighter Wing. US Marine Major John Glenn (three kills) and Air Force First Lieutenant Edwin "Buzz" Aldrin (two kills) were with the 51st Fighter Interceptor Wing (see Stephen Sherman, *Korean War Aces*, http://acepilots.com/korea_aces.html#top).

29.   Email from James Salter to author, August 8, 2011.

30.   "US Air Force Fact Sheet: 334th Fighter Squadron, Seymour Johnson Air Force Base," http://www.seymourjohnson.af.mil/library/factsheets/factsheet .asp?id=4510.

31.   Blesse, *Check Six*, 80.

32.   Ibid.

33.   Salter, *Gods of Tin*, 48, 52; Blesse, *Check Six*, 94.

34.   *Gods of Tin*, 68.

35.   Ibid., 96–97.

36.   Grissom and Still, *Starfall*, 39.

37.   Carpenter et al., *We Seven*, 56.

38.   French and Burgess, *Into That Silent Sea*, 49.

39.   Grissom and Still, *Starfall*, 38.

40.   Salter, *Gods of Tin*, 68.

41.   Blesse, *Check Six*, 86, 95.

42.   Salter, *Gods of Tin*, 68.

43.   Glenn's frequent wingman, Boston Red Sox slugger Ted Williams, was a Marine Corps reservist who survived several close calls during his tour in Korea. Glenn described Williams as a "very active combat pilot." See "As Good a Marine as He Was a Ballplayer," http://mlb.mlb.com/mlb/news/tributes/mlb_obit_ted _williams.jsp?content=military.

44.   Sherman, *Korean War Aces.*

45.   Salter, *Gods of Tin,* 53.

46.   Ibid., 60.

47.   Grissom and Still, *Starfall,* 38.

48.   Salter, *Gods of Tin,* 54.

49.   Ibid.

50.   Ibid., 47.

51.   Salter interview on PBS Newshour, May 28, 2001.

52.   Blesse, *Check Six,* 91.

53.   Grissom and Still, *Starfall,* 39.

54.   Carpenter et al., *We Seven,* 56.

55.   Salter, *Gods of Tin,* 77.

56.   Ibid., 44.

57.   Grissom and Still, *Starfall,* 39.

58.   Salter, *Gods of Tin,* 58.

59.   Besides Grissom, Glenn, and Aldrin, other astronauts who served in Korea included Walter M. "Wally" Schirra Jr. (a naval aviator who was an Air Force exchange pilot), Neil Armstrong, and Frank Borman. Schirra, Gus Grissom's next-door neighbor in the Timber Cove development southeast of Houston, would later serve as the executor of Grissom's estate.

60.   Ray Jones, *Memoir: Dynamite, Check Six* (Bloomington, IN: AuthorHouse, 2013), 1.

61.   Carpenter et al., *We Seven,* 56–57.

62.   It is unclear from the accounts of the incident whether the cadet was flying a propeller aircraft or a jet trainer, although, according to Betty, her husband "did a lot of flying in the T-33 jet trainer and it was good experience." Grissom and Still, *Starfall,* 39.

63.   Ibid.

64.   Sington, *In the Shadow of the Moon.*

5: TEST PILOT

1.   "Long twilight struggle" was among the many memorable phrases from John F. Kennedy's inaugural address on January 20, 1961.

2.   Dwight D. Eisenhower, "Inaugural Address," January 20, 1953. Online by Gerhard Peters and John T. Woolley, *The American Presidency Project*. http://www.presidency.ucsb.edu/ws/?pid=9600.

3.   Ibid.

4.   The "Agreement between the Commander-in-Chief, United Nations Command, on the One Hand, and the Supreme Commander of the Korean People's Army and the Commander of the Chinese People's Volunteers, on the Other Hand, Concerning a Military Armistice in Korea," was signed by US Army Lieutenant General William K. Harrison Jr. and North Korean General Nam II, representing North Korea and China. During the eleven-minute ceremony in a roadside hall built specially by the North Koreans for the occasion, neither man acknowledged the other. The truce went into effect at 10 p.m. that evening. See also "American Documentation" (n.d.), http://dx.doi.org/10.1002/(issn)1936-6108; Lindesay Parrott, "Truce is Signed, Ending the Fighting in Korea; POW Exchange Near; Rhee Gets U.S. Pledge; Eisenhower Bids Free World Stay Vigilant," *New York Times*, July 27, 1953, http://dx.doi.org/10.1002/(issn)1936-6108.

5.   Grissom and Still, *Starfall*, 41.

6.   US National Archives and Records Administration, National Personnel Records Center, St. Louis, "Records of Persons of Exceptional Prominence," Official Military Personnel Files, Virgil I. Grissom.

7.   Gordon Cooper and Bruce Henderson, *Leap of Faith: An Astronaut's Journey into the Unknown* (New York: Harper Collins, 2000), 88–89.

8.   Ibid., 42.

9.   Cooper and Henderson, *Leap of Faith*, 37–39. In a notorious stunt during Project Mercury, Cooper was angered the day before his *Faith 7* flight on May 15, 1963, to find that technicians had made a last-minute modification to his custom-made pressure suit. He vented his anger by buzzing the crew quarters at Cape Canaveral in a F-102 jet. Walt Williams, the legendary Project Mercury operations director, happened to step out of the doorway as Cooper came roaring over a few feet off the ground. Livid, Williams very nearly bumped Cooper from the flight. The stunt was typical of Cooper's career as an astronaut.

10.   Grissom and Still, *Starfall*, 42.

11.   Ibid. See also Martin Caidin, *The Astronauts: The Story of Project Mercury, America's Man-in-Space Program* (New York: E. P. Dutton and Co., 1960), 91. Caidin's account of the accident makes it appear as if Grissom was at fault, noting that it was "Captain Grissom's one flying accident." A brief biographical sketch of Gordon Cooper's career by Caidin, a veteran aerospace and aviation writer and author, makes no reference to the T-33 accident.

12.   Cooper and Henderson, *Leap of Faith*, 22.

13.   US National Archives and Records Administration, National Personnel Records Center, St. Louis, "Records of Persons of Exceptional Prominence," Official Military Personnel Files, Virgil I. Grissom.

14.   Richard Hallion, *Test Pilots: The Frontiersmen of Flight* (Washington, DC: Smithsonian Institution Press, revised edition, 1988), 215.

15.   See website: http://www.colonelrichardcorbett.com/Edwards.html.

16.   Harrison Schmitt interview, *In the Shadow of the Moon*.

17.   "X Marks the Spot: And at Edwards Air Force Base, Every Spot Tells a Story," *Air and Space Collector's Edition*, 2014, 26.

18.   Colin Burgess, *Selecting the Mercury Seven: The Search for America's Astronauts* (Chichester, UK: Springer Praxis, 2011), 151–53.

19.   James Harford, *Korolev: How One Man Masterminded the Soviet Drive to Beat America to the Moon* (New York: John Wiley and Sons, 1997), 108–109.

20.   Ibid., 126.

21.   Ibid., 127–28. Korolev, fearing that *Sputnik*'s instruments would overheat in orbit, insisted that both halves of the metallic sphere first be polished by hand until they shone. This way, the satellite would reflect as much sunlight as possible.

22.   Neil Armstrong, "40th Anniversary of Apollo 11" (John H. Glenn Lecture Series, National Air and Space Museum, Smithsonian Institution, Washington, DC, July 19, 2009).

23.   Clarke, *JFK's Last Hundred Days*, 146.

24.   Armstrong, "40th Anniversary of Apollo 11."

25.   "NASA History in Brief," last updated on May 20, 2011, http://history.nasa.gov/brief.html.

26.   Burgess, *Selecting the Mercury Seven*, 25. The society proposed calling the US civilian space agency the Astronautical Research and Development Agency. Hence, the future NASA could have instead been known as ARDA. See also

"Major Events Leading to Project Mercury, March 1944 through December 1957," http://history.nasa.gov/SP-4001/p1a.htm.

27.   The military countered the civilian assertion of dominance over space exploration by creating the Advanced Research Projects Agency in December 1957 to oversee military space programs and to forestall further technological surprises.

28.   "The Space Race," episode from "The Sixties: The Decade That Changed the World," CNN, 2015.

29.   Caidin, *The Astronauts*, 65.

30.   Ibid., 72.

31.   Burgess, *Selecting the Mercury Seven*, 32.

32.   Grissom, *Gemini*, 21.

33.   Carpenter et al., *We Seven*, 55.

34.   Cooper and Henderson, *Leap of Faith*, 22.

35.   Loudon S. Wainwright, "Grissom: A Quiet Little Fellow Who Scoffs at the Chance of Becoming a Hero," *Life*, March 3, 1961, 28–29.

36.   Carpenter et al., *We Seven*, 55.

37.   Author's interview with Samuel T. Beddingfield, March 23, 2010.

38.   Ibid.

39.   Sam Beddingfield, "Astronaut Virgil 'Gus' Grissom," http://www.ispyspace.com/Gus_Grissom.html.

40.   Grissom, *Gemini*, 16; emphasis added.

41.   Alex Malley, "An Audience with Neil Armstrong," *The Bottom Line, CPA Australia*, May 2011.

42.   Henry Fountain, "Dr. Donald D. Flickinger, 89, A Pioneer in Space Medicine," *New York Times*, March 9, 1997; Burgess, *Selecting the Mercury Seven*, 33.

43.   Grissom, *Gemini*, 21.

44.   Ibid., 22.

45.   Ibid.

46.   Grissom and Still, *Starfall*, 33, 45.

47.   *In the Shadow of the Moon*.

6: MERCURY SEVEN

1.   Dr. W. Randall Lovelace II, who ran the clinic where the astronaut candidates underwent biomedical testing, was said to favor including one woman in the original group of American spacefarers. He was overruled by President Eisenhower,

whose directive to select candidates only from the nation's test pilot schools effectively eliminated women from consideration. See NASA Johnson Space Center Oral History Project interview with Charles J. Donlan, April 27, 1998, http://www.jsc.nasa.gov/history/oral_histories/DonlanCJ/DonlanCJ_4-27-98.htm.

2.   Scott Carpenter and Kris Stoever, *For Spacious Skies: The Uncommon Journey of a Mercury Astronaut* (New York: New American Library, 2004), 185.

3.   Another Air Force test pilot and future Mercury astronaut Donald "Deke" Slayton noted that the early astronauts did nothing as spectacular as flying the X-1 or X-15 rocket planes; they were among the "ninety percent of American test pilots who never got close to stuff like that." He added, "We were working test pilots who happened to get selected" as astronauts." See Donald K. Slayton and Michael Cassutt, *Deke! U.S. Manned Space: From Mercury to the Shuttle* (New York: Thomas Doherty Associates, Forge paperback edition, 1994), 82.

4.   Burgess, *Selecting the Mercury Seven*, 51.

5.   Lamb, *Inside the Space Race*, 79.

6.   Ibid., 78.

7.   Carpenter and Stoever, *For Spacious Skies*, 182–83.

8.   Ibid., 183.

9.   Project Mercury Overview—Astronaut Selection, https://www.nasa.gov/mission_pages/mercury/missions/astronaut.html.

10.   Carpenter and Stoever, *For Spacious Skies*, 169.

11.   Lamb, *Inside the Space Race*, 104.

12.   Walter Cunningham, *The All-American Boys: An Insider's Look at the U.S. Space Program* (New York: Ibooks, 2003), 41.

13.   NASA oral history interview with Charles J. Donlan, April 27, 1998.

14.   Wally Schirra with Richard N. Billings, *Schirra's Space* (Annapolis, MD: Bluejacket Books/Naval Institute Press, 1995), 60.

15.   Carpenter et al., *We Seven*, 58.

16.   NASA oral history interview with Charles J. Donlan, April, 27, 1998.

17.   Burgess, *Selecting the Mercury Seven*, 220.

18.   Slayton and Cassutt, *Deke!*, 72.

19.   Ibid., 73.

20.   Carpenter et al., *We Seven*, 58.

21.   Carpenter and Stoever, *For Spacious Skies*, 180.

22.   Ibid., 187–88.

23.   Grissom and Still, *Starfall*, 56.

24.   Ibid.

25.   Carpenter and Stoever, *For Spacious Skies*, 192, 344.

26.   Nancy Conrad and Howard Klausner, *Rocketman: Astronaut Pete Conrad's Incredible Ride to the Moon and Beyond* (New York: New American Library, 2005), 116.

27.   Schirra and Billings, *Schirra's Space*, 61.

28.   Robert Sherrod, "Apollo Expeditions to the Moon," chapter 8.1, http://history.nasa.gov/SP-350/ch-8-1.html.

29.   Carpenter and Stoever, *For Spacious Skies*, 189.

30.   Burgess, *Selecting the Mercury Seven*, 231.

31.   Ibid.; author's interview with Walter B. Sullivan, May 15, 2012.

32.   NASA History Office, "Awarding the Prime Contract," http://history.nasa.gov/SP-4201/ch6-3.htm.

33.   Carpenter et al., *We Seven*, 65.

34.   Author's interview with Bill Head, July 23, 2011, Mitchell, IN.

35.   NASA oral history interview with Charles J. Donlan, April 27, 1998.

36.   Ibid.

37.   Carpenter and Stoever, *For Spacious Skies*, 175.

38.   Grissom, *Gemini*, 22.

39.   On April 15, 1959, Special Order A-161 was amended to read "CAPT VIRGIL I. GRISSOM."

40.   A series of one-year extensions from the Department of Defense were issued as the Mercury program dragged into 1963 and the two-man Gemini program moved from the drawing board to testing to the launchpad.

41.   Slayton and Cassutt, *Deke!*, 74.

42.   Ibid.

43.   Author's interview with Lowell Grissom, September 1, 2011.

44.   NASA Johnson Space Center Oral History Project interview with Jerome B. Hammack, Seabrook, TX, August 14, 1997. See http://www.jsc.nasa.gov/history/oral_histories/HammackJB/HammackJB_8-14-97.htm.

45.   Beddingfield, "Astronaut Virgil 'Gus' Grissom."

46.   Author's interview with Lowell Grissom, September 1, 2011.

47.   Beddingfield, "Astronaut Virgil 'Gus' Grissom."

48.   Kris Stoever graciously conveyed her ailing mother's recollections in a personal communication dated November 29, 2010.

49.   Grissom and Still, *Starfall*, 66.

50.   Slayton and Cassutt, *Deke!*, 88.

51.   Ibid., 80–81.

52.   Grissom, *Gemini*, 35–36.

53.   Ibid., 36.

54.   Ibid.

55.   Ibid.

56.   Each astronaut family would receive about $70,000 before taxes. Carpenter and Stoever, *For Spacious Skies*, 202.

57.   Loudon Wainwright, "Apollo's Great Leap for the Moon," *Life*, July 25, 1969, 18D.

58.   Carpenter and Stoever, *For Spacious Skies*, 203.

59.   Caiden, *The Astronauts*, 148–49.

7: EXTRACURRICULAR ACTIVITIES

1.   Grissom and Still, *Starfall*, 216.

2.   Neal Thompson, *Light This Candle: The Life and Times of Alan Shepard* (New York: Three Rivers Press, 2004), 268.

3.   Cunningham, *The All-American Boys*, 37.

4.   Young and Hansen, *Forever Young*, 60.

5.   Ibid.

6.   Carpenter and Stoever, *For Spacious Skies*, 207.

7.   Worden and French, *Falling to Earth*, 109.

8.   Ibid., 111.

9.   James Schefter, who covered NASA for a decade beginning in 1963, published the most scurrilous tales about Grissom's infidelities. In his account of the Space Race, Schefter insisted that the "rumors surround[ing] Grissom" were indeed true, repeating one that he was the father of a child, gender unknown, born to a McDonnell Aircraft secretary. Schefter also repeated a tale about Grissom that "was not a rumor." According to Schefter, "There was a certain kind of small black fly that hatches in the spring around the space center south of Houston. Swarms of the bugs can splatter [on] windshields, but their real distinction is that the male and female catch each other in midair and fly happily along mated." Schefter then claimed Grissom told a *Life* magazine reporter: "They do two things I like best in life, flying and fucking—and they do them at the same time."

Thereafter, Schefter claimed the locals referred to the insects as "Grissom Bugs." Why Grissom would make such a statement to a reporter, someone who was bound to repeat it, was not explained. If anything, Grissom avoided journalists whenever he could. See James Schefter, *The Race: The Uncensored Story of How America Beat Russia to the Moon* (New York: Doubleday, 1999), 72.

10. Roger Mudd, *The Place to Be: Washington, CBS, and the Glory Days of Television News* (Philadelphia: PublicAffairs, Perseus Books Group, 2008), 95.

11. Anne Truitt, *Daybook: The Journey of an Artist* (New York: Penguin Books, 1982), 200.

12. In his introduction to JFK's postwar diary published in 1995, reporter Hugh Sidey noted: "There are, I have found, many compartments within the souls of men who rise to great power." *Prelude to Leadership: The Post-War Diary of John F. Kennedy*, introduction by Hugh Sidey, quoted in Clarke, *JFK's Last Hundred Days*, 216.

13. "Composite Air-to-Ground and Onboard Voice Tape Transcription of the GT-3 Mission," NASA, Johnson Space Center, April, 1965. http://www.jsc.nasa.gov/history/mission_trans/GT03_TEC.PDF.

14. Author's interview with Lowell Grissom, September 1, 2011.

15. Mark Grissom comments during fiftieth anniversary observance of the flight of *Liberty Bell 7*, Mitchell, IN, July 21, 2011.

16. NASA Johnson Space Center Oral History interview with Jerome B. Hammack, August 14, 1997.

17. Robert Harlan Moser, *Past Imperfect: A Personal History of an Adventuresome Lifetime in and around Medicine* (Lincoln, NE: Writers Club Press, 2002), 214.

18. The author's Freedom of Information Act request for Gus Grissom's FBI file, if one exists, was fruitless.

19. Grissom and Still, *Starfall*, 15.

20. Ibid., 19.

21. Ibid., 259.

8: THE FLIGHT OF *LIBERTY BELL 7*

1. Carpenter et al., *We Seven*, 247.

2. As a member of the National Advisory Committee on Aeronautics, Doolittle would later help establish NASA.

3. Carpenter et al., *We Seven*, 243.

4. NASA Johnson Space Center Oral History Project interview with Wayne E. Koons, October 14, 2004, transcript, 48.

5. Guenter Wendt, who crammed the astronauts into their spacecraft, observed: "We get the astronaut in with a shoehorn and we get him out with a can opener." NASA Johnson Space Center Oral History interview with Guenter Wendt, Titusville, FL, February 25, 1999.

6. Newport, *Lost Spacecraft*, 139.

7. *Results of the Second U.S. Manned Suborbital Space Flight, July 21, 1961*, Manned Spacecraft Center, National Aeronautics and Space Administration (Washington, DC: US Government Printing Office, 1961), 55.

8. Colin Burgess, *Liberty Bell 7: The Suborbital Flight of Virgil I. Grissom* (Heidelberg, Germany: Springer Praxis Books, 2014), 74–76.

9. John Bisney and J. L. Pickering, *Spaceshots and Snapshots of Projects Mercury and Gemini: A Rare Photographic History* (Albuquerque: University of New Mexico Press, 2015), 16–17.

10. Dr. Fred Kelly, *America's Astronauts and Their Indestructible Spirit* (Blue Ridge Summit, PA: TAB Books, 1986), 51.

11. Moser, *Past Imperfect*, 214.

12. Ibid.

13. James Lewis and Robert Thompson, "Sinking of the *Liberty Bell 7* (Project Mercury), What Really Happened," Space Center Lecture Series, July 21, 2011. https://www.youtube.com/watch?v=oFmNo8UFMjI.

14. Burgess, *Liberty Bell 7*, 91.

15. Ibid., 92.

16. Carpenter et al., *We Seven*, 237.

17. Source for all voice air-to-ground transmissions: "Air-to-Ground Communications for MR-4," in NASA, *Results of the Second U.S. Manned Suborbital Space Flight, July 21, 1961*, appendix, 41–46.

18. Carpenter and Stoever, *For Spacious Skies*, 256.

19. NASA, *Results of the Second U.S. Manned Suborbital Space Flight, July 21, 1961*, 42.

20. Ibid., 51.

21. Ibid.

22.   Loyd S. Swenson Jr., James M. Grimwood, and Charles C. Alexander, *This New Ocean: A History of Project Mercury* (Washington, DC: NASA History Series, 1998), 367, 376; Burgess, *Liberty Bell 7*, 75.

23.   Carpenter et al., *We Seven*, 247.

24.   Accounts vary as to whether Grissom managed to stow the custom-made survival knife designed to cut through the spacecraft hull in an emergency. When *Liberty Bell 7* was recovered in 1999, the knife was found under Grissom's couch. See Newport, *Lost Spacecraft*.

25.   *Results of the Second U.S. Manned Suborbital Space Flight, July 21, 1961*, 46.

26.   The author of *The Right Stuff* did not respond to interview requests.

27.   The Sikorsky helicopter, also designated UH-34D, offered a large payload capacity and "generous center-of-gravity range," according to a Smithsonian National Air and Space Museum profile. "Its weaknesses were a reciprocating engine that struggled in the heat and humidity of Southeast Asia and maintenance intensive mechanical components." See also http://airandspace.si.edu/collections /artifact.cfm?object=siris_arc_373050.

28.   Recorded interview with John Reinhard by Rick Boos, provided to the author on July 8, 2013.

29.   Swenson, Grimwood, and Alexander, *This New Ocean*, 373.

30.   Author's interview with Rick Boos, Celina, OH, March 20, 2014.

31.   http://www.byc.com/files/Basket%20Hoist.pdf (slide 5); see also http:// www.uscg.mil/directives/cim/3000-3999/CIM_3710_4C.pdf; emphasis original.

32.   Naval Helicopter Operations, GlobalSecurity.org, http://www .globalsecurity.org/military/systems/aircraft/rotary-naval-ops.htm.

33.   NASA postflight press conference, Cocoa Beach, FL, July 22, 1961.

34.   The detection mechanism consisted of two prongs, a screw, and a plug at the bottom of the engine's oil sump. A warning light would illuminate in the helicopter cockpit if metal chips moved across the prongs, usually resulting in engine damage.

35.   Carpenter and Stoever, *For Spacious Skies*, 325.

36.   Turner Home Entertainment, *Moon Shot* (Atlanta: Turner Broadcasting System, Inc., 1994).

37.   Ibid.

38.   Chappell, *Seven Minus One*, v.

39.   *In Search of Liberty Bell 7* (Silver Spring, MD: Discovery Channel Pictures, 1999).

40.   Wendt was among those who believed the exterior lanyard probably blew Grissom's hatch. See Guenter Wendt and Russell Still, *The Unbroken Chain* (Burlington, Ontario: Apogee Books, 2008), 41.

41.   Guenter Wendt, 1999 Oral History Interview, C-SPAN, February 25, 1999, http://www.c-span.org/video/?298410-1/guenter-wendt-1999-oral-history -interview.

42.   Moser, *Past Imperfect*, 221.

43.   Lewis and Thompson, "Sinking of the *Liberty Bell 7* (Project Mercury), What Really Happened."

44.   Ibid.

45.   NASA Johnson Space Center Oral History Project interview with Wayne E. Koons, October 14, 2004, transcript, 46.

46.   *Moonshot* (Atlanta: TBS, 1994).

47.   The assertion that Grissom hit the hatch inadvertently is almost certainly incorrect. Robert B. Voas interview, NASA Johnson Space Center Oral History Project, May 19, 2002, 41.

48.   Stephen Clemmons, collectspace.com, August 16, 2004. http://www .collectspace.com/ubb/Forum29/HTML/000082-2.html.

49.   Ibid.

50.   "Grissom Insists the Hatch Was Blown by Accident," *New York Times*, July 23, 1961, 1.

51.   *Moonshot*.

52.   Author's interview with Robert Moser, February 8, 2013.

53.   Carpenter et al., *We Seven*, 246–47.

54.   "Remarks Congratulating Astronaut Virgil Grissom after his Sub-orbital Flight, 21 July 1961," John F. Kennedy President Library, White House Audio Collection. http://www.jfklibrary.org/Asset-Viewer/Archives/JFKWHA-044 -002.aspx.

55.   "Remarks upon Signing Bill Providing for an Expanded Space Program, July 21, 1961," http://www.jfklink.com/speeches/jfk/publicpapers/1961/jfk296_61.html.

56.   Ibid.

57.   Carpenter and Stoever, *For Spacious Skies*, 325–26.

58.   *Results of the Second U.S. Manned Suborbital Space Flight, July 21, 1961*, 52.

59.   Carpenter et al., *We Seven*, 240–41.

60.   Carpenter and Stoever, *For Spacious Skies*, 325.

9: DOWN A PEG

1.   Idiopathic atrial fibrillation.

2.   Carpenter and Stoever, *For Spacious Skies*, 220–21.

3.   Ibid., 181; see also Henry C. Detloff, *Suddenly, Tomorrow Came . . . A History of the Johnson Space Center* (Houston: NASA History Series, 1993), 53.

4.   Robert R. Gilruth, recorded interview by Walter D. Sohier and James M. Grimwood, April 1, 1964, p. 1 of transcript, John F. Kennedy Library Oral History Program.

5.   "Grissom Insists the Hatch was Blown by Accident," 1.

6.   Rik Stevens, "Gus Grissom Letter Showing Astronauts' Jealousy of John Glenn Now up for Auction." *Associated Press*, November 21, 2013.

7.   Carpenter and Stoever, *For Spacious Skies*, 219.

8.   Ibid., 325.

9.   NASA Oral History Project interview with Robert Voas, May 19, 2002, http://www.jsc.nasa.gov/history/oral_histories/VoasRB/VoasRB_5-19-02.pdf.

10.   Matthew H. Hersch, *Inventing the American Astronaut* (New York: Palgrave Macmillan, 2012), 38.

11.   Carpenter and Stoever, *For Spacious Skies*, 325–26.

12.   NASA Oral History Project interview with Walter M. Schirra Jr., December 1, 1998, http://www.jsc.nasa.gov/history/oral_histories/SchirraWM /WMS_12-1-98.pdf.

13.   Carpenter and Stoever, *For Spacious Skies*, 326.

14.   Papers of John F. Kennedy, Presidential Papers, President's Office Files, Speech Files, Remarks to McDonnell Aircraft employees, St. Louis, Missouri, September 12, 1962.

15.   Schirra and Billings, *Schirra's Space*, 94.

16.   Ibid., 218–19.

17.   Thom Patterson, "Apollo's Most Controversial Mission," CNN, July 27, 2011, http://lightyears.blogs.cnn.com/2011/07/27/apollos-most -controversial-mission.

18. NASA Oral History Project interview with Walter M. Schirra Jr., December 1, 1998.

19. Ibid.

20. "Talk Delivered by Major Virgil Grissom at the Society of Experimental Test Pilots East Coast Section Meeting, November 9, 1962, *SETP Newsletter* (November-December 1962), 5–12. Cited in David A. Mindell, *Digital Apollo: Humans and Machine in Spaceflight* (Cambridge, MA: MIT Press, 2008), 83–84.

21. Ibid.

22. "President, Touring Canaveral, Sees Polaris Fired," *New York Times*, November 17, 1963, 1.

23. Clarke, *JFK's Last Hundred Days*, 306.

24. Ibid., 308–309.

25. Ibid., 341.

10: APOGEE

1. Doran and Bizony, *Starman*, 183.

2. Grissom, *Gemini*, 2.

3. Ibid., 3–4.

4. Ibid., 5.

5. Ibid., 6.

6. See especially Walter A. McDougall, *The Heavens and the Earth: A Political History of the Space Age* (Baltimore: Johns Hopkins University Press, 1997).

7. Grissom, *Gemini*, 7.

8. NASA Johnson Space Center Oral History Project interview with Thomas P. Stafford, October 15, 1997.

9. Young and Hanson, *Forever Young*, 64.

10. NASA Johnson Space Flight Center Oral History Project interview with Frank Borman, April 13, 1999.

11. Young and Hansen, *Forever Young*, 62.

12. Grissom, *Gemini*, 74.

13. Cunningham, *The All-American Boys*, 43.

14. *In Search of Liberty Bell 7*.

15. Tom Wolfe, *The Right Stuff* (New York: Farrar, Straus and Giroux, 1979), 123.

16.   NASA Johnson Space Flight Center Oral History Project interview with Robert F. Thompson, August 29, 2000.

17.   The goals of the Gemini program are listed at http://www-pao.ksc.nasa .gov/history/gemini/gemini-goals.htm.

18.   Grissom, *Gemini*, 104.

19.   David M. Harland, *How NASA Learned to Fly in Space: An Exciting Account of the Gemini Missions* (Burlington, Ontario: Apogee Books, 2004), 35; Grissom, *Gemini*, 104.

20.   Grissom, *Gemini*, 106.

21.   All *Gemini 3* crew and ground control conversations throughout this chapter were drawn from "Gemini III Composite Air-to-Ground and Onboard Voice Tape Transcription, April 1965," NASA, Johnson Space Center, JSC History Portal, http://www.jsc.nasa.gov/history/mission_trans/gemini3.htm.

22.   Harland, *How NASA Learned to Fly in Space*, 33.

23.   Each of the hatch windows measured eight inches wide by six inches deep. See Harland, *How NASA Learned to Fly in Space*, 39.

24.   Grissom, *Gemini*, 109.

25.   Ibid., 110.

26.   After his Gemini flight, Grissom was uncharacteristically introspective about what he observed during his three orbits. For example, he recorded in his account of the Gemini program how surprised he was to actually see that the continents looked just as they did on maps. "I never expected to be able to take in almost a whole continent at a time, and that's quit a thrill." The commander said he scoured the tape transcripts of later Gemini missions looking for "some quotable quotes" describing the view from orbit. He found none. The reason was the Gemini crews "were simply too busy with the flight plan to wax poetic about the views." It was the same on later flights. Space shuttle commander George Zamka told the author after his February 2010 flight to the International Space Station that he was utterly consumed with his mission checklist throughout his thirteen-day mission. "You're operating at a high duty cycle right up until 'wheels stop,'" Zamka said, referring to the moment the shuttle rolled to a stop on the runway at the Kennedy Space Center. Astronauts seeking time to appreciate the view from space, Zamka added, would need a six-month crew assignment on the International Space Station. Zamka never got one. Author's interview with George Zamka, NASA Headquarters, Washington, DC, April 23, 2010. See also Grissom, *Gemini*, 108.

27.   "Grissom Maneuvers the Gemini as He and Young Make 3 Orbits in Test for a Space Rendezvous," *New York Times*, March 24, 1965, 1.

28.   Grissom, *Gemini*, 111.

29.   *Project Mercury: Bridge to the Moon* (Houston: NASAFLIX, 2003).

30.   Author's interview with Thomas P. Stafford, July 5, 2012.

31.   Young and Hansen, *Forever Young*, 84–85.

32.   "Grissom Maneuvers the Gemini as He and Young Make 3 Orbits in Test for a Space Rendezvous," 1.

33.   Young and Hansen, *Forever Young*, 82; *Project Gemini: Bridge to the Moon*; "March 23, 1965, Launch of First Crewed Gemini Flight," http://www.nasa.gov/content/march-23-1965-launch-of-first-crewed-gemini-flight.

34.   "Grissom Maneuvers the Gemini as He and Young Make 3 Orbits in Test for a Space Rendezvous," 1.

35.   The USS *Intrepid* is now berthed on the Hudson River in New York City, the centerpiece of the Intrepid Sea, Air and Space Museum Complex.

36.   Grissom, *Gemini*, 113.

37.   Ibid.

38.   "Grissom Maneuver the Gemini as He and Young Make 3 Orbits in Test for Space Rendezvous," 1.

39.   Author's interview with the Honorable Lee H. Hamilton, January 10, 2012.

40.   Ibid.

41.   Rookie astronaut Donn Eisele had originally been assigned to the *Apollo 1* crew, but he was dropped when he sustained a left shoulder separation that required surgery. He was replaced by Ed White and reassigned to the backup crew. Eisele is interred at Arlington National Cemetery several plots over from the graves of Grissom and Chaffee.

11: RISK AND REWARD

1.   Salter, *Gods of Tin*, 114.

2.   President John F. Kennedy, "Address on the Nation's Space Effort," Rice University. University Stadium, Houston, TX, September 12, 1962.

3.   Robert Krulwich, "Neil Armstrong Talks about the First Moon Walk," *National Public Radio*, December 8, 2010.

4.   Andrew Chaikan and Victoria Kohl, *Voices from the Moon: Apollo Astronauts Describe Their Lunar Experiences* (New York: Viking Studio, 2009), 159.

5.   "Glenn: An Unswerving and Self-Denying Man Engaged in a Stern, Dangerous Pursuit," *Life*, March 3, 1961, 26.

6.   Big Ten Network, *The Boilermakers: Gus Grissom*, 2010.

7.   Salter, *The Hunters*, 177.

8.   Burgess, *Selecting the Mercury Seven*, 259.

9.   *Apollo 12 Uncensored: The Untold Story of the 2nd Manned Mission to the Moon* (Beverly Hills, CA: Global Science Productions, 1996), DVD.

10.   Author's interview with Lowell Grissom, September 1, 2011.

11.   Gus Grissom, interview by Jules Bergman, ABC News, December 16, 1966.

12.   Gus Grissom, interview by Nelson Benton, CBS News, December 1966.

13.   Cunningham, *The All-American Boys*, 49.

14.   Alan Bean remarks at the Smithsonian Air and Space Museum, Washington, DC, July 17, 2009.

15.   Charles Donlan, NASA Johnson Space Center Oral History Interview by Jim Slade, April 27, 1998.

16.   Grissom, *Gemini*, 22.

17.   Carpenter et al., *We Seven*, 55.

18.   Malcolm Scott Carpenter, Leroy G. Cooper, John H. Glenn, Virgil I. Grissom, Walter M. Schirra, Alan B. Shepard, and Donald K. Slayton, *The Astronauts: Pioneers in Space* (New York: Golden Press, 1961), 46.

19.   General Chuck Yeager and Leo Janos, *Yeager: An Autobiography* (New York: Bantam Books, 1985), 106.

20.   William Lundgren, *Across the High Frontier: The Story of a Test Pilot, Major Charles E. Yeager, USAF* (New York: William Morrow, 1955), 75–76.

21.   Yeager and Janos, *Yeager*, 164.

22.   Cunningham, *The All-American Boys*, 16.

23.   Brooks, Grimwood, and Swenson, *Chariots for Apollo*, chapter 8.

24.   Jay Barbree, *Live From Cape Canaveral* (Washington, DC: Smithsonian Books, 2007), 123.

25.   Cunningham, *The All-American Boys*, 16.

26.   Young and Hansen, *Forever Young*, 79.

27.   Interview with Paul Recer, February 23, 2011.

28.   Cecile King Grissom, telephone interview by Robert Sherrod, December 31, 1969. Transcribed interview, NASA Headquarters Historical Reference Collection, Washington, DC.

29.   Dennis Grissom died on December 30, 1994, at the age of ninety-one; Cecile King Grissom died on November 8, 1995. She was ninety-four.

30.   Author's interview with Ralph Basilio, June 9, 2014.

31.   C-SPAN interview with Guenter Wendt, February 25, 1999.

32.   Ibid.

12: HOW ASTRONAUTS TALK

1.   Schefter, *The Race*, 248.

2.   Author's interview with Alan Bean, August 31, 2010.

3.   Ibid.

4.   *Apollo 1* preflight press conference, Manned Spaceflight Center, December 1966, https://www.dvidshub.net/audio/32132/apollo-1#.Vtr 8Rse0Hwx.

5.   Howard Benedict, "After Rash of Space Flights, U.S. to Launch Only 1 Or 2 in 1967," *Indianapolis Star*, December 26, 1966.

6.   Email correspondence with Marcia Dunn, February 23–24, 2011.

7.   Cooper and Henderson, *Leap of Faith*, 67.

8.   Henry C. Dethloff, *Suddenly, Tomorrow Came: The NASA History of the Johnson Space Center* (Washington, DC: NASA History Series, 1993), 125.

9.   Loudon Wainwright, *The Great American Magazine: An Inside History of Life* (New York: Ballantine Books, 1986), 301.

10.   Ibid., 310.

11.   Andrew Chaikin, *A Man on the Moon: The Voyages of the Apollo Astronauts* (New York: Penguin Books, 1994), 22–23.

12.   Neil Armstrong, Michael Collins, and Edwin E. Aldrin Jr., *First on the Moon* (Old Saybrook, CT: Konecky and Konecky, n.d.), 49.

13.   John Barbour, *Footprints on the Moon* (New York: Associated Press, 1969), 125.

14.   Cunningham, *The All-American Boys*, 8.

13: FRONT OF THE LINE

1.   Cunningham, *The All-American Boys*, 68.

2.   Ibid., 71.

3.   Ibid., 68.

4.   Author's interview with Lowell Grissom, September 1, 2011.

5.   North American Aviation likely pedaled influence in Washington through its lobbyist Fred Black and his business partner, the political fixer Bobby Baker, to win the Apollo contract over the more qualified aerospace contractor Martin Company, which would eventually become part of the military contracting giant Lockheed Martin Corp. For a thorough discussion of North American Aviation's role in the Apollo program, see Gray, *Angle of Attack*, esp. 117–19.

6.   Besides *Apollo 1*, *Apollo 7* and *8* also lacked a docking mechanism that was included on all other Apollo Block II spacecraft.

7.   Initial plans to launch the first Apollo flight in late 1966, perhaps rendezvousing with the last Gemini flight, were cancelled when it became clear the Spacecraft 012 would not be ready.

8.   Cunningham, *The All-American Boys*, 10.

9.   Donald L. Chaffee and C. Donald Chrysler, *On Course to the Stars: The Roger B. Chaffee Story* (Grand Rapids, MI: Kregel Publications, 1968), 67.

10.   "Donald Chaffee, Astronaut's Father," *Chicago Tribune*, October 31, 1998.

11.   Chaffee and Chrysler, *On Course to the Stars*, 74.

12.   Ibid., 73.

13.   Cunningham, *The All-American Boys*, 54–55.

14.   Chaffee and Chrysler, *On Course to the Stars*, 84.

15.   Eugene Cernan and Don Davis, *The Last Man on the Moon* (New York: St. Martin's Griffin, 2000), 3.

16.   "Crew of Apollo Accepted Risks: 3 Men Believed Space Flight Was Worth Facing Perils," *New York Times*, January 29, 1967, 48.

17.   The beach conversation between Donald and Roger Chaffee in the summer of 1966 is drawn from "A Father's Love, a Nation's Loss, a Reflection," unpublished article by Rick Boos, January 27, 1989.

18.   ABC News special report on the *Apollo 1* fire with science editor Jules Bergman, January 28, 1967.

19.   Young and Hansen, *Forever Young*, 59.

20.   Salter also flew with *Apollo 11* astronaut Buzz Aldrin during the Korean War.

21.   Email to the author from James Salter, August 18, 2011.

22.   Salter, *Burning the Days*, 285–86.

23.   Moser, *Past Imperfect*, 269.

24.   ABC News broadcast interview with Edward White, December 1966.

25.   Salter, *Burnings the Days*, 175.

26.   "Crew of Apollo Accepted Risks," *New York Times*, January 29, 1967, 48.

27.   "Cause of the Apollo 204 Fire," *Report of the Apollo 204 Review Board, Part V, Section 4*, http://history.nasa.gov/Apollo204/invest.html.

28.   NASA ordered North American Aviation to bundle and install spacecraft wiring by hand after the *Apollo 1* fire.

29.   Young and Hansen, *Forever Young*, 65.

30.   Ibid., 114. See also "John Young, Spaceman," *Air and Space Magazine*, September 2005 http://www.airspacemag.com/space/spaceman-7766826 /#ixzz3M7NB1I2h; Sington, *In the Shadow of the Moon*.

31.   Cunningham, *The All-American Boys*, 15.

32.   Lovell provides a detailed description of the Apollo Block I hatch, which he noted was "designed less to permit easy escape than to maintain the integrity of the craft." See Jim Lovell and Jeffrey Kluger. *Lost Moon: The Perilous Voyage of Apollo 13* (New York: Houghton Mifflin, 1994), 14.

33.   Ibid., 2, 17; Slayton and Cassutt, *Deke!*, 189.

34.   Author's interview with former NASA public affairs officer Bob Button, December 3, 2014.

35.   NASA Johnson Space Center Oral History interview with Richard Gordon, June 16, 1999. http://www.jsc.nasa.gov/history/oral_histories/GordonRF /GordonRF_6-16-99.htm.

36.   A fatal Soviet accident involving pure oxygen under pressure was not revealed in the West until 1980.

37.   Kelly, *America's Astronauts and Their Indestructible Spirit*, 154.

38.   Ibid., 154–55.

39.   Letter from Samuel Phillips, Apollo program director, to Mark E. Bradley, vice president of the Garrett Corp., October 12, 1966.

40.   *Chariots for Apollo*, "Preparations for the First Manned Apollo Mission," http://www.hq.nasa.gov/pao/History/SP-4205/ch8-7.html.

41.   *Report of Apollo 204 Review Board, Part V: Investigation and Analyses*; Section 4, "Cause of the Apollo 204 Fire."

42.   *Chariots for Apollo*, chapter 8, "Preparations for the First Manned Apollo Flight," http://www.hq.nasa.gov/pao/History/SP-4205/ch8-7.html.

43.   Cunningham, *The All-American Boys*, 87.

44.   Grissom and Still, *Starfall*, 179.

14: DEATH AT 218 FEET

1.   Field Enterprises also was the publisher of the *World Book Encyclopedia*, a unit of which owned the copyright to Gus Grissom's posthumously published account of the Gemini program.

2.   Grissom and Still, *Starfall*, 183.

3.   Schirra with Billings, *Schirra's Space*, 180.

4.   "Saturn: Launch Complex 34," NASA documentary, circa 1962, posted to Air Space and Missile Museum YouTube channel: https://youtu.be /SAVYzv5Zwwk.

5.   Walter C. Williams, unpublished manuscript, NASA Headquarters History Office, "The Spacecraft 012 Fire," October 26, 1972, draft, 15.

6.   See also Erik Bergaust, *Murder on Pad 34* (New York: G. P. Putnam's Sons, 1968), 30.

7.   Barbree, *Live from Cape Canaveral*, 124–25.

8.   Schirra with Billings, *Schirra's Space*, 182–83.

9.   Ibid., 183.

10.   Defense Video and Imagery Distribution System, https://www.dvidshub .net/audio/32132/apollo-1#.VOveKkKxFUQ at 26.52.

11.   Ibid., beginning at 2:40.

12.   NASA Johnson Space Center Oral History Project interview with Joseph W. Cuzzupoli, Kirkland, WA, January 19, 1999. See also http://www.jsc.nasa .gov/history/oral_histories/CuzzupoliJW/CuzzupoliJW_1-19-99.htm.

13.   NASA Oral History Project interview with Wally Schirra, December 1, 1998.

14.   Ibid.

15.   Kent Demaret, "'Group Think' and 'Go Fever' Brought the Shuttle Down, Says Ex-Astronaut Donn Eisele," *People*, March 24, 1986, http://www .people.com/people/archive/article/0,,20093213,00.html.

16.   NASA Oral History Project interview with Wally Schirra, December 1, 1998. http://www.jsc.nasa.gov/history/oral_histories/SchirraWM/WMS_12-1-98.pdf.

17.   Demaret, "'Group Think' and 'Go Fever' Brought the Shuttle Down, Say Ex-Astronaut Donn Eisele."

18.   Christopher C. Kraft, *Flight: My Life in Mission Control* (New York: Penguin Putnam, 2001), 275.

19.   University of Houston, Center for Public History, Christopher C. Kraft, "Remembering Apollo 8," *Houston History: NASA Johnson Space Center, 1958–1978* 6, no. 1 (Fall 2008): 15. http://www.jsc.nasa.gov/history/HouHistory /HoustonHistory-Fall08.pdf.

20.   Charles Murray and Catherine Bly Cox, *Apollo* (Burkittsville, MD: South Mountain Press, 2004), 183.

21.   Turner Home Entertainment, *Moon Shot.*

22.   Graveline and Kelly, *From Laika with Love*, 157.

23.   Schirra and Billings, *Schirra's Space*, 183.

24.   *Report of the Apollo 204 Review Board*, appendix B, 51.

25.   Kelly, *America's Astronauts and Their Indestructible Spirit*, 128.

26.   Collette Brooks, *Lost in Wonder: Imagining Science and Other Mysteries* (Berkeley, CA: Counter Point, 2010), 101.

27.   Reviewing the audiotapes of the *Apollo 1* fire, some listeners thought Chaffee, or perhaps Grissom, may have said, "Fire!"

28.   Grissom and Still, *Starfall*, 172.

29.   Graveline and Kelly, *From Laika with Love*, 146–47.

30.   *Apollo 1* (Columbus, OH: Spacecraft Films, 2007).

31.   *Report of the Apollo 204 Review Board*, appendix B, B-39.

32.   Ibid.

33.   United States Senate, *Apollo 204 Accident: Report Together with Additional Views.* 90th Cong., 2d sess. Report No. 956. Washington, DC, GPO, 1968.

34.   Author's interview with Rick Boos, March 20, 2014, Celina, OH.

35.   *Report of the Apollo 204 Review Board*, Witness Statements and Releases, Appendix B to the Final Report, B-64.

36.   The record is unclear on the question of the exact cabin temperature during the fire. Some sources indicate it reached as high as 2,500 degrees Fahrenheit. Stainless steel used in the spacecraft was observed to have melted as a result of the fire. The melting range for stainless steel, depending on grade, ranges from 1,325 to 1,530 degrees Celsius (about 2,400 to 2,786 degrees Fahrenheit). See also Young and Hansen, *Forever Young*, 113.

37.   Murray and Cox, *Apollo*, 190.

38.   Willie G. Moseley, *Smoke Jumper, Moon Pilot: The Remarkable Life of Apollo 14 Astronaut Stuart Roosa* (Morley, MO: Acclaim Press, 2011), 103.

39.   The inner hatch was to have been lowered onto the polyurethane pad during the planned egress drill. The highly flammable pad soaked up huge amounts of pure oxygen under pressure and should never have been allowed in the cabin during the plugs-out test.

40.   Young and Hansen, *Forever Young*, 113.

41.   Slayton and Cassutt, *Deke!*, 190.

42.   *Report of the Apollo 204 Review Board*, appendix B, 161–62.

43.   *Live from the Moon: The Story of Apollo Television* (Columbus, OH: Spacecraft Films, 2009).

44.   Ibid.

45.   Gene Kranz, *Failure is Not an Option: Mission Control from Mercury to Apollo 13 and Beyond* (New York: Simon and Schuster, 2000), 197.

46.   "3 Astronauts' Tape Ended With 'Get Us Out of Here!'" *New York Times*, January 31, 1967, 1.

47.   Grissom and Still, *Starfall*, 188.

48.   Cunningham, *The All-American Boys*, 3–4. Schirra recalled it was Joseph Algranti, chief of aircraft operations at the Manned Spacecraft Center, who had broken the news to the backup crew.

49.   Author's interview with Alfred Worden, Washington, DC, July 29, 2011.

50.   Betty Grissom said Charles Berry offered to help notify her in-laws; she declined, saying, "I think they'd rather hear it from me." *Starfall*, 189.

51.   Transcript of Robert Sherrod interview with Cecile Grissom, December 31, 1969, NASA History Office collection, Washington, DC.

52.   Walter C. Williams, unpublished manuscript, chapter 7, October 26, 1972, draft, 14; Gray, *Angle of Attack*, 228–30.

53.   Carpenter and Stoever, *For Spacious Skies*, 326.

54.   Walter Schirra interview with Associated Press reporter Howard Benedict, September 20, 1968.

55.   Author's interview with Rick Boos, July 8, 2013.

15: ABANDON IN PLACE

1.   Harford, *Korolev*, 113.

2.   Clarke, *JFK's Last Hundred Days*, 100.

3.   Ibid., 102.

4.   By now, the United States supposedly had built up a substantial advantage over the Soviets in land-based nuclear missiles. Another cost being considered at the time was whether to spend an additional $80 billion for "blast shelters" along with more offensive and defensive weapons. The Apollo program is estimated to have cost more than $20 billion (see Clarke, *JFK's Last Hundred Days*, 166).

5.   Turner Home Entertainment, *Moon Shot*.

6.   The phrase "train wreck" is apt. According to Richard White, a Stanford University history professor, "In the 19th and early 20th centuries, railroads rejected new technologies that could have improved safety as too complicated and too expensive." "Our Trouble with Trains," *New York Times*, May 18, 2015, http://www.nytimes.com/2015/05/18/opinion/our-trouble-with-trains.html.

7.   Cunningham, *The All-American Boys*, 12.

8.   Mitchell and Williams, *The Way of the Explorer*, 26.

9.   Ibid., 39–41.

10.   Turner Home Entertainment, *Moon Shot*.

11.   James Oberg, "NASA Has to Fight the Forgetting," NBCNews.com, January 28, 2007, http://www.nbcnews.com/id/16830696/ns/technology_and_science-space/t/nasa-has-fight-forgetting.

12.   Cunningham, *The All-American Boys*, 13.

13.   Conrad later gave the original pen-and-ink drawing to Paul Haney, the NASA public affairs chief in Houston. Haney's estate eventually sold the drawing at auction.

14.   Examples of such bureaucratic behavior are rife throughout US history. In the chaotic hours and days following the assassination of President Kennedy, US Deputy Attorney General Nicholas deB Katzenbach wrote and distributed a memorandum that laid the groundwork for establishing the Warren Commission. "We need something to head off public speculation or Congressional hearings of the wrong sort," Katzenbach concluded in a memorandum to President Johnson's aide Bill Moyers, dated November 25, 1963. The Katzenbach memorandum is reprinted in David R. Wrone's *The Zapruder Film: Reframing JFK's Assassination* (Lawrence: University Press of Kansas, 2003), 289.

15.   Astronaut Frank Borman, paying his respects to the White family in El Lago before flying to Cape Kennedy to begin investigating the fire, discovered that NASA officials already were pressuring Pat White to have her husband

buried with his crewmates at Arlington National Cemetery. If anything happened, Ed White had told his wife he wished to be interred at West Point. Borman soon figured out what was going on and instructed the NASA functionaries that White's burial would take place at the Academy in accordance with the family's wishes. NASA was "worrying [more] about what would make it easier on them than on the victims' families," Borman realized. See Frank Borman and Robert J. Serling, *Countdown: An Autobiography* (New York: Silver Arrow Books/William Morrow, 1988), 170. According to the novelist James Salter, a West Point graduate and White's commanding officer while they were stationed together in Europe, White's grave is among the most visited at the West Point Cemetery.

16.   McCullough, *The Wright Brothers*, 190–92.

17.   Ibid., 197.

18.   US Air Force Lieutenant Colonel Virgil Ivan Grissom was buried in Section 3, Lot 2503-E, Grid Q-15-16 at Arlington National Cemetery, VA.

19.   Grissom and Still, *Starfall*, 191.

20.   "For the Heroes, Salute and Farewell," *Life*, February 10, 1967, 28–29.

21.   Gemini astronauts Ted Freeman, Elliot See, and Charles Bassett were killed in training jet crashes: Freeman in October 1964, and See and Bassett in February 1966.

22.   *To the Moon* (Boston: NOVA, PBS, 1999).

23.   Oberg, "NASA Has to Fight the Forgetting."

24.   *Apollo 1*; author's interview with Stephen Clemmons, May 2011.

25.   Ibid.

26.   Ibid.

27.   Borman and Serling, *Countdown*, 175.

28.   *Apollo 1*; author's interview with Stephen Clemmons, May 2011.

29.   Ibid., 182.

30.   The astronauts insisted that North American Aviation also hire Guenter Wendt, the McDonnell "Pad Fuehrer" from the Mercury and Gemini programs, to run Apollo launchpad operations. Only after agreeing to give Wendt complete control did he agree to leave McDonnell and join North American. Wendt oversaw launch operations throughout Apollo, enforcing strict quality control and safety measures.

31.   The BMAG switch incident is drawn from Herbert Kean's commentary posted to the website Collectspace.com, as well as an email exchange with the author.

32. Ibid.

33. Email exchange with David Carey, April 13, 2015.

34. NASA Oral History Project interview with Wally Schirra, December 1, 1998, 12–24.

35. According to Dr. Fred Kelly, NASA had at the time of the fire more than twenty thousand hours of experience with pure oxygen at pressures of five pounds per square inch in altitude chambers and spaceflight. Kelly, "We Have a Fire in the Cockpit," in *From Laika with Love*, 145.

36. Young and Hansen, *Forever Young*, 57–58, 215.

37. Borman and Serling, *Countdown*, 174.

38. Ibid., 175.

39. Ibid., 180.

40. Sington, *In the Shadow of the Moon*.

41. Murray and Cox, *Apollo*, 186; see also *The Apollo Spacecraft: A Chronology*. Vol. IV, Part 1 (H) "Preparation for Flight, the Accident, and Investigation March 16 through April 5, 1967, http://www.hq.nasa.gov/pao/History/SP-4009/v4p1h.htm.

42. Construction of Spacecraft 012 commenced in August 1964 at the North American Aviation plant in Downey, CA. The basic structure was completed in September 1965. Installation, final assembly, and checkout of spacecraft subsystems followed by integrated testing of all subsystems were completed in March 1966. NASA issued a flightworthiness certificate and authorized shipment of the spacecraft despite a long list of problems, particularly with the environmental control system, in August 1966. The spacecraft arrived at the Kennedy Space Center on August 26, 1966. See "Apollo 1 Spacecraft History," http://history.nasa.gov/SP-4029/Apollo_01b_Spacecraft_History.htm.

43. Among them was a former naval aviator and Republican congressman from Illinois, Donald Rumsfeld, who complained that NASA had failed to inform lawmakers of crew safety initiatives. The future US defense secretary during the Iraq war managed to get an amendment passed in 1968, creating an Aerospace Safety Advisory Panel. See Bergaust, *Murder on Pad 34*, 193–95.

44. *Moon Machines*.

45. "Moon Shot Opposed: Vannevar Bush Says Program Not Worth Dangers Involved," *New York Times*, November 17, 1963, E8.

46. Grissom Crater is located at 45 degrees south latitude, 160 degrees west longitude on the lunar far side.

47.   The Presidential Commission on the Space Shuttle *Challenger* Accident, also known as the Rogers Commission, held a lengthy series of public hearings before releasing its report more than four months after the shuttle exploded shortly after launch.

48.   Author's interview with Rick Boos, Celina, OH, March 20, 2014.

49.   Mark Grissom comments during fiftieth anniversary observance of the flight of *Liberty Bell 7*, Mitchell, IN, July 21, 2011.

50.   Grissom and Still, *Starfall*, 249.

51.   Email exchange with Rick Armstrong, eldest son of Neil Armstrong, February 27, 2013.

52.   Grissom and Cooper formed an Indianapolis 500 racing team with former winner Jim Rathmann, the supplier of the Mercury astronauts' Corvettes. "GCR Racing" entered several Indy 500 races.

53.   Grissom and Still, *Starfall*, 220–21.

54.   Alex French and Howie Kahn, "Punch a Hole in the Sky: An Oral History of the *Right Stuff*," *WIRED* magazine, December 2014, 88–106

55.   Rogertebert.com, *Great Movie*, "The Right Stuff," March 12, 2002, http://www.rogerebert.com/reviews/great-movie-the-right-stuff-1983.

56.   Norman Grissom, untitled remembrance of his brother Virgil I. Grissom, observance of the fiftieth anniversary observance of the flight of *Liberty Bell 7*, Mitchell, IN, July 23, 2011.

57.   Time Capsule, *Indianapolis Monthly*, October 2000, 104.

58.   Pad 34 was closed to the public in 2015 for unspecified security reasons. It has been suggested the closure may be related to "environmental remediation" at the site, where chlorinated solvents such as trichloroethylene were poured into the ground for decades. See "That Sinking Feeling," *Space KSC* blog by Stephen C. Smith, October 23, 2015, http://spaceksc.blogspot.com/2015/10/that-sinking-feeling.html?showComment=1445865693442#c8847937808292489762.

59.   Helen Macdonald, author of the prize-winning 2014 memoir *H is for Hawk*, has noted: "When contact with others is made difficult through social or personal circumstance, feeding animals can bring enormous solace." She added, "The birds that choose to come to my garden make my house a less lonely place. And that is why many of us feed animals." Helen Macdonald, "Why Do We Feed Animals?" *New York Times Magazine*, January 6, 2016, 18.

60.   One observer described NASA's half-hearted attempts at preservation as allowing the spacecraft "to rot in glorified tool shed." See *Roger Launius's Blog*, "Whatever Became of the *Apollo 1* Spacecraft?" May 30, 2014, https://launiusr .wordpress.com/2014/05/30/whatever-became-of-the-apollo-1-spacecraft/.

61.   Ibid.

62.   Oberg, "NASA Has to Fight the Forgetting"; author's interview with James Oberg, June 1, 2015. NASA finally placed wreckage from the *Challenger* and *Columbia* on public display at the Kennedy Space Center in the summer of 2015. See Marcia Dunn, "Challenger, Columbia Wreckage on Public Display for First Time," *Associated Press*, August 2, 2015, http://bigstory.ap.org/article /69b86cef13024ea3a0df06bdb0a67965/challenger-columbia-wreckage-public -display-1st-time.

63.   With thanks to James Oberg.

64.   Author's interview with Lowell Grissom, September 1, 2011.

65.   Newport, *Lost Spacecraft*, 149.

66.   Ibid., 150.

67.   Newport also entertained the possibility that static electricity from the recovery helicopter had caused the hatch to blow prematurely; ibid., 87.

BIBLIOGRAPHY

BOOKS

Atkinson, Rick, et al. *Where Valor Rests: Arlington National Cemetery*. Washington, DC: National Geographic, 2007.

Baker, Russell. *Growing Up*. New York: Signet, 1982.

Barbour, John. *Footprints on the Moon*. New York: Associated Press, 1969.

Bergaust, Erik. *Murder on Pad 34*. New York: G. P. Putnam, 1968.

Bisney, John, and J. L. Pickering. *Spaceshots and Snapshots of Projects Mercury and Gemini: A Rare Photographic History*. Albuquerque: University of New Mexico Press, 2015.

Blesse, Frederick C. *Check Six: A Fighter Pilot Looks Back*. New York: Ivy Books, 1987.

Boomhower, Ray E. *Gus Grissom: The Lost Astronaut*. Indianapolis: Indiana Historical Society Press, 2004.

Borman, Frank, and Robert J. Serling. *Countdown: An Autobiography*. New York: Silver Arrow Books/William Morrow, 1988.

Bredeson, Carmen. *Gus Grissom: A Space Biography*. Springfield, NJ: Enslow Publishers, 1998.

Brooks, Collette. *Lost in Wonder: Imagining Science and Other Mysteries*. Berkeley, CA: Counter Point, 2010.

Buckbee, Ed, and Wally Schirra. *The Real Space Cowboys*. Burlington, Ontario: Apogee Books, 2005.

Burgess, Colin. *Liberty Bell 7: The Suborbital Flight of Virgil I. Grissom*. Heidelberg, Germany: Springer-Praxis, 2014.

———. *Selecting the Mercury Seven: The Search for America's First Astronauts*. Heidelberg, Germany: Springer-Praxis, 2011.

Burgess, Colin, and Kate Doolan. *Fallen Astronauts: Heroes Who Died Reaching the Moon*. Lincoln: University of Nebraska Press, 2003.

Burrows, William E. *This New Ocean: The Story of the First Space Age*. New York: Random House, 1998.

Caiden, Martin. *The Astronauts: The Story of Project Mercury, America's Man-in-Space Program*. New York: E. P. Dutton, 1960.

Carpenter, M. Scott, L. Gordon Cooper Jr., John H. Glenn Jr., Virgil I. Grissom, Walter M. Schirra Jr., Alan B. Shepard Jr., and Donald K. Slayton. *We Seven.* New York: Simon and Schuster, 1962.

Carpenter, Scott, L. Gordon Cooper Jr., John H. Glenn Jr., Virgil I. Grissom, Walter M. Schirra Jr., Alan B. Shepard Jr., Donald K. Slayton, and Loudon Wainwright. *The Astronauts: Pioneers of Space.* New York: Golden Press, 1961.

Carpenter, Scott, and Kris Stoever. *For Spacious Skies: The Uncommon Journey of a Mercury Astronaut.* Orlando, FL: Harcourt, 2002.

Cernan, Eugene, and Don Davis. *The Last Man on the Moon: Astronaut Eugene Cernan and America's Race in Space.* New York: St. Martin's Press, 1999.

Chaffee, Donald L., and C. Donald Chrysler. *On Course To the Stars: The Roger B. Chaffee Story.* Grand Rapids, MI: Kregel Publications, 1968.

Chaikin, Andrew. *A Man on the Moon: The Voyages of the Apollo Astronauts.* New York: Viking Press, 1994.

Chaikin, Andrew, and Victoria Kohl. *Voices from the Moon: Apollo Astronauts Describe Their Experiences.* New York: Viking Studio, 2009.

Chappell, Carl L. *Seven Minus One: The Story of Gus Grissom.* Madison, IN: Author, 1968.

Clarke, Thurston. *JFK's Last Hundred Days: The Transformation of a Man and the Emergence of a Great President.* New York: Penguin Press, 2013.

Collins, Michael. *Carrying the Fire: An Astronaut's Journey.* New York: Farrar, Straus, and Giroux, 1974.

———. *Flying to the Moon: An Astronaut's Story.* New York: Farrar, Straus, and Giroux, 1976.

———. *Liftoff: The Story of America's Adventure in Space.* New York: Grove Press, 1988.

Conrad, Nancy, and Howard A. Klausner. *Rocketman: Astronaut Pete Conrad's Incredible Ride to the Moon and Beyond.* New York: New American Library, 2005.

Cooper, Gordon, and Bruce Henderson. *Leap of Faith: An Astronaut's Journey into the Unknown.* New York: HarperCollins, 2000.

Cunningham, Walter. *The All-American Boys.* New York: Macmillan, 1977.

Doran, Jamie, and Piers Bizony. *Starman: The Truth behind the Legend of Yuri Gagarin.* New York: Walker and Co., 1998.

Duke, Charlie, and Dottie. *Moonwalker.* Nashville: Oliver-Nelson Books, 1990.

Fallaci, Oriana. *If The Sun Dies.* New York: Atheneum, 1967.

French, Francis, and Colin Burgess. *In the Shadow of the Moon: A Challenging Journey to Tranquility, 1965–1969.* Lincoln: University of Nebraska Press, 2007.

Glenn, John, and Nick Taylor. *John Glenn: A Memoir.* New York: Bantam Books, 1999.

Grandt, Alten. F., Jr., Winthrop A. Gustafson, and Lawrence T. Cargnino. *One Small Step: The History of Aerospace Engineering at Purdue University.* West Lafayette, IN: Purdue University School of Aeronautics and Astronautics, 2010.

Graveline, Duanne, and Dr. Fred Kelly. *From Laika with Love: Secret Soviet Gifts to Apollo.* Author, 2007.

Gray, Mike. *Angle of Attack: Harrison Storms and the Race to the Moon.* New York: Norton, 1992.

Grissom, Betty, and Henry Still. *Starfall.* New York: Thomas Y. Crowell, 1974.

Grissom, Virgil "Gus." *Gemini! A Personal Account of Man's Venture into Space.* New York: Macmillan, 1968.

Hallion, Richard P. *Test Pilots: The Frontiersman of Flight.* Washington, DC: Smithsonian Institution Press, 1981.

Hansen, James R. *First Man: The Life of Neil A. Armstrong.* New York: Simon and Schuster, 2005.

Harford, James. *Korolev: How One Man Masterminded the Soviet Drive to Beat America to the Moon.* New York: John Wiley and Sons, 1997.

Harland, David M. *How NASA Learned to Fly in Space: An Exciting Account of the Gemini Missions.* Burlington, Ontario: Apogee Books, 2004.

Heller, Joseph. *Now and Then: From Coney Island to Here.* New York: Alfred A. Knopf, 1998.

Hersch, Matthew H. *Inventing the American Astronaut.* New York: Palgrave Macmillan, 2012.

Hunter, Mel. *The Missilemen.* Garden City, NY: Doubleday, 1960.

Johnson, Paul. *Eisenhower: A Life.* New York: Viking, 2014.

Kauffman, James L. *Selling Outer Space: Kennedy, the Media, and Funding Project Apollo, 1961–1963.* Tuscaloosa: University of Alabama Press, 1994.

Kelly, Dr. Fred. *America's Astronauts and Their Indestructible Spirit.* Blue Ridge Summit, PA: TAB Books, 1986.

Kennan, Erland A., and Edmund H. Harvey Jr. *Mission to the Moon: A Critical Examination of NASA and the Space Program.* New York: William Morrow, 1969.

Kraft, Chris. *Flight: My Life in Mission Control.* New York: Penguin, 2002.

Kranz, Gene. *Failure Is Not an Option: Mission Control From Mercury to Apollo 13 and Beyond.* New York: Simon and Schuster, 2000.

Lamb, Lawrence E., MD. *Inside the Space Race: A Space Surgeon's Diary.* Austin, TX: Synergy Books, 2006.

Logsdon, John M. *John F. Kennedy and the Race to the Moon.* New York: Palgrave Macmillan, 2010.

Lovell, Jim, and Jeffrey Kluger. *Lost Moon: The Perilous Voyage of Apollo 13.* New York: Houghton Mifflin, 1994.

Lundgren, William R. *Across the High Frontier: The Story of a Test Pilot—Major Charles E, Yeager, USAF.* New York: William Morrow, 1955.

McCullough, David. *The Wright Brothers.* New York: Simon and Schuster, 2015.

McDonnell, Sanford N. *This Is Old Mac Calling All The Team: The Story of James S. McDonnell and McDonnell Douglas.* St. Louis: Author, 1999.

McDougall, Walter A. *The Heavens and the Earth: A Political History of the Space Age.* New York: Basic Books, 1985.

Mindell, David A. *Digital Apollo: Human and Machine in Spaceflight.* Cambridge, MA: MIT Press, 2008.

Mitchell, Dr. Edgar, and Dwight Williams. *The Way of the Explorer: An Apollo Astronaut's Journey through the Material and Mystical Worlds.* Franklin Lakes, NJ: New Page Books, 2008.

Moseley, Willie G. *Smoke Jumper, Moon Pilot: The Remarkable Story of Apollo 14 Astronaut Stuart Roosa.* Morely, MO: Acclaim Press, 2011.

Moser, Robert Harlan. *Past Imperfect: A Personal History of an Adventuresome Lifetime in and around Medicine.* Lincoln, NE: Writers Club Press, 2002.

Mudd, Roger. *The Place to Be: Washington, CBS, and the Glory Days of Television News.* New York: PublicAffairs, 2008.

Murray, Charles, and Catherine Bly Cox. *Apollo.* Burkittsville, MD: South Mountain Books, 2004.

Newport, Curt. *Lost Spacecraft: The Search For Liberty Bell 7.* Burlington, Ontario: Apogee Books, 2002.

Norberg, John. *Wings of Their Dreams: Purdue in Flight.* West Lafayette, IN: Purdue University Press, 2003.

Norberg, John, ed. *Full Steam Ahead: Purdue Mechanical Engineering Yesterday, Today and Tomorrow.* West Lafayette, IN: Purdue University Press, 2013.

O'Leary, Brian. *The Making of an Ex-Astronaut.* Boston: Houghton Mifflin, 1970.

Pellegrino, Charles R., and Joshua Stoff. *Chariots for Apollo: The Untold Story Behind the Race to the Moon.* New York: Avon Books, 1985.

Peters, James Edwards. *Arlington National Cemetery: Shrine to America's Heroes.* Kensington, MD: Woodbine House, 1986.

Rogers, Robert G. *Round Trip to the Morgue.* Grand Prairie, TX: Semaphore Publishing House, 2006.

Ross, Jerry L., and John Norberg. *Spacewalker: My Journey in Space and Faith as NASA's Record-Setting Frequent Flyer.* West Lafayette, IN: Purdue University Press, 2013.

Sacknoff, Scott, ed. *In Their Own Words: Conversations with the Astronauts and Men Who Led America's Journey into Space.* Bethesda, MD: Space Publications, 2003.

Salter, James. *Burning the Days: Recollection.* New York: Vintage, 1988.

———. *Gods of Tin: The Flying Years.* Washington, DC: Shoemaker and Hoard, 2004.

———. *The Hunters.* New York: Harper and Brothers, 1956.

Schefter, James. *The Race: The Uncensored Story of How America Beat Russia to the Moon.* New York: Doubleday, 1999.

Schirra, Wally, and Richard N. Billings. *Schirra's Space.* Boston: Quinlan Press, 1988.

Scott, David, and Alexei Leonov. *Two Sides of the Moon: Our Story of the Cold War Space Race.* New York: St. Martin's Press, 2004.

Shayler, David J. *Disasters and Accidents in Manned Spaceflight.* Chichester, UK: Springer/Praxis, 2000.

Shepard, Alan, Deke Slayton, Jay Barbree, and Howard Benedict. *Moon Shot: The Inside Story of America's Race to the Moon.* Atlanta: Turner Publishing, 1994.

Slayton, Donald K., and Michael Cassutt. *Deke! U.S. Manned Space: From Mercury to the Shuttle.* New York: Tom Doherty Associates, 1994.

Sorensen, Ted. *Counselor: A Life at the Edge of History.* New York: Harper, 2008.

Stafford, Thomas P., and Michael Cassett. *We Have Capture: Tom Stafford and the Space Race.* Washington, DC: Smithsonian Institution Press, 2002.

Thompson, Neal. *Light This Candle: The Life and Times of Alan Shepard—America's First Spaceman.* New York: Crown Publishers, 2004.

Wainwright, Loudon. *The Great American Magazine: An Inside History of Life.* New York: Alfred A. Knopf, 1986.

Wendt, Guenter, and Russell Still. *The Unbroken Chain.* Burlington, Ontario: Apogee Books, 2001.

Whitfield, Steve. *Project Gemini: Pocket Space Guide*. Burlington, Ontario: Apogee Books, 2007.

———. *Project Mercury: Pocket Space Guide*. Burlington, Ontario: Apogee Books, 2007.

Wilford, John Noble. *We Reach the Moon*. New York: Bantam, 1969.

Wolfe, Tom. *The Right Stuff*. New York: Farrar, Straus and Giroux, 1979.

Worden, Al, and Francis French. *Falling to Earth: An Apollo 15 Astronaut's Journey to the Moon*. Washington, DC: Smithsonian Books, 2011.

Yeager, Chuck, and Leo Janos. *Yeager: An Autobiography*. New York: Bantam, 1985.

Young, John, and James R. Hansen. *Forever Young: A Life of Adventure in Air and Space*. Gainesville: University Press of Florida, 2012.

GOVERNMENT PUBLICATIONS

Apollo 204 Review Board. *Report of the Apollo 204 Review Board to the Administrator, National Aeronautics and Space Administration*. Washington, DC: NASA Historical Reference Collection, NASA Headquarters, April 5, 1967.

Brooks, Courtney G., James M. Grimwood, and Loyd S. Swenson. *Chariots for Apollo: A History of Manned Lunar Spacecraft*. Washington, DC: NASA History Series, 1979.

National Aeronautics and Space Administration, Manned Spacecraft Center. *Results of the Second U.S. Manned Suborbital Space Flight July 21, 1961*. Washington, DC: Government Printing Office, 1961.

———. Manned Spacecraft Center. *Composite Air-to-Ground and Onboard Tape Transcription of the GT-3 Mission*. Houston, Texas: April 1965.

———. NASA Johnson Space Center Oral History Project.

National Archives, National Personnel Records Center, St. Louis.

Persons of Exceptional Prominence Records, Official Military Personnel File of: Virgil I. Grissom. 1 CD-ROM, 2015.

U.S. Senate. *Apollo 204 Accident: Report Together with Additional Views*. 90th Cong., 2d sess. Report No. 956. Washington, GPO, 1968.

ARTICLES

Beddingfield, Sam. "Astronaut Virgil 'Gus' Grissom." *ispyspace.com*, 2007.

Clark, Evert. "Grissom Maneuvers the Gemini as He and Young Make 3 Orbits in Test for a Space Rendezvous." *New York Times*, March 24, 1965, 1.

Editors. "For the Heroes, Salute and Farewell." *Life*, February 10, 1967, 20–31.

———. "Put Them High on the List of Men Who Count." *Life*, February 3, 1967, 18–27.

———. "Space: 'To Strive, to Seek, to Find, and Not to Yield.'" *Time*, February 3, 1967, 13–16.

———. "The Last American Aces." *Air and Space/Smithsonian*, August 2015, 34–39.

Finney, John W. "Pilots Will Control Gemini Spacecraft." *New York Times*, October 15, 1962, 1.

French, Alex, and Howie Kahn. "Punch a Hole in the Sky: An Oral History of *The Right Stuff*." *WIRED*, December 2014, 88–106.

Grissom, Virgil "Gus," and John W. Young. "Pair Picked for Gemini: Astronauts Tell Their Stories." *Life*, June 5, 1964, 113–21.

Joiner, Stephen, et al. "X-Planes: Great Test Pilots Tell Their Stories." *Air and Space/Smithsonian Collector's Edition*, 2014.

Little, Geoffrey. "John Young, Spaceman." *Air and Space/Smithsonian*, September 2005.

Oberg, James. "NASA Has to Fight the Forgetting." *NBCNews.com*, January 28, 2007.

Wainwright, Loudon. "The Chosen Three for First Space Ride." *Life*, March 3, 1961, 24–33.

Witkin, Richard. "Grissom Insists the Hatch Was Blown by Accident." *New York Times*, July 23, 1967, 1.

Yardley, Jonathan. "Attaboy! Booth Tarkington's Rascals." *Washington Post*, August 7, 2004.

MANUSCRIPT SOURCES

Frederick L. Hovde Papers, Archives and Special Collections, Purdue University Libraries.

VIDEO AND FILMS

Alex Malley. "An Audience with Neil Armstrong." *The Bottom Line*, CPA Australia, May 2011.

Apollo 1. Spacecraft Films, 2007.

Apollo 12: Uncensored: The Untold Story of the 2nd Manned Mission to the Moon. Global Science Productions, 1996.

Guenter Wendt 1999 Oral History Interview. C-SPAN, 1999.

In the Shadow of the Moon. ThinkFilm, 2008.

In Search of Liberty Bell 7. Discovery Channel, 1999.

Live from the Moon: The Story of Apollo Television. Spacecraft Films, 2009.

Moon Machines. Science Channel, 2009.

Moon Shot. Turner Classic Movies, 1994.

Project Mercury: Bridge to the Moon. NASAFLIX, 2003.

The Astronauts: Volume 1. Spacecraft Films, 2009.

The Boilermakers: Gus Grissom. Big Ten Network, 2010.

The Right Stuff, Warner Bros., 1983.

Thirty Seconds over Tokyo. Warner Bros., 1944.

INDEX